STUDIES IN IMPERIALISM

general editor John M. MacKenzie

When the 'Studies in Imperialism' series was founded more than twenty-five years ago, emphasis was laid upon the conviction that 'imperialism as a cultural phenomenon had as significant an effect on the dominant as on the subordinate societies'. With more than ninety books published, this remains the prime concern of the series. Cross-disciplinary work has indeed appeared covering the full spectrum of cultural phenomena, as well as examining aspects of gender and sex, frontiers and law, science and the environment, language and literature, migration and patriotic societies, and much else. Moreover, the series has always wished to present comparative work on European and American imperialism, and particularly welcomes the submission of books in these areas. The fascination with imperialism, in all its aspects, shows no sign of abating, and this series will continue to lead the way in encouraging the widest possible range of studies in the field. 'Studies in Imperialism' is fully organic in its development, always seeking to be at the cutting edge, responding to the latest interests of scholars and the needs of this ever-expanding area of scholarship.

Heroic imperialists in Africa

MANCHESTER 1824
Manchester University Press

SELECTED TITLES AVAILABLE IN THE SERIES

WALES AND THE BRITISH OVERSEAS EMPIRE
Interactions and influences, 1650–1830
Huw Bowen (ed.)

EUROPEAN EMPIRES AND THE PEOPLE
Popular responses to imperialism in France, Britain, the Netherlands, Belgium, Germany and Italy
John M. MacKenzie (ed.)

THE COLONISATION OF TIME
Ritual, routine and resistance in the British empire
Giordano Nanni

CULTURES AND CARICATURES OF BRITISH IMPERIAL AVIATION
Passengers, pilots, publicity
Gordon Pirie

FROM JACK TAR TO UNION JACK
Representing naval manhood in the British empire, 1870–1918
Mary A. Conley

Heroic imperialists in Africa

THE PROMOTION OF BRITISH AND FRENCH
COLONIAL HEROES, 1870–1939

Berny Sèbe

MANCHESTER
UNIVERSITY PRESS

Copyright © Berny Sèbe 2013

The right of Berny Sèbe to be identified as the author of this work has been asserted by him in accordance with the Copyright, Designs and Patents Act 1988.

Published by Manchester University Press
Altrincham Street, Manchester M1 7JA, UK
www.manchesteruniversitypress.co.uk

British Library Cataloguing-in-Publication Data is available

Library of Congress Cataloging-in-Publication Data is available

ISBN 978 0 7190 9751 5 *paperback*

First published by Manchester University Press in hardback 2013

This paperback edition first published 2015

The publisher has no responsibility for the persistence or accuracy of URLs for any external or third-party internet websites referred to in this book, and does not guarantee that any content on such websites is, or will remain, accurate or appropriate.

Printed by Lightning Source

To my parents

MITSOU AND ALAIN

Com evident experiència mostra, la debilitat de la nostra memòria, sotsmetent fàcilment a oblivió no solament los actes per longitud de temps envellits, mas encara los actes frescs de nostres dies, és estat doncs molt condecent, útil e expedient deduir en escrit les gestes e històries antigues dels homens forts e virtuosos, com sien espills molt clars, exemples e virtuosa doctrina de nostra vida, segons recita aquell gran orador Tul·li.

As shown evidently by experience, the weakness of our memory, which throws easily into oblivion not only those deeds which have suffered the outrage of time, but also the fresh events of our days, has made it very appropriate, useful and opportune to record in writing the ancient feats and stories of strong and virtuous men. Such men are the brightest of mirrors, examples and sources of virtous instruction for our own life, as said that great orator Tully [Cicero].

Johanot Martorell and Martí Johan de Galba,
prologue to *Tirant Lo Blanch* (late fifteenth century,
translation by the author and Esmeralda Francés-Martínez).

CONTENTS

List of figures—ix
List of tables—xi
General editor's introduction—xiii
Acknowledgements—xvii
Abbreviations and conventions—xxi
Introduction—1

PART I CONTEXTS

1	The emergence of a new type of hero: British and French contexts	27
2	Imperial heroes and the market I: the printed world	54
3	Imperial heroes and the market II: the audiovisual world	96

PART II USES

4	Imperial heroes and domestic politics	139
5	Cross-Channel *entente*? The values embodied by imperial heroes	174

PART III CASE STUDIES

6	The creation of the Marchand legend, 1895–1906	225
7	George Warrington Steevens, Blackwood Publishers and the making of *With Kitchener to Khartoum*	264

Conclusion—290
Biographical sketches—304
Index—321

LIST OF FIGURES

1. Imperial heroes set in stone: statues of General Gordon in Gravesend and Major Marchand in Thoissey — 38
2. Front cover of Michel Morphy's serialized account of the Marchand mission (1900–01) — 77
3. Paul Philippoteaux, *Le Commandant Marchand* (1899) — 102
4. Front cover of the illustrated supplement of *Le Petit Journal*, 19 March 1905 — 104
5. Marchand makes the headlines — 106
6. *Penny Illustrated Paper*, 1 October 1898 — 107
7. *The Graphic*, 12 November 1898, issue 1511 — 108
8. *Penny Illustrated Paper*, 18 March 1911 — 108
9. *Le Rire*, 17 February 1900 — 109
10. *Le Petit Parisien*, 5 April 1896 — 110
11. *The Graphic*, 24 May 1884 — 111
12. Heroism and realism at the time of the cinema. From L. Poirier, *Charles de Foucauld et l'Appel du silence* (1939), p. 221 [Reproduced with kind permission from Robert Darène, Ekwata films, Paris] — 115
13. *Illustrated London News*, 2 May 1931 — 117
14. Exploration as an argument to cleanse oneself: Brazza adorning the *Savon des Explorateurs* produced by the *Société continentale du Cosmydor* — 118
15. Imperial heroes to secure customers' loyalty: General Gordon on Ogden's, Mitchell's and Brooke Bond Tea collectible cards — 119
16. Brazza king of the *chromos*: cards produced by *Chocolats Guérin-Boutron* and *Tisanes du Père Célestin* — 119
17. Kitchener, Great War leader with a clear imperial pedigree: wartime postcard — 121
18. Heroes of 'Greater France': Marshal Lyautey, patron of the 1931 Vincennes exhibition — 122
19. Imperial heroes and the circulation of colonial imagery: postcards representing a statue of Cardinal Lavigerie in Tunis, and the inauguration by Marshal Lyautey of a memorial to Charles de Foucauld, destined to be sent to the metropole — 123
20. Brazza supervises the freeing of slaves — 197

LIST OF FIGURES

21	Fashoda revisited: wartime postcard with Kitchener's portrait adorned by the Union Jack and the tricolour	200
22	Posthumous celebrations reviving heroic reputations: the transfer of the remains of Marshal Lyautey from Nancy to Morocco	207
23	Brazza 'reassuring a young boy who had just shot him'	212
24	Paris celebrates the heroic Marchand, 'The very latest favourite of France'	240
25	*Image d'Epinal* representing Marchand as 'France's hope' (ca. 1898). © Bridgeman Art Library	245
26	'Marchandise': collectible cards produced by *Chocolats Cémoi* and *Félix Potin* shops	259

All items shown in the images (except 1, 3 and 25) belong to the author's or to private collections.

LIST OF TABLES

1	Imperial heroes in G. A. Henty's titles: overall sales from date of release until 31 August 1917	69
2	The Kitchener legend and the publishing industry	70
3	Print-runs, *With Kitchener to Khartoum*	72
4	Print-runs and commercial results of some French books dealing with colonial subjects, 1900–03	75
5	Print-runs and commercial results of some French mainstream books, 1900–07	76
6	Sales figures of Michel Morphy's 28-volume biographical series on Marchand between February 1900 and June 1901	78
7	Print-runs and commercial results of books on Marchand, by authors other than Michel Morphy 1900–01	80
8	Sales figures of a few of Baratier's books sent by Fayard to Mme J. Delorme-Jules Simon, 17 July 1922	81
9	Compared print-runs of two-volume biographies of three different imperial heroes, all by Paul d'Ivoi, and all published by Fayard in 1900	82
10	Print-runs and commercial results of three French books dealing with imperial heroes other than Marchand	83
11	'The most illustrious Frenchmen of the nineteenth century': Nationwide poll carried out by *Le Petit Parisien*, 11 January 1907	196

GENERAL EDITOR'S INTRODUCTION

Empires, for imperialists, have always been realms of fantasy. The outer regions where empires are created and controlled is a fantastical world where larger-than-life events take place, where great victories may be achieved and where fortunes and reputations can be made. Such exotic territories promote the exercise of the standard imperial fantasies of world government, of the allegedly superior attributes of the imperial people, of intellectual and religious ideas as well as technologies that sanctify and enable at the same time, all supplemented by the comforting notion that the violence through which empires are created is justified by the cargoes of good things that are delivered with them. Imperialists always imagine that they are creating order out of chaos, peace out of strife, a peace permitting the export of what they conceive to be more advanced administrative, legal, constitutional, religious and intellectual concepts. The brutalities of empires are thus but passing moments permitting the distribution of their benefits. All of this can be seen as holding true of all empires in many historical periods.

However, there were certain distinctive characteristics associated with the fantasies of nineteenth-century empires. These included the desire to sweep up the natural phenomena of the world (including its human varieties) into global taxonomies, classifying and ordering in a scientific embrace both facilitated and symbolized by the military and technological advances achieved by the imperial people. Moreover, this fantasy of universal knowledge could be reproduced and dispersed through the printed word and new forms of image-construction (such as photography and the emerging capacity to print such visual representations of the world). All this was accompanied by the fantasy of freedom of travel and movement, of information and communications, enhanced by the power of steam and the electro-magnetic miracle of the telegraph. These were bent to the end of incorporating the peoples of the imperial metropolis to its objectives. The elite had to be convinced that empire was an appropriate objective for the state; politicians had to be brought on side; while the generality of the populace had to be convinced of the benefits of an imperial policy, easier perhaps in the case of the 'empire of settlement' than in the 'empire of rule' where settlement was unlikely to take place. Yet in many respects imperial territories in Africa (and also Asia) could be depicted as more exotic, more filled with heroic potential and adventure that colonies rendered almost familiar by white settlement.

GENERAL EDITOR'S INTRODUCTION

Heroes inhabit such worlds of fantasy and this book reveals the ways in which this was true in both the British and the French empires. The projection of heroic reputations became a key component of the policies of incorporation of social classes and policy makers. Heroes were thus crucial in the formation of opinion, in the repeated renewal and confirmation of those imperial fantasies, a phenomenon which can certainly be better understood through such a comparative study. Both the British and the French were swept up in similar processes (and to this we can probably add other European societies implicated in imperial projects at the time). Through this comparative study, Berny Sèbe brings a number of fresh insights to bear – and perhaps offers guidelines for future studies, not least in different countries. Through analysing the similarities and differences of the formation and presentation of British and French heroes, he is able to delineate more clearly the manner in which heroes were both manufactured and marketed.

As he demonstrates, the particular conditions of the late nineteenth century produced a new type of hero, heroes who came to be embedded in the particular market conditions of the period. These were markets characterized by the extraordinary speed of communications, by the existence of a vigorous press, with journalists writing in fresh and vivid styles, achieving immediacy by sending 'copy' back with remarkable speed, supplemented by the possibility of image production and dissemination – through engravings and later photographs. Such images were themselves capable of creating fantasies of exoticism, heroism and drama. And, in addition to all of that, there were new possibilities for the printed word, the speedy production of attractive, exciting and above all cheap books that could condense the essences of heroism within their covers. Such books could be produced in extraordinarily extensive print runs, achieving sales hitherto virtually unheard of, and strikingly extending their reach to most social classes and to both adults and children. Besides, heroes could be celebrated through symbolic arrivals and departures, through appearances and ceremonies which rendered their progress a matter of public spectacle, almost akin to the triumphs of Ancient Rome. Heroic reputations could also be built on the shoulders, as it were, of predecessors – a good example would be the ways in which the manufacture of the Kitchener legend was constructed out of the heroic reputation of General Charles Gordon, perhaps the most iconic hero of late nineteenth-century Britain.

Case studies are clearly exceptionally valuable in the examination of all these processes in a comparative perspective. The author uses the reputations of Colonel Jean-Baptiste Marchand and of General Horatio Herbert Kitchener (with echoes of another hero in that first name) to explore the manifold ways in which their heroic deeds were projected

GENERAL EDITOR'S INTRODUCTION

to the French and British publics. Both became publishing and political phenomena, though in somewhat varying ways and with different results. Each was fortunate enough to be celebrated by 'hero-makers' – Morphy, d'Ivoi and later Daudet and Delebecque for Marchand and the incomparable Steevens for Kitchener. Both had their exploits projected through notable publications. Throughout this study, Sèbe has used a remarkable variety of archives and sources, printed and visual, to demonstrate the significance of his chosen heroes and of their projection to all the imperial constituencies that contributed to the sense of a fantastical world.

It is a particular pleasure to introduce this stimulating work for its inclusion in the 'Studies in Imperialism' series. Heroes have long been an interest of mine, as past publications have revealed. I was privileged to be the external examiner of the author's Oxford D.Phil. thesis of which this book is a much developed version, and that experience led to our becoming collaborators on a number of projects. It is a source of some satisfaction to propose that this book should cement the growing reputation of Berny Sèbe in the field of comparative imperial studies.

John M. MacKenzie

ACKNOWLEDGEMENTS

Since its inception in 2003, this project has benefited from the help of many, and I should like to express my heartfelt thanks to all those who have contributed to bringing the ideas expressed here to fruition. First developed as a D.Phil. thesis submitted in the summer of 2007, this research benefited enormously from the expert supervision of John Darwin, whose erudition and academic acumen have set standards difficult to attain, but which certainly demonstrate the effectiveness of rigorous historical research. The many enlightening comments made by John M. MacKenzie, first in his capacity as the external examiner of this work, and then as an intellectual mentor, have considerably enriched this book, which also profited from the stimulating discussions he led as the editor of the *European Empires and the People* volume, to which I had the good fortune to contribute. His input into this project has been pivotal, not least as a source of intellectual inspiration. Wm Roger Louis has provided constant and competent advice throughout the maturation of this book, and his ample contribution to the field of imperial history has greatly helped me to situate the present work on historiographical maps. Martyn Cornick has generously shared his deep knowledge of the complexity and ambiguities of Franco-British relations, and his familiarity with nineteenth-century French culture and politics. I owe a great intellectual debt to the four of them.

I should also like to thank the organizers, chairpersons or commentators of the many conferences that have given me the opportunity to discuss the outline of the ideas presented in this book: in chronological order, Andy Stafford and the Second Annual Conference of the Society for Francophone Postcolonial Studies; Anthony Hopkins, Peter Cain and Andy Cohen for the First Conference on Imperial and Commonwealth History at Sheffield University; Diana Cooper-Richet and Michael Kelly for the Centenary of the Franco-British Exhibition (London 1908) International Conference at the French Institute in London; Jo Fox and David Welch for the 'Justifying War: Propaganda, Politics and War in the Modern Age' conference at the University of Kent. At the Sixth Harvard Graduate Student Conference at Harvard University (March 2006), Ed Berenson commented on my paper 'Spreading Universality: British and French Imperial Heroes', in which I argued for a comparative framework of analysis for British and French imperial heroes and where I outlined many of the ideas expressed here; David Armitage and Niall

ACKNOWLEDGEMENTS

Ferguson chaired the sessions. I was fortunate enough to present my ideas at the following seminars, and would like to extend my thanks to their convenors for their invitation: Emma Reisz and Rachel Berger for the World History Workshop at Cambridge University; Andrew Porter and David Killingray for the Imperial History Seminar at the Institute of Historical Research in London; the team of the Marc Bloch Institute in Berlin; Julian Jackson for the Modern French History Seminar, Institute of Historical Research, University of London; Wm Roger Louis for the British Studies Seminar at the University of Texas at Austin; Debra Kelly for the Group for War and Culture Studies Seminar, University of Westminster; Peter Jackson and Martin Alexander at the University of Aberystwyth; Xavier Guégan and Claudia Baldoli at Newcastle University.

This research has greatly benefited from the many discussions I had with friends and colleagues over the years. The Oxford Graduate Workshop in Imperial and Commonwealth History was a stimulating platform to test out fresh ideas and new hypotheses. Thanks to Casper Andersen, Andrew Cohen, Andrew Dilley, Vincent Kuitenbrouwer, Alexander Morrison, Ali Parchami and Thomas Welsford for their inspiring remarks and friendship. At the *Maison française d'Oxford*, I would like to acknowledge the unfailing support provided by its director Alexis Tadié (2003–08), as well as the advice generously shared by many of the researchers in residence: Sophie Duchesne-Guilluy, Luc Foisneau, Muriel Leroux, Jean-Frédéric Schaub, Anne Simonin, Stéphane Vandamme. At the University of Durham, Jo Fox, Giles Gasper, Cherry Leonardi, Philip Williamson, Julian Wright and Jane Hogan in the library enlightened my take on British and Sudanese history. In Birmingham, I very much enjoy the stimulating companionship of Daniele Albertazzi, Jennifer Birkett, Craig Blunt, Martyn Cornick, Louise Hardwick, Kate Ince, Corey Ross, Simone Lacqua O'Donnell, Steffen Prauser, Joanne Sayner, Andrew Watts, as well as all my colleagues from the Languages and History departments. In France, I am grateful to Geneviève Berthelot, Raphaëlle Branche, Marie-Thérèse Coudrat, Alexandre Escudier, Marc and Agnès Franconie, Jacques Frémeaux, Daniel Lefeuvre, Michel Leymarie, Marie Nguyen, Michel Rapoport, Daniel and Jacqueline Richelet and Jean-Louis Triaud for their contribution in one way or another to the successful development of this project. I would also like to thank Brigitte and Henri Berg of *Les Documents cinématographiques* for facilitating an interview with French actor Robert Darène, who played the role of Pierre Savorgan de Brazza in 1939. Thanks also go to Michaël Abecassis, Isabelle Avila, Robert Gildea, Christian Goeschel, Max Jones, Pedram Khosronejad, John Strachan, Bertrand Taithe, Martin Thomas and Peter Yeandle for

ACKNOWLEDGEMENTS

the discussions we had in relation to the topics discussed here. Lastly, I would like to acknowledge the pivotal role played by the many archivists in England, Scotland and France who, through their co-operation, enriched the substance of this book.

I would like to thank for their generous support the Arts and Humanities Research Council, the British Council for an 'Entente Cordiale' scholarship, the Keble Association for an Open Scholarship and the Beit Fund for a Beit Fund Research Scholarship in Imperial and Commonwealth History. Travel grants from the Beit Fund, the Keble Association and the Arnold, Bryce and Read Fund have allowed me to travel to archives in France and in Scotland.

Although spines do not acknowledge it, books are collaborative endeavours. In the first place, heartfelt thanks go to Emma Brennan and her team at Manchester University Press for their unwavering support throughout the preparation of this book, as well as to the series editors, John MacKenzie and Andrew Thompson. Thanks also to the anonymous readers, the series editors, and to Martyn Cornick and Daniel Richelet for their insightful comments on the final draft of this book. Earlier versions or chapters were read by Jennifer Birkett, Simon Day, Nicholas Hunter, Kate Ince, Wm Roger Louis, Brian Melican, Ali Parchami and Stéphane Vandamme. Any errors remain strictly mine.

Lastly, I would like to thank for her love and support my partner Esmeralda, who also provided the most inspiring impetus towards the end of this project in the person of our son Robin. But my parents Mitsou and Alain made it all possible in the first place, and for that reason deserve my deepest and loving gratitude. This book is dedicated to them.

Oxford – Birmingham, 2003–2011

ABBREVIATIONS AND CONVENTIONS

AN	*Archives nationales*, Paris
ANOM	*Archives nationales d'outre-mer*, Aix-en-Provence
BL	Central Bodleian Library, Oxford
CS	Christina Steevens
GWS	George Warrington Steevens
IMEC	*Institut mémoires de l'édition contemporaine*, Paris
Marchand	Jean-Baptiste Marchand
MECA	Middle East Centre Archives, St Antony's College, Oxford
NLS	National Library of Scotland, Edinburgh
ODNB	*Oxford Dictionary of National Biography*, Oxford University Press, 2004
PCL	Pembroke College Library, Oxford
PLB	Private Letter Book
PRO	Public Record Office, Kew
PSB	Pierre Savorgnan de Brazza
RHL	Bodleian Library of Commonwealth and African Studies at Rhodes House, Oxford
SAD	Sudan Archive, Durham University Library, Durham
SG	*Sûreté Générale*
WB	William Blackwood III

When referred to in a general context, names of military officers are given with the rank that is most commonly used to designate them: for instance, Major (*Commandant*) Marchand although he became a general in May 1915.

When referred to in the context of French Third Republic politics, Premier or Prime Minister means *Président du Conseil*.

When making direct quotations, the spelling of local names has been kept intact, even if new conventions have arisen since the production of the work cited.

Unless otherwise stated, titles in English were published in London, and those in French in Paris.

If unspecified, translations from the French were made by the author.

INTRODUCTION

Any stroll in London or Paris can take the *flâneur* to far-flung territories, even if hasty visitors rarely realize the significance of this legacy, and many residents only have a hazy understanding of why they populate their everyday space. References are often transparent (such as for example the *Rue d'Alger*, christened only two years after the French landing in Sidi-Fredj, or *Khartoum Road* named the year when Kitchener annihilated the Mahdi's army), but in many cases they are mediated through a powerful figure: the name (or imposing silhouette) of a national 'great man', who conducted himself overseas above and beyond the call of duty, at the risk of his life, at a time when the metropole was engaged in restless territorial expansion. Half a century after the bulk of the British and French African colonies became independent, the pantheon of imperial heroes that roam the streets of these once-hegemonic capitals remains surprisingly varied. Many names linked to the now almost entirely dismantled British and French empires still inhabit the imaginary of millions of people, from the Gallieni *métro* station to Gordon Road (in the London borough of Southwark), from the statue of Livingstone in front of the Royal Geographical Society (opposite the eminently imperial Albert Memorial) to the ten-metre-long bas-relief celebrating Marchand and his men at the *Porte dorée*, opposite the former *Musée des colonies* which has meanwhile become the *Cité nationale de l'immigration*, but which is still surrounded by half a dozen streets bearing the names of noted nineteenth-century empire builders. These are just a few examples among the many that are featured in this book. Imperial heroes are certainly not everywhere in metropolitan France and Britain, but they remain a familiar presence endowed with long-lasting historical significance in the two countries, perhaps outdated, yet providing living testimonies of the colonial 'moment' of the two countries' national history.

Imperial heroes embodied the symbolic implementation of the colonial project and performed a highly mythologized meeting between conquerors and conquered. In short, they were a crucial element of the 'European encounter with Africa' that took place as part of the Scramble for Africa.[1] To the Western public, they personified the arguments of duty, responsibility and justice commonly used in imperial propaganda to support overseas territorial expansion at a time when competitive and antagonistic forms of nationalism blossomed across Europe.[2] These exemplary figures led local soldiers, braved indigenous

[1]

resistance and an inhospitable environment to carry out their explorations or to convert native populations, playing the role of pathfinders propagating the ideals of Christian service and sacrifice, progress, Republican universalism, patriotism or its more acute forms, jingoism or chauvinism. Imperial heroes combined the features of a simple and versatile celebratory construction appealing to popular audiences, and the moral persuasiveness of a justifying principle, whilst conveying an exotic vision of an expanding and successful empire. Above all, the moral paradigm that they conveyed could easily be turned into a justification for colonial conquest and rule from a variety of points of view which could be at odds with each other in a metropolitan context, but became more compatible when they were applied to an overseas setting: to take a French example, different reasons could lead an anti-clerical Republican and a religious proselyte to celebrate with equal enthusiasm the achievements of Brazza in the Congo.

Longue durée socio-cultural and political trends at work since the French Revolution go a long way towards explaining that it was 'during the nineteenth century that [great men] have been the most systematically looked for, celebrated and given as examples', as Maurice Agulhon argued.[3] This historical evolution, largely echoing the changes brought about by the Industrial Revolution, justifies an in-depth and transnational study dedicated to these 'heroic imperialists' who were among the major contributors to this new wave of national figures. In Britain, heroes who displayed personal, moral and religious exemplarity were particularly well-suited to counter the effects of a real or perceived rise of commercialism and spiritual doubt in the late Victorian period.[4] (The irony was that their promotion reflected, and to a large extent built upon, this rise of commercialism.) In France, imperial heroes could contribute to restoring a badly wounded national pride after 1870: the country's honour had to be saved, and individual acts of courage and heroism redeemed its military reputation. General Trochu's remarks in 1867 were telling: the French were able to 'console [themselves] by the memory, faithfully retained from age to age, of some chivalric action or words, which is always at hand to ennoble or poetise the struggle, whatever the outcome'.[5]

Since decolonization, the historical study of European colonial history has witnessed a clear shift from 'a history of conquerors to a history of the dominated', as Sophie Dulucq and Colette Zytnicki aptly put it.[6] British and French imperial heroes may appear at first sight as the antithesis of this trend: they can be seen as a convenient subject to undertake a revisionist appraisal of colonial rule, from the colonizer's triumphant vantage point. Yet limiting the possible use of imperial

INTRODUCTION

heroes to a glorification of the colonial past would dramatically underestimate the multiple historical processes upon which this phenomenon throws light. There is much more to say about them than just recounting their overseas exploits. The purpose here is not to deliver a series of portraits of the 'path to glory' of a handful of significant figures, however instructive each of them can be. In stark contrast with the canon of the genre, which tends to divide chapters along biographical lines, this book offers a genuinely synthetic view which charts the rise of a new type of hero: taken together, these figures reshape the heroic landscape of the two countries.[7] This thematic approach highlights the conditions that led to the blossoming of a new generation of heroes linked to the rise to prominence of Africa in European cultures and to the subsequent conquest of the continent – mostly by Britain and by France, which explains the comparative perspective adopted here. It uses in turn a range of cases to analyse various socio-cultural and technical aspects of the phenomenon, to throw light upon the processes that led as much to the 'invention of Africa' as to the 'invention of Europe'.[8] The purpose here is not to narrate the actions that propelled these heroic deeds to the forefront of the national news, or to embark upon the perilous and anachronistic task of explaining why or if these heroes deserved the recognition they were given. Nor is it to deconstruct critically the various images and myths which developed around imperial heroes in their various guises, as explorers, travellers or conquerors.[9] Rather, the task consists in defining the contours and dynamics of what could be called, in the vein of François Hartog, 'a new regime of heroism' stemming from the coincidence of 'New Imperialism' and what Benedict Anderson called 'print-capitalism'.[10] Fame was certainly not a new phenomenon, but it took a new twist as the geographical scope of European heroism and the means to promote it expanded.[11]

My ambition is to answer two questions: how was an imperial hero 'made'? And what rendered the reputations of the heroes of 'New Imperialism' possible and different from their predecessors?[12] This book deals only occasionally with what made the flesh of these heroic reputations, but it does so only when it allows us to understand better the hero-making processes which remain the primary focus of investigation. The core of the analysis revolves around the factors that allowed them to reach a wide public and to become household names: how they were promoted, disseminated and often commodified at a time when the mass-media came into being, giving unprecedented clout to journalists and a variety of other cultural actors.[13] It is more a study into how heroes were mediated to the public of the two leading imperial powers of the time, rather than a foray into what they consisted of. For all its richness, a semiotic interpretation of the meaning of these representations does not tell us much about the technical, commercial, political and social prerequisites that allowed their existence in the first place. The primary ambition of this book is to explore systematically the multiple outlets through which heroes of the British and French empires were celebrated, how their reputations were made over several decades and who sustained them. This book does not aim to produce a *histoire des mentalités*, and there will probably never be enough statistical material to allow us to reach a definitive conclusion in such a task. Rather, the book explores the intricacies of colonial propaganda and the ways in which attempts to shape public opinion underwent a Copernican revolution with the advent of the massmedia and a variety of new means of communication, which in turn increased the capacity of audiences to react to material.

The relevance of imperial heroes as both agents and reflections of popular attachment to the imperial idea was first identified by John MacKenzie in the early 1990s[14] and has often been mentioned in passing since then,[15] but it has never been approached from a synthetic and contextual perspective as is done here. Little has been said about the often complex mechanics of hero-making, which in an increasingly mechanized media world were a prerequisite to widespread popular attachment: how these heroes came into being, the interests their reputations served and the extent to which they reached ever-wider audiences. This book looks at the managerial aspect of the hero-making process as well as the technical and socio-cultural improvements which made it possible: in other words, the 'logistics' and the 'economics' of imperial hero-making. Looking at the chain of intermediaries who made imperial heroes such a cogent feature of the 'New Imperialism' reveals a protean interface, combining politics, religion and self-interest, which ensured that heroic deeds performed in far-flung territories were mediated to wide audiences in the metropoles. The 'politics' of imperial heroes often reflected a complex web of interests which contributed significantly to bolstering their reputations. Lastly, renewed curiosity towards overseas possessions coincided with a moment when the hero-making business changed radically as the popular press began to exercise its power, and 'found it could create out of not altogether promising material a hero overnight'.[16] As Andrew Thompson aptly put it, 'New Journalism' and 'New Imperialism' had 'a symbiotic relationship'.[17]

Heroic Imperialists in Africa tackles a multi-faceted phenomenon in a Franco-British comparative perspective. As such, it draws upon, and hopes to contribute to, the historiography of several fields: though it relates constantly to imperial history and *histoire coloniale*, it also relies on contributions from French Studies, cultural history or *histoire culturelle* and the history of popular culture – in particular, the history of publishing and the press, with occasional insights from cultural and media studies.[18] Apart from imperial history, all these fields have traditionally left little space to the imperial phenomenon, which has remained for a long time at the periphery of the ex-colonial metropoles, as if conceptual efforts reflected dominant geographical conceptions. Faithful to the intellectual path opened by the series in which it is published, this book is designed to balance the debate, by showing the ways in which imperial expansion gave rise to cultural constructions and projections not only in keeping with the ever-evolving culture and practices of the motherland and in relation with their imperial destinies but also constantly contributing to shape them and redefine their boundaries, symbolically and spatially.[19]

For too long, national and 'colonial' history have tended to ignore each other *superbement*, as if they remained prisoners of parallel lanes condemned never to merge. This remark is valid as much in Britain as in France, where the empire remained apparently alien to national culture.[20] At best, what made British society reluctant to engage in imperial ventures attracted more attention than what made it properly 'imperial'.[21] By examining the manifestations of the imperial idea in British daily life at different social levels from the late nineteenth century until decolonization, John MacKenzie's *Propaganda and Empire* initiated a historiographical turn, emphasizing for the first time the cultural consequences of imperialism on the culture of the British Isles themselves.[22] Two years later, the contributors to *Imperialism and Popular Culture* demonstrated, under MacKenzie's editorship, how popular culture tended to be a vehicle for the dominant ideas of its age, which at the end of the nineteenth century were nationalism and imperialism.[23] Another MacKenzie-edited volume, *Popular Imperialism and the Military*, showed how popular perceptions of the military changed thanks to imperial conquests, which turned the old reputation of 'rapacious and licentious soldiery' into veneration for the patriot and the potential hero.[24] By applying research strategies typical of British social history to the imperial case – especially shifting away from the traditional official documents and products of the 'official mind' to manifestations of popular culture, these works drew a rich intellectual agenda that made the most of a variety of sources which had hitherto remained neglected. This new grid of interpretation made the proofs of attachment to the imperial idea appear more clearly in metropolitan popular culture, defined along similar lines to that of Peter Burke for early modern Europe: the 'system of shared meanings, attitudes and values' of the 'ordinary people'.[25] From the study of the myths and metaphors of imperialism[26] to the visibility and popularization of imperial hierarchies encapsulated in 'Ornamentalism',[27] along with the place of empire in specific cultural productions such as children's book or films,[28] or the impact of empire on politics,[29] the place of the empire in British metropolitan culture has since been meticulously apprehended from a variety of angles. The phenomenon was further amplified by the propoments of the 'new imperial history', which placed material culture at the centre of their attempt to revivify the field.[30] Periods preceding the wave of 'New Imperialism' were also re-examined through this fruitful lens.[31] The numerous connections between metropoles and colonies have become of central importance: their intertwining and reciprocal influences at last found recognition and shaped new historiographical agendas, well exemplified in Ann Laura Stoler and Frederick Cooper's edited collection *Tensions of Empire*.[32] The historiography testifies to the existence of this 'imperial turn', which Antoinette Burton described as the 'accelerated attention to the impact of histories of imperialism on metropolitan societies'.[33] This effort has been echoed, but from a more theoretical and literary perspective and with a different agenda, in the field of 'postcolonial studies', largely initiated by Edward Said's theorization of Western interpretations of the 'Orient' – which coincided with areas of European colonial rule.[34] For Said and the proponents of postcolonialism, empire 'entered the social fabric, the intellectual discourse and the life of the imagination'.[35] Together, these enterprises had far-reaching consequences, incuding that of 'provincializing Europe',[36] at a time when the urge to write global histories of empires was felt strongly.[37] Yet the fact that the existence of a complex cultural relationship between the 'metropole' and the 'periphery' has now become part of the historical *doxa* does not mean that all has been said about it, or that nothing remains to be (re-)examined.

MacKenzie's approach was emulated in other European countries, especially in France where a sustained historiographical current has emerged since the 1990s,[38] in stark opposition to Charles-Robert Ageron's earlier statements to the effect that the empire was never a popular enterprise in France.[39] Martin Thomas rightly pointed out that, until recently, the expression 'popular imperialism' in the French context sounded like an 'oxymoron'.[40] For a long time, 'New Imperialism' appeared as the result of either a handful of men on the spot out of the control of Paris,[41] or of the successful lobbying of the Colonial Party,[42] and the majority of the French public was seen as either aloof or even hostile to the idea.[43] In Pierre Nora's encyclopaedic *Realms of Memory*, the 1931 Vincennes exhibition was the only colonial *lieu de mémoire*.[44] However, recent scholarship has demonstrated the validity of cultural approaches to the empire in France. In a radical re-appraisal, Tony Chafer and Amanda Sackur claimed that 'the empire

INTRODUCTION

was crucial to popular culture' and that it played a pivotal role in the shaping of post-1870 French society and culture.[45] Further works tend to demonstrate the validity of a Gallic interpretation of 'popular imperialism',[46] and the extent to which French social sciences have been influenced by the colonial experience is becoming increasingly clear.[47] In the meantime, France's imperial past has become one of the richest fields of investigation ploughed by French Studies;[48] the Francophone roots of much of postcolonial thinking have reappeared with striking force,[49] and it has become evident that postcolonial cultures and beliefs cannot be fully understood without references to the colonial era.[50]

Yet this avalanche of new material and interpretative effort in relation to the phenomenon of 'popular imperialism' has occasionally attracted expressions of scepticism. In particular, Bernard Porter took issue with the link between imperialism, imperial culture and mentalities, persuaded that empires arose mainly for material reasons and that the classes to which the empire appealed remained somewhat limited, with the colonies' appeal hardly percolating below the elites because, after all, the empire did not need mass support to exist, and it never got it anyway.[51] He called into question the representativeness of the usual proofs of the 'popularity' of imperialism: without enough evidence relating to their distribution and public reception, printed documents would be of little help to demonstrate the prevalence of any feeling among the complex class-stratified British population. If it is true that the statistical material that would provide a definitive answer will never be available for periods when opinion polls did not exist, new sources have emerged to help historians get a clearer understanding of the depth and scale which are attested by cultural artefacts rather than pure numerical evidence. In particular, the print-runs used here, and the close scrutiny of networks of propaganda behind the promotion of heroic legends, allow us to study the background to, and the popularity of, documents conveying imperial messages. With the help of the new material gathered in this book (commented on in more detail later in this chapter), which includes not only quantitative data but also an indication of the social profile of buyers, imperial heroes offer ideal case studies to test the popular reception of imperial messages in the late nineteenth and early twentieth centuries, in the countries possessing the two most extended empires of the period. The Franco-British comparative dimension adds to recent avenues of research opened by trans-European studies of the phenomenon which has come to be called 'popular imperialism'.[52]

The concept and etymology of the word 'hero' is in itself a long journey through time that is on a par with the most adventurous expeditions of nineteenth-century explorers. The substantive 'hero' comes from the classical Latin word *heros* meaning 'half-God', 'man of great value', which itself came from the Greek *hêrôs* which first referred to the military chiefs of the Trojan War before being extended to 'half-God' and 'man elevated to the status of a half-God after his death'.[53] They were later regarded as intermediate between gods and men, sometimes endowed with immortality. Around the eighth century BC, Hesiod wrote that 'Zeus the son of Cronos made yet another [generation of men] which was nobler and more righteous [than the previous ones], a god-like race of hero-men who are called demi-gods'.[54] Ten centuries later, Pausanias noted that the inhabitants of Marathon worshipped 'those who died in the fighting, calling them heroes'.[55]

With the Renaissance came the modern meaning of 'hero' in English, defining 'a man distinguished by extraordinary valour and martial achievements; one who does brave or noble deeds; an illustrious warrior' (first occurrence in 1578). A century later, it was applied to 'a man who exhibits extraordinary bravery, firmness, fortitude, or greatness of soul, in any course of action, or in connexion with any pursuit, work, or enterprise; a man admired and venerated for his achievements and noble qualities'. This meaning prevailed in Thomas Carlyle's 1838 famous series of lectures *On Heroes and Hero-Worship*, which often remains to this day the starting point of studies of heroism.[56]

The French *'héros'* evolved in roughly the same way as its English equivalent, with which it shared the ancient and modern meanings. As early as 1694, the dictionary of the French Academy exemplified the modern use of the word 'hero' with the sentence 'This General is a true hero', attesting a potent link between heroism and military activity.[57] Emile Littré mentioned six different senses of the word 'hero' (including one referring to a butterfly); the first was related to ancient times, and the second was applied to 'those who distinguish themselves through extraordinary value or memorable successes at war'. It quoted among other examples La Bruyère (1645–1696), who argued that 'the hero, it seems, belongs to one profession only, that of arms', and Fénelon (1651–1715), for whom 'we treat as hero a man who conquers, that is to say that unjustly subjugates the domains of a neighbouring state'.[58] In the late nineteenth century, the Academy described the modern meaning of *héros* as 'those who distinguish themselves through extraordinary value, who achieve memorable successes at war, who undertake great and perilous enterprises'.[59] Pierre Larousse's dictionary also stressed that the word was used particularly to describe 'those who distinguished themselves through achievements at war'.[60] The etymology demonstrates that heroism and martiality

INTRODUCTION

were intertwined until very recently: for a long time, the word retained its warlike and supernatural connotations, and it is only recently that this meaning lost its supremacy (coming down to fifth position in a 1981 dictionary).[61] It goes a long way towards explaining why so many of the figures considered in this book were primarily military leaders. Looking at the biographies of most of the heroes discussed here further strengthens the picture, especially on the French side where they all were educated at some point in a prestigious military academy (especially Saint-Cyr).[62]

Most of the entries dedicated to the French *'héros'* as well as the English 'hero' also include a reference to the correlated meaning of 'principal character of a literary or artistic work', reminding us of the close relationship between the heroic deed itself and the narrative fashioned from it. The martial value attached to the masculine hero or *héros* was absent from the feminine heroine or *héroïne*, a fact which might explain why this research has not found any contemporary heroine of empire: they generally remained poorly publicized until the postcolonial period, and, even when they started to attract public attention, the qualifier of 'heroine' was not applied to them.[63]

Beyond these etymological considerations, a more functional and subject-specific definition will be adopted in this book, whereby imperial heroes were leading figures of the colonial expansion, who enjoyed widespread publicity for a variety of reasons in their home countries between the late nineteenth century and the Second World War, and who were viewed and described as heroes by at least a significant fraction of their compatriots, in connection with overseas pursuits. Central to this meaning is the concept of 'heroic reputation', first put forward by Geoffrey Cubitt and Allen Warren, which they defined as 'a translation of the individual existence into imaginative terms which resonate with the structures of meaning and values that compose a given culture'.[64] The 'heroic reputation' is a projection of the 'heroic deeds' of a particular hero (what he did above and beyond the call of duty), and this book examines the modalities, uses and popularity of this 'translation'.[65] Since the cultural celebration of the hero as such matters more here than his actual entitlement to heroism from any philosophical perspective, any hero considered here needs to have enjoyed wide renown in the press on at least one occasion, to have been the subject of biographies and to have been celebrated in statues, engravings, paintings and, preferably, a variety of memorabilia that ensured a wide degree of publicity in his home country. This definition does not take account of the perception of the imperial hero in conquered territories: the material promoting imperial heroes considered here was aimed at metropolitan audiences.

Behind these 'heroic reputations' were efficient 'hero-makers'. War correspondents, journalists, writers, painters or, later in the period, film-makers produced the content of the primary sources mentioned in this book. Yet they were only one link in a larger chain: they worked with, or for, a variety of economic and political actors who had a vested interest in the success of these reputations: publishers, newspaper editors or owners, politicians and many members of the establishment who, for personal or professional reasons, wanted to promote these heroes.

Juxtaposing biographical chapters was a tempting strategy for studying such a protean topic as imperial heroes, offering as it does a straightforward plan. Yet, it could not convey a major point explored in this book, which is the need to develop a synthetic view of the phenomenon of 'imperial heroes'. Boiling the subject down to a handful of case studies would have dramatically impoverished it. By contrast, the contrapuntal strategy adopted in most of the chapters (bar the last two, for reasons explained below) allows us to consider a variety of heroes who match the above-mentioned functional and practical definition. The analysis becomes subtler and more varied as several types of imperial hero emerge thanks to the fifteen or so case studies examined here (whose achievements are sketched out in the biographical section at the end of this volume). David Livingstone, Henry Morton Stanley, Pierre Savorgan de Brazza and Henri Duveyrier exemplify the case of explorers who performed an imperial role.[66] The religious dimension of imperial heroism is exemplified through David Livingstone (alongside his role as an explorer), Cardinal Lavigerie and Brother Charles de Foucauld. Lastly, the most abundant contingent of imperial heroes came from a military background: Charles George Gordon (whose fame also had strong religious undertones), Horatio Herbert Kitchener, Jean-Baptiste Marchand, Joseph Gallieni, Hubert Lyautey and Thomas Edward Lawrence 'of Arabia'. The case of the colonial proconsul Frederick Lugard illustrates how a leading civil servant who could have been regarded as an imperial hero never managed to capture the public's attention. Although he was never directly in competition with French imperial interests, and had no real Gallic equivalent, Cecil Rhodes features in this book for the role he played in the development of British southern Africa, and because he embodied a larger-than-life hero dedicated to imperial expansion through political and economic acumen rather than his own personal military prowess.[67] Garnet Joseph Wolseley is not included here as he never enjoyed the fame of a popular hero, and his reputation was rapidly eclipsed by his rival Lord Frederick Roberts. Although he was 'an icon of late Victorian Britain' and 'his image and reputation were the fruit of a flourishing press and the proliferation of illustrated papers', and he

INTRODUCTION

'knew how to use his popular following for the achievement of political ends', Roberts is not featured here either because his reputation gathered momentum during postings in Afghanistan and India, and his spell as commander-in-chief in South Africa was not enough to make him a hero of the British empire in Africa.[68]

Long-term cultural phenomena such as the one studied here, considered in their globality rather than their individual expressions, fade in and out of popular imagination over extended periods of time. If it is true that heroic reputations often gained momentum through an accumulation of political statements and cultural products over a short period (as in the cases of Marchand and Kitchener, studied in the third part of this book), making it possible to pin down an exact moment when a new household name appeared in the national pantheon, the evolution is much more fluid when considering the phenomenon in its globality. Quite obviously, ancestors to the heroes of 'New Imperialism' can be found before 1870 in the two countries. Livingstone's reputation took off in Britain as early as 1856–57 and the Indian rebellion of 1857 generated its host of new heroic figures like Henry Havelock, the brothers Lawrence and James Outram among others.[69] René Caillié became an explorer hero in 1830, and the conquest of Algeria propelled Bugeaud and his *casquette* to the front of French folklore in the 1840s. Yet the period from 1870 to 1939 represents a turning point in the colonial destiny of each country, with the advent of what Henri Brunschwig called the 'steeple-chase race', more commonly known today as the 'Scramble for Africa', which was the most visible consequence of the expansionist theories often labelled as 'New Imperialism'. This imperial turn in the conceptualization of international relations brought to the forefront, and more systematically than before, a distinct category of hero, the imperial hero. Arguably, a relationship existed between the celebration of imperial heroes and *Torschlusspanik* – the fear that other nations might benefit from the resources of Africa to turn the balance of power in Europe.[70] For the French, these seven decades span the entirety of the Third Republic, covering years of clearly chaotic political life, but within a similar international framework.

The 1870s were the moment when what would be later called the 'mass-media' really took hold of Europe. Even more than in the early to mid-nineteenth century, this period was marked by a new set of political, cultural and technical conditions that had a major impact upon hero-making. Celebrating new heroes was perfectly in keeping with a period that saw the advent of what Eric Hobsbawm called 'mass-producing traditions'.[71] In the political field, these decades were marked by the birth of the French Third Republic, the Gallic controversy about colonial expansion in the following twenty years and the advent of a more triumphant form of imperialism in Britain, powerfully symbolized by the proclamation of Victoria as Empress of India on the occasion of the Delhi imperial assemblage in 1877. Socio-cultural evolutions brought about by the second Industrial Revolution altered the foundations on which heroic reputations were built. The democratization of education and better means of transport and communication increased the awareness of the outside world among European populations, whilst the development of a cheap press and of new publishing techniques and commercial strategies as a consequence of technical inventions made the promotion of heroes more efficient and more desirable from an economic and political point of view.

This book ends when the Second World War begins. This global conflict marked the end of two decades of enthusiastic imperialism for two countries which had seen their resources dramatically tested during the Great War, and clung to their empires as a guarantee of great power status. If the 1914–18 war brought about significant changes to the celebration of imperial heroes as will be seen in the following chapters (with a clear shift towards memorialization), the foundations of imperial rule remained unshaken until 1939 – the British and French colonial ensembles actually expanded as a result of the Treaty of Versailles, and reached their geographical climax.[72] By contrast, the Second World War, with its cohort of radical political, intellectual and symbolic changes and the spectacle of colonizers subjugated by the Axis armies, marked the end of an epoch. It sealed the fate of the French Third Republic, paving the way for the expression of deep political division within France and its empire, whilst it considerably weakened Britain internally and in its relationship with its colonies. Laying the ground for decolonization, these five years of conflict changed the meaning and altered the relevance of imperial heroes to national narratives. After seventy years of celebration in the national imaginations of the two countries, their reputations were not left unscathed by the war. If they did not disappear from the national pantheons, and were even re-used later in the postcolonial period, they became remnants of a distant past which appeared less relevant as the future of empire appeared more uncertain than ever: they became another, more distant, story in the postwar world.

The geographical limits of this book have been drawn to address the paucity of attempts to compare the cultural consequences on metropolitan cultures of the two most important empires in the nineteenth-century.[73] Yet the fact that Britain and France so often competed against each other in their attempts to master large expanses of the world revealed a convergence of purpose which was likely to be translated into the national imagination of each country.[74] The different

INTRODUCTION

traditions, social outlook and political workings of each case add to the appeal of such a parallel perspective which highlights differences *and* similarities, sketching out the main avenues of investigation for a pan-European understanding of European imperialisms and their consequences for national cultures.[75] Rivalry betrays a similarity of goals which can easily be overlooked if the focus remains national – which is the case of most works in imperial history. A genuine comparative framework, looking at aspects of hero-making in the two countries together, shows the extent and mechanisms of mutual influences. French geographical societies started a tradition which blossomed in Britain, whilst the notoriety of Hester Stanhope (1776–1839) and Lawrence of Arabia revealed 'the importance of the British model in the constitution of a modern mystic of adventure in France'.[76] British and French projects in Africa have always been so intertwined that they deserved to be examined from the perspective of an *'histoire croisée'*, an 'entangled history' as conceptualized by Michael Werner and Bénédicte Zimmermann.[77] This book only considers imperial heroes who had acted in Africa and, marginally, the Middle-East, because, as an author of the 1890s noted quite bluntly, it was the continent whose 'time had come' in the period chosen, and the timeline of the British and French conquests was similar.[78] It is also on this continent that the majority of the imperial heroes of the period performed their most important roles – the only other place in a position to compete being the Indian subcontinent, which applies only to the British case.

A chapter breakdown organized solely along national lines or individual heroes is insufficient to deliver a genuinely comparative and synthetic appraisal of the phenomenon of imperial heroism in the two major contenders of the 'New Imperialism'. Instead, this book revolves around three major axes, the first two of which entirely intertwine the narratives of the two countries to deliver a synthetic view organized around key aspects of the phenomenon. The first part of this book, 'Contexts', looks at the general socio-cultural and political trends prevalent in Britain and France in the period under consideration, and considers micro-economic tendencies and technological developments in the cultural industry that accompanied and fostered the development of legends revolving around imperial heroes. It allows the reader to grasp the variety of media, genres and formats through which meanings were conveyed, allowing imperial heroes to reach a 'public presence'.[79] The second part, 'Uses', stems from the underlying assumption that heroism is a content-driven process involving the production of meaning reflecting and informing cultural practices and beliefs. It considers two major aspects that invested imperial heroes with a role in society: the use of their image as political argument or their own political roles; and the values that they embodied through their own personal dedication above and beyond the call of duty. The third section, 'Case studies', uses micro-history to follow step by step the genesis and development of two emblematic heroic reputations of the turn of the century, through the prism of networks of patronage, political sensitivities and crises, and commercial interest informing the promotion of two emblematic heroes, Major Marchand and the Sirdar Kitchener, in the context of the Fashoda incident. Marchand illustrates the case of a hero who promoted his cause himself, while the study of George Warrington Steevens and the Kitchener legend throws light upon the agenda and strategies of a dedicated hero-maker. Each one demonstrates complementary aspects of a successful hero-making campaign leading to the durable establishment of a popular legend: broad overviews and attention to detail complement each other throughout the book.

The book starts with an introductory consideration of the socio-political, economic and technological reasons that allowed in each country the emergence of this new type of hero in the context of heightened imperial activity. The geopolitical background explains the pre-eminence of military heroes among these colonial figures, helped by improvements in the popular image of the army, which gradually became an object of sympathy in the eyes of the public. Generalized urban development offered opportunities for topographical celebrations of town-naming, street-naming, the christening of official buildings and statues displayed on public squares which entrenched imperial heroes in the geographical imagination of large sections of the growing urban population. The chapter also considers how the social, technical and cultural consequences of the Second Industrial Revolution favoured the development of these heroic reputations, and how the extension of the franchise expanded the range of possible uses that could be made of them.

The next two chapters analyse the pivotal role played by the advent of the mass-media in the making of imperial heroes, as a prelude to what would be called 'celebrity colonialism' for a slightly later period.[80] The reputations of imperial heroes resulted from the transmission of information and symbolic content between individuals who were separated from each other in space and time, and this form of 'mediated interaction' explains why this book dedicates so much attention to the media that propelled this new generation of heroes.[81] In the second chapter, the ever-evolving role of the popular press, the publishing world and other printed cultural artefacts is examined. On the basis of print-runs, as well as a detailed contextual interpretation of market trends and publishing strategies, it demonstrates the key influence of

INTRODUCTION

commercial interest on hero-making at the time of 'print-capitalism'. The third chapter, entirely dedicated to the audiovisual worlds where diversity increased as the period progressed, documents how visual, musical and audiovisual depictions of heroic deeds reinforced the place and meaning of these heroes through mass-produced cultural products such as songs, illustrated newspapers, advertisements and films. Paintings, and especially their mechanized reproduction as it became possible, set the scene for this mapping out of the impact of visual depictions of heroic deeds which, again, answered commercial interests which contributed decisively to the growth of the phenomenon in the two countries. Taken together, these two chapters provide an overview of the many 'languages' and systems of representation through which imperial reputations were promoted.[82] They also show how the success of imperial heroes benefited from the unprecedented speed at which the media developed, thanks to never-ending technical improvements in terms of speed of communication, cost effectiveness and content sophistication.

The second section opens with an assessment of the political role assumed by, or political meaning attributed to, imperial heroes in the two countries. Their fame and appeal made them ideal tools to promote colonial expansion, to celebrate national grandeur or to serve for debate in Parliament, especially if the government was accountable for their ultimate failure. In that context, their popularity could be used to serve political purposes, and this chronological chapter evaluates the different political roles they performed: early in the period, as 'indirect promoters of expansion', followed by the 'direct promoters of expansion' at the height of the 'New Imperialism', then as 'pure political arguments', and lastly as 'proconsuls' representing the authority of the colonial state.

The fifth chapter looks at the values embodied by imperial heroes, and the various uses that could be made of their 'exemplarity'. Real or idealized representations of imperial heroes were used to support the concept of the civilizing mission, to illustrate the value of entrepreneurship and to promote religious or patriotic agendas, all typical of the ethos that fuelled the drive towards colonial expansion. The concepts associated with military valour, such as strength, manliness and the ability to achieve victory, have been analysed in less detail as comprehensive research has already been undertaken on this subject, and because they are less specifically imperial than military.[83] Throughout this chapter, the similarity of British and French colonial goals certainly appears as a factor of antagonism until at least the Entente Cordiale, but it also reveals clear patterns of cultural convergence in terms of practice, content and moral beliefs – even if they tended to be overshadowed by the competitive context which pitted each colonial project against each other.

The last part of the book shows the various above-mentioned phenomena at work, through the micro-histories of the making of the legends surrounding the figures of Major Jean-Baptiste Marchand and the Sirdar Kitchener. The former allows us to undertake a study in public relations and large-scale publicity, whilst the latter offers an insight into the mechanics of a publishing project which entrenched the name of Kitchener as one of the major military heroes of the British pantheon. Both exemplify the commercial and political impetus behind successful heroic reputations. They evolved along roughly the same timeline, and came to play a prominent role (for very different reasons) in their respective countries in the aftermath of the Fashoda crisis. The high level of detail in each chapter has been retained in order to follow step by step the transformation of an imperial army officer into an imperial hero, to analyse the role of those who promoted this reputation, the possible participation of the future hero himself and the influence upon hero-making of politics and of the internal situation of the country where the reputation developed.

Chapter 6 considers the development of the heroic reputation surrounding the leader of the Congo–Nile mission between the moment when his network of patronage was powerful enough to ensure he led a major French mission in Africa and the end of his short-lived but highly publicized attempt to use his new fame as a launching pad towards a political career. Rather than recounting the story of the mission (a task already undertaken masterfully by Marc Michel),[84] the aim is to cross-examine a variety of private letters, official reports, memoirs, parliamentary documents, police records and publishers' archives in order to demonstrate the converging interests and networks of patronage that ensured the success of a heroic reputation. It also highlights the role of the Press and the publishing world in translating the colonial officer into a heroic figure.

Chapter 7 follows step-by-step the process that led a book to entrench the Kitchener legend almost by chance. It details how a war correspodent eager to make a name for himself, George Warrington Steevens, and a commercially minded publisher, Blackwood and Sons, seized the opportunity of the fall of Khartoum to turn what could have remained a fleeting media frenzy into one of the most durable heroic reputations of late Victorian and Edwardian times. Steevens was 'after Seeley and Kipling, the most important propagandist of the British "New Imperialism"', while Blackwood was well known as a publisher with imperialist leanings, and their correspondence demonstrates how commercial interest and political convictions were far

INTRODUCTION

from incompatible.[85] By following the winding itinerary that led to the publishing of this book, this chapter reveals a generally overlooked but complex and powerful mechanisms of hero-making, with recurring preoccupations about financial issues and success looming in the background, more than any moral crusading spirit.

The archival material used here demonstrates the pivotal importance of previously little-considered practical aspects of the hero-making process. Several questions are addressed here: how a living individual became a public figure; who were the 'hero-makers' responsible for this 'translation'; why they promoted him and what their *modus operandi* was; and to what extent they became popular figures. Answers to these questions have been found notably by shifting the emphasis away from the representations themselves and looking 'upstream' and 'downstream' of the hero-making process, through a documented analysis of the reasons that led to the production of these representations (lobbies, commercial interest, personal networks of the hero), and to the commercial success of these representations. Following the growth of a heroic reputation from its start reveals the logic, interests and beliefs that sustained the promotion of a series of imperial heroes over several decades, and to appraise the success of these reputations among the British and French publics. The internal dynamics of hero-making reveal that, to those involved in this 'trade', production and profit were the most important elements in the equation, as long as the hero did not contradict their own politics. Beyond the ideological excitement that most of them assuredly felt, they were conducting a business and pragmatic concerns came first. For many of the writers, editors and publishers who formed part of this industry which would later be called 'the mass-media', imperial heroes were a welcome tool for the advancement of their trade.

Printed documents and (mostly unpublished) manuscript sources form the bulk of the original material considered here. The former allow us to include here these powerful vectors of heroic reputations and they bring to light the moral, political or practical reasons that made imperial heroes attractive to hero-makers. The latter throw light upon the motivations of, and strategies implemented by, those involved in the promotion of a particular hero: private correspondence between heroes and hero-makers, or between different types of hero-maker (author to publisher, publisher to journalist, journalist to book author, politician to journalist, etc.), reveal the hidden mechanisms that ensured the success of a heroic reputation.

Printed sources include biographic or hagiographic books, leaflets and pamphlets and school textbooks, as well as newspapers and magazines. These sources were obtained mainly at the Bodleian Library

(Oxford), the British Library (London), the National Library of Scotland (Edinburgh), the *Bibliothèque nationale de France* (Paris) and occasionally at the *Archives nationales d'outre-mer* of Aix-en-Provence (ANOM). Four main areas of publication supported one another to promote new heroes, and they have all been given attention on various occasions: the press, juvenile literature, educational texts and non-fiction writing. Hansard and the *Journal officiel de la république française* have been used to discuss the political impact of imperial heroes in parliamentary debates.

The amount and novelty of new manuscript sources varies for each of the imperial heroes considered. The papers of Major Marchand and Captain Baratier at the French National Archives in Paris (AN) and at the ANOM chart the establishment, development and effects of a powerful network of patronage behind Major Marchand in the context of the 'steeple-chase' race (*'la course au clocher'*) for Africa and the Fashoda crisis. Police records held at the *Archives nationales* reveal the political challenge represented by Marchand upon his triumphant return from Fashoda. The ruthless business of selling popular stories of heroic deeds in the empire is fleshed out in the Baratier papers and, crucially, in the correspondence between George Warrington Steevens and his publisher William Blackwood III, held at the National Library of Scotland. Other sources used to produce this book include the papers of Horace Waller, General Gordon, Lord Lugard, Margery Perham, Marshal Lyautey and Pierre Savorgnan de Brazza held at the Bodleian Library of Commonwealth and African Studies at Rhodes House (Oxford), the Middle East Centre (Oxford), the AN and the ANOM. The Sudan archive of Durham University Library offered valuable testimonies on the reputations of General Gordon, the Sirdar Kitchener and Major Marchand in the Anglo-Egyptian Sudan and among officers. The sales ledgers of Blackwood & Sons at the National Library of Scotland, and those of various French publishers held at the *Institut mémoires de l'édition contemporaine* (IMEC) provided crucial quantitative data. The scrupulously and methodically kept statistics in voluminous leather-bound ledgers provide an invaluable, and apparently reliable, assessment of the success of these heroic reputations in the publishing world. The comparison with other titles of the period, the sales of which were recorded in the same ledgers, is another indicator of popularity. As a rule, print-run figures from the publishing industry have been preferred to newspaper circulation as the variety of articles featured in any daily edition diminished the clarity of the causal link between circulation and the featuring of imperial heroes.

Other, less conventional, sources have also been used. Following a major line of research which has demonstrated the usefulness of less

INTRODUCTION

textual, more concrete sources to evaluate more completely a phenomenon, this book also attempts to evaluate the reception of imperial heroes through commemorative monuments and street names.[86] Whenever possible, preparatory documents and discussions related to these celebrations are used.

Industrially produced visual sources were another major resource. Mechanical reproduction in large quantities, and their exceptionally powerful evocative power, explains that visual materials had a major impact upon hero-making phenomena. Engravings and photographs included in printed sources (some of which were among the best-selling titles of the period) help understand how the authors, and consequently the public, visualized heroic deeds. Photographic archives have not been used as unpublished slides were seen only in very limited circles (if seen at all), and therefore did not influence the popular perception of the heroes. However, the cinema has been explored as filmic re-enactments represented a major promotional device for heroes in the interwar years. Films and directors' memoirs, 'making-of' shots and press-cuttings of these films have been found mainly at the *Bibliothèque du film* and *Gaumont Pathé Archives* (Paris) and the National Library of Scotland (papers of the Livingstone Film Expedition), while further press-cuttings have been released from the private archives of *Les Documents cinématographiques* (Paris).

Taken together, these sources reveal a surprisingly coherent and often co-ordinated effort on the part of a variety of hero-makers who had an interest in promoting legends surrounding the great empire-builders of the time. They also allow us to evaluate their commercial weight at a time when popular entertainment underwent drastic processes of industrialization. Imperial heroes did not enter the pantheon of popular national imagination accidentally, and this book traces the hero-making processes that turned some actors of 'New Imperialism' into national heroes of a new kind.

Notes

1 J. M. MacKenzie (ed.), *David Livingstone and the Victorian Encounter with Africa* (1996). See also R. Robinson and J. Gallagher, *Africa and the Victorians* (1961), and P. Brantlinger, *Rule of Darkness: British Literature and Imperialism, 1830–1914* (Ithaca, NY, 1988).
2 Among the many works dedicated to the development of nationalisms in Europe, see for instance B. Anderson, *Imagined Communities: Reflections on the Origin and Spread of Nationalism* (1983); R. Brubaker, *Citizenship and Nationhood in France and Germany* (Cambridge, MA, 1992); E. Hobsbawm, *Nations and Nationalism since 1780* (Cambridge, 1990); E. Gellner, *Nations and Nationalism* (Ithaca, NY, 1983); A. Hastings, *The Construction of Nationhood* (Cambridge, 1997).
3 M. Agulhon, 'Nouveaux propos sur les statues de "grands hommes" au XIXe siècle', in 'Le grand homme', *Romantisme*, 100 (1998), 11–16.

4   W. E. Houghton, *The Victorian Frame of Mind* (1957, repr. 1979), p.316.
5   Général Trochu, *L'Armée française en 1867* (1867), p.18, quoted in R. Gildea, *The Past in French History* (New Haven and London, 1994), p.119.
6   S. Dulucq and C. Zytnicki, 'Penser le passé colonial français, entre perspectives historiographiques et résurgence des mémoires', *Vingtième Siècle*, 86 (April–June 2005), 59–69.
7   Two examples of recent works based on an individual study of heroes and organized around a biographical chapter breakdown are B. Singer and J. Langdon, *Cultured Force* (London and Madison, 2004), and E. Berenson, *Heroes of Empire* (Berkeley and Los Angeles, CA, 2011).
8   V. Mudimbe, *The Invention of Africa* (Indianapolis, 1988), p.151.
9   Efforts in this direction have been made in relation to Western travel writing in M.-L. Pratt, *Imperial Eyes: Travel-Writing and Transculturation* (1992), and in relation to German and Belgian exploration in Central Africa in J. Fabian, *Out of Our Minds: Reason and Madness in the Exploration of Central Africa* (Berkeley, CA, 2000).
10 F. Hartog, *Régimes d'historicité, présentisme et expérience du temps* (2002); Anderson, *Imagined Communities*.
11 For a historicization of the concept of fame, see L. Braudy, *The Frenzy of Renown* (Oxford, 1986); F. Inglis, *A Short History of Celebrity* (Princeton, NJ, 2010).
12 For a summary of the questions which have driven this research, see B. Sèbe, 'Portedrapeaux de l'Empire: la promotion des héros coloniaux français et britanniques de la conquête de l'Afrique à la Seconde Guerre mondiale', *Synergies Royaume-Uni et Irlande*, 2 (2009), 81–92, and B. Sèbe, 'French and British colonial heroes', in Wm R. Louis (ed.), *Resurgent Adventures with Britannia* (2011), pp.45–60.
13 A considerable amount of scholarship has been dedicated to the study of the political and socio-cultural impact of the mass-media; see for instance J. Theobald, *The Media and the Making of History* (Aldershot, 2004); J. Curran, 'Media and the making of British society, c. 1700–2000', *Media History*, 8:2 (2002), 135–54; A. Berger, (ed.), *Making Sense of Media: Key Texts in Media and Cultural Studies* (Malden, 2005); P. Burke and A. Briggs, *A Social History of the Media: From Gutenberg to the Internet* (Cambridge, 2005); J. Lull, *Media, Communication, Culture* (Cambridge, 1995 and 2000). For a general approach to media theories, see D. Albertazzi and P. Cobley (eds), *The Media: An Introduction* (Harlow, 2010); a good general conceptualization is also offered from a historical point of view in C. Ross, *Media and the Making of Modern Germany* (Oxford, 2008), pp.11–58. On France, see F. d'Almeida and C. Delporte, *Histoire des médias en France* (2003); J.-N. Jeanneney, *Une histoire des médias des origines à nos jours* (1996); J.-P. Rioux and J.-F. Sirinelli (eds), *La Culture de masse en France de la Belle Epoque à aujourd'hui* (2002); D. Kalifa, *La Culture de masse en France. 1/1860–1930* (2001).
14 J. M. MacKenzie, 'Heroic myths of Empire', in J.M. MacKenzie (ed.), *Popular Imperialism and the Military* (Manchester, 1992), pp.109–38.
15 See for instance B. Taithe, *The Killer Trail* (Oxford, 2009), pp.109–39, or E. Deroo and S. Lemaire, *L'Illusion coloniale* (2005), pp.40–55 and 114–23.
16 R. H. MacDonald, *The Language of Empire* (Manchester, 1994), p.83.
17 A. S. Thompson, *Imperial Britain: The Empire in British Politics c. 1880–1932* (Harlow, 2000), p.64.
18 For a definition of *histoire culturelle*, see P. Ory, *L'Histoire culturelle* (2004), and 'Pour une histoire culturelle de la France contemporaine (1870 …). Etat de la question', *Bulletin du Centre d'histoire de la France contemporaine*, 2 (1981), 5–32. The concepts of 'popular culture' and 'mass media' are used in this book without any pejorative connotation.
19 See for instance, in the 'Studies in Imperialism' series, J. M. MacKenzie, *Propaganda and Empire* (Manchester, 1984); MacKenzie (ed.), *Popular Imperialism and the Military* and *European Empires and the People* (Manchester, 2011); J. Richards (ed.), *Imperialism and Juvenile Literature* (Manchester, 1989). Outside this series, see for instance A. Thompson, *The Empire Strikes Back* (Harlow, 2005), or C. Hall and S. O. Rose (eds), *At Home with the Empire* (Cambridge, 2006).

INTRODUCTION

20 C. R. Ageron, *France coloniale ou parti colonial?* (1978).
21 See for instance A. P. Thornton, *The Imperial Idea and Its Enemies* (1959); B. Porter, *Critics of Empire: British Radical Attitudes to Colonialism in Africa 1895–1914* (1968); S. Howe, *Anticolonialism in British Politics: The Left and the End of Empire, 1918–1964* (Oxford, 1993).
22 MacKenzie, *Propaganda and Empire*.
23 J. M. MacKenzie (ed.), *Imperialism and Popular Culture* (Manchester, 1986).
24 MacKenzie, *Popular Imperialism and the Military*, p. 1.
25 P. Burke, *Popular Culture in Early Modern Europe* (1978), p. 270.
26 MacDonald, *Language of Empire*.
27 D. Cannadine, *Ornamentalism: How the British Saw Their Empire* (2001).
28 Richards (ed.), *Imperialism and Juvenile Literature*; J. Chapman and N. J. Cull, *Imperialism and Popular Cinema* (2009).
29 Thompson, *Imperial Britain*.
30 On the 'new imperial history', see for instance S. Marks, 'History, the nation and empire: sniping from the periphery', *History Workshop*, 29 (Spring 1990), 111–19; A. Burton, 'Rules of thumb: British history and "imperial culture" in nineteenth and twentieth century Britain', *Women's History Review*, 3:4 (1994), 483–500; A. Burton (ed.), *After the Imperial Turn: Thinking with and through the Nation* (Durham, NC, 2003); C. Hall, *Civilising Subjects: Metropole and Colony in the English Imagination, 1830–1867* (Cambridge, 2002).
31 See for instance K. Wilson (ed.), *A New Imperial History: Culture, Identity and Modernity in Britain and the Empire, 1660–1840* (Cambridge, 2004); M. Jasanoff, *Edge of Empire* (2005); H. Hoock, *Empires of the Imagination* (2010).
32 A.-L. Stoler and F. Cooper (eds), *Tensions of Empire: Colonial Cultures in a Bourgeois World* (Berkeley, CA, 1997); S. Gikandi, *Maps of Englishness: Writing Identity in the Culture of Colonialism* (New York, 1996); M. Evans and R. Branche, 'Where does colonial history end?', in R. Gildea and A. Simonin (eds), *Writing Contemporary History* (2008), pp. 145–67; M. Silverman, 'Interconnected Histories: Holocaust and Empire in the Cultural Imaginary', *French Studies*, 62:4 (2008), 417–28; C. Hall and K. McClelland (eds), *Race, Nation and Empire: Making Histories, 1750 to the Present* (Manchester, 2010). In recent years, increased attention has also been paid to the development of inter-imperial media networks, which show a level of integration between metropole and colonies which had remained largely ignored beforehand: see S. Kaul (ed.), *Media and the British Empire* (Basingstoke, 2006); S. Potter, *News and the British World: The Emergence of an Imperial Press System 1876–1922* (Oxford, 2003), and *Broadcasting Empire: The BBC and the British World, 1922–1970* (Oxford, 2012).
33 Burton, *After the Imperial Turn*, p. 2.
34 E. Said, *Orientalism* (1978), *Culture & Imperialism* (1993). John MacKenzie provides a magisterial discussion of Said's analysis in *Orientalism: History, Theory and the Arts* (Manchester, 1995).
35 B. Parry, 'Overlapping territories and intertwined histories: Edward Said's postcolonial cosmopolitanism', in M. Sprinker (ed.), *Edward Said: A Reader* (Oxford, 1993), p. 24.
36 D. Chakrabarty, *Provincializing Europe: Postcolonial Thought and Historical Difference* (Princeton, NJ, 2000).
37 See for instance J. Darwin, *After Tamerlane: The Global History of Empire since 1405* (2007), and *The Empire Project: The Rise and Fall of the British World-System, 1830–1970* (Cambridge, 2009), or J. Burbank and F. Cooper, *Empires in World History: Power and the Politics of Difference* (Princeton, NJ, 2010).
38 In particular, N. Bancel, P. Blanchard, A. Chatelier (eds), *Images et colonies* (1993); P. Blanchard, S. Lemaire and N. Bancel (eds), *Culture coloniale en France* (2008). Also, to a lesser extent, Deroo and Lemaire, *L'Illusion coloniale*.
39 Ageron, *France coloniale*.
40 M. Thomas, *The French Empire between the Wars* (Manchester, 2005), p. 185.
41 A. S. Kanya-Forstner, *The Conquest of the Western Sudan* (Cambridge, 1969).

42 See in particular C. M. Andrew and A. S. Kanya-Forstner, 'The French "colonial party": its composition, aims and influence, 1885–1914', *The Historical Journal*, 14:1 (March 1971), 99–128, and 'The *Groupe Colonial* in the French Chamber of Deputies, 1892–1932', *The Historical Journal*, 17:4 (Dec. 1974), 837–66; S. M. Persell, *The French Colonial Lobby, 1889–1938* (Stanford, 1983).
43 For a general appraisal of the imperial activity of the Third Republic, see J. J. Cooke, *New French Imperialism, 1880–1910: The Third Republic and Colonial Expansion* (Newton Abbot, 1973).
44 C.-R. Ageron, 'L'exposition coloniale de 1931. Mythe républicain ou mythe impérial?', in P. Nora (ed.), *Les Lieux de mémoire*, vol. 1 (1984), pp. 493–515.
45 T. Chafer and A. Sackur (eds), *Promoting the Colonial Idea* (2002), pp. 1–9. See also Chapter and Sackur, *French Colonial Empire and the Popular Front* (Basingstoke, 1999), which is based on the same assumption.
46 See for instance M. Evans, *Empire and Culture: The French Experience 1830–1940* (Basingstoke, 2004). For a historiographical overview, see B. Sèbe, 'Exalting imperial grandeur', in MacKenzie, *European Empires and the People*, pp. 19–56.
47 See for instance E. Sibeud, *Une science impériale pour l'Afrique? La construction des savoirs africanistes en France (1878–930)* (2002); O. Saaïdia and L. Zerbini (eds), *La Construction du discours colonial* (2009); S. Dulucq, *Ecrire l'histoire de l'Afrique à l'époque coloniale (XIXe–XXe siècles)* (2009).
48 Among the growing literature in the field, see D. Murphy, 'De-Centring French Studies: Towards a Postcolonial Theory of Francophone Cultures', *French Cultural Studies*, 13:2 (June 2002), 165–85; D. Murphy and C. Forsdick (eds), *Francophone Postcolonial Studies* (2003), and *Postcolonial Thought in the French-Speaking World* (Liverpool, 2009); C. Forsdick, 'On the abolition of the French department? Exploring the disciplinary contexts of *Littérature-monde*', in A. C. Hargreaves, C. Forsdick and D. Murphy (eds), *Transnational French Studies* (Liverpool, 2010), pp. 89–108; A. C. Hargreaves (ed.), *Memory, Empire and Colonialism: Legacies of French Colonialism* (Lanham, MD, 2005); F. Lionnet and D. Thomas, *Francophone Studies: New Landscapes, Modern Language Notes* special issue, 118:4 (2003); H. Lebovics, *True France: The Wars over Cultural Identity, 1900–1945* (1992); K. Ross, *Fast Cars, Clean Bodies: Decolonization and the Reordering of French Culture* (Cambridge, MA, 1996).
49 M. A. Majumdar, *Postcoloniality: The French Dimension* (New York and Oxford, 2007).
50 This is particularly the case in France, as social discontent in some suburbs (*banlieues*) with high levels of population of ex-colonial origin can be traced directly to the country's colonial past. See among others B. Stora, *La Gangrène et l'oubli* (1991); N. Bancel, P. Blanchard and F. Vergès (eds), *La République coloniale. Essai sur une utopie* (2003); G. Manceron, *Marianne et les colonies* (2003); P. Blanchard, N. Bancel and S. Lemaire (eds), *La Fracture coloniale* (2005); and the third part of R. Branche, *La Guerre d'Algérie: une histoire apaisée?* (2005), pp. 255–384. In Britain, the empire is subject to a different type of assessment, and its praise has become a popular subject, as shown notably by N. Ferguson's *Empire: How Britain Made the Modern World* (2003). A more critical appraisal has been recently provided by J. Paxman, *Empire: What Ruling the World Did to the British* (2011).
51 B. Porter, *The Absent-Minded Imperialists* (Oxford, 2004).
52 And in particular MacKenzie (ed.), *European Empires and the People*.
53 A. Rey (ed.), *Dictionnaire historique de la langue française*, vol. 2 (1998), p. 1711.
54 Hesiod, *Works and Days*, 140–65.
55 Pausanias, *Description of Greece*, 1, XXXII, 4.
56 Heroism as understood by Carlyle appears as a widespread phenomenon in the Western world, with cases appearing in Britain, France, the USA and even Chile: A. W. Yarrington, *The Commemoration of the Hero 1800–1864: Monuments to the British Victors of the Napoleonic Wars* (London and New York, 1988); M. Peterson, *The Jefferson Image in the American Mind* (New York, 1960), and *Lincoln in American Memory* (Oxford, 1994); B. Schwarz, *George Washington: The Making of*

INTRODUCTION

an American Myth (Ithaca, NY, 1987); M. Warner, *Joan of Arc: The Image of Female Heroism* (New York, 1981); I. Germani, *Jean-Paul-Marat: Hero and Anti-Hero of the French Revolution* (Lewiston, NY, 1992); W. F. Sater, *The Heroic Image in Chile: Arturo Prat, Secular Saint* (Berkeley, 1973).

57 *Le Dictionnaire de l'Académie françoise*, vol. 1 (1694, repr. 1901), p. 562.
58 E. Littré, *Dictionnaire de la langue française*, vol. 2 (1885), pp. 2013–14.
59 *Dictionnaire de l'Académie française, septième édition*, vol. 1 (1878), pp. 879–80.
60 P. Larousse, *Grand dictionnaire universel du XIXe siècle*, vol. IX (1866–77), p. 241.
61 *Trésor de la langue française, dictionnaire de la langue française du 19e et du 20e siècle*, vol. 9 (1981), pp. 796–7.
62 See the Biographical Sketches at the end of this book.
63 B. Sèbe, 'Aventurières et voyageuses en Afrique de l'Ouest', in R. Little (ed.), *Lucie Cousturier, les tirailleurs sénégalais et la question coloniale* (2008), pp. 163–86.
64 G. Cubitt and A. Warren (eds), *Heroic Reputations and Exemplary Lives* (Manchester, 2000), p. 3.
65 For general considerations on the historical analysis of heroes, see M. Jones, 'What should historians do with heroes? Reflections on nineteenth- and twentieth-century Britain', *History Compass*, 5:2 (2007), 439–54.
66 David Livingstone's heroic reputation obviously started before the beginning of the period covered in this book, but it largely survived him, and epitomized the model imperial hero which inspired later instances of the phenomenon.
67 R. Tholoniat and P. Venier, 'French imperialist perceptions of Cecil Rhodes', in S. Aprile and F. Bensimon (eds), *La France et l'Angleterre au XIXe siècle. Echanges, représentations et comparaisons* (2004).
68 H. Strachan, *The Politics of the British Army* (Oxford, 1997), pp. 92–3.
69 MacKenzie, 'Heroic myths of Empire'.
70 H. A. Turner Jr, 'Bismarck's imperialist venture: anti-British in origin?', in P. Gifford and Wm Roger Louis (eds), *France and Britain in Africa* (New Haven and London, 1971), pp. 47–82.
71 E. Hobsbawm, 'Mass-producing traditions: Europe 1870–1914', in E. Hobsbawm and T. Ranger (eds), *The Invention of Tradition* (Cambridge, 1983), pp. 263–307.
72 C. Andrews and A. S. Kanya-Forstner, *The Climax of French Imperial Expansion, 1914–1924* (Stanford, CA, 1981); Darwin, *Empire Project*, pp. 305–475.
73 With a few exceptions, such as Gifford and Louis (eds), *France and Britain in Africa*; F. Cooper, *Decolonization and African Society: The Labour Question in French and British Africa* (Cambridge, 1996); C. Charle, *La Crise des sociétés impériales 1900–1940: Allemagne, France, Grande-Bretagne. Essai d'histoire comparée* (2001); or Berenson, *Heroes of Empire*. A few general comparisons have been published, but it has remained uncharted territory in the field of popular culture, with the exception of MacKenzie (ed.), *European Empires and the People*.
74 On Franco-British imperial rivalry, see T. G. Otte, 'From "war-in-sight" to nearly war: Anglo-French relations in the age of high imperialism, 1875–1898', in G. Stone and T. G. Otte (eds), *Anglo-French Relations since the Late Eighteenth Century* (Abingdon, 2008), pp. 59–80.
75 See for instance MacKenzie (ed.), *European Empires and the People*, or K. Nicolaidis and B. Sèbe (eds), *Echoes of Empire: The Present of Europe's Past* (forthcoming).
76 S. Venayre, *La Gloire de l'aventure* (2002), p. 142.
77 B. Zimmermann and M. Werner (eds), *De la comparaison à l'histoire croisée* (2004). James Fichter's current research project looks at the entanglement of British and French imperial projects at the time of 'New Imperialism' – see his forthcoming *Passage to India: The Suez Canal and the Anglo-French Empires in Asia, 1798–1885*.
78 J. S. Keltie, 'Mr Stanley's expedition: its conduct and results', *Fortnightly Review*, 48 (1890), 81.
79 C. Gledhill, 'Signs of melodrama', in C. Gledhill (ed.), *Stardom: Industry of Desire* (1991), p. 214.
80 B. Sèbe, 'Colonial celebrities in popular culture: Heroes of the British and French

empire, 1850–1914', in R. Clarke (ed.), *Celebrity Colonialism: Fame, Power and Representation in Colonial and Postcolonial Cultures* (Newcastle, 2009), pp. 37–54.
81 J. B. Thompson, *The Media and Modernity* (Cambridge, 1995).
82 S. Hall (ed.), *Representation. Cultural Representations and Signifying Practices* (1997), pp. 16–19.
83 See for instance G. Dawson, *Soldier Heroes* (1994).
84 M. Michel, *La Mission Marchand* (1972), revised and abridged as *Fachoda. Guerre sur le Nil* (2010).
85 R. T. Stearn, 'G. W. Steevens and the Message of Empire', *Journal of Imperial and Commonwealth History*, 17 (1988–89), 226. On the influence of British publishers on the promotion of an imperial agenda, see L. Howsam, 'Imperial publishers and the idea of colonial history, 1870–1916', *History of Intellectual Culture*, 5:1 (2005), 1–15: www.ucalgary.ca/hic/issues/vol5/5 [Accessed 15 October 2011].
86 Exemplified in particular by Anderson, *Imagined Communities*; Hobsbawm and Ranger (eds), *Invention of Tradition* on the British side and, in France, M. Agulhon, *Marianne au combat, 1789–1880* (1979) and *Marianne au pouvoir, 1880–1914* (1989), and P. Nora (ed.), *Les Lieux de mémoire*, 7 vols (1984, 1986 and 1992, Engl. trans. *Realms of Memory*, New York, 1997).

PART I

Contexts

CHAPTER 1

The emergence of a new type of hero: British and French contexts

Heroes play a vital role in their country's self-confidence. Besides serving to strengthen their nation's cohesion (and self-esteem too) through an exceptional deed that lends itself to idealization and commemoration, they set a proud and glorious precedent that legitimizes the existence of the nation to whom they belong. The national hero is an iconic example, an 'Exemplar Virtutis',[1] who provides guiding principles to society. Although the meaning of heroic behaviour is often presented as universally appealing, it is far from ahistorical. Carlyle's fundamental principle that 'society is founded on hero-worship'[2] implies that the national pantheon of heroes evolves according to the values of the time, which are themselves shaped by technology, science, the general state of culture and the nation's own perception of itself at any given moment. New heroes appear and are added or substituted to earlier Great Men as events unfold, while dominant sensibilities evolve and new means of promotion appear. The Scramble for Africa, one of the most evident expressions of the gigantic land grab that was later termed 'New Imperialism', was one of the defining moments of the end of the nineteenth century, and it provided a context propitious to the rise to fame of a new generation of heroes. The conquest of a continent at a time of shrinking colonial opportunities was well suited to the development of heroic reputations inspired by Romantic thought, according to which heroes were individuals capable of changing the course of history.

Several fundamental changes in nearly all aspects of British and French life help us understand the backdrop against which this new type of hero developed. A unique set of conditions enabled the appearance of imperial heroes in British and French popular culture. First, geostrategic developments linked to the 'Congress system' explain why so many imperial heroes of the period were linked to the army. The absence of any major military campaign on the European continent between the Treaty of Vienna and 1914 (with the notable exception of the Franco-Prussian War) and the wave of 'New Imperialism' reinvigorated interest in overseas deeds, which in turn generated new imperial heroes. Secondly, the geographical expansion of 'New Imperialism', combined with deep urban changes resulting from the industrial revolution, provided new means of promoting the reputations of these heroes. Thirdly, the extension of the franchise meant that policy makers had more potential voters to convince. Colonially minded politicians and geographical societies wishing to advance the cause of 'Greater Britain' or *la plus grande France* could use the political value of imperial heroes to gather support for colonial expansion or simply to massage public opinion. To press their agenda, they could use the power of the press, which had become a 'Fourth Estate', as described by Thomas Carlyle (who attributed it to Edmund Burke without supporting evidence), making more explicit the concept of *quatrième pouvoir* first put forward by Alexis de Tocqueville in *De la démocratie en Amérique* (1833). The last aspect under consideration in this chapter is directly related to this evolution: fundamental socio-cultural changes allowed a greater diffusion, and a better reception, of the promotional material that established the reputations of these heroes. Literacy and wages increased among the working classes, creating markets for cheap popular products, which will be studied in the subsequent two chapters.

From the French navy officer Brazza to Marshal Lyautey, from General Gordon to the 'Sirdar' Kitchener, many of the imperial heroes featured in this book gained their heroic status through military deeds (a quick look at the Biographical Sketches at the end of this book shows that many British figures discussed here, and all the French except for one, underwent specialist military training). To understand this trend, we must remember that a significant number of encounters between Europeans and Africans in the nineteenth century happened through colonial warfare, the details of which were reported to the European public, sometimes in much detail. In his famous indictment of European imperialism, John A. Hobson once referred unflatteringly to 'hero worship and sensational glory, adventure and the sporting spirit' as 'current history falsified in coarse flaring colours, for the direct stimulation of the combative instincts'.[3]

As was implied by Hobson's remark, the appearance of military heroes who acted in Africa was closely linked to changes in the image of the army in Britain and in France, and the geopolitical context in which these two armies operated. In the two countries, the army was made of interlocking and sometimes overlapping communities which gradually enhanced their reputation outside the barracks. At an individual level, the reasons why officers might have sought active service overseas should not be overlooked – what David Cannadine called the 'lust for titles'.[4]

Up to the end of the Napoleonic wars, British and French military heroes had risen to prominence confronting European enemies on European or, exceptionally, North American battlefields: Québec, Trafalgar, Waterloo, Austerlitz and Wagram, to name but five great battles, consecrated the names of Wolfe, Nelson, Wellington and Napoleon respectively. The Treaty of Vienna in 1815, and the concerted attempt to favour diplomacy over war in the conduct of European affairs, rendered the European continent unsuitable for warfare. As a consequence, motives for military advancement, official rewards and popular veneration had to be sought overseas. This coincided with a new period of European expansion, in Asia, Oceania and Africa. If most of the African interior remained *terra incognita* in 1800, by 1914 all the continent (apart from Ethiopia and Liberia) had been shared between Britain, France, Belgium, Germany, Italy, Portugal and Spain, the first two having carved the largest shares at the price of a sharp and constant competition between their explorers, officers and traders.

These conquests were conducted on the ground by armed forces composed of European troops or native troops led by European officers. Such campaigns contributed to enhancing the image of the army in Britain, where its reputation had been traditionally bad, in particular in the decades of peace following the Napoleonic wars, when most of the European powers shaped their forces as much for use in the suppression of insurrection at home as for fighting abroad.[5] During most of the nineteenth century, 'suspicion of, and disregard for, the army was widespread throughout all levels of [British] society', and the army was considered nothing more than 'the dustbin of the nation'.[6] The army was unpopular, soldiers were looked at with contempt and enlistment was frequently considered degrading by family and friends of the new recruit. This disdain for the soldier was only sometimes softened by the fact that ultimately 'as a symbol, the uniform, above all, represented the traditions which Victorian society sought to uphold'.[7] This situation changed from the mid-nineteenth century onwards: the army was less involved in the repression of public unrest at home, and the widely publicized logistical shortcomings of the Crimean War attracted public sympathy with the plight of the army.[8] This coincided also with an enhancement of the army's image in Victorian literature, which had been under way for at least a couple of decades.[9] It came to be perceived as a factor of unification of the peoples and classes of the United Kingdom, while the usual respect for officers, who traditionally came from aristocratic stock, helped to improve the institution's overall image. V. Kiernan noted that 'as an organization combining all classes, the army made a suitable emblem of national unity, of the nation as a big family'.[10] Concomitantly, several writers and publicists, the most famous of whom was Rudyard Kipling, helped to raise the status of the army (in particular its imperial version) in the eyes of the British public, who finally came to recognize it as an intrinsic part of Victorian society.[11] Imperial campaigns greatly enhanced the prestige of military officers and their soldiers, who were 'at the forefront of the action' when foreign and colonial policy were concerned, and upon whom 'the security of the Empire depended'.[12]

For officers starting their careers in a period of European peace, overseas campaigns proved to be the easiest, if not the sole, means of securing official rewards. The changes in the international backdrop against which military heroes became famous explain why the eighteenth- or early nineteenth-century military hero (like Wellington or Napoleon) was succeeded by the mid- to late nineteenth-century imperial hero. In a society cemented by elaborate systems of honour, reaping the rewards of a successful African campaign could be an attractive prospect, especially for those intending to climb the social ladder. The 'most successful British proconsuls and imperial soldiers' became 'veritable walking Christmas trees of stars and collars, medals and sashes, ermine robes and coronets'.[13] Neither General Gordon nor the Sirdar Kitchener came from the aristocracy, but their successful military assignments overseas opened them the doors of the upper strata of British society: Gordon died CB, and Kitchener was created Baron of Khartoum and Aspall following his successful leadership in the 1898 Sudan campaign. Lord Lugard was appointed KCMG in 1901, and was raised to the peerage in 1928. The prestige and social recognition conferred by these rewards can partly explain the attractiveness of imperial campaigns to promising officers, who could occasionally indulge in lobbying and promotional campaigns that had the potential to generate new heroic narratives.

Whereas the British never felt themselves to be under the threat of invasion (apart from brief and unfounded outbursts of anxiety about a possible French landing), post-1870 France lived with the fear of the growing German menace. Sympathy for the armed forces after the defeat in the war against Prussia stemmed from the desire to avoid another catastrophe.[14] The army was to the French what the navy was to the British: seemingly, the only guarantee for the territory's safety. Unlike its British counterpart, the French army enjoyed a favourable image among large groups of the population, the only notable exception being the *Communards* and their sympathizers.

THE EMERGENCE OF A NEW TYPE OF HERO

British forces relied upon enlistment, and for that reason the army was perceived as the only choice for those who lacked the qualities, or the temperance or knowledge required to lead a decent and normal civil life. By contrast, the French army relied heavily upon conscription (following the 1872, 1873 and 1875 military laws which established universal five-year military service and put an end to the practice of substitution) and was perceived as a unifying factor in a country with marked regional differences. Embracing a career in the army was generally considered a respectable choice, applauded for its patriotic value. Socialist anti-militarism remained marginal until at least the turn of the century. The primary education system taught children to respect and admire the army; pupils were asked to practise their writing skills on subjects related to the life of soldiers and their families during wartime.[15] Children or grandchildren of officers or soldiers eagerly shared with their comrades and teachers family narratives of metropolitan or colonial war campaigns.[16] Military commanders, as much as their troops, were reluctant to repress too violently popular unrest or strikes when they were asked to restore order (for instance, General Boulanger celebrated the 'fraternity' between soldiers and miners on the occasion of the strike of Decazeville in 1886). Such moderation was a motive of sympathy in the eyes of the French public.[17]

Opportunities for the French army to take pride of place in the last third of the nineteenth century were limited as the Prussian-led army was undeniably superior and waging war on Germany would have been simply suicidal. French troops were not involved in any European campaign between 1870 and 1914 (French strategic plans in Europe were always defensive, never offensive), which prevented them from gaining opportunities for popular publicity. Consequently, colonial campaigns were popular among ambitious officers seeking quick advancement and wishing to escape the boring routine of garrison life. Numerous future generals or marshals had gained experience in the *bureaux arabes* of Algeria even before the Prussian war,[18] but the post-1870 situation offered unprecedented opportunities for campaigning that brought to the forefront new names such as Gallieni, Marchand, Gouraud or Mangin, who 'added new episodes to France's war epic [*épopée guerrière*]'.[19] Henri Brunschwig remarked rightly that 'a new school of colonizing officers-men of outstanding ability' emerged under the Third Republic.[20] A hierarchy of prestige between colonies existed, the most attractive to officers being those where fighting (*le baroud*) was likely to happen: for instance, Tunisia was judged a rather uninteresting and unpromising posting by the future General Laperrine.[21]

As in Britain, the wish to secure official rewards was a significant incentive. In France, state-sanctioned recognition took the form of the

Légion d'honneur. With its five different levels, it ranked and classified military and civilian service to the State.[22] For example, Major Marchand joined the 'elite of the living' (as de Gaulle later called it) as a *'Chevalier'* further to his action in West Africa in 1889, but was promoted to the rank of *'officier'* in 1895 and *'commandeur'* following Fashoda in March 1899.[23] Obtaining the Legion of Honour, and subsquent promotion among its ranks, could encourage officers to accomplish great deeds, whose narratives in the press could captivate audiences beyond military circles.

Exemplary British imperial successes, widely (if sometimes envyingly) publicized in France (especially through translations of Rudyard Kipling, who quickly became 'the most widely read of the Anglo-Saxon writers' in France)[24] also helped to popularize among the French audience the image of the 'empire builder', as did, later, the extensive literature of the interwar period celebrating the officers of the Saharan camel corps (see Chapter 2). The examples of Gallieni and Lyautey, who both laid down their theories of conquest and colonization,[25] were increasingly echoed among the military, and the public took more and more interest in the 'civilizing mission' undertaken by the French soldiers turned apprentice colonizers by the circumstances.[26]

Lastly, the slow but steady development of the image of the 'imperial hero' in France resulted from a governmental tendency to send specifically colonial troops overseas. The Third Republic proved reluctant to risk its new 'metropolitan' army of short-service conscripts in perilous imperial adventures: unlike the conquest of Algeria, which had been undertaken mostly by regular regiments, imperial expansion beyond North Africa fell almost exclusively to colonial units raised specifically for that purpose.[27] For instance, the French Foreign Legion took part in the conquest of Dahomey and Madagascar, while French marines traditionally operated in sub-Saharan Africa. These divisions gave rise to several enduring heroic legends attached to the French Foreign Legion (in particular in novels and movies, including in Britain under the guise of P. C. Wren's *Beau Geste*), while officers of the French navy, like Brazza, came into the limelight as imperial builders.

In France as much as in Britain, the military hero appears as the major figure of imperial heroism for the period under consideration. Not only was he one of the main agents of expansion on the spot, but his image came to enjoy prestige and affection among both officials and the general public.

The rise to fame of this new type of hero took place against the backdrop of a period of unprecedented urban growth, and relatively new practices of official celebration, which provided many opportunities to commemorate new figures in public space. The expansion of towns and cities allowed the christening of public places or even new towns after exemplary characters among the pantheon of national history. Imperial heroes became part of everyday life though their imprint on urban landscapes.[28]

Because they proceed from a selective and constructed perception of history that 'writes an official view of the past onto the landscape',[29] street names amount to 'a national honorific system'.[30] As 'manifestations of a community's collective memory' and 'external signs of notoriety', they tell the historian about 'the establishment's representations of the national memory and the nation's great men as well as about the means of promoting those representations'.[31] Even if local inhabitants sometimes knew little about the great person celebrated in their neighbourhood, street naming states durably the nation's recognition of the hero's achievements: the population refers to it on a daily basis, and further publicity is ensured through maps and many other references to the place.

In France, the monarch monopolized street naming at the same time as the right to use violence and to tax, in the early seventeenth century. In 1760, only three out of some eight hundred public streets in Paris paid homage to the great men of the nation (excluding the royal family and great noble houses). The proportion of great men increased regularly, until Napoleon officially set up street naming as a national honorific tradition which the Third Republic reinforced. Although the Republic could create an atmosphere favourable to the celebration of certain national heroes or themes, street naming remained within the competence of municipal councils: the initiative ultimately remained within the power of the local authorities. With its cohort of new streets, the urban growth of the late nineteenth century left room for imperial heroes to join the national pantheon of urban toponymy: for instance, the fourth commission of the Municipal Council of Paris decided to name after Brazza one of the alleys of the *Champ de Mars* that were built in 1907.[32] In Paris as much as in the *province*, the proportion of colonial street names became far from trivial as metropolitan cities expanded at a time of imperial growth. Because they evocatively connected colonial enterprise with the greatness of France, explorers, conquerors, colonially minded government figures or writers or scientists linked to the empire proved to be a popular choice.[33] France still counts at least eighteen street names and a harbour referring to Major Marchand.[34] Marchand's name was even given to one of the main avenues of the new business district built in Paris in the 1960s, *La Défense*. The Paris underground has a Gallieni metro station, while in France there are many streets named after Lyautey (at least twenty),[35]

Brazza (seventeen),[36] Laperrine (nine)[37] or Charles de Foucauld (twenty-five).[38] Although these imperial heroes never reached the almost universal notoriety of names such as Victor Hugo, Léon Gambetta, Louis Pasteur or Jean Jaurès, it is evident that the development of the habit of christening streets after great men of the nation asserted, expanded and consolidated the fame of the French imperial heroes who came to prominence for their action in Africa during the height of 'New Imperialism'. It is not a coincidence if the request for the naming after Brazza of a Parisian street was made by the *Société de propagande coloniale*:[39] publicizing the work of imperial heroes in that way helped to justify the imperial effort.

The British public could also feel the presence of imperial heroes throughout the United Kingdom. A study in street name frequencies based on the *Complete London Street Atlas* and the *A–Z Manchester Street Atlas* has shown that, in 1991, British imperial heroes were still significantly present in the urban landscape of these two major English cities. In Greater London, there were still seventy-one streets bearing the name of Gordon and seventy-five that of Stanley – well above Nightingale and Nelson, with forty-nine and forty-six respectively. In Greater Manchester, forty-seven were named after Stanley and twenty after Gordon (which put Stanley slightly above Wellington who got forty-five registered streets, and well above Nelson and Vernon, who each got twenty-nine).[40] Today, many British places still bear the names of Livingstone (about twenty-five),[41] Rhodes (nineteen)[42] or Kitchener (twenty-five),[43] and Aldershot celebrates its former military student with a Gordon Road too. Though some street names might have occasionally referred to homonyms (e.g. Gordon Street in Bloomsbury referred to the Duke of Gordon, and Stanley can also refer to the Earls of Derby), in the overwhelming majority these streets expressed the recognition of the above-mentioned imperial heroes by local town-dwellers. These statistics say a lot about the level of support that these figures enjoyed even at local level, reflecting the prevalence at all echelons of society of a belief system in which colonial conquerors were viewed highly.[44] The Towns Improvement Clauses Act 1847, part III, ensured that street naming was a statutory function of local authorities,[45] which meant that, as in France, decisions about street names did not result from a centralized, concerted decision at government level: the celebration of imperial heroes did not reflect a top-down initiative but more a grassroots expression of reconnaissance. This feature was even strengthened by the Public Health Act of 1925 which acknowledged the need to consult and involve affected owners. The nature of street names as mirrors of local opinion was thus asserted throughout the period 1870–1939, and the appearance of imperial heroes in British towns and cities both reflected and reinforced the popularity of those who had made the empire, or who were linked to it.

At the same time as they appeared on the metropolitan scene, colonial officers entered the realms of memory in the empire itself – if Pierre Nora's concept of 'realms of memory' can be stretched to encompass the overseas experience.[46] Colonizers brought to Africa a European conception of infrastructures, creating new towns and settlements, opening and naming new streets. The toponyms of colonial cities were deeply marked by imperial heroes. Dakar had its *Rue Laperrine* and its *Rue du Commandant Marchand* alongside its *Avenue Faidherbe*, Algiers its *Avenue Bugeaud*, *Rue Charles de Foucauld* and *Rue Savorgnan de Brazza*, while Brazzaville had its *Rue Lyautey*, *Rue Charles de Foucauld* and, naturally, its *Avenue de Brazza*, and Djibouti its *Rue du Commandant Marchand* and its *Avenue Lyautey*. Khartoum had the *Gordon Gardens* and, naturally, Cape Town got its *Rhodes Street*, and Dar es-Salaam later got its *Livingstone Street*. Colonial officers, expatriates, visitors, and indeed the native population, could not escape the memory of those who had built the British or French empires. The same way as street naming ensured the 'powerful and widespread sense of the royal presence throughout the [British] empire',[47] imperial heroes celebrated throughout imperial urban space created a web of meaning that tied the newly founded colonies to a pantheon of founders that was singularly coherent and separate from earlier conquerors.

In addition to street names, commemorative plaques could further legitimize imperial heroes by turning metropolitan places where they were born, or where they lived, into sites of memorialization. For instance, passers-by on the Place de Broglie in Strasbourg are still reminded that Charles de Foucauld was born in a house that was later demolished, and Cecil Rhodes's stay in Oxford is commemorated through an imposing portrait bust and plaque on King Edward Street.

But the place of imperial heroes could be even more prominent in the colonies, and have a direct impact on the metropolitan popularity of these names. Contrary to Europe, where most of the human settlements pre-existed the Industrial Revolution, European activity overseas offered opportunities to christen new cities after imperial heroes. One Algerian town thus bore the name of the archbishop of Algiers (1867–92), Charles Lavigerie (it is called today Djendel), as did a district of Algiers (near *Maison carrée*, it is now called Mohammadia). The Algerian settlement of Laperrine (today Djebahia) remembered the conqueror of the Sahara, General Laperrine, while Lyauteyville (today Khénitra), on the Atlantic coast of Moroccco, did the same with the architect of the French protectorate over Morocco. Brazzaville, capital of the French Congo, honoured the founder of the colony. French forts in the Sahara mostly referred to the colonial conquerors of the region: Fort-Lamy (today N'Djamena) bore the name of the co-leader of the Foureau–Lamy mission (1898–1900), Fort-Flatters (today Bordj-Omar Driss) paid tribute to the leader of the ill-fated Flatters mission slaughtered by the Tuaregs in 1881, Fort Largeau (today Faya) celebrated a military explorer of the Congo and Chad, and Fort Gouraud (Zouérate) was named after a key actor of the conquest of Morocco and the French Sudan. These names were almost invariably mentioned on the maps shown to schoolchildren to teach them *la grandeur de la France*, and such prominence reinforced their fame in the metropole whilst at the same time entrenching the empire into national consciousness. These place names were regularly cited in the numerous novels about Saharan adventure, that proved so popular in France in the interwar period, and helped to root the imperial ethos in the hearts of their readers.

In the British case, missionary activities led to the local celebration of imperial heroes (David Livingstone in particular), sometimes even before the official colonial authorities had arrived. As early as 1874, fifteen years before a British protectorate was established over Nyasaland, the Free Church of Scotland[48] named one of its mission stations Livingstonia, although its founder, James Stewart, had been one of Livingstone's staunchest detractors: this commemorative value helped his project gain momentum, and his views about the missionary subsequently softened.[49] It was followed in 1876 by the founding of a Church of Scotland mission bearing the name of Livingstone's birthplace, Blantyre, which has grown to become Malawi's most important town.[50] Northern Rhodesia's capital city was called Livingstone, until the founding of Lusaka in the 1930s. Indeed, the country name Rhodesia was itself a tribute to Cecil Rhodes, while Nigeria came close to being named after the founder of the National African Company, George Dashwood Goldie (which would have made Goldesia).[51] Imperial topography, and its cartographical consequences, greatly contributed to asserting the importance attached by Britain and France to their imperial heroes, and to entrench their names in the national psyche of each country.[52]

Although town and street naming was one of the most efficient ways of celebrating imperial heroes in the everyday life of the population, in particular because maps and city plans relayed their message, it did not dwarf the influence of statues and monuments. The opening scene of Jean-Paul Paulin's 1939 movie *Les Chemins de l'honneur*, where the Foreign Legion and the *Zouaves* play a pivotal role, convincingly exemplified the role of statues: it showed at length the equestrian statue of Marshal Lyautey in Casablanca, before ending the sequence with a close-up on the plinth where a plaque remembered his name in large letters. Inaugurated in 1938, four years after Lyautey's death, the statue represented the Resident General at his best, valiant conqueror mounting an elegant and thoroughbred horse. Significantly, it was the cornerstone of Casablanca's *Place de la Victoire*. This statue, like many others, had the purpose of celebrating the hero, and above all of being 'worthy of him', to quote a civil servant of H.M. Office of Works to Lady Haig during the discussions about the statue of Douglas Haig.[53]

Statues combine the prestige of official state recognition with the impact of a larger-than-life representation that is presented to all passers-by. As such, they are powerful propaganda tools which embody 'the idiom of symbolic discourse'.[54] (It is not a coincidence that the anti-conformist Jean Genet later ridiculed the power of statues in his play *Les Paravents*, deeply influenced by events of the Algerian war of decolonization.) The urban growth of the nineteenth century required town planning, and it was not unusual to include recreational spaces which could be ornamented with statues of local or national great men. This 'mass production of public monuments' (to quote Eric Hobsbawm again) was decisive in clearly granting imperial heroes exceptional status (which, in France, also contributed to the development or the 'invention' of a Republican tradition).

The period from 1870 to the Second World War was marked by a significant increase in the number of official statues erected on both sides of the Channel. In Britain and its colonies, marble sculptures or bronze casts of kings and queens frequently ornamented city squares and the entrance of government houses, a fact which reduced the potential for imperial heroes to be statufied. However, John MacKenzie argues that a significant shift towards military heroes connected with the empire happened as early as 1759, when General Wolfe was celebrated by the dedication of an obelisk in Lord Cobham's gardens at Stowe.[55] Some imperial heroes, such as Henry Havelock, featured in statues in later decades, although the trend remained somewhat marginal until the 1870s. Public sculpture may appear as seldom inclined to promote great men of the Empire in the pre-1870 period; yet the forty years before the First World War saw 'more statues of imperial heroes [appear] in the streets', as Bernard Porter noted.[56] General Gordon's first statue, by Sir William Thornycroft, was erected in Trafalgar Square only three years after his death[57] and another statue (by Edward Onslow Ford) quickly followed in 1890 in Gordon's own Corps (Royal Engineers) in Chatham. Gravesend also celebrated its famous resident with a statue inaugurated in 1893 (Figure 1). Onslow Ford's statue was replicated in 1902 to be displayed in St Martin's Place, London and, eventually, in Khartoum.[58] To support the widespread myth of Gordon's faculty of adaptation, this bronze statue represented him riding a camel and wearing the uniform

1   Imperial heroes set in stone: statues of General Gordon in Gravesend and Major Marchand in Thoissey

and tarbush of an Egyptian general.[59] The statue became so central to colonial Khartoum's life that the *Sudan Star* ran a daily chronicle (by the pseudonymous 'The Hump') under the title *Round Gordon's Statue*.[60] As early as 1907, the Sudan Church Notes indicated that 'the British Community [had] been much increased during the last two months by weekly arrivals of visitors whose chief object seem to be a kind of pilgrimage to the Gordon Statue'.[61] An equestrian statue of Lord Kitchener was also on display next to Gordon's in Khartoum, and he was also remembered after his death through a statue on the Horse Guards Parade. Livingstone memorials were built in Chitambo in March 1900,[62] and in Tabora and Ujiji between 1919 and 1930,[63] while statues were erected in his birthplace, in Victoria Falls and lastly, in 1953, in London, at the Royal Geographical Society's headquarters in Kensington Gore. In Glasgow, an imposing statue of Livingstone with a Bible in the left hand, by John Mossman, was unveiled just outside the city's cathedral in 1879, and he is also celebrated in Edinburgh's Princes Street Gardens.[64] Cecil Rhodes was also remembered through sometimes monumental statues in Rhodesia and in

THE EMERGENCE OF A NEW TYPE OF HERO

South Africa, particularly in Cape Town, where a statue depicting him in pensive pose welcomes the visitor to the University of Cape Town, and where the Rhodes Memorial was built between 1906 and 1911.[65] A statue of Cecil Rhodes still dominates the High Street entrance to the Rhodes building of Oriel College, Oxford, conspicuously above those of Edward VII and George V.

In France, although the Revolution and the Restoration had been marked by a certain interest in statues, the Third Republic appeared to be 'the most statue-obsessed of all the regimes' (*'le régime statuomaniaque par excellence'*). From a Republican perspective, statues should not only 'pay an homage' but be 'an instructive homage'.[66] The *Secrétaire d'état aux beaux-arts* Henri Dujardin Baumetz stated that 'the monuments which have been raised to the men who have best served the country do not only bear witness to the gratitude of the public, but also show new generations an example of their life and their deeds'.[67] Politically, statues were initially more an ideal of the left, although the right came to accept their pedagogical value (*'une pédagogie de l'exemple'*). The fact that, as Maurice Agulhon put it, the French Third Republic was 'the Republic of statues' considerably helped to promote the French empire builders who distinguished themselves after 1870. Numerous statues of Faidherbe (e.g. in Lille, Bapaume and Saint-Louis, Senegal), Lavigerie (in Bayonne, Algiers, Tunis and Biskra), Gallieni (in his native Saint-Béat, one in Trilbardou on behalf of the city of Paris and a later one on the *Champ de Mars*, and also one in Antanarivo) or Marchand (in his native Thoissey and in Paris, on the occasion of the 1931 colonial exhibition) were ordered by the municipalities or the State.

Imperial heroes also entered national imaginaries through national institutions named after them (a relatively new trend). The Gordon Boys School in Woking was founded in 1886 by public subscription, at the express wish of Queen Victoria in person, who wanted it to be the National Memorial to General Gordon. Similarly, the creation of the Gordon Memorial College of Khartoum was one of the first organizational steps taken by the Sirdar Kitchener, after the re-conquest of the Sudan. The school which was called at times 'the Eton of the Sudan' had been purposely named in memory of General Gordon, as its 'brown-brick imposing building of Gothic tendencies' would shelter 'many of the sons and grandsons of those savages learning diligently and bowing to the discipline of the hated white man', as a newspaper chronicler remarked at the time.[68] Many primary and secondary schools were named Livingstone in Southern Africa. Higher education institutions could also honour the memory of imperial heroes, as was the case of Rhodes University in Grahamstown (established in 1904), or the Kitchener School of Medicine of Khartoum, founded in 1916.

In France and in the French empire, a significant number of primary and secondary schools, launched to cater for expanding educational needs, remembered imperial heroes: Marshal Lyautey (*Lycée Lyautey*, Casablanca; *Ecole Lyautey*, Allonnes, Caen, Riedisheim,Vittel; Oran); Charles de Foucauld (*Lycée Charles de Foucauld*, Brest, Lyon, Nancy, Schiltigheim, Strasbourg and Casablanca, *Ecole Charles de Foucauld*, Le Havre, Le Pontet, Nancy, Paris, St Maur des Fossés); Jean-Baptiste Marchand (*Ecole Marchand*, Arras, *Lycée camp Marchand*, Rufisque); Pierre Savorgnan de Brazza (*Ecole de Brazza*, Auxerre, *Lycée de Brazza*, Brazzaville, Algiers). This association between the names of imperial heroes and official buildings where learning was dispensed was highly symbolic, as free education for all was one of the main achievements of the Third Republic. Remembering implicitly the role of imperial heroes as pioneers of the expansion of French culture and language, it also reinforced the claims of the civilizing mission and celebrated their achievements as founders of 'Greater France'.

The names of imperial heroes penetrated deeply into the fabric of British and French culture throughout the period, as they entered the public space in various forms. Streets, avenues or squares were christened after famous conquerors or explorers of Africa, creating landmarks that referred to its conquest in the metropole, while the same happened on a larger scale (sometimes including town names) on the African continent itself. Imperial heroes progressively pervaded the world's geography, 'inventing' a tradition of imperial heroism, to borrow Eric Hobsbawm and Terence Ranger's description of this powerful 'process of formalization and ritualization, characterized by reference to the past, if only by imposing repetition'.[69]

Beyond the above-mentioned processes of symbolic recognition that had reached an unprecedented level of prevalence throughout the nineteenth century, political, social, cultural, technical and economic changes provided a fertile terrain to ensure the enduring success of imperial heroes in the two countries. The development of the British and French African empires took place against the backdrop of an industrial revolution that had far-reaching consequences: the phenomenon of imperial heroes has to be set in the context of radical political, socio-cultural and technical breakthroughs.

Politically, the continuous extension of franchise throughout the period (achieving in both cases universal suffrage, by different paths) increased the political weight of public opinion, making imperial heroes a potentially valuable source of legitimacy for pro-imperial politicians and organizations, in an attempt to perform what Bagehot called 'the co-ordination of judgements'.[70] Although Chamberlain denied the existence of 'manufactories of political opinion, where zeal and unanimity are produced to order',[71] there is significant evidence to the contrary, and imperial heroes were a good asset for the 'manufacturers' of Greater Britain. In Britain, the Chartist movement had asked for parliamentary reforms (including universal suffrage, as early as 1838), but ran out of steam in the 1850s. However, the Reform Act of 1867 extended the right to vote down the class ladder, adding nearly a million voters, including many working men. The 1884 Bill and the 1885 Redistribution Act trebled the electorate, giving the vote to most agricultural labourers, before the 1918 Act enfranchised all men over twenty-one and all women over thirty. Universal suffrage regardless of gender was finally obtained in 1928.

In France, the establishment of the Third Republic dramatically changed the relationship between the government and the population. While the disastrous outcome of the expedition to Mexico did not result in the fall of Napoleon III, Jules Ferry was voted out of office by the deputies as a consequence of the failure of a French expeditionary force in the Tonkin. Universal male suffrage was reinstituted in France in 1871, setting the basis for a parliamentary democracy.[72] Universal male suffrage, an elected Chamber of Deputies, and parliamentary cabinet responsibility gave importance to the opinion of the French masses in political decisions.[73] Colonial propagandists soon realized that they had to promote their convictions to the public, and those 'pioneers of Adventure, their national Flag and Civilization' provided convincing examples apt to create a certain *'état d'esprit'* among the population.[74] Their evocative examples had to be swiftly enlisted as it was widely believed that French energies had to be geared towards the 'blue line of the Vosges' (i.e. the re-conquest of Alsace and Lorraine), rather than overseas expansion. In post-1870 France, all politicians agreed that France needed regeneration to claim back its 'rank', but they disagreed about methods. Defending a concept of 'continental patriotism', the Right systematically opposed colonial expansion in the 1880s, while the 'Opportunists' (moderate Republicans) supported it, in spite of public aloofness or occasional open hostility. Colonial advocates were adamant that colonization reasserted France's power and prestige, and fostered the moral and physical value of its citizens. To them, imperial heroes showcased the qualities of the colonizer, contributed to fuelling patriotic pride in French achievements and offered a good excuse to spread geographical knowledge about new or future colonies.

The organization of a clearly structured colonial movement in the 1890s provided an efficient promotional platform for the likes of Brazza, Foucauld and Marchand. As early as 1874, Paul Leroy-Beaulieu produced the best nineteenth-century doctrinal exposition of colonialism in *De la colonisation chez les peuples modernes*. It took a few more years for what became known as the *Parti colonial* to take shape. Contrary to what its name suggested, it was never a proper political party but a group whose members, of various political affiliations, shared a common interest in France's expansion. The first club of colonially minded politicians, intellectuals and officers, the *Comité de l'Afrique française*, was set up in 1890. In 1892, a group of pro-imperial deputies was founded at the National Assembly. Chaired by the representative of Oran (Algeria), Eugène Etienne, and vice-chaired by the prince d'Arenberg (also president of the *Comité de l'Afrique française* and a member of the board of the Suez Canal), the *Groupe colonial* expanded quickly from 22 to 113 members in its first year, with a strong representation of moderate Republicans.[75] The launch of the *Union coloniale* in 1895 was the last step towards the creation of an efficient network of colonial supporters.[76] The members of these small but comparatively powerful groups, which were closely intertwined and enjoyed privileged connections with the geographical societies, intended to twist the government's arm and raise public awareness about the colonies (or at least reduce public opposition to colonial expansion).[77] Through their action, imperial heroes gave them good examples of national determination to support their arguments and to disqualify Clemenceau's claims.

Colonial advocates could also count on geographical societies to reach this goal, and they too created a context propitious to the promotion of imperial heroes. Not only did they occasionally lobby politicians into embarking upon the colonial conquest of Africa, for ideological, religious and/or economic reasons,[78] therefore advancing the case of ambitious imperial heroes, but they were also prone to using leading explorers or conquerors as a means of drawing public support to their cause.[79]

The London Royal Geographical Society was the meeting point of British explorers and conquerors, who found at 1 Savile Road (Kensington Gore after 1911) the maps and information they needed to carry out their African plans. Above all, the Society was the place where new discoveries were made public and several heroes were 'manufactured' through an efficient system of public lectures, dissemination of knowledge (through journals and personal contacts with decision makers) and official recognition (e.g. the gold medal). To fulfil its remit to 'advance [...] geographical science', it promoted nearly all British explorers who came to embody the heroic discovery of Africa: Richard Burton, John Hanning Speke, David Livingstone or Henry M. Stanley, among others. The RGS's involvement with the Livingstone legend was so deep that the Revd Horace Waller wrote to Livingstone, in 1869, that the interest in this country about you is as intense as I ever would wish it to be and no one has a better chance of grasping it than yourself. The Geographical Society might in short be called the Livingstone Society for the last two years.[80]

Membership shows that societies like the RGS, or the Royal Scottish Geographical Society, and many other regional geographical societies, became increasingly popular in the late nineteenth century. Their committed promotion of figures who furthered European knowledge of Africa transformed British geographical societies into conscious promoters of imperial heroes – particularly Livingstone.[81] A blatant demonstration of this role was offered in April 1874, when the Royal Geographical Society organized the highly publicized, and deeply symbolic, burial for Livingstone in Westminster Abbey.[82]

Founded in 1821 (nine years before the RGS), Paris's geographical society was more a lobbying club than a professional association.[83] Its interest in Africa became apparent as early as 1825, when a public subscription was opened for a prize to reward the first French explorer who reached Timbuktu. In 1838, it was awarded to René Caillié, celebrated as a hero after completing a journey to the mythic city: Caillié's popularity was such that Louis-Philippe received the self-taught explorer at the Tuileries. The society remained actively involved in rewarding explorers through its golden medal, which distinguished several eminent explorers or conquerors of Africa, regardless of whether their deeds had been achieved militarily: Livingstone was awarded the supreme French geographical distinction in 1857, Stanley in 1878, Brazza in 1879, followed by the officers Binger in 1890, Gentil in 1899, Marchand in 1900 and Foureau in 1901.

The *Société de géographie* remained the only one of its kind for more than half a century; but this monopoly gave way to a blossoming of regional societies in the mid-1870s. The second French geographical society was founded in Lyon in 1873, followed by twenty-five provincial openings in the following ten years. Membership of geographical societies rocketed from 240 in 1864 (Paris only) to between 15,000 and 16,000 (all the abovementioned societies) at the end of the 1880s, making France the leading country in terms of membership of geographical societies.[84] In 1875, the second international congress of geography met in Paris.[85] Sustained interest in geographical knowledge generated curiosity and, inevitably, support for imperial heroes, whom societies could use to make a case for 'greater France' at the same time as they promoted their own activities.[86] In 1879, the *Société de Géographie de Lyon* made its intentions clear to Brazza:

Please let us know which day you intend to come so that we can arrange everything for the conference. All the city will come to listen to you, hence we need to ensure we have the appropriate place.[87]

The work of geographical societies was advertised to the public not only through their own prestigious journals but also through national newspapers (in the French case, for instance, the *Journal des débats*, *Le Constitutionnel* and *Le Siècle*). This was an efficient channel of public promotion that contributed to making many reputations. In France, the Paris Geographical Society was an exceptionally efficient propagandist, enjoying 'considerable overlapping of officialdom in the French government, the Geographical Society, and the staff of the *Journal officiel*'.[88] In parallel with geographical societies, chambers of commerce also promoted imperial expansion while undertaking their primary purpose, namely increasing awareness of business opportunities abroad, sometimes in connection with imperial heroes.[89]

Geographical societies, the activities of which increased considerably throughout the nineteenth century, appear as key vectors of the reputations attached to imperial heroes. Their role was enhanced by the growing importance of public opinion against a changing political backdrop; colonial advocates measured how imperial heroes, used in conjunction with the geographical establishment, could help them win over public support at a time when political awareness grew steadily.

A third major contextual change helped the development of heroic legends of empire: the reception of promotional material was significantly enhanced by deep socio-cultural mutations, in terms of readership composition and numbers and the industrial production of cultural material. The development of an industrial society and the progressive distantiation of men from the soil changed radically the structures of British and, to a lesser extent, French societies, creating new markets of readers. In 1851, England and Wales counted 63 cities of over 20,000 inhabitants, totalling 6,265,011 inhabitants. Forty years later, there were 185 such cities, bringing together a population of 15,563,834, to the astonishment of their contemporaries.[90] In France, the *exode rural* led to the growth of towns until the First World War, followed by the expansion of larger cities. While the urban population accounted only for 25 per cent of the total French population in 1850, France had 17 cities of over 100,000 inhabitants and 681 of between 5,000 and 20,000 inhabitants in 1936.[91]

Urban growth, and the reconfiguration of social practices that it brought about, took place at a time when marked efforts were made in the educational field. Government officials and philanthropists (who followed the path opened by the Sunday school movement in the late eighteenth century) viewed illiteracy as an obstacle to the social (and, sometimes, spiritual) improvement of society. In the nineteenth century, it became a widely accepted gauge of social and economic progress, with a significant impact on international prestige.[92] The need to ensure a minimal level of education for the French population was first asserted by the Guizot law on education voted in the aftermath of the July Revolution, followed more than three decades later by provisions made specifically for girls (laws Duruy in 1867 and Sée in 1878). The decisive step came from a pro-colonial leader, Jules Ferry, who believed that there could be no democracy without proper education. In the early 1880s, he laid the ground for a free, compulsory and non-religious education for all, which considerably widened the potential readership of books and newspapers, and reinforced feelings of nationhood, as he clearly stated: 'It is important to a society like ours, to today's France, to put on the same school benches the children who will later mix under the motherland's flag.'[93] The policy delivered good results: it brought literacy to the country as a whole. In the rural department of Morbihan, the literacy rate rose from 36.75 to 76.54 per cent between 1850 and 1890.[94] Even in the more agricultural departments, peasants agreed to break their routine in order to let their children become literate.[95] According to the *Statistique générale de la France*, the illiteracy rate nationwide dropped from 43.4 per cent in 1872 to 19.4 per cent in 1901 and 11.2 per cent in 1912 – and 96.2 per cent of females and 96.6 per cent of males in the age range 10-20 years were literate at the latter date.[96] Primary school education created a 'new popular culture'[97] where patriotism was carefully cultivated, efficiently percolating down to the working classes.[98] It also secured the steady development of printed material for mass consumption,[99] which would have a decisive influence on a few imperial legends that made it into the national curriculum. Undergoing a revolution in purpose, some actors of the publishing industry avowedly intended to foster literacy: six million copies of G. Bruno's *Le Tour de la France par deux enfants*, which formed the basis of the curriculum in geography, were printed between 1877 and 1901,[100] and borrowing from school libraries means that many more people read it.[101]

In Britain, reformers such as Matthew Arnold called for the establishment of secondary education similar to the French system, and complained that English children of 'middle and professional classes' could not find in Britain an equivalent to the French institution of the *lycée*.[102] The opening of new public schools, the development of a state schooling system and the role played by religious associations and other charities inspired by the ideas of philanthropists such as Walter Besant or Lady Bell considerably improved literacy rates in Britain, especially after attending school became a legal obligation.[103] Forster's Education Act of 1870 established a framework for compulsory elementary education; literacy rates grew from 70 per cent for 20 to 24 year olds and 50 per cent for 45 to 49 year olds in the period 1859–74 to almost 100 per cent and 80 per cent respectively in the period 1899–1914.[104] Before the First World War, approximately 96 per cent of the English and Welsh population was able to read, and public libraries or bookshops were available to most of them.[105] As early as 1892, the leading newspaper editor W. T. Stead asserted that 'the Education Act has practically created a new reading public'.[106] This increase in literacy rates allowed for the rise of the popular press and publishing activities, which offered imperial legends the means to reach wide audiences, as will be seen in Chapters 2, 6 and 7.

Closely linked to improved literacy rates, school textbooks efficiently contributed to the promotion of imperial heroes. In Third Republic France, Ernest Lavisse, head of the *'hussards noirs de la République'*, played a pivotal role in the shaping of a national identity[107] as his textbooks intended for primary and secondary education generated a powerful 'mythological French history'.[108] Beyond Lavisse, school textbooks in general increasingly sought to advocate the benefits of the colonies to their young readers.[109] It was not unusual to read in schoolbooks that 'in the cities and villages of France, the stories of battles in Africa were remembered. We were proud of the bravery of our soldiers'.[110] In 1904, a textbook for the last year of primary school trumpeted that 'the history of our colonial expeditions since 1880 is a great school of heroism and patriotism'.[111] The combination of improved printing techniques that made images more appealing and less costly, the extension of primary education and the need to compensate for the humiliating defeat of 1870 favoured the development of a nationalist and militarist glorification that made imperial heroes all the more desirable in the eyes of authors of textbooks.[112]

Having been through an informal and sometimes involuntary, yet influential, process of censorship and selection, British history textbooks taught schoolchildren opinions about social class, political opinions, morality, religion and the place of England in the world, all subjects which included national heroes as part of their demonstrative process. With a few exceptions, British school history textbooks adopted an increasingly imperialist stance throughout the nineteenth century: more jingoistic, they stressed the grandeur of British dominions and the ideal of empire, and described at length a noble national stereotype compared to supposedly inferior races while they recalled the patriotic duty of all Britons, strengthening their determination in case of external aggression. Authors used material about heroes, from Drake, Wolfe, Nelson and Wellington to Gordon, to make their case.[113] The development of school textbooks, especially from the 1870s onwards, which promoted a 'highly simplified message of racial and cultural superiority, breeding a sense of self-satisfaction', and occurred in the context of the transmission of the dominant imperial ideology,[114] was an important factor in the popularization of the legends attached to imperial heroes.

Not only were more people able to read: more could also buy cultural products that had hitherto remained beyond their purse. With daily wages of unskilled workers rising threefold between 1830 and 1938, and above all with the salaries of white-collar positions increasing on average ten times, more families could afford expenses beyond accommodation and food.[115] Perhaps Victorian working-class families had little time for leisurely activities (their intrinsic interest in the empire still remaining a matter of debate)[116] and they enjoyed limited access to cultural products, but leisurely reading was not an activity unheard of as early as the seventeenth century,[117] and the improvement of the working-class living standards over the period encouraged the development of this habit in industrial environments.[118] In spite of several recession-driven slumps, between 1860 and 1875 working-class real incomes rose by 40 per cent, and between 1875 and 1900 by a further 50 per cent: with disposable incomes increasing, items of popular culture became more affordable.[119] Workers also had more spare time available: the Factory Acts of 1867 and 1874 extended to much larger groups of workers those clauses from the Act of 1833 which ruled against work on Christmas Day or Good Friday. During the period, Saturday became a half-holiday, enabling workers to shop on that day, leaving Sunday free for leisure. Leisure, defined as residual time beyond work and other obligations, spread more widely, offering more opportunities to make use of cultural products.[120] Criticism and fear of 'wasted time' not only on Sundays but on patronal festivals or holidays contributed to the wish to 'reform the lives of illiterate Englishmen and women',[121] a key target for Sunday schools. Philanthropists promoted the diffusion of popular literature, including many educational works which featured imperial heroes such as General Gordon, Field Marshal Kitchener, Lord Roberts or Lawrence of Arabia (some of them were given away as Sunday School prizes). Circulating libraries and the opening of public libraries, usually using collections donated by private benefactors,[122] expanded the readership of such books, in particular among unemployed men from the working classes.[123]

In France, the working class paid the consequences of the late industrialization of the country, combined with the alliance between the bourgeoisie and the rural world in the Third Republic. Wages certainly increased but unemployment remained a serious threat hampering access to the world of culture. However, this did not prevent the French working class from reading: increasingly popular newspapers allowed to practise skills learnt at the *Ecole de la république*.[124] Thus French heroes were more efficiently promoted through the press and its mass readership than through books, the latter remaining one of the favourite pastimes of the bourgeoisie (in spite of a few exceptions, such as Victor Hugo, who appealed across all classes). But other means of promoting heroes could reach the population as a result of the development of leisure, such as songs and ballads played by local bands on Sundays. The growth of a working class and a lower middle class easily reachable within an urban context favoured the appearance of a new type of commercially driven popular culture in place of the more traditional and more local cultures of predominantly agricultural communities. The taste for news from the outside world was less pressing in the countryside than in town, which made the latter a comparatively more fertile breeding ground for popular books and newspapers.[125]

Although the British and French socio-cultural contexts presented marked differences, the period between 1870 and 1930 witnessed in the two countries unique geostrategical and political changes that created favourable conditions for the arrival of a new type of hero, the 'imperial hero'. The differences between the two countries resulted principally from the later industrialization of France, the Gallic attachment to agricultural values (a legacy of geography) and the deeper attachment to class that prevailed in Britain. Until the Great War, the French embraced the colonial project of some of their leaders more cautiously than the British. However, the context of the two countries also presented many similarities. The European urge to colonize and, later, to develop, Africa in a context of sharper international competition brought about the 'Scramble for Africa' under the leadership of the two countries. This 'Scramble' offered an opportunity to celebrate in the world's topography, and through urban street names in the metropoles the generation of explorers and conquerors who advanced the interests of their nation on the spot, therefore durably inscribing their memory in the everyday geography of millions. Changing political conditions gave more weight to public opinion (a relatively new concept at the time), and imperial heroes could help justify colonial expansion in the eyes of a population that was not always inclined to costly overseas ventures. On that account, a more detailed analysis of the conditions prevalent in each country (which will appear clearly in Chapters 6 and 7) reveals significant differences: if British imperial heroes were nearly unanimously celebrated in their homeland, the fame of their French counterparts was less universal, and was used and fostered by the advocates of colonial expansion to serve a cause which remained far from popular for several decades.

Lastly, unprecedented social improvement and the tide of urbanization that stemmed from the industrial revolution created the appropriate conditions for the emerging of imperial heroes in both countries. The nineteenth century witnessed a rapid increase in literacy among the lower classes, whilst urban growth created more unified, and easily accessible, markets that fostered the development of cheaper cultural products aimed at the masses. Heroes were a means of reasserting their country's pride and the valour of its nationals, and they were quickly promoted through all the new means which became available over the period, and which made the most of markets that they contributed to creating themselves. Written works, which had been a major vector of heroic accounts in Western cultures, reached wider constituencies. The press and the publishing world, which underwent profound changes over the period, will be the subject of the next chapter, while audio-visual means of promotion, such as war paintings, lantern slides, songs, ballads and films, will be studied in Chapter 3. Popular culture gained an unprecedented momentum in the late nineteenth century, and the commercial opportunities that arose for promoters of imperial heroes are a key element to illuminate our understanding of the phenomenon.

Notes

1 G. Karl Galinsky, *The Herakles Theme* (Oxford, 1972), p. 10.
2 T. Carlyle, *On Heroes and Hero-Worship* (1841), p. 193.
3 J. A. Hobson, *Imperialism: A Study* (1938 edn), p. 222.
4 D. Cannadine, *Ornamentalism: How the British Saw Their Empire* (2001), p. 88.
5 M. Howard, *The Franco-Prussian War* (1962), p. 8.
6 A. R. Skelley, *The Victorian Army at Home* (London and Montreal, 1977), pp. 243–7.
7 G. Harries-Jenkins, *The Army in Victorian Society* (Hull, 1993), p. 10.
8 Skelley, *Victorian Army*, pp. 31 and 241.
9 J. Peck, *War, the Army and Victorian Literature* (1998); S. Walton, *Imagining Soldiers and Fathers in the Mid-Victorian Era* (Aldershot, 2010), p. 27.
10 V. Kiernan, 'Working class and nation in nineteenth-century Britain', in M. Cornforth (ed.), *Rebels and Their Causes* (1978), p. 126.
11 S. Attridge, *Nationalism, Imperialism, and Identity in Late Victorian Culture: Civil and Military Worlds* (Basingstoke and New York, 2003), p. 45.
12 Skelley, *Victorian Army*, p. 17.
13 Cannadine, *Ornamentalism*, pp. 95 and 267.
14 A. Horne, *The French Army and Politics, 1870–1970* (1984), pp. 14–19.
15 R. Girardet, *Le Nationalisme français* (1992), p. 79.
16 Thanks to Daniel Richelet for sharing this testimony which is well-known among families historically linked to the army.
17 W. Serman, *Les Officiers français dans la nation, 1848–1914* (1982), pp. 58–9.

CONTEXTS

18 W. Serman, *La Vie professionnelle des officiers français au milieu du XIXe siècle* (1994), p. 21.
19 R. Girardet, *La Société militaire dans la France contemporaine* (1953), p. 297.
20 H. Brunschwig, *French Colonialism 1871–1914: Myths and Realities* (Engl. trans., 1966), p. 164.
21 R. Pottier, *Laperrine: conquérant pacifique du Sahara* (1943), p. 27.
22 Three grades (*chevalier, officier* and *commandeur*) and two *dignités* (*grand officier* and *grand croix*).
23 AN, Dossiers Légion d'honneur, LH/1729/36.
24 A. H. Rowbotham, 'Rudyard Kipling and France', *The French Review*, 10:5 (March 1937), 365–72.
25 J. Gallieni, *Instructions de pacification, 22 mai 1898*, 'Gallieni à Madagascar et Lyautey au Maroc: deux œuvres de "pacification" complémentaires', *Cahier de la recherche doctrinale* (June 2011), p. 43, available (www.cdef.terre.defense.gouv.fr/publications/cahiers_drex/les_cahiers_recherche.htm [accessed 20 April 2012]; H. Lyautey, *Du rôle colonial de l'armée* (1900) and *Lettres du Tonkin et de Madagascar* (1920), pp. 273–97.
26 One such example being officers of the *bureaux arabes*, whose action on the spot shaped French colonial practices in Algeria and beyond (through the expansion of colonial doctrines beyond the Algerian 'laboratory'). See J. Frémeaux, *Les Bureaux arabes dans l'Algérie de la conquête* (1993).
27 D. Porch, *The French Foreign Legion: A Complete History* (1991), p. 170.
28 A. Thompson, *The Empire Strikes Back* (Harlow, 2005), pp. 181–6; R. Aldrich, *Vestiges of the Colonial Empire in France* (Basingstoke, 2005), pp. 157–95.
29 R. Aldrich, 'Colonial names in Paris streets', in T. Chafer and A. Sackur (eds), *Promoting the Colonial Idea* (2002), pp. 211–23.
30 D. Milo, 'Street names', in P. Nora (ed.), *Realms of Memory* (Engl. trans., New York, 1997), p. 369.
31 Milo, 'Street names', pp. 365–6.
32 The decision, taken on 24 June 1907, was widely reported in the press. See for instance *Le Journal des débats*, 2 February 1907.
33 Aldrich, *Colonial names in Paris streets*, pp. 214–5 and 222.
34 There is a *Rue Marchand* or *Rue Commandant-Marchand* in Arnouville-les-Gonesse, Bordeaux, Cachan, Corbeil-Essonnes, Givet, La Défense, Lyon, Nogent-sur-Marne, Paris, Toulon, Vannes, Villejuif, Vannes, Villenave d'Ornon. *Rues Mission Marchand* can be found in Argenteuil, Courbevoie, Houilles and Paris. The *Port Marchand* is situated in Toulon.
35 *Rue Lyautey*: Charleville-Mézières, Frouard, Geneville, La Roche sur Yon, Maxéville, Montigny-les-Metz, Nancy, Paris, Sainte-Clotilde (Réunion). *Avenue Lyautey*: Blois, Brest, Cavalaire, Dijon, Garches, Gray, Grenoble, Hyères, La Celle-Saint-Cloud, Nice, St-Maur-les-Fossés.
36 *Rue Brazza*: Auxerre, Caen, Bellegarde sur Valserine, Béziers, Bruges (near Bordeaux), La Rochelle, Mantes-La-Jolie, Montpellier, Nîmes, Paris, Puteaux, Perpignan. *Quai de Brazza*: Bordeaux. *Avenue Brazza*: Grand Quevilly, La Varenne, Le Mans, Marvejols.
37 *Rue Laperrine*: Carcassone, Castelnaudary, Nice, Pau, Quimper, Tourcoing, Valence. *Avenue Laperrine*: Caen, Paris.
38 *Rue Charles de Foucauld*: Alençon, Amiens, Douarnenez, Guer, Landivinau, Le Passage, Lille, Maizières-les-Metz, Mantes-la-Jolie, Meyzieu, Montbrison, Nancy, Nice, Niort, Paris, Pau, St-André-Les-Vergers, St-Avold, St-Germain-du-Puy, St-Médard'en-Jalles, Strasbourg, Valmont, Villeneuve-d'Ornon. *Avenue Charles de Foucauld*: Caen, Corenc.
39 *Bulletin Municipal Officiel*, 12 October 1905, in ANOM, Brazza Papers, PA 16 VIII.
40 A. Room, *The Street Names of England* (1992), pp. 199–205.
41 *Livingstone Avenue*: Birmingham, Blackburn, Broadstairs, Derby, Doncaster, Gillingham, Hull, Long Lawford, Mossley, Portswood, Rugby, Perton, Southampton, Wolverhampton, Wythenshawe, Yaxley. *Livingstone Street*: Beaconsfield, Blantyre,

Leicester, Norwich. *Livingstone Place*: Edinburgh, Galashiels, Maindee, Newport, St Andrews.
42 *Rhodes Avenue*: Blackburn, Helmshore, London, Mowbray, Oldham, Swansea. *Rhodes Street*: Castleford, Hillsdale, Hull, Hyde, Goodwood, Halifax, Newcastle upon Tyne, Shipley, Smallbridge, Stoke on Trent, Warrington. *Rhodes Place*: Milton Keynes, Oldham.
43 *Kitchener Avenue*: Chatham, Derby, Dulwich, Gloucester, Gravesend, Leeds, London, Manchester, Salford. *Kitchener Street*: Barrow-in-Furness, Belfast, Darlington, Gateshead, King's Lynn, Leeds, Oakenshow, Selby, St Helens, Sunderland, Swindon, Wishaw, Woodlesford, York. *Kitchener Place*: Bedford, Leeds.
44 Room, *Street Names of England*, p. 192.
45 A. Rosset and H. Daniels, 'Mixing and matching: a study of the Woking street-namestock', *Journal of the English Place-Name Society* (Nottingham), 33 (2000–1), 117.
46 Nora, *Realms of Memory*.
47 Cannadine, *Ornamentalism*, p. 103.
48 Anon., *Welcome to Blantyre: A Handbook to Blantyre and Limbe* (Nairobi, 1969), p. 45.
49 J. McCracken, *Politics and Christianity in Malawi 1875–1940: The Impact of the Livingstonia Mission in the Northern Province* (Cambridge, 1977), pp. 27–8.
50 B. Lamport-Stokes, *Blantyre, Glimpses of the Early Days* (Blantyre, 1989), p. 13.
51 H. Wesseling, *Le Partage de l'Afrique* (French trans., 1991), p. 408.
52 On the impact of imperial maps on newspaper audiences, see M. Heffernan, 'The cartography of the Fourth Estate: mapping the New Imperialism in British and French newspapers, 1875–1925', in J. R. Akerman (ed.), *The Imperial Map* (Chicago and London, 2009), pp. 261–99.
53 NLS, Acc. 3155, H328j, George Lansbury to Lady Haig, 22 January 1931.
54 E. Hobsbawm, 'Mass-producing traditions: Europe 1870–1914', in E. Hobsbawm and T. Ranger (eds), *The Invention of Tradition* (Cambridge, 1983), p. 304.
55 J. M. MacKenzie, 'Nelson goes global', in D. Cannadine (ed.), *Admiral Lord Nelson: Context and Legacy* (Basingstoke, 2005), pp. 148–9; on representations of Wolfe as a hero, see N. C. Rogers, 'Brave Wolfe: the making of a hero in mid-eighteenth century Britain and America', in K. Wilson (ed.), *A New Imperial History: Culture, Identity and Modernity in Britain and the Empire, 1660–1840* (Cambridge, 2004), pp. 239–59.
56 B. Porter, *The Absent-Minded Imperialists* (Oxford, 2004), pp. 147 and 176.
57 It was removed from Trafalgar Square during the Second World War, and moved to the Victoria Embankment gardens in 1953: http://yourarchives.nationalarchives.gov.uk/index.php?title=Thornycroft,_Sir_William_Hamo_(1850–1925)_Knight_Sculptor [Accessed 15 June 2012].
58 SAD, Evans Papers, 714/10/22.
59 SAD, Evans Papers, 714/10/24.
60 SAD, Vokes Papers, 610/1.
61 *Sudan Church Notes*, 15 February 1907.
62 Anon., 'The Livingstone monument at Chitambo', *The Geographical Journal*, 61:5 (1923), 366–9.
63 C. H. B. Grant, 'The Livingstone-Stanley memorials in Africa', *The Geographical Journal*, 79:4 (1932), 318–19.
64 Thanks to John M. MacKenzie for this reference.
65 P. Maylam, *The Cult of Rhodes* (Claremont, South Africa, 2005), pp. 31–62.
66 M. Agulhon, 'La "statuomanie" et l'histoire', *Ethnologie française*, 8:2–3 (1978), 148–9.
67 From a speech given on the occasion of the unveiling of a statue of Eugène Fromentin in La Rochelle, 1 October 1905, in H. Dujardin-Baumetz (F. Dujardin-Baumetz, ed.), *Discours prononcés de 1905 à 1911* (1913). For an extensive survey of colonially inspired statues in France, see Aldrich, *Vestiges of the Colonial Empire*, pp. 158–74.

68 *Sphere*, 12 November 1904.
69 Hobsbawm and Ranger (eds), *Invention of Tradition*, p. 4.
70 W. Bagehot, 'History of the unreformed parliament, and its lessons' (1858), in *The Works and Life of Walter Bagehot*, vol. VI (1915), p. 273.
71 M. Ostrogorski, *Democracy and the Organization of Political Parties*, vol. I (1902), p. 211.
72 On universal suffrage in France, see P. Rosanvallon, *Le Sacre du citoyen: histoire du suffrage universel en France* (1992).
73 W. H. Schneider, *An Empire for the Masses, The French Popular Image of Africa, 1870–1900* (1982), p. 5.
74 R. Girardet, *L'Idée coloniale en France* (1972), p. 179.
75 C. M. Andrew and A. S. Kanya-Forstner, 'The *Groupe Colonial* in the French Chamber of Deputies, 1892–1932', *The Historical Journal*, 17:4 (Dec. 1974), 837–66.
76 J. M. Mayeur, *Les Débuts de la Troisième République, 1871–1898* (1973), pp. 226–7.
77 C. M. Andrew and A.S. Kanya-Forstner, 'The French "colonial party": its composition, aims and influence, 1885–1914', *The Historical Journal*, 14:1 (March 1971), 99–128.
78 D. Lejeune, *Les Sociétés de géographie en France de 1871 à 1962* (1993).
79 For a more substantial development of this argument, see B. Sèbe, 'The making of British and French legends of exploration, 1821–1914', in D. Kennedy (ed.), *Exploration: A Reassessment* (forthcoming, New York, 2013).
80 RHL, Waller Papers, MSS. Afr. S. 16, I/B, f. 219, Waller to Livingstone, 25 October 1869.
81 J. M. MacKenzie, 'Geography and imperialism: British provincial geographical societies', in F. Driver and G. Rose (eds), *Nature and Science: Essays in the History of Geographical Knowledge*, Historical Geography Research Series, 28 (1992), pp. 49–62.
82 D. O. Helly, *Livingstone's Legacy* (Athens, OH, 1987), p. 26.
83 M. F. Taylor, 'Nascent expansionism in the Geographical Society of Paris, 1821–1848', *Proceedings of the Annual Meeting of the Western Society for French History*, 6 (1978), 229–38.
84 Lejeune, *Sociétés de géographie*, pp. 82–5.
85 A. Murphy, *The Ideology of French Imperialism, 1871–1881* (Washington DC, 1948), p. 8.
86 On the link between the development of geographical science and imperialism, see P. Singaravélou, *L'Empire des géographes* (2008); F. Driver, *Geography Militant: Cultures of Exploration and Empire* (Oxford, 2000); R. A. Butlin, *Geographies of Empire: European Empires and Colonies, c. 1880–1960* (2009).
87 ANOM, Brazza Papers, PA 16 VII, box 10, letter from Louis Desgrand, *Société de géographie de Lyon* to PSB, 21 January 1879.
88 D. McKay, 'Colonialism in the French geographical movement, 1871–1881', *The Geographical Review*, 38 (1943), 214–32.
89 For instance, the director of the *Journal des Chambres de commerce* introduced Brazza to the journal's remit, namely to be the 'propagator of foreign trade and commerce with our colonies'. ANOM, Brazza Papers, PA 16 III, Box 4, Director of the *Journal des Chambres de commerce* to PSB, 20 January 1883.
90 A. F. Weber, *The Growth of Cities in the Nineteenth Century* (New York, 1899), p. 43.
91 P. Ariès, *Histoire des populations françaises* (1971), pp. 274–311.
92 D. Vincent, 'The progress of literacy', *Victorian Studies*, 45:3 (Spring 2003), 405–31.
93 Quoted in F. Ponteil, *Histoire de l'enseignement 1789–1965* (1966), p. 287.
94 F. Furet and J. Ozouf, *Lire et écrire* (1977), p. 334.
95 E. Weber, *Peasants into Frenchmen: The Modernization of Rural France, 1870–1914* (Stanford, 1976), p. 331.

96 J.-Y. Mollier, 'Un parfum de la Belle Epoque', in J.-P. Rioux and J.-F. Sirinelli (eds), *La Culture de masse en France de la Belle Epoque à aujourd'hui* (2002), p. 77.
97 M. Crubellier, *Histoire culturelle de la France, XIXe–XXe siècle* (1974), p. 228.
98 J. and M. Ozouf, 'Le thème du patriotisme dans les manuels primaires', *Le mouvement social*, 49 (Oct.–Dec. 1964), 5–31.
99 M. Lyons, *Le Triomphe du livre: une histoire sociologique de la lecture dans la France du XIXe siècle* (1987), p. 76.
100 The actual name of the author was Mme Augustine Fouillée (*née* Tuillerie). For an analysis of the *Tour de France*, see J. Strachan, 'Romance, religion and the Republic: Bruno's *Le Tour de la France par deux enfants*', *French History*, 18:1 (2004), 96–118.
101 J. and M. Ozouf, 'The little red book of the Republic', in Nora, *Realms*, p. 126.
102 M. Arnold, *A French Eton* (1892), p. 7.
103 D. F. Mitch, *The Rise of Popular Literacy in Victorian England* (Philadelphia, 1992), p. 201.
104 D. Vincent, *Literacy and Popular Culture, England 1750–1914* (Cambridge, 1989), p. 27.
105 A. Weedon, *Victorian Publishing: The Economics of Book Production for a Mass Market 1836–1916* (Aldershot, 2003), p. 33.
106 Cited in P. A. Dunae, 'New Grub Street for boys', in J. Richards (ed.), *Imperialism and Juvenile Literature* (Manchester, 1989), p. 14.
107 P. Nora, 'Ernest Lavisse: son rôle dans la formation du sentiment national', *Revue historique*, 228 (1962), 73–106.
108 C. Billard and P. Guibbert, *Histoire mythologique des Français* (1976). The power of images and stereotypes transmitted by school textbooks has been studied by M. Ferro, *The Use and Abuse of History or How the Past Is Taught* (Engl. trans., 1984).
109 As shown in some revealing examples collected in Musée national de l'éducation, *Les Colonies dans les manuels scolaires de la Troisième République* (1982).
110 Girardet, *Le Nationalisme*, p. 84.
111 Gauthier-Deschamps textbook for the *cours moyen* (1904), cited by Y. Gaulupeau, 'Les manuels d'histoire à l'école primaire', in J.-P. Rioux (ed.), *Dictionnaire de la France coloniale* (2007), pp. 779–88.
112 C. Amalvi, 'Les manuels d'histoire et leur illustration', in H.-J. Martin and R. Chartier (eds), *Histoire de l'édition française*, vol. III (1985), pp. 432–3.
113 V. Chancellor, *History for Their Masters: Opinion in the English History Textbook, 1800–1914* (Bath, 1970), pp. 73–4 and 112–38; K. Castle, *Britannia's Children: Reading Colonialism through Children's Books* (Manchester, 2006), pp. 112–14.
114 J. M. MacKenzie, *Propaganda and Empire* (Manchester, 1984), p. 194.
115 J. Smith Allen, *In the Public Eye: A History of Reading in Modern France, 1800–1940* (Princeton, 1991), p. 65.
116 Porter, *Absent-Minded*; Thompson, *Empire Strikes Back*.
117 M. Spufford, *Small Books and Pleasant Histories: Popular Fiction and Its Readership in Seventeenth-Century England* (Cambridge, 1981).
118 D. Vincent, 'Reading in the working-class home', in J. K. Walton and J. Walvin (eds), *Leisure in Britain 1780–1939* (Manchester, 1983), pp. 207–26.
119 C. Bull, J. Hoose and M. Weed, *An Introduction to Leisure Studies* (Harlow, 2003), p. 14.
120 For a definition of leisure, see J. Dumazedier, 'Leisure and the social system', in J. F. Murphy (ed.), *Concepts of Leisure* (Englewood Cliffs, NJ, 1974), pp. 129–44.
121 P. Langford, *A Polite and Commercial People, England 1727–1783* (Oxford, 1989, 1998), pp. 499–500.
122 J. Lowerson, *Time to Spare in Victorian England* (Hassocks, 1977), p. 110.
123 R. McKibbin, *Classes and Cultures, England 1918–1951* (Oxford, 1998), p. 155.
124 Mayeur, *Débuts de la Troisième République*, pp. 70–3 and 154.
125 Mollier, 'Parfum de la Belle Epoque', p. 82.

CHAPTER 2

Imperial heroes and the market I: the printed world

Marshall McLuhan famously argued that 'the medium is the message', highlighting the way in which the medium used to convey information contributes to its shape and conditions its impact.[1] To this we can add that the medium is closely linked to the market, with which it has a close relationship of reciprocity: the two shape each other to a large extent. The nineteenth century was not the century of the 'Gutenberg revolution', but it witnessed fundamental improvements in reproduction techniques which eased the spreading of texts and images, some of which powerfully supported the fame of imperial heroes when the context was favourable (whether for social or circumstantial reasons, as we have seen in the previous chapter). Throughout the nineteenth century, printing techniques constantly improved in quality and quantity, whilst enhanced paper production processes dramatically reduced costs by two-thirds between 1866 and the end of the century.[2] In Britain, this came in addition to the abolition of stamp duties on the press in 1855, and of paper duties in 1861. Such profound changes in the newspaper industry created conditions propitious to the large-scale promotion of imperial heroes, driven by the 'invisible hand of the market' which had been made more powerful as the period was witnessing the acceleration of a form of 'print-capitalism' which had started earlier but the rhythm of which was accelerated by the unprecedented industrialization of the trade.[3] This chapter will look at aspects of the market evolution (from technical as well as financial points of view) of the press and the publishing worlds between 1870 and the Second World War that are relevant to our understanding of hero-making processes.[4] In so doing, it will also highlight the complex relationship between producers and consumers at the beginning of the era of the mass media, depicting a situation of mutual influence which was much more dynamic than has been acknowledged, for instance, by the Frankfurt School.[5]

In the nineteenth century, the press witnessed gradual but steady technical revolutions which had far-reaching consequences in terms of content and circulation, two key aspects for the nationwide diffusion of heroic legends. In the press, the first vertical rotary press used by the London *Times* from 1848 doubled the hourly output of the newspaper. The American development of the rotary was first used by *The Times* in 1857, and, in 1866, the Walter Press, prefiguring offset printing, was patented. By 1908, the Goss and Hoe octuple presses acquired by *The Times* were capable of printing a thirty-two-page paper at the rate of 25,000 copies an hour.[6] Such large-scale machinery, combined with improvements in the mechanization of letterpress printing such as the Linotype composing machine, allowed quicker production, and a wider diffusion of printed culture. The French printing world followed the same evolution as its British counterpart: the two countries had old traditions in the book trade and the press. For instance, in 1867, when the first rotary press arrived in Paris, it printed 18,000 copies of the *Petit Journal* per hour.[7]

Mechanization and industrialization of newspaper production went alongside the appearance of increasingly sophisticated techniques of image reproduction, which changed the content of newspapers through the addition of visual representations (a medium that was particularly fitting to imperial heroes). Following attempts at reproducing photographs through wood block printing in the 1870s, the first practicable photographic half-tone process for letterpress printing was invented in 1882.[8] The appearance of images made newspapers more appealing to a wider readership, and purely visual magazines were launched (the *Illustrated London News* dated back to 1842, but the first daily illustrated newspaper, the *Daily Graphic*, was launched in 1890). The use of realistic images in the press turned the average Briton into a 'socially omniscient citizen of the world'.[9] In an increasingly competitive market, newspapers found that including an appealing image on their front cover increased their commercial prospects (famously exemplified by the front cover of the illustrated supplement of the *Petit journal* in France). Many newspapers came to feature their artists' personal interpretations of heroic deeds (mostly military action) as a means of attracting attention, confirming E. M. Spiers's argument that 'coverage of the army in the national press paralleled the massive expansion of the newspaper industry'.[10] These highly evocative images were often associated with the national flags, either as part of the scene or as decoration in the margin. Visual representations of imperial heroes (either in action, or wearing their newly acquired decorations) proved popular as well when they became technically possible at a reasonably low cost. Kitchener's portrait was widely featured in the British press as early as November 1898, the *Illustrated London News* published a special supplement with a portrait in colour,[11] while the *New Penny Magazine* featured 'Lord Kitchener of Khartoum' in a special issue,[12] stressing proudly that he came 'from a fighting race'.

The market segmentation was re-shaped by these technological advancements, as the possibility of achieving higher circulation at a lower price, and of making newspapers attractive to a wider public through the recourse to images, considerably expanded the popular reach of the press. This was attained not through the expansion of existing elite titles (*The Times* never became a mass journal)[13] but through the development of a powerful popular press. Imperial topics featured in both the popular press and 'quality newspapers', and the places of heroic figures of overseas expansion reflected both an editorial line and a market strategy.

Among the upper- and middle- class papers, imperial expansion remained firmly advocated throughout the period by the London *Times*. Lord Lugard himself implicitly acknowledged the role of the English newspaper of reference when, writing to his wife Flora Shaw, former head of the colonial section of *The Times*, he reflected upon 'how much the "Imperial idea" owes to you'.[14] The *History of The Times* openly demonstrates that 'the paper became one of the principal agencies by which the nation was taught to "think imperially"'.[15] Although the respectable press only reluctantly praised individuals and preferred a penetrating political analysis to a piece of hagiography, in certain circumstances it contributed to the promotion of imperial heroes, for political or ideological as much as commercial reasons. This was particularly the case with General Gordon in 1884–85. *The Times*'s leading article of 21 January 1884 thus placed its confidence in Gordon's powers of pacification, and the dispatches sent by *The Times*'s correspondent in Khartoum, Frank Power, were regarded as representing Gordon's opinion.[16] More than sixty years after the fall of Khartoum, a chapter of the *History of The Times* was given the title 'Empire and Imperialism: Gordon', thus making Gordon the embodiment of the colonial ethos forcefully promoted by the newspaper.[17]

But the popular press appears as the key element of the story behind the widespread success of the genre of imperial heroes in the last decades of the nineteenth century. A new-style cheap press, the penny press, quickly became the most powerful propaganda tool available at that time – actually, the first mass-medium worth the name. Crucially, this powerful means of shaping public perceptions sustained imperial feelings across all classes of society. It was also prone to celebrating the triumphs of imperial heroes, who allowed journalists to put the emphasis on individual achievements (as a way of justifying the

European domination of the world,) rather than on sheer technological superiority.[18]

Launched in 1896, the *Daily Mail* promised to 'explain, simplify, clarify': within just three years it had doubled the circulation of any other national newspaper,[19] notably thanks to its 'positive coverage of Britain's imperial wars'.[20] This was confirmed at the outbreak of the Boer War: whereas 430,000 people on average bought the *Daily Mail* every day in 1898, the figure increased to almost a million in 1900. Overall, annual circulation figures increased from 85 million in 1851 to 5,604 million in 1920.[21] In reality, circulation figures were below the actual number of readers: the same copy was often read by several individuals in public houses or cafés or even in the workplace. Imperial heroes were featured in the inside pages as well as on front covers, frequently under bold headlines and accompanied by evocative engravings (often in colour). This *mise en scène* was meant to appeal to the reader's imagination, especially in the case of imperial wars, when imperialism, warfare and nationalism coalesced. Although there were obvious commercial benefits to be gained, some newspapers, such as the *Daily Mail*, avowed their commitment to the promotion of the imperial idea: its founder Alfred Harmsworth 'insisted that the Empire was central to the *Mail's* mission'.[22] Their affordability ('a penny newspaper for one halfpenny') ensured them the widest circulation in the country, and their impact on the fame of imperial heroes among the population was decisive. It is revealing that the main maker of the 'Kitchener legend' in the aftermath of the re-conquest of the Sudan, George Warrington Steevens, was a war correspondent for the *Daily Mail* (his role in the making of the Kitchener legend will be studied in more detail in Chapter 7).

In France, *Le Petit Journal* and *Le Petit Parisien* pioneered mass circulation. Founded in 1863 by Moïse Millaud, *Le Petit Journal* revolutionized the market by reaching as many readers as possible thanks to its low price of one *sou*.[23] Thirteen years later, the *Petit Parisien*, founded by a committee of twelve Republican supporters all linked to Adolphe Thiers and Léon Gambetta, followed the assumption that 'the taste for reading increases in proportion with the easiness with which the public can satisfy it'.[24] With the Third Republic, newspapers became *un produit de consommation courante* (an everyday consumer product) thanks to the industrialization of their production and the modernization of their distribution, which steadily expanded the market available to them.[25] In 1870, the top four cheap daily newspapers together sold nearly 600,000 copies per day in Paris, while in 1880 the *Petit Journal* alone sold 583,000 copies in Paris (it was to reach a million nationally around 1890), and in 1910 the *Petit Parisien* reached a daily circulation of 1,400,000 copies. Overall, the Parisian population bought five times more newspapers in 1939 than in 1870. Outside Paris, the increase was even sharper: if in the late 1860s the sales figures in the *province* did not exceed 250,000 copies, the quantities rose to 500,000 in 1875, a million in 1885 and 4 million on the eve of the Great War. Between 1870 and 1939, the increase in circulation figures outside Paris was twelvefold; the overall output of the French press eightfold, with 1.5 million in 1870 as opposed to 12.5 million in 1939. The law on the freedom of the press of 29 July 1881 gave the French press an unprecedented sense of power.[26] Concomitantly, it tried to sell cheaply, and to exploit the railway and the telegraph in order to cater to the huge demand for literature characteristic of the period.[27] This increasingly powerful propaganda machine did not play the same role in France and in Britain as far as imperial subjects were concerned: while very few newspapers criticized imperialism in England (it was even a major staple for some of them), several major French newspapers remained staunchly hostile to colonial expansion, like *Le Petit Parisien* until Jean Dupuy became director in 1888.[28] In a hotly debated political context, newspapers played a far less unanimous role in France regarding imperial heroes, but they remained a powerful medium that could enable heroic reputations to develop among the public – in particular because cheap books took longer to appear in France.

Compared to the British popular newspapers, the French press had a more literary approach to journalism and enjoyed a closer relationship with '*le monde des lettres*', hence leaving more room for fiction, short stories and poetry than its British equivalents. Because politics was also widely discussed and used up a lot of space, this literary bias came at the expense of news (especially when it came from abroad) and sensational features such as imperial heroes. In addition, colonial ventures only intermittently attracted readers' attention until the turn of the century. Before the interwar years, imperial heroes appealed to the French public more efficiently if they were linked to another significant topic of the moment, such as Anglophobia (Fashoda and Marchand) or Germanophobia (Lyautey in Morocco). Although imperial enthusiasm was nowhere near the level it reached in the *Daily Mail*, colonial matters were far from absent in the French press.[29] *Le Matin* opened a public subscription to fund the building of the trans-Saharan railway.[30] The most respectable of French newspapers, *Le Temps*, under the leadership of Paul Bourde and Pierre Mille, played a key role in the promotion of the imperial ethos, through a variety of articles on colonial life, despatches on colonial campaigns and personal contacts with colonial explorers such as Brazza, Binger and Gallieni.[31] *Le Petit Parisien* resolutely supported colonial expansion from 1888 onwards, under the editorship of Jean Dupuy and his followers.[32] But in all the instances mentioned above, journalists intended more to educate the population, to convert their readers to the colonial agenda, than to make the most of a commercial trend. Imperial heroes did not rank very high compared to the *roman-feuilleton*, such as *La Petite Mionne* or *Roger-la-honte* (by Emile Richebourg and Jules Mary, respectively), which guaranteed steady success to the newspaper which had the luck to serialize it.

Last but not least, the very concept of 'hero' was problematic among Republican newspapers as the potent attraction exerted by a hero increased the risk of a *coup d'état*, should the Great Man be manipulated by opponents to the Republic. Further to the crisis generated by the success of the Boulangist movement (which stemmed entirely from the popularity of its blue-eyed, attractive and apparently resolute leader), moderate or Republican newspapers, such as *Le Petit Parisien* under Jean Dupuy, systematically abstained from promoting any personality cult: although he was, as previously seen, favourable to colonial expansion, he did not press his agenda through the evocative argument of imperial heroes.[33]

This comes in stark contrast to the British situation, where the emphasis could easily be placed on individual qualities displayed within the framework of colonial activity, therefore lending itself more often to Carlylean forms of imperial 'hero-worship'. It was achieved through the intercession of two major novelties of the period: the war correspondent and the interview, two 'inventions' that drastically influenced the content of newspapers and subsequently the manufacturing of notoriety.

The English-speaking press in general, and the British in particular, pioneered the genre of live coverage of important events through the figure of the war correspondent. The development of overland telegraphic lines and undersea cable facilities by the British, or with British help and capital, gave Britain the upper hand on information from far-flung corners of the globe. *The Times* took a decisive turning point when it decided, in 1854, to send a member of its staff in his mid-thirties, William Howard Russell, to report on the situation in Crimea just before the war with Russia broke out. In so doing, the newspaper commissioned the first ever war correspondent, as stated on his memorial plaque in the crypt of St Paul's cathedral.[34] Russell was the first of many British war correspondents sent to report on operations of the British army abroad, a list so long that it became a characteristic feature of British journalism in the late nineteenth century and inaugurated a tradition of (often dangerous) proximity between war and the media.[35]

War correspondents played a pivotal role in the promotion of new heroic reputations, as they were the first to report vividly the actions of the men who defended Britain's interests, praising British troops as a whole but usually naming officers and, not uncommonly, celebrating the 'thin red line of heroes'. With war correspondents, the emphasis naturally shifted away from a theoretical and literary approach to what was actually happening on the battlefield, and eyes subsequently turned to the great 'man on the spot' who knew how to lead his men to victory, visibly to the great delight of readers. R. T. Stearn has shown that 'war correspondents contributed much to the making of popular military heroes' and that 'the press [even] promoted a cult of the war correspondent as hero'.[36] War correspondents and special artists – the ancestors of war photographers – who naturally identified with army officers, served not only what they believed was a moral duty of patriotism but also their financial and personal interest when they promoted new heroic reputations, while newspapers were pleased to find in war correspondents good aides in their continual competition for readership. Both respected the logics of the market.

It is thus hardly surprising that, until the First World War, the number of war correspondents grew steadily. Whereas Frank Power of *The Times* was the only correspondent with Gordon in Khartoum in 1884, '30-odd journalists covered Kitchener's campaign' of 1898,[37] and no fewer than fifty-eight newspaper correspondents accompanied the British army to South Africa (*The Times* alone had sent twenty of them).[38] Such growth indicates that war correspondents were financially profitable, and that the costs involved (salary and travel expenses) were justified by the increase in profits that their reporting generated. For the war correspondents themselves, it was a means of earning a living while enjoying themselves (most of them felt close to the officers, although the feeling was not always reciprocated). Dispatches from the war correspondents sent to report on imperial campaigns were particularly sought by the public: William Howard Russell, Archibald Forbes, Bennet Burleigh or Francis Scudamore were not anonymous (unlike most of their colleagues), and some of them even became famous.[39] Occasionally, they could also earn a substantial amount of money very rapidly through the sale of their eyewitness accounts in book form, as we shall see in Chapter 7. It has been argued that the decline of the popular broadsides and the concomitant development of the popular press gave the latter so much power that it 'boosted the careers and reputations of several senior officers'.[40]

The second factor that helped imperial heroes enter British national consciousness was the advent of 'New Journalism', which marked the beginning of media interest in the lives of famous people: a prototype of 'celebrity coverage',[41] prefiguring the 'human interest' story in popular magazines and newspapers.[42] Largely shaped after W. T. Stead's innovative ideas set out in the late 1870s, it put the emphasis on individuals and their personality, especially through interview, which was intended to put the interviewee's character and special abilities to the forefront. In the process, it could also promote the interviewer's reputation and this tended to make 'larger-than-life' portraiture desirable, as it enhanced the reporter's own status and gave more weight to his arguments (which was also a means of implementing the 'government by journalism' facet of the 'New Journalism'). Above all, such articles attracted the attention of the general public in a way that more serious, more elaborate political analyses could not. One blatant example of the power of the interview (and of New Journalism) was the appointment of General Gordon by Gladstone as a way of solving the 1884 Sudan crisis. Whereas a letter from Sir Samuel Baker calling for the appointment of 'an Englishman' to solve the thorny issue of the Sudan, published in the *Pall Mall Gazette* on 27 November 1883 under the title 'What should be done in the Soudan', did not attract much attention (nor did an article by the same in *The Times* on New Year's Day 1884 calling for the appointment of 'Gordon Pacha'), Stead's 9 January 1884 article entitled 'Chinese Gordon to the Soudan' had such an impact on British readership that it altered the course of national policy making, forcing the Gladstone government to appoint Gordon. Unlike Baker, Stead had focused his attention on a well-known, outstanding individual, whom he skilfully interviewed: General Charles George Gordon, known at the time as 'Chinese Gordon' but who would later become the heroic 'Gordon of Khartoum'. Stead's interview, featured in the 'quality' newspaper *Pall Mall Gazette*, quickly spread in the popular press and won popular acclaim. The interviewer and editor Stead, then thirty-four, enhanced his own reputation and increased its market value.

Although they were new as a doctrine, Stead's techniques were not unprecedented; rather, 'New Journalism' crystallized into a coherent journalistic strategy an approach that had been adopted intermittently beforehand. Apparently, the first occurrence of an interview, due to James Gordon Bennett Sr, took place in the US in 1836. However, the idea was not taken up in Britain before the second half of the nineteenth century, when personality cults, typical of the Victorians and closely linked to their fascination with history and their propensity to learn lessons from the past, developed steadily.[43] Readers became eager to discover worthy characters through edifying stories, and heroic deeds sensational enough to catch the public's eye were eagerly promoted with a view to generating commercial benefit. Submitting to the increasingly irresistible appeal of what Virginia Berridge has called its 'commercialization', the press seized the opportunities offered by these new techniques of image-shaping, which allowed it to manufacture celebrity.[44]

The figure of David Livingstone was at the centre of one such instance. James Gordon Bennett Jr, the son of the American inventor of the interview, set a precedent when he commissioned the ambitious journalist of working-class origin, Henry Morton Stanley, in his early thirties, to find David Livingstone, dead or alive, as the climax of a series of sensational reports on the opening of the Suez Canal, Sir Samuel Baker's Nile expedition, Jerusalem, the old battlefields of the Crimea, Persia and India.[45] From the outset, Stanley's expedition had been clearly orchestrated as a journalistic endeavour designed to generate the greatest publicity to its commissioner, the *New York Herald*. Livingstone's wanderings in the interior of Africa had generated many worries for his health in London, and several relief expeditions supported by the Royal Geographical Society and its president Sir Roderick Murchison (a close friend of Livingstone's) had intended to find him. One such expedition, led by the gunner E. D. Young in 1867–68, was a complete success, but failed to attract much public attention although it (rightly) claimed that Livingstone was still alive, contrary to what authoritative figures such as Dr John Kirk and Sir Samuel Baker had asserted. The situation was glaringly different four years later, at the end of May 1872, when Stanley returned to England from Central Africa, where he had accompanied Livingstone for four months: then, he was acclaimed as a hero by almost the whole of the British and international public and press. Although he was sometimes scorned in higher class circles because of his modest origins, Stanley managed to become a popular icon alongside the hero he had helped to promote. His stories and reports in the *New York Herald* had aroused public curiosity in a way no other follower of Livingstone's had. Livingstone's reputation had reached such a status, not least under Stanley's impetus, that, when his body was repatriated in April 1874, it was buried with full national honours in the nave of Westminster Abbey. The 'death of a National Hero in Darkest Africa'[46] captivated the Victorian public's mind and established his legendary status among the public (as in Gordon's case, his death had made him a Christian martyr whose legend owed much to the religiosity of the period).[47] Helped by a powerful press behind him, Stanley had achieved his aim of making as big as possible a story out of his encounter with Livingstone, not least because 'he was also a man well able and willing to blow his own trumpet', unlike his predecessor E. D. Young who had apparently not adopted self-publicity strategies.[48] Without the clout of the press and a conscious strategy of self-promotion, Stanley's story would have remained relatively unknown. But the combination of the interests of a newspaper, which could increase its circulation thanks to sensational stories, and the willingness of a journalist like Stanley to indulge in self-promotion at the same time as he celebrated his missionary hero ensured the growth of Livingstone's popularity – to such an extent that it can be argued that 'without Stanley and the famous meeting, we would probably not remember Livingstone'.[49] By setting such a memorable precedent, this journalistic scoop greatly influenced the evolution of the market for heroic accounts and their related paraphernalia, showing the popularity of imperial heroes in Britain, and inducing journalists (and editors) to find more opportunities to create new heroic reputations for their own benefit.

If 'New Journalism' had a famous predecessor in the unlikely duo formed by David Livingstone and Henry Morton Stanley, it found an epilogue in the promotion of Thomas Edward Lawrence.[50] Another instance of promotion of a British hero by an American journalist, Lawrence became famous in the interwar period owing to a series of successful lectures by the American reporter Lowell Thomas, illustrated by photos and short feature films by his cameraman Harry Chase (the impact of which will be studied in Chapter 3). Endowed with $100,000 of private sponsorship, Thomas and Chase first intended to report from the glorious battlefields of Allied campaigns in Europe. Appalled by the horrors of war in France and in Italy, they asked John Buchan, then working for the Ministry of Information, to find an alternative. He suggested transferring them to Allenby's headquarters in Palestine. An anonymous writer, probably Lawrence's brother Arnold Walter Lawrence, describes the rest of a process that started on a Sunday in March 1919 in the Century Theater (near Central Park), with publicity courtesy of the New York *Globe*:[51]

> After the war, they put on a two man lecture-show in New York, first in a Theatre and later at Madison Square Gardens: and it was here that their programme featuring Allenby and Lawrence first drew the crowds. The English impresario, Percy Burton, saw their performances and heard of Lawrence the 'great hero' for the first time. He brought Lowell Thomas to Covent Garden, and later to the Albert Hall, originally for a short season, which was extended to six months and was seen by over a million people, followed by a three-year tour of the English-speaking world. I set out this story in some detail because it is important to realise that until this dramatic tour-de-force, Lawrence was only known among the Arabs and to the select few: after it, his fame was almost worldwide and inescapable; and coloured by the nature of the programme that made it so.[52]

In Lawrence's case, as in Livingstone's, the American influence upon hero-making in Britain can be felt. Enjoying wider audiences, more advanced technologically and able to attract inventors and implement new techniques, wealthier, exceptionally skilled at anticipating the dominant tastes of the public, the American cultural industry was more prone to influence the British market through the knock-on effect of internationally famous contributions – especially because Thomas's talk benefited from the backing of the English-Speaking Union.[53] US-based hero-makers such as Stanley or Lowell Thomas were no exception and they succeeded in generating interest in newly discovered national figures who were soon turned into attractive subjects for British journalists themselves: a sort of free English-speaking market for heroic material seems to have taken shape as the concept of mass media was imported from the US into Britain. This process was made all the easier since the first transatlantic telegraphic cable was laid in 1866, allowing for the development of a 'new global Anglo-American public sphere'.[54]

In large part because of linguistic and cultural barriers, the French market was less influenced than the British by the pioneering American hero-making business.[55] Although there was in Paris a Stanley club, Stanley was considered in France a dangerous colonial rival, especially after he had confronted Brazza in Central Africa on behalf of his employer the Belgian King Leopold II. The Livingstone legend did reach France, but its development did not result directly from the orchestration designed by Stanley and the *New York Herald*, nor did it achieve the same level of popularity as in English-speaking countries. Comparatively few biographical printed works on Livingstone were published in France in the late nineteenth century.[56] As for Lawrence, Lowell Thomas limited his talks to English-speaking countries, a fact that slowed down the development of the legend in France. It did not earn any real market value until the American film *Lawrence of Arabia* (David Lean, 1962) was swiftly dubbed into French.

In general, the French press proved to be less innovative than the British or Americans when it came to promoting imperial heroes, in particular because they fitted less easily in the French journalistic tradition which put the emphasis on literature and politics, and only reluctantly agreed to follow the path of *l'américanisation*. Besides, the French press was, overall, reluctant to engage in sensationalism (which was commonly referred to as *'newyorkheraldisme'*, showing quite clearly how this practice was seen as alien).[57] Gallic heroes were neither at the centre of journalistic scoops nor featured in illustrated slide shows produced by reporters, even in the later decades of the period. Imperial heroes were more likely to appear in certain categories of the French press when they could serve a cause, such as the French conquest of the Congo in Brazza's case or merely the end of the Third Republic when it came to Marchand.[58] They appeared more frequently in the press when public opinion had to be comforted after a defeat or a bitterly felt downturn: hence, Brazza's Makoko treaty helped the French national psyche to forget the humiliation of leaving the British Fleet to act alone in Egypt,[59] while Marchand's supporters sought a compensatory hero after the loss of prestige which followed the evacuation of Fashoda.

Although, as seen above, the Republican press was rather reluctant to celebrate individuals anyway, other currents of thought in the French press, and particularly the nationalists, did promote their specific heroes, such as Boulanger, Déroulède or Marchand. The nationalist press did not hesitate to celebrate its heroes to serve both its beliefs and its commercial interests. Renowned for its Anglophobic, anti-Panama and anti-Clemenceau stance (under the influence of its editor Ernest Judet), *Le Petit Journal* frequently featured imperial heroes on the engravings illustrating the cover of its weekly *Supplément Illustré*, first published in June 1884 (there was at least one colour engraving from 1891 onwards). Imperial heroes suited well the nationalist, militaristic and often simplistic tone of the publication, which drew heavily upon the tradition of the *image d'Epinal*.[60] With a circulation of more than a million in 1895, it brought imperial heroes to large constituencies. Celebrations of imperial heroes in the press could also result from specific events which provided unique opportunities to increase sales or produce special issues. On 31 May 1899, the day Marchand set foot in Toulon, the self-styled '*Journal anti-maçonnique*' *A bas les tyrans* (an anti-Freemason newspaper) celebrated the return of the explorer hero. In so doing, it reduced its unsold bulk to 2,800 copies as opposed to an average of 10,000 per day (for instance, 11,788 on 29 June 1899). Special supplements dedicated to the celebration of national-imperial heroes were also a good source of profit as they remained on the newsagents' stalls longer than daily issues. On 30 May 1899, there were just 250 unsold copies of a supplement on *Colonel Marchand* returned to the *Messageries Hachette*, as opposed to 20,258 unsold copies of *Le Gaulois*, 25,386 of *La Patrie* or 40,973 of *La Liberté* that same day.[61] Although Republican weariness towards great men suggests that the French public was less unanimously inclined than the British to revere imperial heroes (a journalist of the *Comité de l'Afrique française* even went as far as saying in the interwar years that the French '[did] not worship great men in general, nor great colonial leaders in particular'),[62] there are clear proofs that some parts of the public could find heroic accounts appealing, and their taste was diligently catered for by nationalist newspapers.

Yet, even for those newspapers that dedicated space to imperial heroes, their promotional strategies did not borrow much from the New Journalism. Instead of interviews, readers found long hagiographic articles combining attacks on the 'corrupted government' and praise of the hero (alongside a celebration of the civilizing values he embodied). If imperial heroes often featured prominently in the press on both sides of the Channel, French strategies of promotion and image-making in the press differend significantly from those prevalent in Britain. Although interviews became more popular in the French press after 1890 (especially under 'Anglo-Saxon' influence, as it was called in Paris), they did not prove instrumental in generating new imperial legends. Journalists generally preferred to write their own articles about imperial heroes, as a means of conveying their views. Even Ernest Judet, who was a close friend of Marchand's, never published a formal interview of the hero of Fashoda in *Le Petit Journal*. Tellingly, no interview followed a long meeting they had in Barbizon in September 1899.[63] When Marchand resigned from the army in April 1904 as a consequence of the French government's decision to dismiss him from an official mission to Russia, he wrote a mere letter to the editor of *La Patrie*, and was not interviewed.[64] The special correspondent in Berlin of the aristocratic, royalist newspaper *Le Gaulois* conducted Marchand's only published interview. He recounted his meeting with Tsar Nicholas II, in an attempt to disqualify his government's decision not to send him to advise the Russians on the occasion of the Russo-Japanese War.[65] In all fairness, the fact that the hero of Fashoda was not a gifted communicator did not help. A few months later, when *Le Figaro* published Marchand's memoirs of the Fashoda encounter, the editor was reportedly so disappointed with the poor quality of the material that he considered stopping the publication of the colonel's recollections altogether.[66] In spite of this circumstantial evidence, it remains beyond doubt that French newspapers were not prone to featuring interviews and, instead, seemed to prefer carefully crafted articles where the hero's argument and image could be sharpened at leisure.

Noises in the press about an imperial hero could easily turn into a publisher's dream: media interest tended to draw large audiences, with some readers willing to open their purses to know more about the great man of the moment. The publishing market was influenced by the trends of the newspaper market as a result of the similarity of their target audience: many newspaper readers were also book-buyers. Most of the technical improvements mentioned earlier in this chapter were also beneficial to book printing. Publishing multiplied the effects of these developments: books appear as a primary factor for the promotion of imperial heroes, prolonging the action of newspapers and fuelling public interest over the *longue durée*. Not only did a book have an incomparably longer shelf-life than a newspaper, but it had a deeper effect as it was traditionally kept in households or lent many times by libraries. Books had the potential to turn an ephemeral reputation into an enduring one.

Increased mechanization allowed book releases to soar whilst market demands expanded: the quality of upmarket books improved, while at the same time the quantity of cheap books rocketed.[67] This had direct consequences on the material relating to imperial heroes in the two countries. Writing about France, W. H. Schneider remarked that 'the old pattern, whereby new information about Africa was made available only to a small educated elite, was broken after 1870, and important African events were reported to the French masses almost as quickly as they happened'.[68] This statement applies equally well to the British case. The public's widening horizons prepared the ground for, and fostered, the legends attached to empire builders. Authors of juvenile literature found in the conquest of Africa edifying subjects; young readers could identify themselves with the famous conquerors who conveyed a patriotic message and showed moral or physical superiority over indigenous populations, and contributed to the making of an 'imperialist genealogy of hegemonic masculinity'.[69] The fate of General Gordon attracted British interest in the barren desert of the Sudan, while the story of Charles de Foucauld deeply entrenched the Hoggar mountains into French minds, long before oil was discovered in the Sahara.

Travel literature and exploration accounts were not new to the British and French public: eighteenth-century readers had proved genuinely interested in state-sponsored explorations of the southern hemisphere, such as those undertaken by Byron, Wallis, Cook, La Pérouse, Dumont d'Urville and Bougainville. Aware of the public's taste for this type of literature, publishers offered substantial royalties for such travel accounts. John Hawkesworth, who was given the task of writing the official version of the early voyages of Byron, Wallis, Carteret and Cook by Lord Sandwich, the First Lord of the Admiralty, asked the publishers Strahan and Cadell for a fee of £6,000 for the three volumes, making this venture one of the most remunerative of the century. Paul Langford has gone so far as describing Cook's voyages 'a literary eldorado'.[70] With America decolonized, the South Seas already under European control, India unpopular after the 1857 uprising and the major European Powers trying to maintain or expand their influence overseas, Africa, alongside China and the Middle East, was ready to become a new 'literary eldorado'. The interaction between the white man and the African environment and the Africans captured the reader's imagination, making imperial heroes the ideal topic for successful books, testified by the rise to prominence of the literary genre of travel writing throughout the period.[71]

Similarly, the market for edifying biographical books already existed in the eighteenth century,[72] but its importance grew throughout the nineteenth century, as a consequence of the decisive improvements in printing processes which, for instance, made it possible to publish about seventy-five biographies of General Gordon in the months following the fall of Khartoum. The productivity of biographers, hagiographers and publishers about Gordon coincided with a general frenzy for Gordon in the press, generated by the siege and fall of Khartoum.[73] Even in the publishing world, speed of production had apparently become a determining factor: it was observed in the 1970s that 'the rapidity with which the authors got into print following Gordon's death in January, 1885, would be envied today'.[74] In the last two decades of the nineteenth century, both the output of books and the market demand for writing upon military or quasi-military themes reached new heights.[75]

Most of the time, these works appeared to be primarily commercially driven. They usually lacked originality and failed to bring new evidence or anecdotes on the subject. Paul Maylam observed that the 'degree of recycling' of biographies about Cecil Rhodes was 'extraordinary', a fact that tends to show that the authors of these unoriginal works primarily sought to make money out of a subject that could potentially sell well (no fewer than twenty-six biographies of Rhodes appeared between 1897 and 1996).[76]

Famous imperial heroes could generate steady sales for publishers as the public felt a strong appeal towards the names of the great men of the day, whose deeds had been widely reported in the press. Some authors seem to have made this subject their speciality. Harold F. B. Wheeler announced on the title pages of his book on Kitchener that he was the author of *The Story of Napoleon, The Story of Wellington, The Story of Nelson, The Story of Lord Roberts* and *The Story of Lord Kitchener*:[77] the way in which heroes of the Napoleonic wars dovetail into imperial figures in this list of titles supports this book's view that imperial heroes represented a new category of national heroic figures. In her book on Stanley published in 1890 (immediately after he had come back from the Emin Pasha Relief Expedition which had attracted significant media attention), Eva Hope's name was followed by the mention 'by the author of "The Life of General Gordon", as if she wanted to stress her literary specialization in great figures, and perhaps to foster the development of a 'heroic genealogy' through her works.[78]

One of the most established authors of juvenile literature in the period, G. A. Henty was also prone to using the names of famous imperial

Table 1 Imperial heroes in G. A. Henty's titles: overall sales from date of release until 31 August 1917

Title	Release date	Copies sold
Non-African imperial heroes		
With Clive in India	September 1883	38,238
With Wolfe in Canada	May 1886	17,662
With Lee in Virginia	August 1889	11652
By right of conquest (Pizarro in Mexico)	October 1890	14,370
African imperial heroes		
The Dash for Khartoum	July 1891	23,432
With Buller in Natal	July 1900	25,808
With Roberts to Pretoria	August 1901	23,731
With Kitchener in the Soudan	May 1902	19,909
Other titles		
Bonnie Prince Charlie	June 1887	16,759
Under Wellington's Command	June 1898	26,537
With the British Legion	August 1902	9,095

Source: P. Newbolt, *G. A. Henty 1832–1902, A Bibliographical Study* (Aldershot, 1996), Appendix VII.

heroes in the titles of his books (which usually featured fictional heroes with whom young readers could identify more easily). Sales figures of the six-shilling versions of Henty's novels show that titles bearing the names of imperial heroes generally sold very well. Although *With Clive in India* appears as the clear best-seller of the list, many books bearing the name of imperial heroes who acted in Africa, or referring to their action, feature among the best-selling titles. The fact that eight of the Henty novels were set in Africa testifies to the enduring appeal of the Dark Continent to his young readers.[79] Although it did not bear the name of General Gordon explicitly, *The Dash for Khartoum* (first published in July 1891) generated a spontaneous association with Gordon, only five years afer his highly publicized death in Khartoum. Referring to the Wilson expedition, which had been sent to rescue General Gordon, the book praised British military superiority and Christian and British values. In line with the dominant view of the time, it criticized Gladstone for sending General Wolseley too late to save Gordon: it was clearly part of the Gordon industry. As Table 1 demonstrates, Henty books dedicated to British imperial heroes who had acted in Africa performed well commercially, especially when bearing in mind that these figures rcfcr only to the six-shilling editions: almost all of these titles were re-issued in a 'New and Popular edition' (e.g. *With Kitchener in the Soudan* in 1916), which was followed in the

CONTEXTS

Table 2 The Kitchener legend and the publishing industry (number of titles published, from the Bodleian and British Library catalogues)

	1898–99	1900–15	1916 (d.)	1917	1918–25	1925–40	after 1940
On Kitchener's strategy	3	5	–	–	3	4	3
Biographies	2	8	11	7	5	11	23
Songs	4	2	3	1	–	–	–

1920s by a closely related series entitled 'The New Popular Henty' (in which *The Dash for Khartoum* could be found among others), but there are no figures for them. In certain cases, such as that of *With Roberts to Pretoria*, the publisher did not release the book in any of the above-mentioned cheaper series because 'demand remain[ed] strong enough for Blackie to maintain the original six-shilling price'.[80]

Driven by the wish to find topics likely to ensure steady sales, publishers were eager to make the most of (and, as a result, to contribute to) the public's taste for contemporaneous 'exemplary lives'. They usually reacted in two steps. First, they published accounts of the heroic deed for which the individual had become famous. Less ambitious (or smaller) publishers contributed more ephemeral *pièces de circonstance* such as songs. This phase could exceptionally include critical works about the hero. One such example was a book by the editor of *Punch*, mocking Stanley's claimed philanthropic ambitions after the Emin Pasha relief expedition, and arguing that it was nothing more than a publicity stunt: it was so successful that in 1891 it had already reached its sixth edition.[81] The second editorial phase came a few months (or sometimes years) later: if the hero had not fallen into oblivion, authors and publishers attempted longer biographies. This two-stage reaction resulted from the time it took to collect the data necessary to write an extended biography, design the book, and produce it. A survey of the bibliography about Lord Kitchener in the years following his re-conquest of the Sudan shows the multiplication of biographies over time, whilst songs and books on the Sirdar's strategy decreased (Table 2).

When Kitchener gained for the first time a heroic status in Britain, after the battle of Omdurman and the subsequent publicity campaign led by the *Daily Mail* correspondent George Warrington Steevens (see Chapter 7), popular songs and studies of his strategy in the Sudan (quicker to document and write than full accounts of his life) outnumbered biographies. In the following fifteen years, the most popular 'Kitchener products' were biographies. Kitchener's death in 1916 probably accelerated the publishing of biographies which were already being written given his political pre-eminence at the time. In 1917, the flow of biographies remained steady, but songs were no longer on the agenda. In the interwar period, the rhythm of biographies was close to one per year.

The Kitchener legend offered Blackwood publishers one of its most resounding commercial successes, surpassed only by Laurence Oliphant's *Altiora Petio* (1883). The hardback version of the book generated benefits 'second only to profits gained from the magazine [Blackwood's so-called *Maga*] and the 1890s reprints of George Eliot's works'.[82] Between September 1898 and January 1901 52,337 copies of the original edition at six shillings were printed, with 99 per cent of them sold by then. In addition, 1,050 copies of a 'colonial edition' were printed in February 1901. More significantly, 184,425 copies of the sixpenny edition were printed in March 1899, and this one-off print sold steadily. In total, 236,762 copies of *With Kitchener to Khartoum* were put on the British market in a year and a half. These figures show that the success of the book was due in large part to its topicality, but, at the same time, it can be argued that its wide diffusion in Britain, supported by a relatively significant advertising campaign which cost Blackwood £100, durably strengthened the fame of Lord Kitchener, transforming what could have been ephemeral glory into memorable heroism (Table 3).

Publishers involved in the promotion of imperial heroes could sometimes count on an established tradition in the field, which allowed them to anticipate the public taste. Before *With Kitchener to Khartoum*, Steevens's publisher, Blackwood and Sons, had already had some experience in publishing books on imperial subjects, which had sold steadily. The firm had published John Hanning Speke's *Journal of the Discovery of the Source of the Nile* in December 1863, printing more than 10,000 copies within four months, and making a substantial profit of £3031 5s out of it.[83] In 1885–86, Blackwood sold nearly 6,000 copies of *From Korti to Khartoom* by Wolseley's Chief of the Intelligence Department, Charles Wilson – with a net profit of £262 9s 2d.[84]

Yet, success could never be guaranteed: the dedication of a publisher to the promotion of an imperial hero was not enough to secure a place in the pantheon of national celebrities. Several books celebrating imperial figures, published in the wake of Steevens's *With Kitchener to Khartoum*, proved to be commercial failures. They demonstrated that a successful imperial hero resulted from the convergence of a variety of favourable circumstances, and that a publishing enterprise alone was often not enough to reach the critical mass necessary to achieve widespread fame. General Gerald Graham had been a great military figure of the late nineteenth century, who had successfully fought the Mahdi's

Table 3 Print-runs, *With Kitchener to Khartoum*. NLS, MS 30864, Sales ledger, p. 347 and p. 395

Edition	Date	Print run
1	Sept. 1898	1,050
2	Oct. 1898	1,050
3	Oct. 1898	1,052
4	Oct. 1898	1,660
5	Oct. 1898	2,003
6	Oct. 1898	2,100
7	Oct. 1898	3,199
8	Nov. 1898	2,100
9	Nov. 1898	2,110
10	Nov. 1898	3,165
11	Nov. 1898	3,150
12	Nov. 1898	2,100
13	Dec. 1898	5,416
14	Dec. 1898	3,175
15	Dec. 1898	5,316
16	Dec. 1898	5,251
17	Jan. 1899	2,140
18	Mar. 1899	1,050
19	Apr. 1899	1,025
20	Apr. 1899	1,075
21	Jan. 1900	1,050
22	May 1900	1,050
23	Jan. 1901	1,050
Total 65 ed.	**As to Jan. 1901**	**52,337**
Colonial edition	**Feb. 1901**	**1,050**
Sixpenny edition	**Mar. 1899**	**184,425**

troop to such an extent that he returned to England to 'something of a hero's welcome'.[85] Blackwood published a biography of him in June 1901, a year and a half after his death. No more than 294 copies of R. H. Vetch's book *Life, Letters and Diaries of Sir Gerald Graham VC* were sold in the first six months: out of a print-run of 788 copies, 439 were still in stock on 31 December 1901.[86] Similarly, *Cecil Rhodes: A Study of a Career* by Howard Hensman did relatively poorly: apart from a bulk 1,000 copies sold to the American distributor Harper Bros, just 1,056 copies were sold in bookshops between December 1901 and June 1903.[87] Reception of material about imperial heroes varied according to the subject, title, author, timing and the general mood of the public. The sales figure above (all from the same publisher) tend to show that the British public was receptive to imperial heroes under certain conditions, and profitability could not be taken for granted. The lack of success of General Graham's biography resulted from the combination of several factors: his glorious days had long passed, he died in retirement rather than in action and his death was subsequently not publicized (it gave rise to obituaries rather than plain articles). Graham was no longer in the hero-making circuit: the days when he was seen as exceptional had long gone. Cecil Rhodes's relative unpopularity among book buyers at the turn of the century is more difficult to explain; the painful news of the South African war might have diverted the public's attention from the main activist of British expansion in southern Africa, and lassitude might have overcome the British public following two successive campaigns in the Sudan and South Africa. This was probably a temporary decrease in interest, as the 1930s saw the publication of several Rhodes biographies.

Publishers were part of a wider cultural – or propaganda – network, which included official propaganda, the press, theatres,[88] popular songs and later the radio, the cinema and the television. The commercial attractiveness of any given hero depended upon the combination of these media: chances of success were indeed maximized if they all celebrated the same imperial hero at the same time. This happened to Lord Kitchener after the re-conquest of the Sudan, when he was unanimously celebrated in the press (in spite of the jealousy of fellow officers and rather strained relations with journalists), granted the freedom of the cities of London and Cambridge, awarded many honours, celebrated in songs and indeed presented as a 'man of destiny' in G. W. Steevens's book, stemming from his *Daily Mail* articles.

French publishers faced a more unpredictable situation. Geographical subjects were reputedly less popular in France than in other European countries, in spite of the ceaseless efforts of the *Société de géographie de Paris*. Besides, hero-worshipping traditions were not as deeply entrenched in France as they were in Britain (at least in their Carlylean sense). Carlyle himself was not famous in France: sales figures from the *Mercure de France* records show that both the biography of him by Edmond Barthélémy and the French translation of *Sartor Resartus* sold poorly.[89] Carlyle's ideas on heroes and heroism were not unknown in France, but nowhere near as influential as in Britain. Late nineteenth-century French historians or philosophers, such as Augustin Thierry, Guizot, Lavisse, Michelet, Fustel de Coulanges or Auguste Comte, were not particularly interested in the biographical genre as they preferred holistic approaches to history, from the perspective of societies, civilizations, peoples or institutions.[90] The ground for imperial hero-worship was decidedly less fertile in Paris than in London.

Geographical or colonial topics were not particularly successful in French bookshops until the Great War. The public often remained ignorant of the extent of the French empire (an attitude mirrored by the Minister of the Colonies Clémentel who, upon taking office, recognized bluntly that he did not know France had so many overseas territories),[91] and colonial expansion remained often unpopular – at least until the turn of the century. It is therefore hardly surprising that publishers met limited success with their books on colonial topics, as shown by Table 4 (sales figures of one of the main French book distributors, Louis Hachette & Cie, in the early 1900s).

The market for books on imperial subjects was still embryonic in France at the beginning of the twentieth century, and the evocative power of exotic names in the title seemed the only factor likely to improve the commercial fate of some books. The only title of the list which did reasonably well was *Tombouctou la mystérieuse* (Mysterious Timbuktu), which referred to one of the few famous West African places where a Frenchman outdid a British rival. But even the most successful of these titles did poorly compared to mainstream titles. The average sale of any paperback published by Fayard was nearly 2,500 copies (Table 5), and a new edition of Maupassant's *Pierre et Jean* still sold more than 5,000 copies twelve years after it had first been issued.

Although colonial subjects did not sell satisfactorily, statistics show that imperial heroes were not absent from French publishers' catalogues. In the period, Major Marchand was one of the successful heroes who attracted publishers, biographers and hagiographers (his rise to fame is studied in detail in Chapter 6). Within a few months after his return to France following the French withdrawal from Fashoda, some 'opportunistic' authors came into action: a plethora of booklets, songs and postcards on 'the hero of Fashoda' were published following his return from Djibouti. As early as February 1900, the first books on the subject were launched, most notably by Jules Poirier,[92] Paul d'Ivoi (the alias of Paul Deleutre),[93] Paul Bourdarie[94] and Michel Morphy.[95]

The author of a *National History of Joan of Arc*, Michel Morphy published an ambitious serialized biographical acount of Marchand's heroic deeds in Africa, in 28 volumes totalling 2,240 pages (Figure 2). He described in detail the African environment and the Africans whom Marchand and his men encountered, but he stressed above all the personal qualities of the leader, a 'future General of France' according to Morphy.[96] The first five volumes proved highly promising; the following ones remained relatively successful although a significant erosion of the market could be noted. In total, 62,000 volumes at fifty *centimes* each were released between February 1900 and June 1901 (Table 6). This was a considerable improvement of this author's usual sales

Table 4 Print-runs and commercial results of some French books dealing with colonial subjects, 1900–03. IMEC, Hachette Papers, S2/C16B2, *Registres volumes retour et mise en vente, 1898–1908*

Date	Title	Author	Publisher	Released	Re-orders	Total sent	Unsold	Sold
1900	Femmes au Congo	Castellani	Flammarion	225	175	400	135	265
1900	Bou Saada et M'sila	Galland	Flammarion	120	0	120	114	6
1900	Tombouctou la mystérieuse	Dubois	Flammarion	575	125	700	266	434
1901	Femme chez les Sahariennes	Pommerol	Flammarion	175	0	175	103	72
1901	Haleine du désert	Pommerol	Flammarion	175	0	175	149	26
1901	Campagne de Madagascar	Espérou	Espérou	200	0	200	189	11
1902	Algérie Aujourd'hui	Gay	Combet	175	0	175	119	56
1902	Fils de grande tente	Ben el Oumra	Ollendorf	308	0	308	274	34
1903	2 ans chez les anthropophages	Montrozier	Plon-Nourrit	125	0	125	64	61
1903	Tour d'Afrique	D'Orléans	Plon-Nourrit	225	0	225	124	101
1903	Siestes d'Afrique	Vigné d'Octon	Flammarion	150	0	150	83	67

Table 5 Print-runs and commercial results of some French mainstream books, 1900–07. IMEC, Hachette Papers, S2/C16B2, *Registres volumes retour et mise en vente, 1898–1908*

Date	Title	Publisher	Released	Re-orders	Total sent	Unsold	Sold
1900	50 asserted paperbacks, (FF. 10)	Fayard	106,800	45,931	152,731	29,704	123,027
1900	*Pierre et Jean* (Maupassant)	Ollendorf	2,500	3,675	6,175	1,131	5,044
1901	*Almanach du Petit Parisien*	Petit Parisien	3,991	1,800	5,791	1,210	4,581
1902	*Almanach du Petit Parisien*	Petit Parisien	5,000	1,800	6,800	1,669	5,131
1902	*Almanach de la Libre Parole*	Lib. Antisémite	3,000	0	3,000	1,538	1,462
1903	*Almanach du Petit Parisien*	Petit Parisien	10,350	0	10,350	3,698	6,652

2 Front cover of Michel Morphy's serialized account of the Marchand mission (1900–01)

Table 6 Sales figures of Michel Morphy's 28-volume biographical series on Marchand between February 1900 and June 1901. IMEC, Hachette Papers, S2/C16B2, *Registres volumes retour et mise en vente*, 1898–1908

Date	Volume	Released	Re-orders	Total sent	Unsold	Sold
February 1900	Vol. I	4,800	1,650	6,450		
February 1900	Vol. II	3,000	1,100	4,100		
February 1900	Vol. III	2,500	1,000	3,500		
February 1900	Vol. IV	2,500	600	3,100		
February 1900	Vol. V	2,500	350	2,850		
Total vols I–V		**15,300**	**4,700**	**20,000**	5,787	14,213
June 1900	Vol. VI	2,500	200	2,700		
June 1900	Vol. VII	2,000	200	2,200		
June 1900	Vol. VIII	2,000	100	2,100		
June 1900	Vol. IX	2,000	100	2,100		
June 1900	Vol. X	2,000	100	2,100		
June 1900	Vol. XI	2,000	100	2,100		
June 1900	Vol. XII	2,000	100	2,100		
Total vols VI–XII		**14,500**	**900**	**15,400**	7,566	7,834
October 1900	Vols XIII–XXII	20,000	0	20,000		
February 1901	Vols XXIII–XXVI	8,100	0	8,100		
June 1901	Vols XXVII and XXVIII	4,100	0	4,100		
TOTAL	**Vols I–XXVIII**	**62,000**	**5,600**	**67,600**		

figures: a year later, another of his books, *Première nuit de noces*, sold just 1,100 copies.[97] The unquestionable success of Morphy's volumes indicates that a sizeable market for 'Marchand products' existed in France in 1900, although it seemed by no means able to match its British equivalent for Kitchener.

The public's taste for this type of 'Marchandise' quickly bolstered a steady stream of productions: writing and publishing about the right imperial hero was commercially rewarding. Numerous authors endeavoured to write about Marchand, and quickly found publishers. In *De l'Oubanghi à Fachoda: Marchand et la mission Congo-Nil* (which featured on the first page a portrait of Marchand wearing a kepi), Jules Poirier sought to tell the facts that led the 'heroic soldier' Marchand to be so eloquently celebrated by the *Académie des sciences morales et politiques* – whose laudatory report on the Major was extensively quoted in the short foreword. The author emphasized the character and qualities of his hero. Following the same pattern, Paul d'Ivoi's book featured among its opening pages an engraving depicting the 'heroic explorer' (p. 6) in full colonial officer's gear – which was particularly fitting given that it was meant to start a new series, *Great Explorers*, commissioned from d'Ivoi by Fayard, with the avowed purpose of telling the stories of a 'whole host of heroes'.[98] The writer obviously wished to stir nationalistic feelings and to show Marchand's greatness against the backdrop of English conspiracy, embodied in the story by the fictional British spy Mr Bright. The conclusion reminded the reader of the hero's welcome given to Marchand in Paris. Ivoi was also one of the major authors published by *Le Journal des Voyages*, a weekly dubbed 'the eulogist of the French colonial epic'.[99] With *Fachoda*, the still relatively unknown Paul Bourdarie contributed to the Marchand legend with the help of the little-known publishing house Jacques Strauss. He later became a well-known journalist and writer and, in his capacity as founder of the French Overseas Science Academy in 1922, he contributed to the promotion and study of colonial subjects. The illustrator Charles Castellani, who had published in 1898 a fanciful account of the beginning of the Marchand mission (Marchand soon sent him back for disobedience),[100] produced an unofficial biography of Marchand in 1902, two years after an unsuccessful book on the Congo (see Table 4).[101] Although none of these books matched Morphy's success, nearly all of them performed reasonably well (Table 7). The only exception was Louis Guétant's anarchist pamphlet debunking the military prowess of the hero of Fashoda (whom the author called 'a new and more shameful *boulange*'[102]), calling for an end to overseas colonial campaigns, and published by the anarchist publisher *Administration des Temps Nouveaux*. With 76 copies sold out of a print-run of 500, it confirms that hagiographies, with their

Table 7 Print-runs and commercial results of books on Marchand, by authors other than Michel Morphy 1900–01. IMEC, Hachette Papers, S2/C16B2, *Registres volumes retour et mise en vente*, 1898–1908

Date	Title	Author	Publisher	Released	Re-orders	Total sent	Unsold	Sold
1900	*Marchand-Fachoda*	Guétant	Adm. des Temps Nouveaux	500	0	500	424	76
1900	*Fachoda*	Bourdarie	J. Strauss	2,600	100	2,700	542	2,158
1900	*Mission Marchand, v. I*	D'Ivoi	Fayard	2,200	1,200	3,400	–	–
1900	*Mission Marchand, v. II*	D'Ivoi	Fayard	1,250	900	2,150	–	–
1900	*Fachoda*	Caix	J. André	302	0	302	184	118
1900	*Colonel Marchand*	–	Bodard	2,992	0	2,992	467	2,525
1901	*Ct Marchand à Fachoda*	Louis Noir	Fayard	2,200	–	–	–	–
1901	*Drame militaire Fachoda*	Louis Noir	Fayard	2,200	–	–	–	–
1901	*Mission Marchand Congo*	Louis Noir	Fayard	2,200	–	–	–	–

Table 8 Sales figures of a few of Baratier's books sent by Fayard to Mme J. Delorme-Jules Simon, 17 July 1922 (AN, 99 AP 6, Baratier papers)

Date	Title	Print run	Unsold	Sold	Percentage sold
1912	*A travers l'Afrique*	48,500	1,250	47,250	97.5
1914	*Madagascar*	72,000	3,500	68,500	95.2
1920	*Serment de l'explorateur*	19,000	3,000	16,000	85.0

rich ideological projection and mythical speculation, were much more successful than untimely attacks on the Marchand legend.

The complex cultural and financial mechanisms involved in book buying explain why critical pamphlets did not sell as well as hagiographies. Opponents are not prepared to spend money on a subject they dislike, while supporters are naturally more inclined to indulge in the object of their passion. This situation tends to make golden legends more attractive to both authors and publishers, as hagiographies are likely to attract a wider potential audience. The sales of Guétant's book indicate that critical works about Marchand were not commercially successful, yet it cannot be inferred that the low number of buyers reflects the average proportion of the population hostile to Marchand. On the other hand, it explains why anti-Marchand propaganda was only a tiny fraction of the literature on Marchand.

The success of the 'Marchandise' literary vein (that strand that held positive views) survived the aftermath of the Fashoda crisis. Among them, Albert Baratier was a striking example. Baratier performed the role of official writer of the Marchand mission: he was close to Marchand (whom he called 'his brother', and this feeling was reciprocated),[103] and proved to be the most prolific witness of the mission. Emily, the mission's doctor, published his own accounts,[104] and the officer-interpreter's logbook was published in the 1990s,[105] but these testimonies did not compare with Baratier's in fame or length. In the absence of Marchand's own book (which Baratier repeatedly called for), the accounts of the mission's third-in-command became the major source on the subject. Baratier's books on the mission and its leader were very successful and show the enduring power of the Marchand legend – especially bearing in mind that the first of them was published more than a decade after Fashoda (Table 8).

The turnover of Baratier's books was so high and regular that his publisher often reordered from his printer 5,000 copies at once. The French Ministry of Education once ordered two hundred copies, suggesting that Baratier's writings reached governmental circles. Baratier in June 1910 joined the *Société des gens de lettres*, which was a clear statement of his literary ambition. Although he remained primarily an officer, his literary interests were looked after in the same way as those of a well-established author. His 'agent' was a woman of letters, Mme Delorme-Jules Simon, author of five military novels and a text on heroes with a foreword by the well-known nationalist Maurice Barrès, called *Visions d'héroïsme*. The correspondence Delorme and Baratier exchanged betrays financial preoccupations, showing how the invisible hand of the market twisted even the most altruist hero-makers. Baratier often complained that Mme Delorme failed to defend his interests properly; he ended a letter with a reproachful 'Do you like M. Fayard so much that you side with his interests?' Yet he earned from Fayard FF. 8,000 for the first 75,000 copies of his book. This was a considerable sum: five years earlier he had rented a seven-bedroom house in Auxonne for FF. 900 a year.[106] Beyond the obvious intellectual and political beliefs at stake, commercial reasons could also be a good incentive to hone an imperial legend.

Yet the success of Marchand hagiographies does not mean that imperial heroes were universally popular. From an author's perspective, Ivoi offers a very good case study. He swiftly published several two-volume biographies for the Fayard series 'Les grands explorateurs' ('Great Explorers'), which the publisher had launched with the above-mentioned two-volume biography of Marchand. Another two-volume biography of Gallieni (who was then just returning from Madagascar) followed shortly, as well as another one on Lieutenant Parfait-Louis Monteil, who had explored the Niger area and the Fezzan. Of the three biographies, which all dealt with imperial heroes who were still alive and who had just accomplished great deeds for their country, Marchand's was by far the most successful, doubling or even trebling the score of the other two (Table 9).

Table 9 Compared print-runs of two-volume biographies of three different imperial heroes, all by Paul d'Ivoi, and all published by Fayard in 1900. IMEC, Hachette Papers, S2/C16B2, *Registres volumes retour et mise en vente, 1898–1908*

Date	Title	Released	Re-orders	Total sent
February 1900	*Mission Gallieni, vol. I*	1,250	100	1,350
February 1900	*Mission Gallieni, vol. II*	1,250	100	1,350
February 1900	*Mission Marchand, vol. I*	2,200	1,200	3,400
February 1900	*Mission Marchand, vol. II*	1,250	900	2,150
June 1900	*Lieut. Col. Monteil, vol. I*	1,200	50	1,250
June 1900	*Lieut. Col. Monteil, vol. II*	1,000	50	1,050

Table 10 Print-runs and commercial results of three French books dealing with imperial heroes other than Marchand. IMEC, Hachette Papers, S2/ C16B2, *Registres volumes retour et mise en vente, 1898–1908*

Date	Title	Author	Publisher	Released	Re-orders	Total sent	Unsold	Sold
1900	*Général Gallieni*	Ellie	Jugen	100	0	100	88	12
1901	*Madagascar*	Gallieni	Tallandier	375	0	375	257	118
1904	*Serment de l'explorateur*	Binger	Tallandier	350	25	375	310	65

The relative lack of success of the biographies of Gallieni and Monteil tends to indicate that books on imperial heroes could be successful only in certain circumstances, and that they did not automatically become best-sellers, as is further demonstrated in Table 10. These figures indicate that neither Gallieni nor Binger could match Marchand's popularity. Louis-Gustave Binger, who had played a key role in the creation of the French colony of Côte d'Ivoire, and who was Director of African Affairs at the Ministry for Colonies when he published his *Serment de l'explorateur*, attracted little interest – to say the least. Gallieni did not particularly captivate the public either – as an author or as a biographical subject. Real or perceived differences of character cannot explain this difference, since both Marchand and Gallieni were cold-tempered and distant, and favourite in Conservative circles. However, the circumstances that made them eligible for heroic status were different. Madagascar was certainly less appealing to the public than Central Africa and the upper Nile, which presented the added value of being a site of imperial rivalry. Because Gallieni had conquered the Malagasy colony with the prior agreement of Britain and Germany, he was less likely to attract Anglophobic sympathy than Marchand, who had stood up against the English. In addition, each episode was invested with different symbolic meaning: Gallieni had conquered an island at the head of a regular army and carried out primarily administrative tasks, a fact which lacked panache when confronted with Marchand's fearless crossing of Africa with a small party. Coincidental explanations may have played a role as well. The timing of their return home meant that Gallieni's arrival in France was heavily overshadowed by Marchand's a few days later. The political circumstances also changed dramatically, since Marchand's return coincided with the trial of Déroulède and Habert. The nationalists were subsequently tempted to use Marchand as an implicit support for Déroulède and the anti-Dreyfusard camp, as is analysed in Chapter 6. Lastly, Marchand's humble family background in the Ain department boosted his popularity among the general public, whereas Gallieni was the son of an Italian officer. Confidential police reports observed that 'the arrival of General Gallieni did not give rise to the warm welcome that [the nationalists] expected from the crowds'.[107] This difference in the reception of the two heroes shows that 'print-capitalism' was certainly a key element in the development of heroic legends, but that other parameters had to be factored in: successful imperial heroes resulted from a subtle alchemy involving not only the effect of media framing but also the political context and the charismatic value (or at least popular appeal) of the hero as well as, in some cases, coincidental circumstances.[108] Marchand epitomized the successful imperial hero who enjoyed wide popularity in his country, fuelled public interest in the areas he had explored and conquered, was widely discussed in the press and could hence become a publishing success in bookshops. Although he recruited most of his support among the nationalists and other *chauvins* (most of the hagiographies written about him had nationalist tones), the wider appeal of his reputation and achievements ensured he mobilized a steady customer base which guaranteed significant commercial possibilities. Such commercial prospects were enhanced by advertising campaigns in the press in select newspapers. The *Journal des Voyages* advertised in *Le Temps* a special issue entirely dedicated to the detailed account of the mission by Auguste Terrier, sold at fifteen centimes per copy: as usual, the geographical establishment did its bit to promote an imperial hero, this time through the Secretary of the *Société de géographie*.[109] For instance, the publisher Geffroy advertised Morphy's biography of Marchand in the ultra-nationalist newspaper *L'Intransigeant*, as well as in *Le Drapeau* and *Le Figaro*, just a few days before the hero's return to France, while Fayard promoted the book by Paul d'Ivoi in *Le Figaro* and *Le Gaulois*. Obeying the law of business, publishers invested in such book projects and spent on advertising because they had good reasons to expect a significant return on investment – they usually reminded readers that their books were available at 'all bookshops, newsagents and in stations'.[110]

Bold, daring, profoundly nationalist, and certainly not an Anglophile, Marchand prefigured the future hero of the Sahara, as it appeared during the following decades, particularly in the interwar years. Largely shaped by the nationalist and mystic example set by Ernest Psichari, who died in the Belgian Ardennes in the first days of the Great War, this new type of hero was based upon military glory and Christian sacrifice.[111] The assassination and subsequent legend of Charles de Foucauld (first generated by a highly popular biography by René Bazin in 1921 and strengthened by a wide variety of interwar publications, notably by Paul Lesourd, Georges Gorée and Léon Poirier),[112] and the place the empire had come to occupy in French national consciousness following the decisive intervention of colonial corps during the Great War,[113] further contributed to the nascent fascination for the French officer who acted in the wilderness of the Sahara, performing heroic deeds and setting a spiritual example. This trend gave rise to the tradition of the *roman saharien* (Saharan novel), which proved very popular in the interwar period with authors such as Pierre Benoît (*L'Atlantide*) and Joseph Peyré (*L'Escadron blanc, Croix du Sud, Le Chef à l'étoile d'Argent, La Légende du Goumier Saïd, Sahara éternel, Sous l'étendard vert, Proie des ombres*) and was readily exploited by many eminent Parisian publishers.[114] Such novels certainly depicted an ideal type of hero rather than a real-life character, but they deeply influenced the French conception of the imperial hero and attest a significant change in the publishing market after the Great War. Africa had then been fully incorporated into the intellectual background of the metropolitan public, Frenchmen venturing into this continent were admired and inspired young people to follow in their footsteps, while publishers sought to publish more books on 'heroes of the Sahara'[115] as they now ensured steady sales: for instance, René Bazin's biography of Charles de Foucauld achieved a print-run of 76,000 copies in just three years.[116] The literary and cultural feelings of a rising *Saharomania* that swept across France worked well to promote the reputations of imperial heroes in interwar France.[117]

More generally, the period between the Great War and the 1940s saw the blossoming in France of a publishing trend revolving around biographies of imperial heroes (and especially those who had shone in Africa), against the backdrop of a level of popular interest in the colonies which had never been witnessed before.[118] A plethora of books about French colonies appeared on the market, and among them imperial heroes were given a place of choice by many publishers. In the early 1930s, as the centenary of French Algeria (1930) and the Colonial exhibition of Vincennes (1931) beat the drum for Greater France, *Le Petit Parisien* produced a series of biographies on Lyautey, Bugeaud, Gallieni (among others) under the heading '*Nos gloires coloniales*',[119] whilst Hachette included in its famous series '*Les vies illustres*' titles on colonial heroes written by eminent officers, with a book on Lyautey produced by General Gouraud and another on Bugeaud by Marshal Franchet d'Espérey.[120] The famous Great War general also performed for the publisher *Les Publications coloniales* the role of patron for a series entitled *Le Panthéon colonial*, which counted books on Mangin and Lyautey among others.[121] The *Librairie Larose* published a biography of Brazza by the imperial propagandist Henri-Paul Eydoux (with a preface by Marshal Lyautey), in a series entitled *Médaillons coloniaux*.[122] The future member of the French Academy André Maurois wrote the biography of Lyautey in the prestigious series *Les Maîtres de l'histoire* published by Plon,[123] which also produced the series '*Grandes figures coloniales*', quite clearly dedicated to the biographical celebration of imperial heroes, with books on Bugeaud, Faidherbe, Brazza and Gallieni.[124] The founder of the White Fathers and Sisters inspired several successful publishing ventures: Lavigerie's life appeared as the opening title of the Flammarion series '*Les grands cœurs*',[125] and a book on his achievements, first published in 1894, reached its fifteenth edition in 1926, desmontrating the extraordinary resilience of imperial heroes over the period.[126] The juvenile literature of the interwar years also sought to educate young readers through the exemplary lives of colonial figures, with titles such as *Brazza* in Hachette's highly successful children's book series, the *Bibliothèque verte*, written by the hero's brother-in-law, Aldebert de Chambrun. Teenagers also got their share of imperial heroism, with lavishly illustrated albums such as Marcel Souzy's two-volume *Les Coloniaux français libres*, introduced by a preface by Georges Hardy, honorary director of the *Ecole coloniale* and the rector of the Academy of Algiers.[127]

Although finally successful in both cases, the itineraries that led to the blossoming of imperial heroes on the British and French publishing markets were markedly different. The path to glory proved to be longer and more long-winded for French heroes than for their British counterparts. Yet the strings tended to be pulled by comparable players on each side of the Channel: publishers, authors and journalists were pivotal in mediating the image of these heroes to the public. Whilst some of them did not fully realize their pivotal role, hero-makers were the interface that ultimately made the reputations of imperial heroes possible. If war correspondents were the powerhouse of imperial hero-making in the press, the phenomenon was driven in the publishing world by biographers. They sold their books to educated readers who wanted to delve into the life of an outstanding individual, or to popular audiences who sought entertainment and excitement. In some instances, especially when they catered for less educated (or younger) admirers, some biographers lacked critical distance and presented a very simplistic and Manichean sketch of the lives of imperial heroes. In France, in stark contrast with the market for literature on colonial subjects, biographies were more likely to earn royalties for their authors. Not without reason did Charles-Robert Ageron remark that colonial history had been marked for long by 'the triumph of biography'.[128]

Hero-makers came from various backgrounds and acted for different reasons, but all had to take account of the markets and their evolution.

IMPERIAL HEROES AND THE MARKET I

They could try to bend the public's taste, to follow it, or to do a mixture of both. The mechanics of the market meant that those who did not obey this law almost inevitably failed. Authors could not afford to write – let alone publish – in isolation from market demands. Close friends, relatives, biographers and hagiographers were aware of the potential financial benefits that could be reaped from imperial heroes in the publishing world. One of the key promoters of the Livingstone legend, the Rev Horace Waller, informed Agnes Livingstone that her father's *Last Journals* were worth at least £10 000 for her.[129] This was hardly surprising, given that her father's *Missionary Travels* had earned their author over £8,500 in the first six years of publication.[130] The popularity of Lowell Thomas's two biographies of Lawrence (*With Lawrence in Arabia* went through more than a hundred printings between its launch in 1924 and 1995) also generated comfortable royalties for their author.[131] In France, Captain Baratier (author of numerous books on the Marchand mission) did not neglect financial considerations when he discussed the details of his contract with Fayard, complaining in particular that M. Fayard offered lower royalties beyond the first 75,000 copies printed: 'It would be a thing never seen before! The author would be paid less as his success increases! [...] I will never accept an agreement where the following editions would be paid less than the first edition!'[132] Financial considerations were an important element in the mechanics of imperial heroism at the level of the hero-makers.

When family or friends sought to generate interest in a person whom they considered a potential hero, but the commercial profitability of a biography remained uncertain, publishing projects could take several years before being completed, if they were ever completed. Lady Lugard, who had lent herself to an exercise in hero-making when she wrote Cecil Rhodes's biography for the eleventh edition of the *Encyclopaedia Britannica*, conceived the project to have a life of her husband written. To that purpose, she approached in 1926 Sir Reginald Coupland (who had already written the lives of Sir Samuel Wilberforce and Sir John Kirk), but he declined the offer. Following the death of Lady Lugard (Flora Shaw), Lord Lugard wanted to fulfil his wife's wishes and looked for a biographer for himself. Approached again, Reginald Coupland finally agreed to write the biography, as 'it seemed to me [...] that I should be rendering, in my little way, some service to Africa and the Empire if I could make myself the vehicle of carrying on for the coming generation the example of your great work and the ideals for which you have stood'.[133] However, finding no time to write it, Sir Reginald recommended that a student of his, Margery Perham, should produce it. Her biography in two volumes (published in 1956 and 1960 respectively) became *the* reference on the subject, not only because it had been well-researched but above all because no competitors appeared after the release of the second voume, for the simple reason that it failed commercially.[134] Lord Lugard apparently did not match the taste of the moment, and Margery Perham bitterly resented this lack of success which also meant an unpleasant financial shortfall:

> The whole situation is extremely depressing. I understood you to say when we were discussing the book that you thought it was pretty certain to bring in something between £1-2,000. I certainly never expected such an infinitesimal return especially when, judging by reviews, the book might be regarded as having had a favourable reception. It makes me survey the whole position about writing books of this kind.[135]

Margery Perham's confession reveals how biographers remained inevitably influenced by market demands and resented the consequences of choosing topics that did not appeal to a sizeable audience. With such an attitude witnessed from an academic with a guaranteed income, it is easy to infer that biographers who earned their living from royalties were even more prone to taking this parameter into account. The amount of work required to produce an accurate account of a hero's life contributed to self-regulating the market for biographies: through a process of self-selection, potential heroes who did not appeal to the public disappeared from bookshop shelves because biographers were unwilling to invest their time (and publishers their money) in them.

Beyond any material consideration, success remains a constant preoccupation of any author, and the expectation to gain personal satisfaction through the sale of large numbers of books should not be overlooked. Writing about her new book on imperial affairs, Lady Lugard (who, unlike many authors, did not need royalties to live comfortably) confided to her husband Frederick that she 'shall be disappointed if the book is not widely read'.[136] Undoubtedly, the displeasure that poor sales inevitably inspire can be a strong disincentive that accelerates the editorial death of any fledgling imperial legend.

In the second half of the nineteenth century, the press and the publishing worlds underwent deep transformations which offered new commercial opportunities with far-reaching consequences for imperial heroes. The press became a potent cultural, political and financial power in the two countries, and it contributed to the cultivation of what Felix Driver has called 'cultures of exploration'.[137] Yet, at the same time it had to obey and shape market demands in a double movement of reflection and inspiration of public trends: media were both 'actors [and] agents in the events and processes which they purport[ed] only to be describing'.[138] The time when modern journalism blossomed (with its cohort of innovations, such as the interview) was also that of unprecedented rigorous industrial and capitalistic imperatives. Increasingly integrated markets and marketing strategies created an environment favourable to the development of heroic legends around key figures linked to the development of the British and French empires.

Relying upon improved printing techniques and distribution networks, making the most of their commercial intuition, late Victorian publishers enjoyed an unprecedented opportunity to fuel and exploit the market of hero-workship which, according to John MacKenzie, became 'even more important than the classics'.[139] Concomitantly, imperial expansion offered a vast range of activities likely to attract the curiosity of the European public, especially when it also involved a compatriot embattled in a quest for knowledge, territories or converts. The close intertwining of systemic drive and individual agency of the 'man on the spot' in nineteenth-century colonial conquests explains why 'the cult of personality [...] was an inseparable part of imperialism'.[140] The structuring of European markets for printed materials around capitalistic logics, on the one hand, and the heyday of imperial self-confidence on the other, explain the success and longevity of the reputations of imperial heroes in Britain. David Livingstone, whose posthumous legend had been carefully shaped,[141] set a precedent which was regularly repeated in the following half-century, giving rise to a series of potent cultural constructions that raised awareness about imperial matters whilst also meeting the financial and personal expectations of a variety of intermediaries such as journalists, war correspondents, newspaper editors, biographers and publishers, among others.

The French publishing market for imperial heroes changed more significantly throughout the period than its British counterpart. If the British public had developed a growing fascination for heroes since the Napoleonic wars, and 'sympathy for imperialism was widely diffused through British society' through 'free trade, utilitarianism, evangelical Christianity and anti-slavery',[142] the French lacked the Victorian tradition of heroes, and their interest in overseas matters remained marginal for many years. This is why, until the First World War, imperial heroes could become so only under special circumstances, and notably as a consequence of acute rivalry with Britain (Brazza after the British intervention in Egypt, Marchand following Fashoda). Franco-British rivalry was a structuring force in the late nineteenth century, and it is clearly reflected in hero-making histories related to the empire: it is not a coincidence if Fashoda, which provided the backdrop to the two case studies broached in this book, was an apogee of military imperial heroism in books. For political reasons as much as intellectual tradition, the French press was less prone to hero-making than its British counterpart, which did not help the promotion of heroes when no external threat could boost their relevance to the national project. Although the publishing world was far from inactive in the promotion of national heroes of the colonies, and a marked increase could be noted towards the turn of the century, print-run figures remained considerably lower in France than in Britain.

Successful imperial heroes became household names thanks to adequate publicity (combining various means of propaganda, most notably the press and the publishing industry, which have been under close scrutiny in the present chapter). This entrenchment in popular culture at various levels was at least as important as the hero's performance itself: to a large extent, once notable achievements had been accomplished, the media made the hero. Their pivotal place explains why, after this examination of the press and publishing networks, the next chapter will look at the market dynamics prevalent in the audiovisual worlds that took shape at the time.

Notes

1. M. McLuhan, *Understanding Media* (1964).
2. A. Weedon, *Victorian Publishing: The Economics of Book Production for a Mass Market 1836–1916* (Aldershot, 2003), p. 67.
3. B. Anderson, *Imagined Communities: Reflections on the Origin and Spread of Nationalism* (1983), ch. 3. On the general development of the popular press, and its consequences, see A. J. Lee, *The Origins of the Popular Press 1855–1914* (1976); L. Brown, *Victorian News and Newspapers* (1985); M. W. Summers, *The Press Gang: Newspapers and Politics 1865–1878* (1994). For France, see T. Ferenczi, *L'Invention du journalisme en France* (1993); C. Charle, *Le Siècle de la presse (1830–1939)* (2004); C. Delporte, *Les Journalistes en France 1880–1950. Naissance et construction d'une profession* (1999).
4. There are many studies of the media revolution of the second half of the nineteenth century which offer a general overview. See for instance A. Briggs and P. Burke, *A Social History of the Media* (Cambridge, 2002).
5. D. Cook, *The Culture Industry Revisited* (Lanham, MD, 1996); D. Strinati, *An Introduction to Theories of Popular Culture* (1995), pp. 51–86.
6. *Printing in the Twentieth Century, A Survey. Reprinted for the Special Number of The Times, October 29, 1929* (1930), pp. 15–17.
7. M. Crubellier, *Histoire culturelle de la France, XIXe–XXe siècle* (1974), p. 170.
8. C. Clair, *A History of European Printing* (1976), p. 404.
9. T. H. S. Escott, *Social Transformations of the Victorian Age* (1897), quoted in W. Hamish Fraser, *The Coming of the Mass Market, 1850–1914* (1981), p. 208.
10. E. M. Spiers, *The Army and Society* (1980), p. 211.
11. *Illustrated London News*, 5 November 1898.
12. *New Penny Magazine*, No. 5, vol. I (1898).
13. Briggs and Burke, *Social History of the Media*, p. 107.
14. RHL, Oxford, Perham Papers, 309/3, f. 11, Lord Lugard to Lady Lugard, 15 July 1909.
15. Various authors, Office of The Times, *The History of The Times, 1884–1912*, vol. III, (1947), p. 17.

16 *The Times*, 2 April 1884.
17 *History of The Times*, ch. 1.
18 D. Kalifa, *La Culture de masse en France. 1/1860–1930* (2001), pp. 6–7; J. Curran and J. Seaton, *Power without Responsibility: The Press and Broadcasting in Britain* (1991), p. 46.
19 T. Jackson, *The Boer War* (1999), p. 80.
20 D. Judd and K. Surridge, *The Boer War* (2002), p. 251.
21 Jackson, *Boer War*, p. 80; Curran and Seaton, *Power without Responsibility*, p. 43.
22 A. S. Thompson, *Imperial Britain: The Empire in British Politics c. 1880–1932* (Harlow, 2000), p. 63.
23 Kalifa, *Culture de masse*, pp. 9–10.
24 L. Gambetta, *La République française*, 27 October 1876.
25 C. Bellanger, P. Guiral and F. Terrou (eds), *Histoire générale de la presse française* (1972), pp. 140 and 300.
26 Figures come from Bellanger et al., *Histoire générale de la presse française*, pp. 239–405, and R. de Livois, *Histoire de la presse française* (1965), vol. II.
27 H. Cunningham, *Leisure in the Industrial Revolution* (1980), p. 177.
28 F. Amaury, *Histoire du plus grand quotidien de la IIIe République: Le Petit Parisien (1876–1944)* (1972), vol. II, p. 656.
29 See for instance R. Girardet, *L'Idée coloniale en France* (1972).
30 Livois, *Histoire de la presse française*, vol. II, p. 355.
31 V. Goedorp, Figures du *'Temps'* (1943) and Bellanger, *Histoire générale de la presse française*, p. 355.
32 Amaury, *Le Petit Parisien*, vol. II, p. 656.
33 Amaury, *Le Petit Parisien*, vol. II, p. 854.
34 Although, according to P. Haythornthwaite, the first journalist who accompanied an expedition was C. L. Grüneisen, during the First Carlist War (1833–40). P. Haythornthwaite, *The Colonial Wars Sourcebook* (2000), p. 331.
35 See for instance S. L. Carruthers, *The Media at War* (Basingstoke, 2000), or S. L. Carruthers and I. Stewart (eds), *War, Culture and the Media Representations of the Military in Twentieth Century Britain* (Trowbridge, 1996).
36 R. T. Stearn, 'War correspondents and colonial war c. 1870–1900', in J. M. MacKenzie (ed.), *Popular Imperialism and the Military* (Manchester, 1992), pp. 139–61.
37 H. Cecil, 'British correspondents and the Sudan campaign of 1896–98', in E. M. Spiers (ed.), *Sudan: The Reconquest Reappraised* (1998), p. 102.
38 Jackson, *Boer War*, p. 81.
39 Stearn, 'War correspondents', p. 139.
40 Spiers, *Army and Society*, p. 213.
41 R. Salmon, 'Signs of intimacy: the literary celebrity in the age of interviewing', *Victorian Literature and Culture*, 25:1 (1997), 159–77.
42 J. Evans, 'Celebrity, media and history', in J. Evans and D. Hesmondhalgh, *Understanding Media: Inside Celebrity* (Maidenhead, 2005), p. 24.
43 A. Dwight Culler, *The Victorian Mirror of History* (New Haven and London, 1985), p. 33.
44 V. Berridge, 'Popular Sunday papers and mid-Victorian society' in G. Boyce, J. Curran and P. Wingate (eds), *Newspaper History from the Seventeenth Century to the Present Day* (1978), pp. 247–64.
45 On Stanley, see T. Jeal, *Stanley: The Impossible Life of Africa's Greatest Explorer* (2007); J. Bierman, *Dark Safari: The Life behind the Legend of Henry Morton Stanley* (1990); F. Mc Lynn, *Stanley, the Dark Genius of African Exploration* (2004).
46 P. A. Cole-King, 'Searching for Livingstone: E. D. Young and others', in B. Pachai (ed.), *Livingstone: Man of Africa* (1973), p. 158.
47 On the making of the Livingstone legend, see J. M. MacKenzie, 'David Livingstone, the construction of the myth', in G. Walker and T. Gallagher (eds), *Sermons and Battle Hymns: Protestant Popular Culture in Modern Scotland* (1990), pp. 24–42.

CONTEXTS

48 Cole-King, *Searching for Livingstone*, p. 153.
49 C. Pettitt, *'Dr. Livingstone, I Presume?' Missionaries, Journalists, Explorers and Empire* (2007), p. 11.
50 Thomas Edward Lawrence 'of Arabia' has generated considerable literary and biographical interest since the end of the First World War. Readers interested in the detail of his life are invited to consult, among others, the most documented biography to date by J. Wilson, *Lawrence of Arabia: The Authorised Biography of T. E. Lawrence* (1989). The 'Lawrence legend' can be traced back in L. Thomas, *With Lawrence in Arabia* (London, 1921); B. Liddell Hart, *T. E. Lawrence in Arabia and After* (1934); A. W. Lawrence (ed.), *T. E. Lawrence by His Friends* (1937). The Lawrence legend has been analysed by J. M. MacKenzie, 'T. E. Lawrence: the myth and the message', in R. Giddings (ed.), *Literature and Imperialism* (1991), pp. 150–81. Also worth noting for its psychoanalytical angle, H. Orlans, *T. E. Lawrence, Biography of a Broken Hero* (Jefferson, NC, 2002). For a critical point of view upon Lawrence's achievements, see R. Aldington, *Lawrence of Arabia* (1955), as well as an analysis of the latter study: F. D. Crawford, *Richard Aldington and Lawrence of Arabia* (Carbondale, IL, 1998).
51 J. C. Hodson, *Lawrence of Arabia and American Culture* (Westport, CT, 1995), pp. 14 and 27–8.
52 BL, Lawrence Papers, Anonymous account of the Lawrence story (possibly by Lawrence's brother, A W L), MS Eng. c. 6752, ff. 36–7.
53 J. Portes, 'L'horizon américain', in J.-P. Rioux and J.-F. Sirinelli (eds), *La Culture de masse en France de la Belle Epoque à aujourd'hui* (2002), pp. 29–71. On the involvement of the ESU, see Hodson, *Lawrence of Arabia and American Culture*, p. 30.
54 Pettitt, *Dr. Livingstone*, p. 48.
55 J. Portes, *Fascination and Misgivings: The United States in French Opinion, 1870–1914* (Cambridge, 2000).
56 Two notable exceptions are the 21-page article on Livingstone's exploration of the African Great Lakes, written by the famous French explorer H. Duveyrier in the *Bulletin de la Société de géographie de Paris*, October 1872, and H. Chotard, *Livingstone, Cameron, Stanley* (1879). The next French biography of Livingstone deposited at the French National Library is T. D. Pache, *David Livingstone* (Lausanne, 1926), published, quite significatively, by the *Librairie Protestante*.
57 Ferenczi, *Invention du journalisme*, pp. 15, 19–46 and 237–40.
58 B. Sèbe, 'From Thoissey to the capital via Fashoda: Major Marchand, partisan icon of the Right in Paris', in J. Wardhaugh (ed.), *Paris and the Right in the Twentieth Century* (Cambridge, 2006), pp. 18–42.
59 R. E. Nwoye, *The Public Image of Pierre Savorgnan de Brazza and the Establishment of French Imperialism in the Congo* (Aberdeen, 1981), p. 112.
60 Bellanger, *Histoire générale de la presse française*, pp. 303–4.
61 IMEC, Hachette Papers, S2/C1B6, *Récapitulation annuelle des invendus presse 1899–1913*.
62 AN, Eydoux papers, 546 AP 11, Bartel-Noirot, *Atlantide Prix modérés, d'un bord à l'autre du Sahara* (1937), p. 24.
63 AN, F/7/15981/1, SG, 4e Bureau (Police record), folder 'Commandant Marchand à Barbizon' (Barbizon, 18 September 1899).
64 *La Patrie*, 13 April 1904.
65 *Le Gaulois*, 17 April 1904.
66 AN, F/7/15981/1, SG, 4e Bureau (Police record), report No. P480 (Paris, 9 September 1904).
67 See Weedon, *Victorian Publishing*, and E. Parinet, *Une histoire de l'édition contemporaine, XIX–XXe siècle* (2004).
68 Schneider, *Empire for the Masses*, p. 5.
69 J. Bristow, *Empire Boys: Adventures in a Man's World* (1991), p. 166.
70 P. Langford, *A Polite and Commercial People. England 1727–1783* (Oxford, 1989, 1998), p. 512.

71 See for instance T. Young, *Travellers in Africa: British Travelogue 1850–1900* (Manchester, 1994); M.-L. Pratt, *Imperial Eyes: Travel-Writing and Transculturation* (1992).
72 A good example is Mrs Pilkington's *Biography for Boys, or Characteristic Histories Calculated to Impress the Youthful Mind, With an Admiration of Virtuous Principles and a Detestation of Vicious Ones* (1799).
73 R. Hill, 'The Gordon literature', *The Durham University Journal*, XLVI:3 (June 1955), 97–103.
74 C.-F. Behrman, 'The after-life of General Gordon', *Albion: A Quarterly Journal Concerned with British Studies*, 3:2 (Summer 1971), 47–61.
75 Spiers, *Army and Society*, p. 216; see also J. Peck, *War, the Army and Victorian Literature* (1998).
76 P. Maylam, *The Cult of Rhodes* (Claremont, South Africa, 2005), pp. 1–3.
77 H. F. B. Wheeler, *The Story of Lord Kitchener* (1916), title page.
78 E. Hope, *Stanley and Africa* (1890). Eva Hope was also the author of books such as *Our Queen* and *New World Heroes*.
79 M. K. Logan, *Narrating Henty* (1999), p. 80.
80 P. Newbolt, *G. A. Henty 1832–1902: A Bibliographical Study* (Aldershot, 1996), p. 368.
81 F. C. Burnand, *A New Light Thrown Across the Keep it Quite Darkest Africa* (1891).
82 D. Finkelstein, *The House of Blackwood* (University park, PA, 2002), p. 105.
83 NLS, MS 30860, Publication ledger 1861–1874, ff. 362–4.
84 NLS, MS 30862, Publication ledger 1881–1889, f. 24.
85 James Lunt, 'Graham, Sir Gerald (1831–1899)', *ODNB* [Accessed 15 July 2007].
86 NLS, MS 30864, Publication ledger, 1895–1907, f. 369.
87 NLS, MS 30864, Publication ledger, 1895–1907, f. 369.
88 On imperial plays, see J. S. Bratton, *Acts of Supremacy: The British Empire and the Stage, 1790–1930* (Manchester, 1991).
89 IMEC, Hachette Papers, S2/C16B2, *Liste retours février 1900*.
90 A. Gérard, 'Le grand homme et la conception de l'histoire au XIXe siècle', in 'Le grand homme', *Romantisme, Revue du dix-neuvième siècle*, 100 (1998), 31–48.
91 J. Marseille, *Marianne*, December 2004.
92 J. Poirier, *De l'Oubanghi à Fachoda: Marchand et la mission Congo-Nil* (1900).
93 P. D'Ivoi, *Les Grands Explorateurs. La mission Marchand* (1899–1900).
94 P. Bourdarie, *Fachoda. La mission Marchand* (1899).
95 M. Morphy, *Le Commandant Marchand et ses compagnons d'armes à travers l'Afrique* (1899).
96 Morphy, *Commandant Marchand*, vol. XXVIII, p. 2240.
97 IMEC, Hachette Papers, S2/C16B2, sales figures for Henri Geoffroy, October 1901.
98 D'Ivoi, *Mission Marchand*, back cover presenting the next title in the series: *General Gallieni: Pacification of Madagascar*.
99 M. Palewska, 'Le Journal des Voyages (I)', *Le Rocambole, Bulletin des amis du roman populaire*, Autumn 1998, 9.
100 C. Castellani, *Vers le Nil français* (1898).
101 C. Castellani, *Marchand l'Africain* (1902).
102 Play on words: phonetically, *boulange* evokes the bakery trade, but in these circumstances, referring to General Boulanger, it suggested phonetically he had been nothing but a vile bakery trader.
103 A. Baratier, *Au Congo. Souvenirs de la Mission Marchand de Loango à Brazzaville* (1914); AN, 99 AP 6, Colonel Cherfils to Mme J. Delorme, 31 July 1922: 'I was Albert's [Albert Baratier] brother, but Marchand was his brother as much as myself'.
104 J. Emily, *Mission Marchand* (1913).
105 M. Landeroin, *Mission Congo-Nil (mission Marchand), carnets de route* (1996).

106 AN, 99 AP 4, Baratier papers, box 4, Fayard to Baratier, 6 November 1913, and Baratier to Mme J. Delorme-Jules Simon, 24 February 1914.
107 AN, F/7/15981/1, Police records of the SG, report from 'Jean M. 726', *La Libre Parole et le Retour de Marchand*, 29 May 1899.
108 On media framing, see D. A. Scheufele and D. Tewksbury, 'Framing, agenda setting, and priming: the evolution of three media effects models', *Journal of Communication*, 57 (2007), 9–20.
109 *Le Temps*, 30 May 1899, p. 3.
110 An example of this advert can be found in *L'Intransigeant*, 24 May 1899, p. 4.
111 F. Neau-Dufour, *Ernest Psichari. L'ordre et l'errance* (2001), pp. 293–312. On the content of Psichari's work, see A. C. Hargreaves, *The Colonial Experience in French Fiction* (1981).
112 R. Bazin, *Charles de Foucauld. Explorateur au Maroc, ermite au Sahara* (1921); P. Lesourd, *La Vraie Figure du Père de Foucauld* (1933); G. Gorrée, *Sur les traces de Charles de Foucauld* (1936); L. Poirier, *Charles de Foucauld et L'Appel du silence* (1936).
113 About the place of colonial soldiers in the Great War, see G. Meynier, *L'Algérie Révélée. La guerre de 1914–1918 et le premier quart du XXe siècle* (Lille, 1979); M. Michel, *L'Appel à l'Afrique: contributions et réactions à l'effort de guerre en AOF, 1914–1919* (1982); E. Deroo, 'Mourir: L'appel à l'Empire', in P. Blanchard, S. Lemaire and N. Bancel (eds), *Culture coloniale en France* (2008), pp. 163–72.
114 On Joseph Peyré, see P. Delay, *Joseph Peyré 1892–1968* (1992), and J. Frémeaux, 'Joseph Peyré, documentaire et légende', in J.-R. Henry and L. Martini (eds), *Littératures et temps colonial* (Aix-en-Provence, 1999), pp. 147–54.
115 Title of a book by the Sonia E. Howe, originally published in French in 1931.
116 A copy of Bazin, *Charles de Foucauld*, dated 1924, held at the *Bibliothèque nationale de France*, bears the statement '76e mille'.
117 On French attachment to the Sahara and its inhabitants, see B. Brower, *A Desert Named Peace* (2009), ch. 10, as well as P. Pandolfi, 'La construction du mythe touareg', *Ethnologies comparées*, 7 (2004), http://alor.univ-montp3.fr/cerce/r7/pl.p.htm [Accessed 15 July 2006].
118 For more background information on 'popular imperialism' in the interwar years, see B. Sèbe, 'Exalting imperial grandeur', in J. M. MacKenzie (ed.), *European Empires and the People* (Manchester, 2011), pp. 35–42.
119 P. Azan, *Bugeaud et l'Algérie* (1930); P.-B. Gheusi, *Gallieni et Madagascar* (1931); L. Barthou, *Lyautey et le Maroc* (1931).
120 H. Gouraud, *Lyautey* (1938); L.-F. Franchet d'Espérey, *Bugeaud* (1938).
121 P. Moreau-Vauthier, *Un chef: le Général Mangin* (1936); Y. de Boisboissel, *Lyautey, maréchal de la plus grande France* (1937).
122 H.-P. Eydoux, *Savorgnan de Brazza, le conquérant pacifique* (1932).
123 A. Maurois, *Lyautey* (1931).
124 A. de Chambrun, *Brazza* (1930); G. Grandidier, *Gallieni* (1931); A. Lichtenberger, *Bugeaud* (1931); A. Demaison, *Faidherbe* (1932).
125 F. Jammes, *Lavigerie* (1927).
126 X. de Préville, *Un grand Français: le cardinal Lavigerie* (first ed. 1894, 15th ed. 1926).
127 Général de Chambrun, *Brazza* (1930); M. Souzy, *Les Coloniaux français illustres* (1940).
128 C. R. Ageron, *France coloniale ou parti colonial?* (1978), p. 298.
129 NLS, Stanley Papers, Stanley to Agnes Livingstone, 18 March 1874, quoted in D. O. Helly, *Livingstone's Legacy* (Athens, OH, 1987), p. 67.
130 A. D. Roberts, 'Livingstone, David (1813–1873)', *ODNB* [Accessed 18 November 2004]
131 Hodson, *Lawrence of Arabia*, p. 50.
132 AN, Baratiers Papers, 99 AP 4, Captain Baratier to Mme Jules Simon-Delorme, 24 February 1914.

133 RHL, Perham Papers, 293/1, f. 43, Reginald Coupland to Lord Lugard, 25 December 1929.
134 Though a single-volume biography was published after the launch of Perham's first volume, but before her second: A. Thomson, *Lugard in Africa* (1959).
135 RHL, Perham Papers, 18/5, f. 2, Margery Perham to Mr Bonham Carter (Collins Publishers), 30 April 1957.
136 RHL, Perham Papers, 309/1, f. 33, Lady Lugard to Lord Lugard, 22 November 1905.
137 F. Driver, *Geography Militant: Cultures of Exploration and Empire* (Oxford, 2000), pp. 117–69.
138 J. Theobald, *The Media and the Making of History* (Aldershot, 2004), p. 6.
139 J. M. MacKenzie, *Propaganda and Empire* (Manchester, 1984), p. 18.
140 MacKenzie, *Propaganda and Empire*, p. 18.
141 See Helly, *Livingstone's Legacy*.
142 J. Darwin, 'Imperialism and the Victorians: the dynamics of territorial expansion', *English Historical Review*, June 1997, 627.

CHAPTER 3

Imperial heroes and the market II: the audiovisual world

Visual representations have played a major role in human culture ever since *Homo sapiens sapiens* has felt the drive to record thoughts and leave lasting testimonies of emotions (whether admiration, anxiety or a spiritual quest). After all, rock art paintings or engravings are proofs of prehistoric conceptual activity that was not practically useful, and they clearly predate written statements. For all their limitations in terms of realism and attention to detail, they, together with later documents from the Antiquity to the Renaissance, testify to the pivotal role that visual representations play in the production of meaning.[1] It is no wonder that the celebration of Great Men almost always included, one way or another, visual material – from Ancient Egyptian temples to twentieth-century statues. This chapter tries to put this phenomenon into a historical perspective, paying attention to the technological developments in the period under consideration in this book which allowed the mechanized reproduction of images, and therefore amplified the echo among the population of the heroes they featured. Improvements in sound and image reproduction combined with older, more traditional but still widespread means of celebrating heroic deeds, allowing for a more efficient dissemination of these reputations. If Walter Benjamin argued that technical reproducibility threatened the status of artworks,[2] whilst Chris Bayly saw in mechanization in the arts a 'leveling force',[3] it is beyond doubt that in the case of imperial heroes it enhanced the popular resonance of their legends.

We have seen in the previous chapter that the large-scale dissemination of written messages was facilitated by the mechanization of printing, first implemented by Gutenberg and gradually improved until it reached the industrial stage of 'print capitalism' in the late nineteenth century. However, writers and journalists were not the only hero-makers who could powerfully convey the greatness of a hero: painters, engravers and songwriters could also contribute decisively to the making of a legend attached to imperial heroes, especially because references to the empire in popular culture were far from limited to the written world. Extensive historiographical work has demonstrated how the empire penetrated into metropolitan mindsets through a variety of audiovisual cultural products.[4]

In particular, images became one of the most powerful means of promoting a hero, as visual representation made the heroic deed gain in credibility and appeal. This was even more so as the exoticism of African colonies was increasingly popular over the period.[5] Much of the population had had little contact with images prior to the development of efficient means of reproduction, a fact which reinforced their impact when they were first issued on a large scale. Not only did the public discover an environment that had remained little known before, but they did so through images which seemed sharper and more realistic than ever before. The effect of these images was amplified by the various media in which they were reproduced: newspapers, but also advertisements, posters, postcards or even cigarette cards. The cultural consequences of New Imperialism at home owed a lot to the popularization of images. They drew on established (but generally more elitist) traditions such as war paintings, which had prevailed on both sides of the Channel for a long time, and which provided a vital (and already powerful) starting point.

Most of the military heroes of the Seven Years War or the Napoleonic campaigns had been celebrated through monumental paintings: Benjamin West's *Death of Wolfe* and *Death of Nelson* or John Singleton Copley's *Death of Major Peirson* were the epitome of visual heroization in Britain while, in France, the Napoleonic legend also relied heavily upon graphic representations (engravings, or giant paintings by Antoine-Jean Gros or Jacques-Louis David).[6] Although both Britain and France had been heavily involved in the tradition of military art previously, the British produced many more famous war paintings during the conquest of Africa than the Third Republic ever did.[7]

In Britain, frequent colonial campaigns led to the development of a 'small but flourishing school of military and battle painters'[8] inspired by the early success of Lady Elizabeth Butler, whose depiction of colonial wars had paved the way for the triumphalist representations of British victories produced by the likes of Richard Caton Woodville, William Barnes Wollen, Robert Talbot Kelly, Alphonse de Neuville or Charles Edwin Fripp, alongside W. H. Dugan and B. Fayel in the case of the Zulu War or John Charlton for the 1882 Egypt expedition. These paintings vividly celebrated famous battles won by British troops in Africa, and relished in depicting British military superiority.

Occasionally, they turned military defeats into moral victories – an attitude especially prevalent at the time of the retreat from the Sudan in 1885 and the battles of Isandlwana and Rorke's Drift in 1879. Others celebrated the bravery and loyalty of British soldiers engaged in remote battlegrounds. This last genre was epitomized by John Evan Hodgson's *The Queen, God Bless Her!* (1885), where two soldiers could be seen merrily drinking to the health of the Queen in the middle of the wilderness. Arguably, the empire played a pivotal role in the visual representations of the army in the nineteenth century,[9] and this encouraged the production of images of military imperial heroes, such as Gordon or Kitchener.

The late Victorian fascination with heroes and the appeal of exotic settings which had suddenly emerged explains why Joan Hichberger described the period between the death of General Gordon and the First World War as 'the most prolific time for the production of battle paintings and other celebrations of the military glory of the empire'.[10] In some cases, that also meant imperial heroes. A case in point is General Gordon, whose death gave rise to a wide variety of visual celebrations over the twenty years following his tragic end (and even beyond), some of which were produced by leading Victorian artists such as Frederick Goodall (a member of the Royal Academy since 1852), the portrait specialist Lowes Cato Dickinson (who was well-connected within the establishment) or the former student of John Everett Millais, George W. Joy.

Frederick Goodall chose to refer to Gordon obliquely – but quite obviously – in his *Gordon's Last Messenger*. Having spent extended periods of time in Egypt which inspired many of his works between the 1870s and the 1890s, he produced in 1885 this painting of a boy riding in the middle of the night through the Sudanese desert on his camel, on his way to Wadi Halfa, the bearer of 'a piece of paper no bigger than a postage-stamp, which had been stitched up in his linen garment'.[11] *Gordon's Last Messenger* had been commissioned by Thomas Blackwell, a friend and admirer of Goodall's.[12] The artist's memoirs offer a unique insight into the financial logic that presided over the production of such visual material:

> I commenced a sketch about this time of Gordon entering Khartum for the last time, but never finished it. Although I nearly obtained a handsome commission to paint it, the matter fell through because it was thought that public interest in Gordon would lapse after his death. This was absurd: the public interest in Gordon will never die. His career possessed those elements of romance and mystery which impress the popular imagination. I ought to have had the courage of my convictions and gone on with the picture.[13]

He hastened to add that 'perhaps it may be taken as a rule that an artist paints most successfully, at all events, *con amore*, subjects which have occurred to his own mind'. In spite of this attempt to claim some independence in the choice and development of his subjects, it seems beyond doubt that the opinion of wealthy patrons (who had the power to commission – or not – a painting of an imperial hero) played a key role in the production of most of the works discussed here.

By a process of emulation highlighted in Goodall's above-mentioned quote, visual representations stemmed from the hero's existing popularity (and the belief on the part of potential patrons that it would not be a fleeting popular infatuation), whilst at the same time they contributed to entrenching the legend more deeply and durably in the national pantheon. The news of Gordon's death, and the subsequent lionization of his reputation, inspired either realistic representations of his last months (or moments) in the Sudan or a revival of public interest in the celebrations of earlier feats which had suddenly become topical again as a result of the fall of Khartoum.[14] In the latter category, Val Prinsep's portrait of *Chinese Gordon* (1866) was given a new lease of life, whilst Stanley Berkeley produced in 1885 his *General Gordon and the Slave Dealers of Darfour*, referring to his former anti-slavery activity in the Sudan more than his last military mission. However, the most numerous representations were topical and depicted the hero in the run-up to his death. Lowes Cato Dickinson's *Gordon's Last Watch*, Alexander Melville's *General Gordon in His Palace Writing His Journal and Last Dispatch, December 14, 1884* and Walter J. Allen's *Gordon's Dream* all contributed to manufacturing the image of a serene and competent Gordon ready to sacrifice himself for his cause (regardless of the fact that he had clearly exceeded the orders he had received from Gladstone). The impact of these paintings should not be downplayed: they achieved public prominence through public presentations, and were given wider diffusion through mechanized reproductions as engravings which sold fast, adorning the walls of many homes. Official recognition and commercial success could go hand in hand. For instance, Dickinson's painting was first exhibited at the British Gallery, Pall Mall, as 'The Gordon Memorial Picture', and it was viewed by Queen Victoria on 6 July 1885. The painting was also published in mezzotint by Arthur Dickinson (print made by Samuel Cousins) with the statement 'In memoriam', the artist's initials and the date of production (1885), a step that widened its resonance.[15]

By and large, the painting that entrenched the legend of General Gordon so vividly in British consciousness was George William Joy's monumental *Death of Gordon* (3.00 by 2.10 m), painted eight years after the events and presenting a highly personal interpretation of the

General's end – in spite of the artist's insistence upon his attempt to 'secure the absolute fidelity and truth of [his] representation'.[16] However, its evocative power (due in part to the low-angle view and the perfect, although historically inaccurate, composition) has ensured its author and subject long-lasting fame, at a moment when he recognized that 'times ha[d] sadly changed since those days when [...] there was a mad rush of eager buyers'.[17] It was one of the artist's few works whose copyright was the property of the art merchants Frost & Reed of Bristol (according to Joy's illustrated autobiography), which may indicate a commission. If so, it was a successful initiative: it was presented at the Royal Academy (1894) and the Paris Salon (1895), the Gordon Boys School was endowed with a specifically made copy and it has remained the artist's best-known painting to this day. The artist recognized the influence of pre-existing Gordon imagery on his work, claiming in his memoirs that he had 'obtained copies of every portrait that was known to exist of the General'.[18]

This abundant visual material on General Gordon was given a new lease of life on the occasion of the re-conquest of the Sudan, when images of Gordon and Kitchener were presented alongside each other on many occasions. In late September 1898, sensing a commercial opportunity arising again thirteen years after Gordon's death (and four years after the painting's production), Frost and Reed produced a new series of prints of Joy's *Gordon's Last Stand* in late September 1898, while Lowes Dickinson's painting was re-displayed one month later.[19] Stanley Berkeley depicted another scene of Gordon's action in Darfour with *General Gordon Quelling a Riot in Darfur* (1898), which was reproduced through photogravures. One of the most emblematic depictions of the aftermath of the re-conquest of Khartoum, Richard Caton Woodville's oil painting commissioned by Queen Victoria and exhibited at the Academy, was revealingly entitled *Gordon's Memorial Service at His Ruined Palace in Khartoum, the Day after the Battle of Omdurman* (1899). The Gordon legend proved to be exceptionally resilient in visual terms, through its fusion and recycling on the occasion of the re-conquest of the Sudan. This moment marked the beginning of Kitchener's legend, which will be studied in detail in Chapter 7.

Because the main *modus operandi* of New Imperialism was military (rather than exploration or missionary activity), few civilians were represented in majestic paintings over the period. Yet non-military heroes were not entirely absent from the easels of painters. Precedents included William Scott's painting of Robert Moffat in 1842, or Henry Wyndham Phillips's depiction of John Hanning Speke and Augustus Grant in Africa (ca. 1864), with a young African and a prominent Union Jack in the background. The 1857 portrait of David Livingstone by Henry Wyndham

Phillips was another instance of visual celebration of an imperial hero outside of a military context. Later, George Frederick Watts produced a vivid portait of Cecil Rhodes in 1898, as did Mortimer Ludington Menpes (who made a biographical portrait of Lord Kitchener in 1915).

If British artists were prone to depicting a handful of select imperial heroes of New Imperialism, their French counterparts seemed to limit themselves to colonial battle painting, rather than imperial heroism. The conquest of Algeria was the first to offer French artists (especially under Louis-Philippe and Napoleon III) the opportunity to expand the realm of military painting to colonial themes. Théodore Chassériau, Théodore Gudin and Horace Vernet were among the painters who immortalized the early phases of French involvement in Africa – up to the crushing of Abd-el-Kader's revolt, remembered by Vernet's famous *Prise de la smala d'Abd-el-Kader par le duc d'Aumale à Taguin* (1845). Deeply attached to Africa and to the French colonial project in Algeria, Vernet blurred the disctinction between military painting and *scène de genre*, often exoticizing the background against which French troops were operating. His *Combat de Somah* (1839), based on a battle fought during the campaign that led to the conquest of Constantine, depicted a heroic charge against local fighters which very much anticipated the style of triumphalist depictions of African campaigns that Caton Woodville would adopt a few decades later. The subject remained popular under Napoleon III, with works by Jean Adolphe Beaucé (*Assaut et prise de Laghouat par le général Pélissier*, 1853) or Jules Rigo (*Assaut et prise de Zaatcha par les zouaves commandés par le colonel Canrobert*, 1853) depicting battles fought to expand French control over the Algerian hinterland. Yet portraits of military leaders of the operations were produced only occasionally: Marshal Randon by Horace Vernet (1857), or the Algerian leader Abd-el-Kader by Ange Tissier (1852). Later, the Third Republic seemed singularly unpropitious to the celebration of colonial battles or imperial heroes. One exception was Major Marchand, who inspired a full-length portrait by Paul Philippoteaux as early as 1899 (Figure 3). Depicting Marchand standing near the marshy banks of the Nile, an overscale French flag flying over a hill in the background, it was exhibited at the Salon of 1899. During the Great War, Marchand attracted once again the attention of an artist: in 1915, Georges Bertin Scott depicted in an oil painting the Major (then a General), gravely wounded, in the process of being returned to the rear. This was certainly an imperial hero in everyone's minds, but he was operating in northern France at the time.

The under-representation of imperial heroes in commemorative paintings may reflect the dominant artistic leanings of the country as much as, perhaps, networks of patronage which were unwilling to

3 Paul Philippoteaux, *Le Commandant Marchand* (1899)

commission this type of painting. To put it simply, the market did not seem to exist. As might be expected, the Orientalist school was not interested in the subject either. Its members depicted a supposedly authentic (although in reality heavily idealized) vision of the colonies, where Westerners had no place: there is no trace of any imperial hero in the works of Gustave Guillaumet, Etienne Dinet or Jean-Léon Gérôme. Yet this did not mean that the topic was absent from French visual culture. Whereas not many imperial heroes made it to the walls of galleries or the matrices of printmakers, the rapid sophistication of printing made possible their presence in a growing body of printed visual material enjoying large-scale distribution.

Geographically orientated publications such as *Tour du Monde* (launched in 1860) paved the way for the inclusion of illustrations into travel accounts. For instance, accounts of Brazza's explorations were illustrated with highly detailed engravings by a leading French illustrator, Edouard Riou.[20] In some cases, illustrated newspapers featured engravings depicting an African landscape, as well as an imperial hero, alongside a map and the running text – all on the same page.[21] But it was the arrival of illustrated popular newspapers that made imperial heroes enter the realm of mass communication. The launching of the *Petit Journal*'s *Supplément illustré*, sold for 5 *centimes*, on 15 June 1884 and featuring two engravings on its cover (one of them in colour after 1891), paved the way for the often naive and prejudiced, but always patriotic and proud, celebration of heroic deeds, among which colonial figures featured prominently. Its direct competitor, the *Supplément* of *Le Petit Parisien*, was launched in 1889 and reached a circulation peak of 800,000 copies at the turn of the century. These two powerful promoters of highly evocative images remained close to the tradition of the *images d'Epinal*, but this did not prevent them from conveying visually powerful messages to wide audiences at a time when they were among the sole sources of both entertainment and information.[22] Although not fundamentally inaccurate, their representations of imperial heroes or heroic battles of the French conquest of Africa were artist's interpretations which did not rely upon direct observation or reporting. In addition, in the French tradition, the journalist had to be a literary thinker more than a reporter, and as a consequence drawing skills were not considered essential. The fact that French *grands reporters* did not accompany military columns as closely as British war correspondents did, and that access to rapid means of communication was more problematic for them, meant that representations of imperial heroes in the Gallic press came long after events had taken place, and with a different emphasis: French scenes seemed more posed, less realistic, and featured less action than their British counterparts. French imperial heroes were less frequently shown fighting battles, and more often receiving the submission of local chiefs. Scenes tended to emphasize the ceremonious nature of the encounter, and the tricolour was always carefully positioned. Non-military scenes stressed the benefit bestowed by French rule, as when the *Petit Journal* featured on its front cover an engraving depicting Brazza, his left hand resting on the barrel of his rifle, ceremoniously meeting Africans in the colony which he had founded some twenty years earlier (Figure 4). Pointing doctorally his right finger towards a half-bent African who seems to be seeking advice from him, Brazza, who

CONTEXTS

4 Front cover of the illustrated supplement of *Le Petit Journal*, 19 March 1905

[104]

stands next to a stool on which lies a map, displays a singularly august (if not natural) pose. The supplement featured this engraving two weeks before Brazza and his wife left Marseilles on their investigative (and fatal) journey to the Congo following the Gaud-Toqué colonial scandal. The barbaric practices of these two officers had damaged the reputation of French colonialism at home, and Brazza had been dispatched by the Ministers of the Colonies Clémentel, and President Loubet, to report on the situation in an attempt to calm down public outcry. The image conveyed by the newspaper whitewashed Brazza's reputation by putting the emphasis on his humanitarian designs, rather than on the concessionary system which he had helped to establish, and which had been responsible for widespread abuse (into which he had been sent to enquire). As we have seen in the previous chapter, the print-run of newspapers such as Le Petit Journal or Le Petit Parisien could exceed one million copies from the 1890s onwards (and reached about 1.5 million by 1910), which means that such an image gave widespread publicity to an imperial hero like Brazza.

French newspapers often carried scenes of the return of the imperial hero, as happened when Major Marchand was given a hero's welcome upon his return from Djibouti, a few months after the Fashoda incident. Successive official receptions and landmarks in the elaborate trail of celebrations were vividly depicted on front covers.[23] In little more than a month, the Petit Journal featured on its front cover Marchand's arrival in Paris, his reunion with his father in his hometown of Thoissey and the farewell to his men. The day when the Petit Journal featured Marchand's walkabout near the Gare de Lyon, the Petit Parisien preferred to depict the Major's toast to France, the Republic and the army from the balcony of the Cercle militaire, in front of a large crowd. All these engravings contributed decisively to turning the 'hero of Fashoda' into a household name, as they mediated official consecrations into national events that reached a significant proportion of the country's households (Figure 5).

Visual representations of Marchand's opposite number in the Fashoda incident were also frequent in British newspapers. Engravings depicting the progress of the Anglo-Egyptian army had appeared in the illustrated press since 1896, and the autumn of 1898 saw the appearance of many depictions of Kitchener's role in the victory against the Mahdi, quite similar to the engraving carried by the Penny Illustrated Paper on 1 October, which described the Sirdar ordering the line to avance during the decisive battle of Omdurman (Figure 6).

As in Marchand's case, the ceremonies organized to celebrate the return of the hero to the home country were also widely depicted in the illustrated press, conveying the emotional charge of such celebrations

5   Marchand makes the headlines: front covers of the illustrated supplements of *Le Petit Journal* (11 June, 2 July and 30 July 1899) and *Le Petit Parisien* (11 June 1899)

IMPERIAL HEROES AND THE MARKET II

6 *Penny Illustrated Paper*, 1 October 1898

to a much wider public than those present at the event itself. National recognition of the hero's outstanding deed were mediated to the population through the visual depictions featured in high-circulation newspapers, such as *The Graphic* (Figure 7).

The presence of imperial heroes in the illustrated press was not limited to these somewhat conventional representations (though they already go a long way to demonstrating the popularity of these heroes). Occasionally, heroes of the colonies could also be an object of satire in the press (Figure 8). If the *Penny Illustrated Paper* displayed a mischievous interpretation of Kitchener as a public figure in the years following his rise to prominence as the hero of Khartoum[24], the French newspaper *Le Rire* had a much more caustic appraisal of Cecil Rhodes's role during the South African war. The leading caricaturist Charles Léandre (he obtained a gold medal at the 1900 Paris Universal Exhibition) sketched a greedy Rhodes sitting atop a fortified tower meant to hold a treasure made of shares, diamonds and gold mines. Whilst the cartoon was entitled 'Monsieur Cécil Rhodes', the caption

CONTEXTS

7 *The Graphic*, 12 November 1898, issue 1511

8 *Penny Illustrated Paper*, 18 March 1911

IMPERIAL HEROES AND THE MARKET II

N° 276. 6° année. 17 Février 1900.   15 centimes.

Le Rire

JOURNAL HUMORISTIQUE PARAISSANT LE SAMEDI

LE GOTHA DU RIRE. — N° XXVIII   Monsieur CÉCIL RHODES

Le complice de Chamberlain aura fait verser plus de sang en Afrique que de champagne à Kimberley.
Dessin de Ch. Léandre.

9 *Le Rire*, 17 February 1900

read 'Chamberlain's accomplice will have poured more blood in Africa than champagne in Kimberley' (Figure 9).

Such innuendoes, which often betrayed envy, mockery or outright rivalry, were not systematic. For instance, they did not appear in the illustrated coverage of imperial deeds which sometimes crossed the Channel. Thus, the Anglo-Egyptian advance in the Sudan in 1896 was

[109]

10   *Le Petit Parisien*, 5 April 1896

IMPERIAL HEROES AND THE MARKET II

11 *The Graphic*, 24 May 1884

illustrated on the front cover of the *Petit Parisien* with an engraving showing Kitchener standing sternly in front of a marching camel-mounted army (Figure 10). Three years later, the *Illustrated London News* featured on the front cover of its edition of 10 June 1899 a full-page engraving entitled 'Reception of Major Marchand at the Arsenal'. Published only a few months after Britain and France were on the brink of war, this depiction showed how much importance Marchand was given in Britain. One may also infer that the British were fair players after winning the Fashoda argument, or that they relished the opportunity to remember their triumph once again.

That the British illustrated press was so prone to representing heroes who had shone on the African continent is hardly surprising. The English-speaking world (inspired by marketing strategies first devised in the United States) seized from very early on the commercial opportunities opened up by the appearance of images in newspapers, and the development of illustrated newspapers. Even in the early 1870s, the famous meeting between Stanley and Livingstone in Ujiji was reproduced in illustrated journals such as the *Graphic* and the *Illustrated London News* thanks to wood engraving (see for instance *The Graphic* of 3 August 1872, featuring G. Durand's interpretation of the event). The shrewd publicity-seeker Henry Morton Stanley, advised by his boss James Gordon Bennett Jr, knew how to use images to their full

[111]

potential to sensationalize his action in Africa, not only in the *New York Herald* but also beyond.

Later, the fate of General Gordon gave rise to a series of vivid engravings in the illustrated press, which contributed to placing the General securely on the imaginary map of many British people whilst commenting on current news. One such case was J. Nash's engraving entitled 'Deserted!', published in *The Graphic* of 24 May 1884 (Figure 11). This was the time when the Gladstone government had not yet decided to send the relief expedition – it did not bow to mounting public pressure until August. Although it did not explicitly refer to Gordon in its caption, Nash's picture certainly raised awareness of the General's fate as the dying soldier leaning against the rock clearly bore Gordon's features.

The Graphic later contributed to the Gordon legend with more conventional images, such as a formal portrait of Gordon in civilian attire, with the caption summarizing the three major actions in his life for which he was to be remembered: 'Suppressor of the Taeping rebellion (1863), pacificator of the Soudan (1874–5), defender of Khartoum'.[25] *The Times* contributed to Gordon-mania when it advertised a 'beautiful oleography portrait of the hero of Khartoum', which Bernard Ollendorff sold for sixpence.[26] In the wake of Gordon's assassination, the *Penny Illustrated Paper* advertised an 'illustrated life of General Gordon, the Hero of Khartoum, with portrait gallery of our Soudan heroes', quoting a *Daily News* review which saw in it 'a cheap publication, which is sure to interest a great number of people and to secure a wide sale', putting the emphasis on the fact that 'the text [was] materially assisted by a variety of illustrations'.[27]

As was the case with grand paintings, the re-conquest of the Sudan gave rise to a spate of new celebrations of General Gordon which appeared in the illustrated press. Caton Woodville contributed a watercolour of 'The Memorial Service to Gordon at Khartoum' on the front cover of the *Illustrated London News*.[28] It seems to have inspired some later representations of the same scene, such as the one which was featured on the front cover of the *Aberdeen Weekly Journal* entitled 'In Memory of Gordon', with the caption 'The historic memorial service at Khartoum, on the spot where Gordon met his death'.[29] whilst *The Graphic* featured a few months later, on the anniversary of Gordon's death (and the first to be celebrated after the re-conquest of Khartoum), an image of the memorial service at Khartoum which would later become the annual 'Gordon memorial service'.[30]

An explanation of the growing significance of visual representation of imperial heroes in the British press can be found in the figure of the 'war

IMPERIAL HEROES AND THE MARKET II

artist' – the visual equivalent of war correspondents (who were discussed in the previous chapter), or the precursor of today's war photographers. Undoubtedly, the typically British 'war artists' ('artists-correspondents' sent to the battlefield to report and sketch for their newspaper the scenes they witnessed) contributed significantly to imperial legends. They were a pure product of their age, making the most of significant improvements in the means of communications between London and the frontlines. The original sketches were usually redrawn by the journal's London-office artists, or at least interpreted by an engraver. The results obtained revealed a marked enthusiasm about imperial wars: 'special artists [...] selected, omitted, and portrayed war as dramatic and heroic' – and, understandably, heroes looked as heroic as possible.[31] The doyen of war correspondents, Archibald Forbes, recognized in his memoirs that 'war correspondents should record how our countrymen, our dear ones, [...] vindicate Britain's manhood, and joyously expend their lives for Queen and fatherland'.[32] War artists enjoyed the freedom of creation of the traditional war painter as well as the efficiency of a new age of quicker (although not yet instantaneous) communications. The British public sought to discover new works by Melton Prior, Caton Woodville and Stanley Berkeley in a context of high competition between British newspapers, who all 'tried to gain maximum advantage from their expenditure, by boosting their war reports and correspondents'.[33] In their attempt to appeal to the widest possible public, many of these artists contributed to the reputations of British imperial heroes.

Invented in the late 1830s, but difficult to use in the field for a long time, photography also had far-reaching consequences on the promotion of imperial heroes. The French painter Paul Delaroche exclaimed, upon learning about its invention: 'From now on, painting is over.' Initially, long exposure times (up to a few hours) prevented photography from reproducing living subjects. However, the invention of more sensitive emulsions and better lenses significantly reduced the time of exposure, making it possible to use it for human portraits. Although processing was still encumbering, teams of photographers travelled the world to record exotic scenes as early as the 1850s.[34] In the mid-nineteenth century, famous photographs of Livingstone by Maull & Polyblank (1857) or Thomas Annan (1864) were an integral part of the Livingstone hero-making process. Annan's portrait became one of the most famous images of Livingstone as a result of its being featured as the frontispiece of *The Last Journals of David Livingstone*. Besides being used in books, reproductions of photographs could also be sold to the public. In 1872, the London Stereoscopic Company, which was a thriving business specializing in the sale of stereoscopic photographs, published a series of nine albumen carte-de-visite photographs of Henry Morton Stanley, some of which featured him with his valet Kalulu, with captions such as 'Mr Stanley, in the dress he wore when he met Livingstone in Africa' or 'Discoverer of Livingstone'.[35]

The arrival in the 1860s of flexible negative film, much easier to use than plates, and handheld cameras (George Eastman first launched his Kodak camera in 1888) made the practice of photography in Africa more practical, but did relatively little to promote imperial heroes since spontaneous action shots were still out of the question. The situation changed after the First World War, when technical progress allowed photographs to be taken less cumbersomely. The consolidation of the 'Lawrence of Arabia' legend was a direct result of the progress of photographic techniques: the success of Lowell Thomas's worldwide tour, which launched the global reputation of T. E. Lawrence, was also thanks to the stills of Harry Chase which vividly illustrated Thomas's talk and turned it into a show in its own right, with the added benefit of the typically Henty-esque title *With Lawrence in Arabia*.[36] Photography was a key component in the making of the Lawrence legend, through the Thomas–Chase illustrated talk (alongside short film features), but also because some of Chase's images gained worldwide fame: the 1919 full portrait of T. E. Lawrence wearing Bedouin headgear quickly became a famous shot which reinforced the iconic status of the leader of the Arab revolt and placed him well above and beyond the fleeting status of a piece of news.

Yet photography came too late for nineteenth-century imperial heroes: either photographers would have to turn their sights on other topics or they would have to re-enact the most famous scenes in the hero's life. This was usually the case when a film was being made: the real hero was replaced by an actor, but the re-enactment of the scene made it more evocative. This solution combined the accuracy of photography with the freedom of interpretation of a painting. Although the situation was not real, it looked realistic. A good example of such truth-twisting is Léon Poirier's series of photos published in his book *Charles de Foucauld et L'Appel du silence, photographies du film*, where the re-enactment of Charles de Foucauld's life gave the public the feeling they were seeing *real* scenes, although they were primarily the film-maker's own interpretation (Figure 12).[37] Poirier, a nephew of the impressionist painter Berthe Morisot, had started his career in drama (as the general secretary of the *Théâtre du Gymnase* and the founder of the *Comédie des Champs-Elysées*) and this may well have helped him increase the verisimilitude of each scene he orchestrated, which he called an *évocation*.[38] In spite of the highly evocative and obviously symbolic meaning of these images, they could be perceived as plausible, which increased their commercial appeal. They provided a much sought-after feeling of

> L'APPEL DU SILENCE 221
>
> A l'intérieur, on hisse le drapeau français en présence des Touareg. C'est le Père qui, d'un ordre donné en tamachek, commande le salut au drapeau.

12 Heroism and realism at the time of the cinema: Foucauld exalting patriotic instincts in Léon Poirier's *L'Appel du silence*. The text reads: 'Inside, the French flag is raised in the presence of Tuaregs. It is the Father who gave in Tamachek [Tuareg language] the salute to the flag.'

authenticity which informed, entertained and recalled exemplary destinies: the French public showed clear enthusiasm for Poirier's shots of the film, as no fewer than 110,000 copies of the album were sold in the first two years following its launch.[39]

War artists, photographers and newspaper editors were not the only image producers seeking the attention of potential 'customers': at a time when commercial advertisement strategies were taking shape, the appeal of imperial heroes was not left unused. Throughout the period, propaganda products coming from, or linked to, the colonies spread in the two metropoles, and promotion of the empire (and imperial products) was made more effective.[40] Commercial advertisements represent the other major feature of newspapers, and for that reason the presence of imperial heroes in these adverts is not insignificant, as it could echo or reinforce reputations. Eno used a supposed quotation from General Gordon ('The stomach governs the world') to promote their Fruit Salts in the *Illustrated London News*, between the summer of 1885 and the end of 1887, and then again on the occasion of the reconquest of the Sudan, in 1897 and 1898.[41] The Gordon legend proved remarkably resilient over time, and it seemed to remain a safe commercial bet. As late as 1931, the Hero of Khartoum was used to promote the launch of the 'Britannia and Eve' magazine (Figure 13).

Other adverts using imperial heroes could be openly jingoistic. Such was Bovril's advertisement featuring the headline 'How Lord Roberts spells Bovril', where the itinerary followed by Lord Roberts to Kimberley and Bloemfontein was plotted so as to spell the brand Bovril with the meanders of the hero's route in his fight against the Orange Free State.[42] Famously, Alfred Leete's portrait of Kitchener pointing his almost accusing finger at potential recruits, with the headline 'Your country needs you', represents another instance of imperial heroism used for publicity purposes – this time, to build up what would become the Kitchener armies in wartime Britain. Leete's recruitment poster derived from a design which first appeared on the cover of the weekly magazine *London Opinion* on 5 September 1914 with the line 'Your country needs you'. The Parliamentary Recruiting Committee subsequently adopted this powerful portrait of Kitchener, and chose a slightly different slogan: 'Britons, [Kitchener] wants you'.[43] The poster was later issued with the slogan 'Your country needs you' which posterity recorded. If the real efficiency of the first, unofficial, poster is still a matter of controversy, the fact that 145,000 copies of a second, official, poster were produced in 1915 testifies to the place that the hero of Khartoum had come to occupy in Britain by the beginning of the First World War, and how actively this popularity was used to recruit several million volunteers.[44]

13 *Illustrated London News*, 2 May 1931

14 Exploration as an argument to cleanse oneself: Brazza adorning the *Savon des Explorateurs* produced by the *Société continentale du Cosmydor*

Beyond advertising, imperial heroes proved to be versatile promotional devices. In some instances, visual representation of imperial heroes could be used directly on the products offered by the brand, so that the image of the imperial hero would end up directly on a shop shelf. Such was the case of the Discovery Matches manufactured by Dixon, Son & Evans in the 1870s, which featured a portrait of David Livingstone on the top of the matchbox.[45] Similarly, the Paris-based *Société continentale du Cosmydor* made a portrait of Savorgnan de Brazza in explorer's gear the centrepiece of the label of its aptly named '*savon des explorateurs*' ('Soap of the explorers') (Figure 14). Brazza's appeal was even acknowledged on the other side of the Channel, where the Birmingham-based pen nib manufacturers D. Leonardt & Co. produced (presumably for the French market) the 'plume de Brazza' around the turn of the century. The vast array of commercial uses made of imperial heroes tends to demonstrate that they added value in the eyes of the consumer. In so doing, they also made these figures household names, quite literally.

Smaller visual products revolving around imperial heroes also contributed to promoting the reputations of great men of empire, and testify that, if imperial heroes were not ubiquitous, they certainly remained a frequent topic for a variety of popular products that reached a mass audience of all ages, and contributed decisively to shaping the mental landscapes of millions of people. Postcards, cigarette cards and *chromos* frequently carried portraits (in action or in studio) of the heroes of the exploration or the conquest of Africa (Figure 15). Ogden's Guinea Gold Cigarettes cards featuring a static portrait of General Gordon described him as a 'Great soldier and philanthropist' who 'died heroically in

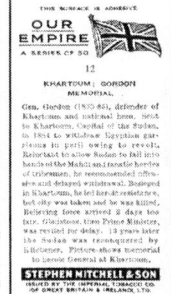

15 Imperial heroes to secure customers' loyalty: General Gordon on Ogden's, Mitchell's and Brooke Bond Tea collectible cards

Khartoum Jan. 1885'. In the late 1930s, a whole half-century after the fall of Khartoum, the Gordon legend was still alive, but this time through the intercession of an official monument: as late as 1937, Stephen Mitchell & Son released a cigarette card featuring the Gordon Memorial in Khartoum, the twelfth of a series of fifty entitled 'our Empire'. On the back of the card, Gordon was presented as 'defender of Khartoum and national hero', and the biographical paragraph stated that the 'picture show[ed] memorial to heroic general at Khartoum'. This trend even survived the Second World War, with Gordon still

16 Brazza king of the *chromos*: cards produced by *Chocolats Guérin-Boutron* and *Tisanes du Père Célestin*

[119]

among those selected to appear on the postwar Brooke Bond Tea cards. The symbolic place of the statue (discussed in Chapter 1) is evident in both cases. Kitchener was also featured on many tobacco cards: for instance, Churchman's Tortoise-Shell smoking mixture included a studio portrait of 'Lord Kitchener' in military uniform as part of its Boer War Generals series (1901).

In France, scenes depicting the hero's action and set-up portraits were the usual ways of representing an imperial hero (Figure 16). Some of the *chromos* combined both approaches, such as the one produced by the *Tisane des Pères Célestins*, as part of its series on famous explorers, among whom Brazza was featured. The front of the card brought together a portrait of Brazza surrounded by a crown of laurels, and an artist's impression of the crossing of marshes during the 1879 expedition (wrongly situated by the caption in the Sudan), whilst the back of the card featured a factual biography (where Brazza's end was not mentioned, suggesting that it was produced during his own lifetime). Other *chromos* celebrating Brazza included those of *Chocolats Guérin-Boutron* or those of the *Félix Potin* stores ('Collection Félix Potin'), both of which displayed rather bland studio portraits.

The flourishing industry of the *chromos*, which carried a commercial message under the guise of information, entertainment and the pleasure of collecting, offered a cultural environment where imperial heroes appeared among other noteworthy historical and topical subjects. This is not to say that they monopolized the attention of collectors, but their prevalence among these widely distributed ancestors of loyalty cards shows how they featured among the topics that the young (and not so young) cared about for their collections. Even if they entered homes alongside other topics, as part of thematic series, the inclusion of imperial heroes demonstrates that they featured among the subjects which deserved to be depicted on *chromos*, and that they formed part of the cultural and historical background that this type of popular product contributed to shaping.

Postcards offered a comparable case: the corpus of postcards representing imperial heroes is not exceptionally significant when put in relation to the overall output of the period. Yet this 'influential form of ephemera', as much as the cigarette or tea cards, placed these heroes in the imaginary pantheon of generations who grew up collecting, exchanging or sending them.[46] Postcards fell into two categories. In the case of heroes whose career went on after their African exploits, their imperial dimension was recalled as the starting point of their national odyssey. Thus, a postcard of Kitchener produced during the First World War mentioned alongside the crown of laurels eight imperial postings of the hero, seven of which were in Africa (Figure 17).

17 Kitchener, Great War leader with a clear imperial pedigree: wartime postcard

CONTEXTS

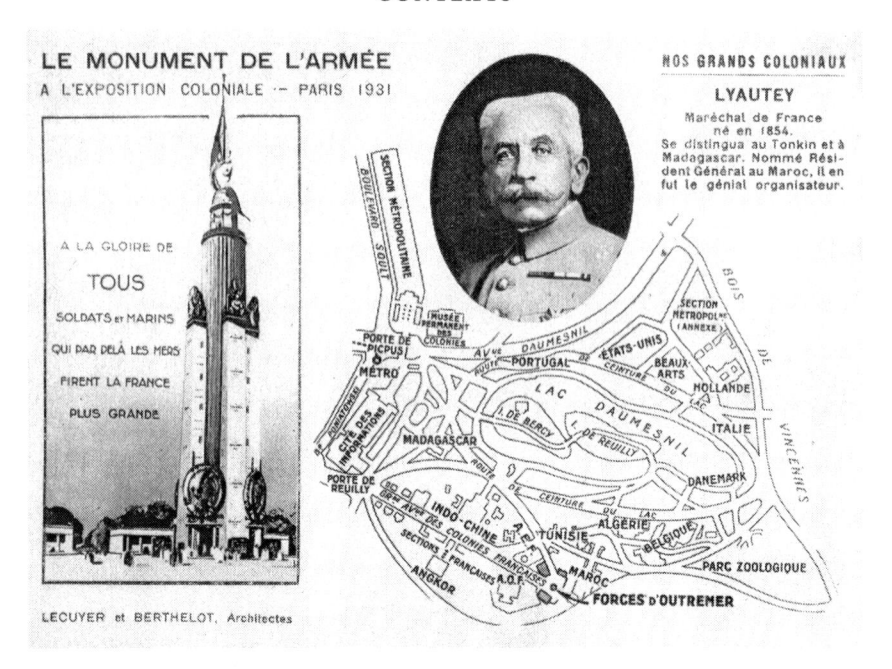

18 Heroes of 'Greater France': Marshal Lyautey, patron of the 1931 Vincennes exhibition

The second category of postcards celebrating imperial heroes had a predominantly imperial theme, but illustrated its relevance to the national narrative through the example of glorious conquerors. This was the case of a 1931 postcard produced on the occasion of the Vincennes *Exposition coloniale*, which displayed a portrait of Lyautey alongside a map of the exhibition, and under the heading 'Nos grands coloniaux' (Figure 18).

Occasionally, postcards of sites of commemoration would strengthen the reputation of the imperial hero through a powerful *mise en abyme*, whereby the image featured a statue of the hero. The postcard conveyed the celebratory message indirectly, and the caption made sure that both sender and receiver were clear as to the identity of the great person that was celebrated. This type of situation arose frequently in the case of monuments erected in the colonies: not only were the statues deemed to be worthy of touristic interest, but they were also a reminder of the glorious epic of the conquest, with a symbolic force which few other visual representations could match (Figure 19).

Although the 'audiovisual worlds' to which this chapter refers were overwhelmingly dominated by fixed images (and especially

19 Imperial heroes and the circulation of colonial imagery: postcards representing a statue of Cardinal Lavigerie in Tunis, and the inauguration by Marshal Lyautey of a memorial to Charles de Foucauld, destined to be sent to the metropole

engravings) throughout the period, other forms of promotion of imperial heroes, involving either sound or moving images (or both), also reflected (and at the same time fuelled) popular interest in the legends surrounding the great men of New Imperialism. The nascent audiovisual industry had not achieved the economic importance and socio-cultural status that it would enjoy later, but it was a novel, powerful and evocative way of conveying heroic deeds to the public. It is also a significant gauge of the popularity and longevity of heroic legends of empire.

Music offered the opportunity to celebrate actively the subjects it referred to: whether a local band, an opera or an individual striking up a song, it allowed the vivid (although ephemeral) exaltation of the theme it covered. Although the phenomenon was not new in itself, the means through which such songs and ballads (and, crucially, their lyrics) were propagated changed over the period. The ability to play an instrument became more widespread among both the middle and educated working classes, as a consequence of the belief of the middle classes that 'singing constituted an important part of the search for rational recreation'.[47] Local bands were more numerous, and singing became compulsory in schools from the 1870s, while choral competitions and choral participation came to characterize the period. The same new printing techniques that we examined for newspapers also allowed for a greater diffusion of the scores and lyrics. Edison's invention in 1877–78 paved the way for the recording of sound and its rediffusion: for the first time music no longer had to be live. The appearance of the gramophone and of the radio in the interwar years permitted the distribution and production of music with unparalleled speed and ubiquity. Imperial heroes sometimes featured as the subject of ballads or songs (especially on the occasion of victories or commemorations), which were more efficiently disseminated throughout the country as a result of improved recording and broadcasting technology.

Songwriters found an easy market each time a heroic figure came to the limelight. In Britain, imperial campaigns often inspired composers in search of themes of current and national relevance. For instance, in the wake of the Sudan campaign, they quickly endeavoured to produce songs for music-halls.[48] Compositions based on colonial campaigning sometimes referred to imperial heroes, such as *Chinese Gordon's March, Gordon's Safety, England's Honour, The Garnet Wolseley March, Kitchener!* or *Kitchener's Karol*. The religious undertones of the legend attached to the death of General Gordon gave Sir Edward Elgar the idea of a 'Gordon symphony' which, although never completed, heavily influenced his *Dream of Gerontius*.[49] The death of Gordon was also remembered in the song *Too Late, Too Late*, composed by G. H. MacDermott, who insisted upon the image of the sacrificial Christian martyr.[50] Numerous songs were written in honour for Kitchener before and after his death, the scores of which were published in the form of pamphlets easily marketable in a world always more eager for memorabilia: three between 1896 and 1901, followed by fifteen in 1915 and 1916 alone, when the imperial hero had become a national saviour.[51]

In France, the exoticism of the empire seemed somewhat more attractive than imperial heroes. Alain Ruscio perceived three main trends in French colonial songs, distinguishing between the 'comic', the 'romantic' and the 'epic' tones.[52] Relatively few French popular songs were written about imperial heroes; rather, they celebrated genres of soldiers or conquerors: the *Zouave*, the *Marsouin* and, above all, the *Légionnaire*. However, among the notable exceptions were Brazza and Marchand, who both seem to have attracted significant interest from songwriters. Brazza was mentioned in songs about heroes such as *Patriotisme*,[53] and was the subject of the patriotic song *Brazza et le Congo*.[54] Both praised the peaceful conquest of Central Africa, devoid of any bloodbath, whilst developing an Anglophobic stance and expecially stressing the patriotic value of Brazza's action for France:

> If de Brazza gives us his conquests
> If he suffered to give us the edge
> We will recall that on the days of our defeats
> He served our outraged standard
> Because in the Congo the Tricolour
> Pre-empted any rival
> Here is Brazza, of whom France is proud.
> Oh Black people, here is Freedom.[55]

This lyric owed its existence to a versatile publisher, Paris-based P. Tralin, whose catalogue included a large variety of titles, from religious sermons and funeral orations to a guide to Paris cabarets and houses of ill repute.

A decade and a half later, it was Marchand's turn to become a subject of musical interest. At the height of the Fashoda crisis, the patriotic march *Fachoda ou la France en Afrique* was frequently sung to the tune of another famous song, *Vous n'aurez pas l'Alsace et la Lorraine* ('You will not get Alsace and Lorraine'). The end of its first chorus read: 'Glory to Marchand, the heroic soldier / Who knew how to stand up to the English furore / When he told them: "In Africa / In Fashoda, never will you dare to come!"' The booklet of lyrics featured on its cover a portrait of Marchand and two scenes showing him leading his men against a fort and during a mounted battle against Arabs.[56] G. Chavanne wrote *La Mission Marchand* in 1898, Emily issued his *Chanson de la Mission Marchand* in 1899, while an anonymous writer contributed to the Marchand myth (and certainly to the Anglophobic sentiment of the moment) with an *Hommage au Commandant Marchand à Fachoda*.[57] Joseph Grégoire celebrated the 'valiant and sublime commandant' in 1899 with an opus sold cheaply at twenty centimes (ensuring it the widest distribution).[58] Other popular songs included *Gloire à Marchand* by Antonin Louis, which was to be sung on the tune of the *Pioupious d'Auvergne*, and the highly ironic *Allocution de M. Lockroy aux membres de la mission Marchand*, by D. Bonnaud and Mévisto Sr, which praised Marchand highly whilst mocking the navy Minister Lockroy. The writer of patriotic songs Georges Fragerolle and the poet Léon Durocher together created the *Marche au Soleil* about the mission, which was shown at two famous Parisian theatres, *La Bodinière* and Caran d'Ache's famous *Epopée*. Another national march, *Le Commandant Marchand*, was played at various Parisian cabarets, notably the *Eldorado* (the French equivalent of Canterbury Hall), the *Petit Casino*, the *Ambassadeurs* and the *Jardin de Paris*. Another cabaret, *Fachoda*, was scheduled at the *Ambassadeurs* and the *Eldorado*. Given the circumstances, a special version of the *Marseillaise* was offered to the audience: *'La Marseillaise de Marchand'*. The most famous of the songwriters to contribute to the Marchand legend was the famous cabaret singer of the time, Aristide Bruant: shortly after his unsuccessful attempt to launch his political career in a district of northern Paris (Belleville), he wrote *'La Patrie française, chanson-marche dédiée au Commandant Marchand'*, a song and march described in the preamble to Morphy's book as 'the great success of the day'.[59]

Yet the entertainment industry had more to contribute to the legends surrounding imperial heroes than cabaret marches, courtesy of an artist who entered posterity mostly thanks to Toulouse-Lautrec's artwork. This nascent industry witnessed a major turning point with the appearance of the cinema, which became a major player in the 'circuit of culture' of the twentieth century.[60] The cinema bore the seeds of a radical shift in the visual depiction of heroic deeds. The succession of projected images, at the heart of the process, had been implemented in magic lantern slides with notable success for David Livingstone. Invented in the seventeenth century, the magic lantern was not a properly 'photographic' process (the slides were drawn rather than exposed, and then coloured by hand-painting or transfers), but it featured scenes realistically (like photography), and was projected (like the future cinema). In the late nineteenth century, magic lantern slides were used to show travel and missionary subjects, especially by the London Missionary Society. They were also a powerful means of propagating the Livingstone legend in an entertaining and appealing manner: the sets devoted to his life were the most successful, and were shown widely throughout Britain.[61] By contrast, the system does not seem to have been used at all to promote French heroes.

The invention of the *cinématographe* by the brothers Lumière in 1895 did not immediately transform the reputations of imperial heroes. The new system was initially used to record everyday life rather than exceptional circumstances, and technical constraints limited the possibilities of recording real military action. When Frederic Villiers attempted to record the battle of Omdurman on cine film from a gunboat, the vibrations of the vessel upon opening fire blew down his camera and exposed his film.[62] Secondly, because films were seen as a new form of music-hall or cheap theatre, once the bland reproduction of everyday life (a hallmark of early films) was exhausted, they drew heavily upon the imagination of a handful of creators such as Georges Méliès, who preferred to invent surreal stories like *Le Voyage dans la lune* (1902). Lastly, films tended to be rather short during the first two decades following the invention of the system, and this limited the technical possibility of celebrating the life of a hero. Yet, in the wake of the First World War, films started to tell longer stories set in more exotic places, and a few pioneers (such as Léon Poirier) tried shooting them on location. This marked the advent of what Jeffrey Richards called the 'cinema of Empire'.[63] For the first time, imperial heroes could fit in motion pictures. They did not do so in the nascent genre of the documentary, which often intended to introduce the metropolitan public to developmental efforts in the colonies and was therefore more interested in recent developments than in the epic of

IMPERIAL HEROES AND THE MARKET II

the conquest,[64] but as subjects of re-enacted scenes in feature films designed to entertain as much as to inform and shape beliefs about the colonial order. Naturally, no footage was available of the real actions that had given rise to these heroic reputations (except in the case of T. E. Lawrence, thanks to Harry Chase's camerawork), but re-enactment brought them to life for the first time for many viewers. Imperial heroes were given a new lease of life in popular imagination when they were shown apparently *accomplishing* their deeds in front of the viewer, in the cosy darkness of a cinema or a theatre. With the advent of films, the public shifted from a *belief* in heroic deeds (they relied on accounts produced for them) to an actual feeling of *perception* (through their own senses, although it was mediated by a film). This was one of the key explanations for the unprecedented success of the Thomas–Chase shows, which projected short films interspersed in the lecture to the greatest effect on the audience: in the four years that their worldwide tour lasted, Thomas is said to have delivered his lecture around four thousand times, to an estimated four million people.[65] Yet the Lawrence legend was the exception rather than the rule: it was the only case of hero-making which included live footage of real action; in most cases film producers had to induce the public to forget about the inevitable re-enactment, and give viewers the sensation of seeing *real* deeds and the *real* hero. When, after 1927, films came with sound as well, the actor's voice could easily become the hero's true voice for the public.

The appearance of imperial heroes in a few major feature films was far from incidental. As years went on, the cinema increasingly contributed to the shaping of popular culture (of which it became a major expression), and any appraisal of the place of imperial heroes in British and French culture has to take this new medium into account when it comes to the interwar years. The cinema became the 'most important medium of popular culture' in these years in Britain and, arguably, 'the English went to the cinema more than any other people'.[66] Significantly, the popularity of the cinema very often brought with it a celebration of the empire and its ethos.[67] In France, a 'massive and popular cinephilia' was perceptible as well.[68] Yet Britain was considerably ahead of France in infrastructural terms, and this makes the resounding success of a few French films dedicated to imperial heroes even more remarkable. By 1917, the National Council of Public Morals established that between 4,000 and 4,500 custom-built cinemas were already operating in Britain,[69] whilst France counted only 1,444 cinemas in 1918 and 2,300 in 1921.[70]

It was against this backdrop of growing cinephilia that a number of films retracing the exemplary lives of imperial heroes appeared on

[127]

each side of the Channel. Their quantity may not look exceptional when compared to the global output of the period, but their immediate success contributed to the perpetuation of these legends among younger generations, and their long-lasting influence demonstrated the appeal of the topic.

The technical and financial means necessary to recreate the context of the exploration or conquest of Africa, as well as the heroic deeds themselves, go a long way to explaining why what we would call today 'biopics' of imperial heroes were not so common. In Britain, although there is no record of any intentional promotion of an imperial hero by the Colonial Office Films Committee or the Empire Marketing Board Unit,[71] several directors delivered visually striking accounts of British Great Men in the colonies: *Livingstone* (1925) directed by Marmaduke Arundel Wetherell (with the director in the leading role), *Rhodes of Africa* (1936) by Berthold Viertal (with Walter Huston in Rhodes's role), *David Livingstone* (1936) by James A. FitzPatrick (with Percy Marmont in Livingstone's role) and *Stanley and Livingstone* (1939) by Henry King, which placed the emphasis on Stanley rather than Livingstone. Wetherell's film was initially silent, but was released with a soundtrack in 1933. In France, fifteen years after the first ever successful film to feature French officers in the Sahara (Jacques Feyder's *L'Atlantide* in 1921), Léon Poirier set a precedent in hero-making with his record-breaking *L'Appel du silence* (1936). This film 'extended and deviated from French colonial films of the mid-1930s such as Jacques Feyder's *Le Grand Jeu* and Julien Duvivier's *Pépé le Moko*,'[72] and it paved the way for Poirier's later films on imperial heroes, *Brazza ou l'Epopée du Congo* (1939) and *La Route inconnue* (1947) which returned to the theme of Charles de Foucauld, but this time putting the spotlight on his 1880s reconnaissance in Morocco. Poirier's films appear as exceptions in a French film industry which was not particularly prone to celebrating imperial heroes, but they enjoyed considerable popularity, which compensated for the relative weakness of the genre in France.

These films hoped to cash in on relatively recent heroic episodes which had taken place in singularly exotic places likely to attract the public's attention. The producer Pierre Marcel summed up his ideas on the subject to Léon Poirier, who was then directing the account of the *Croisière noire* organized by Citroën, and which was in itself a modern version of imperial heroism:

> Bear in mind breath-taking films, which will be remembered not only in the history of the cinema but in history, those which Stanley and Brazza could have brought back if the Lumière brothers had invented their *cinématographe* fifteen years earlier.[73]

But in spite of what this quotation implies, it was not all about putting the romance of exploration on film: these undertakings were at the core of a nexus of commercial interests that could increase their profitability. On that account, the correspondence surrounding the 1925 *Livingstone* film is revealing.[74] The main organizer of the Livingstone Film Expedition was eager to stress that an 'exceptional arrangement [had] been made with one of the foremost American companies' that 'guarantees the success of the film in North America', before adding that the film could be shown in the '100,000 Schools and Churches in the United States which exhibit films' and in the majority of the 25,000 British Free Churches that 'could be made available for the purpose of its display'. The likely popularity of the film, which has a direct impact on its rentability, was carefully appraised, and as well as the availability of 'various other sources of revenue [...], such as Lantern Slides from still pictures, photographs and literary matter for publications'.[75] Questions of profitability were clearly on the agenda before the film was shot.

Profitability (or its forecast absence) was also a central (and thorny) issue when Léon Poirier launched his project of a film celebrating the life and example of Charles de Foucauld. In spite of Poirier's success with the First World War epic commemoration *Verdun, visions d'histoire* (1928, re-issued in 1931 with a soundtrack), and his experience at directing the filmic accounts of two major trans-continental Citroën expeditions, film producers had cold feet when he offered them *L'Appel du silence*. Doubtful about its commercial potential, they all declined to fund it: one of them declared 'not a single penny, do you understand?, not a *centime*. Waste your time if this amuses you, but I do not want to waste my money.'[76] Although the film-maker sometimes turned this situation into a deliberate decision to avoid profit-driven traditional commercial circuits,[77] he later recognized that he had had to overcome 'mountains of difficulty' to produce the film.[78] Inspired, on his own account, by fundraising strategies used to erect statues, Poirier resorted to patronage and public subscription to palliate the lack of faith of professional producers in the commercial prospects of the idea. The committee that Poirier launched in an attempt to finance *L'Appel* counted on the support of several influential publicists and officers, including Marshal Lyautey in its early stages. The *Comité d'action Charles de Foucauld* evidently leaned towards the Right and conservative Catholic circles. Presided by Marshal Franchet d'Espérey, it included eminent officers (including Marshal Pétain, General Weygand, Lieutenant de La Rocque), clergymen (some of them high-ranking), politicians (including former President of the Republic Alexandre Millerand, who had been a socialist before he moved towards conservatism, two ministers and several MPs), men of letters (five members of the French Academy were among them), diplomats, lawyers, musicians, medical professors, colonial figures (including Louis Rollin, Minister of the Colonies, the secretary of the Paris geographical society, and the French general residents in Morocco and Tunisia), journalists (among others, Lucien Romier, director of *Le Figaro*), entrepreneurs (Marcel Michelin) and wives of influential officers or noblemen.[79] Members of the French elite who supported colonial expansion were thus mobilized to provide direct financial support (fundraising dinners were organized), but also to use their celebrity to back a nationwide subscription appeal. Poirier relentlessly defended his idea everywhere in France, embarking on a one-year lecturing tour in eighty-two French, Belgian and Swiss cities and towns, during which he secured enough funds to proceed with the production of the movie, which he claimed came from about a hundred thousand French people (essentially Catholic admirers of the hermit).[80] Contributions varied between FF. 10 and 10,000, with the majority comprising between 50 and 100 francs.[81] Contrary to the financial doom that producers had forecast, the film, which was awarded the *Grand prix du Cinéma français* in 1936, proved to be a resounding success, with ten million viewers in eight months, which placed it second in the French box-office receipts of the year.[82] Merchandizing was also a key component of the financial rewards that Poirier was able to reap, with Mame publishers producing many editions of the book published before the film was made (for fundraising purposes), as well as the illustrated books produced on the basis of stills from the film (which have been discussed earlier in this chapter). Poirier himself acknowledged that this film had been 'very profitable'.[83] Poirier had announced that the film's profits would be used to develop Catholic missions in the Sahara, and, in the absence of data on this question, it seems fair to believe that it was the success of *L'Appel du silence* which made it possible to produce two more 'visual biographies' (as a journalist of *Le Matin* called Poirier's films)[84] featuring French imperial heroes.

The nationalist content of the film is beyond question (Poirier recognized that he wanted to 'spread throughout the world the fame of France and the quality of its elite'),[85] but this aspect cannot fully account for its remarkable success. The appeal of the Sahara and its exotic emptiness, the mysterious Tuaregs with whom Foucauld had lived and worked, the spiritual example set by his story, the tragic circumstances of his death and the interest in colonial possessions following the centenary of the conquest of Algeria and the Vincennes exhibition, all contributed to enhancing the attractiveness of this 'ode to the colonial enterprise'.[86] Referring to *L'Appel du silence*, a journalist of the *Comité de l'Afrique française* believed that the French public '[understood] that the big screen [could] sometimes depict something different than the inanities which Hollywood [poured] on us'.[87] Poirier's success story shows conclusively that the cinema offered valuable opportunities for hero-makers, even if it was not until the interwar years that producers realized it. *Brazza ou L'Épopée du Congo* mixed similar ingredients and stemmed from the same desire to promote the French colonial epic, but its career was cut short by the Phoney War and the Second World War, and it never reached the same level of popularity as its predecessor. Poirier tried to revive the trend after the war, with *La Route inconnue* (1947), which never matched the popularity of *L'Appel du silence*. Taken together, these three films 'paid homage to [...] French colonialism's heroic, and largely imagined, past'.[88] A few years later, Americans largely out-performed Poirier by propelling two British imperial heroes to worldwide stardom: David Lean's *Lawrence of Arabia* (1962) and Basil Dearden and Eliot Elisofon's *Khartoum* (1966), where the towering figure of General Gordon featured prominently.

The cinema represented the latest stage in the attempt to represent heroic deeds as realistically and as evocatively as possible, which has been a characteristic feature of modern hero-worshipping (although the gap between *vraisemblance* and *vrai* – verisimilitude and reality – so famous in theatre, was never really bridged). Imperial heroes were not the main staple of mainstream cinema, but the few highly successful films that arose out of heroic reputations linked to the empire testify the relevance of this topic in interwar cinematographic production.

Evidence suggests that the unprecedented mass production of visual material that took place in the West between 1870 and 1939 contributed decisively to sustaining popular interest in imperial heroes at a time when the waves of 'New Imperialism' were about to swallow the interior of the African continent into European empires. The development of this new type of hero is inseparable from this affordable and quickly expanding imagery, which could be found in a variety of books, newspapers, illustrated magazines and advertisements and everyday items ranging from cigarette cards to postcards. Hero-worshipping could occasionally become genuinely audiovisual, thanks to breakthroughs in music reproduction and the appearance of moving images, which all dramatically re-shaped popular entertainment. The fact that imperial heroes were featured in all these media indicates that the topic deeply penetrated the metropolitan cultures of the two countries, and was appealing enough to be promoted through innovative means of communication when they appeared.

Britain and France experienced the impact of this nascent audiovisual culture differently, depending on traditional preferences, commercial opportunities and also the fortunes of individual entrepreneurship. If the French led the way in terms of large-format color illustrations for Sunday supplements thanks to the pioneering *Le Petit Journal* and *Le Petit Parisien*, there was no exact French equivalent to the British war correspondents who covered colonial battlefields, their sketchbooks in hand, ensuring vivid depictions of war scenes in the English-speaking illustrated press. Large-scale publicity stunts *à la* Stanley remained unmatched in Paris (although they inspired many a French *grand reporter*, and inspired admiration or loathing among Gallic journalists):[89] looking at the cases of Stanley and, later, Lowell Thomas, it seems that the English-speaking world was more efficient at turning imperial heroes into worldwide commercial entertainment. Yet, if films about imperial heroes were more numerous in Britain than in France, Léon Poirier was the only director of the period who succeeded in achieving the status of a blockbuster of his time for a film about a colonial hero.

The significance of all the audiovisual material mentioned in this chapter stems mostly from the many promotional channels which produced and distributed these varied celebratory messages to overlapping or parallel constituencies of the public. The variety of media involved in the promotion of imperial heroes further entrenched them in the imagination of many through a process of accumulation, but it also ensured that they reached diverse audiences.

Deeply influenced by commercial strategies, the production of these visual artefacts reflected attempts to satisfy public taste as much as to arouse interest in colonial subjects. The tension between market demands and political, moral or philosophical convictions was frequently palpable. Having seen the international background and market realities against which the figures of imperial heroes emerged, it is vital to consider the various political and moral values that they carried with them.

Notes

1 On the development of human images since prehistory, see W. Davis, 'The origins of image making', *Current Anthropology*, 27:3 (June 1986), 193–215.
2 W. Benjamin, *L'œuvre d'art à l'époque de sa reproductibilité technique: version de 1939* (2008).
3 C. Bayly, *The Birth of the Modern World* (2003), pp. 371–3.
4 Especially J. M. MacKenzie, *Propaganda and Empire* (Manchester, 1984), and *Orientalism: History, Theory and the Arts* (Manchester, 1995); J. M. MacKenzie (ed.), *Imperialism and Popular Culture* (Manchester, 1986), and *Popular Imperialism*

      and the Military (Manchester, 1992); J. Richards, *Imperialism and Music: Britain 1876–1953* (Manchester, 2001).
5 Visual representations of the empire have attracted much scholarly attention in the last fifteen years. For the French colonies, see in particular J. Marseille, 'Les images de l'Afrique en France, 1880–1930', *Canadian Journal of African Studies / Revue Canadienne des Etudes Africaines*, 22:1 (1988), 121–30; N. Bancel, P. Blanchard and A. Chatelier (eds), *Images et colonies* (1993); E. Deroo and S. Lemaire, *L'Illusion coloniale* (2005). For Britain, see J. R. Ryan, *Picturing Empire: Photography and the Visualization of the British Empire* (1997); T. Barringer, 'Fabricating Africa: Livingstone and the visual image, 1850–1874', in I. M. MacKenzie (ed.), *David Livingstone and the Victorian Encounter with Africa* (1996), pp. 169–200; P. S. Landau and D. Kaspin (eds), *Images & Empires: Visuality in Colonial and Postcolonial Africa* (Berkeley and London, 2002).
6 On eighteenth- and early nineteenth-century visual celebrations of British and French heroes, see among others A. Boime, *Art in an Age of Revolution, 1750–1800* (Chicago, 1987); D. H. Solkin, *Painting for Money: The Visual Arts and the Public Sphere in Eighteenth-Century England* (New Haven, CT, 1993); H. von Erffa and A. Staley, *The Paintings of Benjamin West* (New Haven, CT, 1986); H. Hoock, *Empires of the Imagination* (2010).
7 J. W. M. Hichberger, *Images of the Army* (Manchester, 1988), pp. 69–70.
8 C. Wood, *Victorian Painting* (1999), p. 352.
9 Hichberger, *Images of the Army*.
10 Hichberger, *Images of the Army*, p. 104.
11 F. Goodall, *The Reminiscences of Frederick Goodall R.A.* (1902), p. 181.
12 N. G. Slarke, *Frederick Goodall, R.A.* (Peterborough, 1981), p. 59.
13 Goodall, *Reminiscences*, pp. 181–2.
14 On the contemporary meanings of Gordon's death, see J. Wolffe, *Great Deaths: Religion and Nationhood in Victorian and Edwardian Britain* (Oxford, 2000), ch. 5.
15 Web resource: www.britishmuseum.org/research/search_the_collection_database/search_object_details.aspx?objectid=1601977&partid=1&searchText=general+gordon&numpages=10&orig=%2fresearch%2fsearch_the_collection_database.aspx&currentPage=1 [Accessed 14 July 2011].
16 G. W. Joy, *The Work of George W. Joy, with an Autobiographical Sketch* (1904), p. 22.
17 Joy, *Work of George W. Joy*, p. 13.
18 Joy, *Work of George W. Joy*, p. 21.
19 P. Harrington, *British Artists and War* (1993), pp. 264–5.
20 On Riou, see G. Gauthier, *Edouard Riou, dessinateur. Entre le* Tour du monde *et* Jules Verne: 1860–1900 (2008).
21 M. Heffernan, 'The cartography of the Fourth Estate: mapping the New Imperialism in British and French newspapers, 1875–1925', in J. R. Akerman (ed.), *The Imperial Map* (Chicago and London, 2009), pp. 261–99.
22 C. Bellanger, P. Guiral and F. Terrou (eds), *Histoire générale de la presse française* (1972), pp. 303–8.
23 On the celebrations of Marchand upon his return from Fashoda, see B. Sèbe, 'From Thoissey to the capital via Fashoda: Major Marchand, partisan icon of the Right in Paris', in J. Wardhaugh (ed.), *Paris and the Right in the Twentieth Century* (Cambridge, 2006), pp. 18–42.
24 Thanks to Rebecca Crites for drawing my attention to this source.
25 *The Graphic*, 14 February 1885.
26 Harrington, *British Artists*, pp. 223–7.
27 *Penny Illustrated Paper*, 4 April 1885.
28 *Illustrated London News*, 1 October 1898.
29 *Aberdeen Weekly Journal*, 11 January 1899.
30 *The Graphic*, 28 January 1899.

CONTEXTS

31 R. T. Stearn, 'War correspondents and colonial war c.1870-1900', in J. M. MacKenzie (ed.), *Popular Imperialism and the Military* (Manchester, 1992), p. 151.
32 A. Forbes, 'War correspondents and the authorities', *The Nineteenth Century*, 7 (1880), 190-1.
33 Stearn, 'War correspondents', p. 141.
34 I. Jeffrey, *Photography: A Concise History* (1981), pp. 62-4.
35 Scottish National Portrait Gallery, Edinburgh, NPG x128738, NPG x46623, NPG x76513, NPG x12934, NPG x32118, NPG Ax46283, NPG x32119, NPG x27584, NPG x45981 – all issued in 1872.
36 See Chapter 1 (pp. 63-4), as well as J. C. Hodson, *Lawrence of Arabia and American Culture* (Westport, CT, 1995). See also J. M. MacKenzie, 'T. E. Lawrence: the myth and the message', in R. Giddings (ed.), *Literature and Imperialism* (1991), pp. 150-81.
37 L. Poirier, *Charles de Foucauld et L'Appel du silence. Photographies du film* (1937).
38 L. Poirier, *24 images à la seconde* (1953), p. 243.
39 A copy of Poirier, *Charles de Foucauld*, printed in 1939 bears the statement '*110e mille*' on its front page (author's collection).
40 For an analysis of the racist connotations of advertising linked to the British empire, see A. Ramamurthy, *Imperial Persuaders: Images of Africa and Asia in British Advertising* (Manchester, 2003); A. McClintock, *Imperial Leather: Race, Gender and Sexuality in the Colonial Context* (New York and London, 1995), ch. 5. For the French case, see Blanchard and Chatelier (eds), *Images et colonies*, and Deroo and Lemaire, *L'Illusion coloniale*. For a case-study of the appeal of imperial products in the metropole, see J. Garrigues, *Banania, histoire d'une passion française* (1991).
41 *Illustrated London News*. The advert appeared thirteen times between 25 July 1885 and 24 December 1887, and three more times (but with a different layout) between 20 November 1897 and 15 January 1898.
42 Bovril advertisement, 1900, repr. in W. Hamish Fraser, *The Coming of the Mass Market, 1850–1914* (1981), plate 15.
43 J. Evans, *Alfred Leete* (Woodspring, 1985), pp. 10-11.
44 On Kitchener as a military hero, see K. Surridge, 'More than a great poster: Lord Kitchener and the image of the military hero', *Historical Research*, 74 (2001), 298-313.
45 MacKenzie, *David Livingstone*, p. 168.
46 MacKenzie, *Propaganda and Empire*, p. 23. The role of French postcards as a means of conveying an image of exotic sexuality has attracted much attention; see in particular M. Alloula, *Le Harem colonial: images d'un sous-érotisme* (Anglet, 2001); L. Sebbar and J.-M. Belorgey, *Femmes d'Afrique du Nord. Cartes postales (1885–1930)* (Saint-Pourçain-sur-Sioule, 2002); C. Taraud, *Mauresques. Femmes orientales dans la photographie coloniale, 1860–1910* (2003); R. J. Deroo, 'Colonial collecting: women and Algerian *cartes postales*', *Parallax*, 4:2 (1998), 145-57.
47 MacKenzie, *Propaganda and Empire*, p. 30.
48 Harrington, *British Artists*, p. 265.
49 Richards, *Imperialism and Music*, pp. 60-1.
50 On the image of Gordon as a Christian hero and his link with martyrdom, see K. E. Hendrickson, *Making Saints: Religion and the Public Image of the British Army, 1809–1885* (Madison, NJ, 1998), p. 15. Among popular biographies exploring this theme, A. Nutting, *Gordon of Khartoum: Martyr and Misfit* (1966) is probably the most obvious case.
51 See in particular *Lord Kitchener's Grand Parade March* (1896); *Kitchener! Patriotic Song* (1898); *Kitchener... Song, Words and Music* (1901), and between 1915 and 1916 *Britannia Has Call'd to Her Sons o'er the Seas: Kitchener's Host*; *Irish Song of K of K*; *Kitchener: Stand by Him!*; *The Kitchener Army Song Book*; *Kitchener's Boys*; *We All Trust Kitchener*; *Kitchener's Men*; *Kitchener's Prayer*; *Kitchener's Chaps*; *Kitchener's Question*; *The Immortal Kitchener*; *Kitchener's Army*; *Kitchener*; *Lord Kitchener*; *Lord Kitchener Song*.

52 A. Ruscio, 'Littérature, chansons et colonies', in P. Blanchard and S. Lemaire (eds), *Culture coloniale, 1871–1931* (2003), p. 78.
53 J. Blanchard, *Patriotisme* (Saint-Paul-Trois-Châteaux, 1884).
54 C. Val (lyrics), C. Bourdeau (music), *Brazza et le Congo* (undated).
55 Val and Bourdeau, *Brazza*, stanza 5.
56 L. Lelièvre (lyrics), Ben-Tayoux (music), *Fachoda ou la France en Afrique. Chanson patriotique* (1898).
57 A. Ruscio, *Que la France était belle au temps des colonies* (2001), pp. 129–33.
58 J. Grégoire (lyrics and music), *'Dédié aux Membres de la Mission Congo-Nil' – Le Commandant Marchand – Retour au Pays* (Châtillon sur Chalaronne, 1899).
59 M. Morphy, *Le Commandant Marchand et ses compagnons d'armes à travers l'Afrique* (1899), pp. 2227–39.
60 On the concept of 'circuit of culture', see P. Du Gay, S. Hall et al. (eds), *Doing Cultural Studies: The Story of Sony Walkman* (1997).
61 J. M. MacKenzie (ed.), *David Livingstone and the Victorian Encounter with Africa* (1996), p. 171.
62 P. J. Haythornthwaite, *The Colonial Wars Source Book* (1995), p. 348.
63 J. Richards, *Visions of Yesterday* (1973).
64 On French colonial documentary films, see P. J. Bloom, *French Colonial Documentary: Mythologies of Humanitarianism* (Minneapolis MN, 2008) and A. J. Murray Levine, *Framing the Nation: Documentary Film in Interwar France* (2010).
65 Q. Howe, *The News and How to Understand It* (New York, 1968), p. 40. On the impact of feature films on the audience, see A. Bott, 'A Yankee Captures London', in N. R. Bowen (ed.), *Lowell Thomas, The Stranger Everyone Knows* (New York, 1968), pp. 30–6.
66 R. McKibbin, *Classes and Cultures, England 1918–1951* (Oxford, 1998), p. 419.
67 J. Chapman and N. J. Cull, *Imperialism and Popular Cinema* (2009), p. 1.
68 C.-M. Bosséno, 'Le répertoire du grand écran. Le cinéma "par ailleurs"', in J.-P. Rioux and J.-F. Sirinelli (eds), *La Culture de masse en France de la Belle Epoque à aujourd'hui* (2002), pp. 157–219.
69 R. Low, *The History of the British Film* (1971), p. 47.
70 Bosséno, 'Répertoire'.
71 R. Smith, 'The development of British colonial film policy, 1927–1939', *Journal of African History*, 20:3 (1979), 437–50; A. Higson, *Waving the Flag: Constructing a National Cinema in Britain* (Oxford, 1995), p. 177.
72 S. Ungar, 'Léon Poirier's *L'Appel du silence* and the cult of imperial France', *Journal of Film Preservation*, 63 (2001), 41–6.
73 Quoted by M. Oms, 'L'imaginaire colonial au Cinéma', in Bancel, Blanchard and Chatelier, *Images et colonies*, pp. 103–7.
74 On the film itself, see D. Rapp and C. W. Weber, 'British film, Empire and society in the twenties: the "Livingstone" film, 1923–25', *Historical Journal of Film, Radio and Television*, 9:1 (1989), 3–17.
75 NLS, MS 7875, f. 124, description of the Livingstone Film project on letterhead 'The Livingstone Film Expedition' by J. Aubrey Rees, 10 November 1923.
76 Poirier, *24 images*, p. 236.
77 L. Poirier, *Pourquoi et comment je vais réaliser L'Appel du silence* (Paris and Tours, 1935), p. 35.
78 L. Poirier, *A la recherche d'autre chose* (1968), p. 294.
79 Poirier, *Pourquoi et comment...*
80 Poirier, *Charles de Foucauld, photographies du film*, p. 64.
81 Poirier, *Pourquoi et comment...*, Annex.
82 P. Boulanger, *Le Cinéma colonial de 'L'Atlantide' à 'Lawrence d'Arabie'* (1975), p. 124; D. H. Slavin, *Colonial Cinema and Imperial France, 1919–1939* (Baltimore and London, 2001), p. 47.
83 *Le Jour*, 15 July 1939.
84 *Le Matin*, 21 February 1940.
85 *Le Journal de Roubaix*, 17 February 1940.

CONTEXTS

86 Ungar, *Cult of Imperial France*. Slavin argues in *Colonial Cinema*, p.220, that 'the film has become a cult classic for contemporary France's racist Right', which seems at least to over-estimate the modern reputation of the film, which has almost fallen into oblivion among the general public. Writing in 1975, Boulanger thought that it remained 'touching in spite of its evident wrinkles' (p.124).
87 AN, Eydoux papers, 546 AP 11, Bartel-Noirot, *Atlantide Prix modérés, d'un bord à l'autre du Sahara*, p.24.
88 Slavin, *Colonial cinema*, p.170.
89 T. Ferenczi, *L'Invention du journalisme en France* (1993), p.47.

PART II

Uses

CHAPTER 4

Imperial heroes and domestic politics

The first part of this book demonstrated that the fundamental changes European societies witnessed during the Industrial Revolution had far-reaching consequences for hero-making processes: they created conditions propitious to the appearance of a new type of hero. Imperial heroes had the opportunity to become more present in everyday life (through statues, official tributes, street naming etc.) and more commercially attractive, thanks to a self-sustaining and self-fuelling phenomenon that saw the odds of success for heroic reputations increase dramatically over the period. Africa, imperial expansion and colonial conquerors became more appealing to an increasingly literate and educated public. But the consequences of this trend encouraged by capitalist strategies went far beyond the realm of entertainment: crucially, this growing audience became more aware politically.

The British and French public went through distinct phases, but in both cases the entry of imperial heroes into public space loaded them with political value for several reasons. First, their action resulted from, and at the same time influenced, general policies that were meant to evaluate, serve and defend national interests in a context of heightened international competition, well exemplified by the surge of 'New Imperialism'. This is particularly significant if we agree with the appraisal that places imperialism, alongside the welfare state, among the major factors of change of the British political system.[1] Secondly, their names were meaningful to many segments of population that politicians were likely to address, and the temptation to use them as arguments in political speech was difficult to resist. In particular, colonial propagandists were aware that imperial heroes, whose stories generally flattered national pride, could help them promote a pro-imperial agenda. They anticipated the often-overlooked link between 'the domain of politics and entertainment' which has been identified, for a later period, in the case of celebrities.[2] In some instances, such

USES

as General Gordon or Major Marchand, imperial heroes became major subjects of national debate in a context of heated political controversy. Politicians in opposition did not resist the temptation to use them against the ruling party or the political regime, which they accused of betraying the true interest of the country, conveniently embodied by the heroes whom the government had failed to support. The reputation of imperial heroes could be used as a means of promoting a political vision, to influence governmental decisions, or to enhance the popularity of a party: to a large extent, the rise to fame of imperial heroes reflected the advent of a phenomenon that has been called elsewhere 'populist democracy'.[3]

The rise to prominence of imperial heroes was one of the many variables in the ever-changing landscape of national politics, which in turn shaped their meaning and relevance as arguments to be used in the political arena. Historical contextualization is key to our understanding of the place of imperial heroes in domestic politics, and this chapter distinguishes between four major types of politically influential hero, which roughly follow each other chronologically (with a few overlaps). First came the *indirect promoter of expansion*, of the early years of 'New Imperialism', with figures such as David Livingstone or Mgr Lavigerie, who did not expand the British and French empires themselves, but whose action contributed to their formal development. Second was the *direct promoter of expansion*, product and actor of the peak of 'New Imperialism', best represented by Pierre Savorgnan de Brazza or Cecil Rhodes, who played an active role in creating or expanding British and French possessions in Africa. The two decades between the 1880s and the 1900s saw the *hero used as political argument*, best exemplified by General Gordon or Major Jean-Baptiste Marchand, who were used by opposition parties to win over the electorate by attempting to show through their example the supposed incompetence of the government in power. The last figure to emerge was the *proconsul turned hero*, essentially post-1900, with the Sirdar Kitchener, Marshal Lyautey and to a far lesser extent Lord Lugard (who never became a truly popular figure), who embodied the slow shift from conquest to administration.

To set the scene, it is important to remember that the political cultures of the two countries underwent deep changes which mirrored those of the industrial revolution. Although popularity had already been turned into political advantage by Pitt the Elder in the eighteenth century in spite of the inability of the people to have an impact on the conduct of politics, the influence and weight of public opinion became more mechanical with the extension of franchise which the two countries experienced in the nineteenth century.[4] Better education improved the population's ability to grasp political issues; politicans perceived that they were more accountable to the public. This growing influence of public opinion on ruling elites led Lord Salisbury to confide to Lord Cromer that 'it is easier to combat with the rinderpest or the cholera than with a popular sentiment'.[5] For his part, the French ambassador to London Paul Cambon recognized in a letter to Delcassé that even a common decision such as tariff reform depended upon 'the state of French public opinion'.[6] From the Revolution of February 1848 onwards, public space and political opinion became more closely intertwined in France, giving public opinion its modern sense in politics.[7]

The press was a major promoter of change, building its growing success on the willingness of the public to become more involved in national affairs, which implied to be better informed. The 'scandal of the decorations' which cost his job to the first President of the Third Republic, Jules Grévy, or the Panama Canal scandal of the autumn 1892, clearly showed that the press was emerging as a powerful fourth power. When Marchand was born, under the Second Empire, journalists censored themselves tightly so as to avoid the risk of being given a 'warning', as the third of such warnings led to the disappearance of the newspaper. Twenty years later, under the Third Republic, the 1881 law guaranteed complete freedom of the press: a new era had begun. The evolution was comparable in the United Kingdom; Gladstone's decision to send General Gordon to Khartoum was a good example of what the Earl of Cromer called 'newspaper government'.[8]

In spite of a similar rise of the fourth power (which cannot be separated from the success of 'print capitalism'), the political situation of the two countries differed significantly. The British system, which gave pre-eminence to Parliament over king, had existed for nearly two centuries, in stark contrast to the double political instability that the French constantly experienced (instability of systems of government since the Revolution, and instability of governments under the Third Republic). The Third Republic lacked legitimacy as it had been set up by a series of 'constitutional laws' instead of a proper constitution. The 'Wallon amendment' establishing formally, in just one sentence, a republic and the function of president, had been passed with a majority of one. The regime was called by its detractors *'la Gueuse'* (the slut), and had to face during its first decades of existence international isolation, political unrest and constant controversies as to how France could maintain its status as a world power after the defeat of 1870. On the other hand, Victorian Britain was prosperous under the guidance of the longest-serving monarch in its history, and was by far the first power in the world. For Britain, the colonial question was linked to the preservation of its commercial and world supremacy (which became dangerously threatened after the First World War), while France struggled to regain its status, and was unsure about the best course of action, toying for a long time with the ideas of an *entente* with Germany, a *rapprochement* with Britain or an overseas expansion that would certainly alienate the two.

Furthermore, the way in which the British and French parliaments worked differed. If the life of the British Parliament was mainly marked by the antagonism between Conservatives and Liberals, the French political landscape was much more fragmented and unstable as a result of ever-changing alliances (which were reflected in governments being regularly voted out of office by the same legislature). Some form of parliamentary co-operation was achieved through all-party *commissions parlementaires*. Although, as C. M. Andrew and A. S. Kanya-Forstner have demonstrated, the *Groupe colonial* was predominantly moderate Republican, it also included members ranging from the *Légitimistes* to the *Radicaux* and the *Socialistes*.[9] All in all, between the 1880s and decolonization, the colonial question crossed party lines and generated many political twists and turns, with the Left and the Right alternately defending the principle of colonial expansion (though the reasons to support or oppose colonialism varied each time).[10] This difference in the nature and organization of political fault lines in Britain and in France influenced considerably the ways in which the reputations of imperial heroes could be used for political purposes.

Naturally, the two countries had a different political agenda most of the time (except when they were at odds with each other, somewhat paradoxically making bilateral relations a common preoccupation). Electoral reform and Irish Home Rule dominated the British political scene in the last two decades of the nineteenth century, while France was marked by the Boulangist crisis (1887–89), the Panama scandal (early 1890s), the anarchist unrest (mid-1890s), and above all the Dreyfus affair (1894–1906), which further developed nationalist agitation.

Although British and French imperial heroes were set against such different backdrops, and the nature, reputation and claimed objectives of these figures varied notably, they had in common that the meaning associated with their names gave them an unquestionable value on the political scene. Their role and significance evolved as colonial developments took place in Africa, and their fame was used to different ends depending on the period.

David Livingstone represents the first instance of an imperial hero who had an impact upon political decisions – as an indirect promoter of expansion. As J. MacKenzie has shown, Livingstone's action and reputation significantly influenced the establishment of European colonies in East and Central Africa: not only did he promote the anti-slavery cause among the European public but he also directly inspired the action of several actors of the Scramble for Africa in the region, such as Sir Bartle Frere, Sir Harry Johnston, John Smith Moffat and the Revd John Mackenzie.[11] Following the success of his *Missionary Travels* (1857), David Livingstone used his newly acquired iconic status to promote several ideas which he feared were not popular enough in Britain. Beyond the abolition of the slave trade, he advocated the benevolence of free trade in Africa, white emigration to the continent (he himself had shown the example) and the promotion of technology in less advanced African societies. Together with missionary action (which he called for), all these projects had clear political implications of which he was fully aware.

The growth of the Livingstone myth in the following decades, notably under the impulse of Sir Roderick Murchison and the Revd Horace Waller, who pruned the *Last Journals* quite considerably in an attempt to present an idealized and simplified version of Livingstone, significantly helped popularize, and entrench among the European public, the belief that Europe had the duty to intervene in Africa: 'Livingstone's impact on the course of history in Africa was immense', not so much 'from the impact of personal contacts which he made with African groups and individuals while in their territories, but from the impact his character and way of life made in Europe'.[12] Facing Victorian ministers cautious about embarking upon expensive colonial projects, pro-imperial lobbyists sought the support of public opinion as a means of exciting parliamentary zeal. As John Darwin has argued, 'foreign policy could easily be derailed by a press campaign or an appeal to patriotic prejudices', and this could mean more empire if the appropriate arguments were put forward.[13] In her study of the making (and pruning) of the *Last Journals*, Dorothy Helly came to the conclusion that Waller protected Livingstone's fame 'in order to use that fame as the basis for an anti-slavery crusade in East Africa – as he believed Livingstone would have wished him to do'.[14] Waller and his successors made full use of the evocative power of the Livingstone legend in support of British imperial intervention in tropical Africa (notably in Nyasaland and on the East African coast), where, according to the *Oxford Dictionary of National Biography* entry, it 'redeemed the colonial project'.[15]

The same Waller was also a fervent admirer of General Gordon, whom he was eager to praise to his correspondents. Writing to the vice-consul of Zanzibar Sir John Kirk in 1880, Sir William MacKinnon, founder of the East Africa Company, acknowledged that Horace Waller 'had told [him] everything' about Gordon.[16] Waller worked closely with Gordon to eradicate the slave trade in East Africa, and presumably felt he could make the most of the General's well-established reputation. Gordon was already well known when he came back from China in late 1864: in 1865, a British officer described Gordon to a correspondent as 'the man of whom you may have read in articles headed "China"',[17] and the Italian explorer Romolo Gessi, in his *Seven Years in the Soudan*, mentioned that 'Colonel Gordon was known to all Europe by his campaign in China, so that in England, to distinguish him from other Gordons, he was called "Chinese" Gordon'.[18] Unsurprisingly, Waller was very interested in using this extremely evocative figure, who was 'a totem of the cult of the Christian military hero in the mid-1860s' and who was widely believed to have shown a strong commitment to the anti-slavery cause while performing the role of governor-general of the Sudanese province of Equatoria.[19]

But Waller was not the only anti-slavery crusader who used Gordon to promote a cause that had political implications. The fourth biographical book on 'Chinese Gordon', *Life of Chinese Gordon* (published in 1884), was written by the Secretary of the British and Foreign Anti-Slavery Society, C. H. Allen. It was designed to reach the widest possible audience (recommended retail price one penny), and met with notable success: the copy available at the Bodleian Library in Oxford reads on the top left corner '300th thousand'. Although he was still only 'Chinese Gordon' (as opposed to 'Gordon of Khartoum', who will be studied below), Charles Gordon was consciously used by anti-slavery campaigners, who hoped to wrest direct intervention against the slave traders out of the British government. Ultimately, his reputation and exemplarity reinforced the arguments of colonial advocates. It is therefore arguable that both David Livingstone and Charles Gordon had an impact upon British foreign policy in the 1870s, as they raised awareness of the slave trade problem in Africa among both decision makers and the public, and the latter exerted extra pressure upon the former so that direct action was taken, which was conducive to imperial expansion.

The hero himself could sometimes disagree with the use made of his reputation. Gordon was aware that Waller was capitalizing on his name, and he asked him to 'kindly keep my property, viz my name out of any letters you may write to the papers'.[20] Gordon was also critical about the work of the Anti-Slavery Society, writing to Waller '*I do not believe in you all*, you say this, and that, and you do not do it.'[21] These protests did not prevent Waller or other anti-slavery campaigners from using his legend to serve their cause.

Although the French did not have an exact equivalent to Livingstone, who performed the role of explorer, missionary and promoter of the anti-slavery cause, and whose reputation ultimately contributed to political decisions of annexation, Charles-Martial Allemand-Lavigerie (1825–92), Archbishop of Algiers (1867–92) and Carthage (1884–92), had a political influence in France in the 1880s that bore similarities to Livingstone's and made him a French 'indirect promoter of expansion'. The founder of the Society of Missionaries of Africa (or 'White Fathers') and the Missionary Sisters of Our Lady of Africa (the 'White Sisters'), Lavigerie was given in 1868 by Pope Pius IX the task of evangelizing the Sahara and the French Sudan. Not only did Lavigerie generate numerous vocations among religious priests who in turn made the White Fathers and Sisters a force to be reckoned with, he also personally took a leading part in the promotion of the imperial idea in a country that was doubtful about colonial expansion and where anti-clerical feelings were growing.

Lavigerie showed an evident talent for real-world action alongside religious concerns when, still a young prelate, he took part in the organization and delivery of relief to Maronite Christians following the massacres perpetrated by the Druzes in the Ottoman Empire in 1860. The successful implementation of the co-operation between the *Œuvre des écoles d'Orient* and the French Government in Lebanon and Syria won him nomination as the French Auditor of the Roman Rota in 1861. Although his promotion to the bishopric of Nancy in 1862 seemed to pave the way for a very traditional religious career in metropolitan France, Lavigerie's vocation returned to the Muslim world when Marshal MacMahon, then Governor-General of Algeria, offered him the See of Algiers in November 1866. This appointment was to turn Lavigerie into a religious imperial hero with a significant political influence in France and abroad.

The action of the new Archbishop of Algiers soon took a political turn, when he opposed the French government's scheme to segregate the indigenous people of Algeria from French and Christian influence. A firm advocate of the restoration of Christianity in North Africa, Lavigerie believed in the complementarity of Church proselytism and French colonial expansion. By advocating an openly assimilationist policy that included the conversion of the Muslim populations to Christianity, Lavigerie challenged the traditional attitude of the *Bureaux arabes*, who, under both Louis-Philippe and Napoleon III, sought to prevent any apostolic activity in French-administered Algeria to avoid clashes with indigenous beliefs.[22] Indeed, when Napoleon III ordered Lavigerie to conform to the governmental line, he had already launched a vast press campaign that won him wide public support in France and among Europeans in Algeria. Newspapers favourable to his cause included the moderate Catholic *Le Journal des villes et des campagnes*, the Ultramontanist Catholic *Le Monde* and *L'Univers* and the legitimist *La Gazette de France* as well as *La Patrie* and, to a certain extent, *Le Siècle*. An observer of the time, Countess de Las Cases, reported that it was evident that public opinion supported Lavigerie, confirming that the Bishop of Algiers had already become a public figure in France.[23]

Yet Lavigerie's influence went far beyond the mere relation between France, the Church and the Muslim populations of Algeria. A few years later, the Third Republic having replaced the Second Empire, he sought to expand French influence over Tunisia against Italian interests. From 1873 onwards, he used to that purpose the St Louis Chapel of Carthage, the custody of which had been granted to the White Fathers upon his request to the Vatican. This policy of episcopal control prior to military and political conquest greatly facilitated the establishment of the French protectorate over Tunisia in 1881 and, more importantly, played a significant role in making the Tunisian venture accepted by a French public opinion always reluctant to embark upon expensive colonial campaigns.[24] The true significance of this achievement is highlighted when one remembers that Ferry's great-niece acknowledged that in 1880 her great-uncle's colonial policy was supported by neither public nor parliamentarian opinion.[25] Prime Minister Jules Ferry and the political director of the Foreign Ministry also regularly sought Lavigerie's advice during the French operations in Tunisia.[26] Lavigerie's promotion of the French conquest of Tunisia is better understood in the light of one of the Cardinal's statements:

> The true civilizer, the only effectual preacher at this present time [1880–1881], is the action of events which change the political aspects of the country. Unwittingly, unwillingly even, our Commandants, our soldiers are the chief factors in this change. They represent force, and force to the Mussulman [sic] is the hand of God.[27]

Curiously, this role was contrary to what Lavigerie advocated publicly in 1883, when he warned that missionaries were about to find themselves, in the centre of Africa, 'at the heart of competitions, divisions, passions, often justified, of all nations engaged in quarrels that will shape the future of Africa', and that they should 'never side with any political cause' as the 'only interest they ought to support [was] faith and humanity'.[28] Confronted with the realities of contemporary struggles, the Cardinal had to make some exceptions: he accepted to play a political role when his designs required him to do so.

Africa south of the Sahara was the next region on which Lavigerie set his sights. In 1878–79, Lavigerie had sent two groups of White Fathers to Central Africa, where they founded missions around lakes Nyanza-Victoria and Tanganyika. After a pause, the third contingent to East Africa, in 1881, was more successful and the Catholic mission in Central Africa took root. Subsequently receiving alarming reports from his missionaries, Lavigerie made the fight against the slave trade a priority. He endeavoured to continue Livingstone's crusade by raising awareness of the extent of the slave trade in Africa, and called for an international Armed Brotherhood, modelled on the Knights of St John, designed to fight slave traders. He campaigned with the utmost energy to promote his views, notably in Paris and London in the late 1880s.[29] He convinced Pope Leo XIII to include a long reference to the horrors of the African slave trade in his encyclical *In Plurimis* of May 1888 published on the occasion of the abolition of slavery in Brazil. An early biographer of the prelate argued that '[Lavigerie] stirred public opinion worldwide and, through it, stirred the Powers. He founded anti-slavery committees and organised congresses.'[30]

His fight against slavery made Lavigerie an ever more prominent figure in France, in the international anti-slavery circles and in Europe in general. He used his fame to support his call for direct French or European intervention in Africa. In an 1888 lecture in Brussels, Lavigerie openly defended European paramountcy in Africa as a means of putting an end to the slave trade, and wished his advice had been followed:

> In my past lectures in France and in England, [...] I limited myself to exposing my principal opinion, namely that European governments have the duty to suppress the slave trade, in this Africa that they have seized, and that it is only because of their inefficiency that we have to use private associations.[31]

Lavigerie was also aware that public opinion was a powerful means of forcing governments into action, as he stated in the same lecture that 'my first call is to [public] opinion. It is the Queen of the world. Soon or later, it forces all powers to follow her and to obey her.'[32] His views were even more clearly explained in a private memorandum:

> In every country, those in power, however absolute their authority, must respond to public opinion when this is active and persistent. And opinion in turn will respond to those who are prepared to devote themselves to the service of what is just. [...] Our principal task is to arouse a contagious pity in the hearts of the public by spreading knowledge of facts. Once we have won the public conscience, the rest will follow. When we have convinced the people of Europe and touched their hearts, we shall have raised an army sure of victory. Political leaders will do what public opinion orders them to do.[33]

It is therefore not surprising that Lavigerie relentlessly sought to stir public opinion. In a sermon he preached at the church of St Sulpice in Paris, on 1 July 1888, Lavigerie called for public opinion to influence government action in Central Africa. Dorothy Helly considered that Lavigerie 'successfully caught the public attention'[34] which is understandable since, at his own request, his speech was reported in the secular as well as the Catholic press – with the sole exception of Radical newspapers.[35] Such a role made him a key political player as he endeavoured to bend the policies of European governments and actively encouraged the French government into action in Tunisia and elsewhere in Africa.

Beyond his role as a colonial propagandist, Cardinal Lavigerie exerted a broader influence on internal politics, always keeping an eye on the often thorny relations between the Church and the French State. For the 1885 general elections, Lavigerie published in the French press a call to Catholics urging them to vote against anti-clerical candidates; the conservatives improved their score by two million votes, which indicates that the Cardinal's words had had an echo.[36] Lavigerie also worked to bridge the growing gulf between the Vatican and the increasingly anti-clerical Third Republic. Famously, he encouraged French Catholics to end their boycott of the Republican government, an idea that culminated in the famous 'toast of Algiers' ('the most formidable act of [his] life') on 12 November 1890, when he seized the opportunity of a visit to Algiers of the Admiral of the French Mediterranean Fleet to express the *ralliement* of French Catholics to the Republic.[37] The evidence gathered above confirms that Lavigerie 'influenced the direction of affairs in the Church and in French politics' in the late nineteenth century, in a way that was even more assertive than Livingstone's in mid-nineteenth-century Britain.[38]

If both David Livingstone and Cardinal Lavigerie consciously developed and used a heroic status in order to promote the anti-slavery cause (to the extent to which it could induce formal imperial expansion), and therefore exemplified imperial heroes who made indirectly a case for imperial expansion, in other instances colonial heroes could directly bring their popularity into play to expand their country's empire, playing the role of direct promoters of expansion. During the second of a series of three expeditions to the Ogoué River that won him fame in France, the Italian-born explorer Pierre Savorgnan de Brazza concluded, on behalf of the French government (but without the Chambers' prior consent and without any official role to justify his signing the document), a protectorate treaty with the Congolese King Makoko, founding the future French colony of the Congo, north of Stanley Pool. The initial reluctance of the French Chambers to approve the treaties of protectorate was overcome by the combined effect of the widespread frustration felt in France at the successful British unilateral intervention in Egypt and, above all, by the charisma displayed by Brazza on the occasion of a remarkably effective public relations campaign. Brazza's highly publicized confrontation with Stanley at the Paris Stanley Club, on 21 October 1882, combined with a vigorous lobbying effort led by former Premier Léon Gambetta and his Republican friends, won Parliament over to the cause of the French Congo.[39] Brazza's ability to stir public opinion about his exploits, and the ensuing popular interest in Central Africa, proved to be decisive factors. The newspaper *Le Rappel* admired the fact that he had 'united the press behind his work, in a truly patriotic unanimity, above personal rivalries'.[40] Beyond lobbying geographical societies, the press, and the Chambers, Brazza sent a detailed report to the Minister of Marine Jauréguiberry, making his case for a French colony in the Congo.[41]

Upon his return to France from his first expedition, in December 1878, Brazza had been fêted all over Paris, and 'newspapers and politicians had made him the man of the hour', notably because he was seen as the French answer to Stanley's successful exploration from East Africa to the Congo mouth.[42] He had used his nationwide fame in the newspapers (which he sustained and constantly expanded through articles, lectures, face-to-face meetings and even romantic photographs of him in explorer's dress) to fund his second expedition.[43] He already had several high-level advocates, including the Education minister and colonial lobbyist Jules Ferry (under the premiership of Waddington, Freycinet and himself) who, according to Brazza, told him 'Go on. Never restrain your freedom of action. If you succeed, we will support you.'[44] Brazza followed Ferry's advice. He signed these pivotal treaties with King Makoko just before Stanley had had time to reach the north bank of Stanley Pool, and before Leopold II had managed to obtain the recall of the French explorer through the intercession of Ferdinand de Lesseps, the brain behind the Suez Canal and the Chairman of the French committee of the *Association internationale africaine*, who actually spied and manoeuvred for the benefit of the Belgian king. Brazza bitterly resented Leopold II's attempt to outmanoeuvre him (Brazza had declined an earlier offer of collaboration), and this disgruntlement led him to state quite clearly his own political agenda:

> I believed that there was a political idea beneath the humanitarian sentiments of the King of the Belgians. I was far from blaming him for this, but it did not stop me from having my own political idea as well. And mine was rather simple. If there was an advantage in taking hold of the Congo, I would rather have the French flag flying on it than the 'international' Belgian one.[45]

For Brazza, the Makoko treaties were only a step towards grander designs in the Congo area, and he fully realized the potential influence of his speeches upon his return from the second expedition. When the *Société de géographie de Paris* invited him to give a speech at the *Grand amphithéâtre* of the Sorbonne to an audience that Brazza described as 'a scientific elite', he did not fail to make his case for the ratification of the treaties he had signed on behalf of France, and for the construction of a railway line in the Congo. He ended his speech with a vibrant appeal to decision makers:

> You will lend our project the support of your influence, if you think that it may serve the interests of our motherland while serving the causes of science and civilization! And as far as I am concerned, the greatest honour you could grant me would be to tell me: 'Go ahead!'.[46]

The 'great man of whom everyone talked about those days', and his friends and followers, cashed in on this successes and led a powerful press campaign.[47] Stressing Brazza's pacifism, they sought to lobby the government for funds for a third expedition, the *Mission de l'ouest africain*. The explorer reported to the Senate, where he urged 'Let us not neglect the opportunity that is offered to us, namely to secure at little cost a huge outlet for our trade and industry'.[48] Fully aware of the role they could play, journalists contributed to the development of the hero's legend when they felt it worthwhile or necessary. The son of the editor and owner of *Le Phare de la Loire* wrote to Brazza on the off-chance, after having assured him that his newspaper 'had done its best to be useful to you as soon as you came back [from your second expedition]':

> What I wanted to know from you, rather than from one of your friends, was how the newspaper could help you while you are away, what was the overall direction to follow in order to serve your designs, which I feel are patriotic and beautiful. I also wanted to ask you to let us know what you would like the public to know while you are away.[49]

The sheer popularity and intellectual stature of Brazza could easily give colonial propaganda more credibility. Approaching Brazza further to a meeting at the house of the prominent politician and journalist Joseph Reinach, the editor-in-chief of the *Revue bleue, Revue politique et littéraire*, Alfred Rambaud, sought from the explorer an article on his expedition in the Congo, and above all, 'a statement *ex professo* of twenty pages for [his] *France coloniale*' as a substitute for a similar article written by one Dubreuil de Rheims: the editor obviously judged that Brazza's fame would give more weight to his views.[50] Such an approach was far from exceptional. The Political Director of the *Moniteur des colonies et des pays de protectorat* wrote to the explorer:

IMPERIAL HEROES AND DOMESTIC POLITICS

> We are delighted to count among our subscribers the *Commissaire général de la République au Congo* and his main assistants.
> You can count on our help for the difficult patriotic task which you have accepted to lead. We would welcome with the utmost interest all notes and communications which you would be kind enough to send us from Africa.[51]

Brazza's reputation was seen as a powerful means of promoting the imperial idea, which gave his reputation political value at a time when colonial expansion remained controversial. Even if colonial questions did not rank high on electoral pamphlets, propaganda crystallized around Brazza's figure: his becoming a household name had political implications concerning future colonial policies.

Brazza himself enjoyed various contacts with leading politicians of the time such as Jules Ferry, Léon Gambetta or Charles de Freycinet.[52] The future socialist leader Jean Jaurès even happily referred to Brazza, declaring that 'in the Congo, M. de Brazza could cross vast expanses of territories and warlike tribes without a single shot fired, because he knew how to be loved'.[53] A colonial publicist remarked that for the first time in French contemporary history, 'all political parties from the far right to the far left have been filled with enthusiasm for the same cause [i.e. Brazza's]'.[54] Brazza also had a wide range of contacts through the Masons, whom he joined at the end of his life. His letter of application stated his views about his role:

> I had been working for a long time to promote peace, civilization and progress in the Congo, when a pamphlet from the *Grand Orient de France* fell in my hands. The similarity between the ideal of fraternity and tolerance that was advocated and my own aspirations struck me, and that was the reason why I asked to be admitted among you.[55]

Brazza's appealing image as a tactful conqueror who knew how to be loved by Africans was again used when the Gaud-Toqué scandal drew media attention to colonial abuse in the French Congo. President Loubet, quickly followed by the Minister of the Colonies Clémentel, decided at once to dispatch Brazza to the Congo in order to inquire into the concessionnal regime established in the colony: the political weight carried by Brazza's legend was such that both hoped that his reputation would protect their administration.[56] Brazza's enquiry into systematic abuse of indigenous populations in the French Congo was cut short by his death, which his wife (who accompanied him) attributed to poisoning organized by the many colonial interests which were threatened by the explorer's humanitarian concerns. Regardless of the circumstances, his death gave rise to official celebrations which enshrined his status as a national figure.[57] In the subsequent decades, his legend remained a powerful argument when it came to public debate. When in 1911 France ceded to Germany two substantial triangles of Congolese territory in exchange for a free hand in Morocco, opponents to the scheme made ample use of references to Brazza to justify their hostility to the agreement, and some of them even publicized his widow's protest against the scheme to strengthen their case.[58]

In spite of his Italian origins, Brazza was one of the few French heroes who crossed partisan lines and generally appealed to the metropolitan population as a whole. By contrast, the power of attraction of most of the other French cases studied in this book depended more on political sensitivities. Brazza seems to owe this unique appeal to the multiple meanings of his action and personality. In the first place, his contribution to the expansion of the French empire delighted colonial partisans. Having successfully repelled Belgian ambitions unpalatably embodied by an 'Anglo-Saxon' (Stanley) flattered the national ego, and therefore blurred the boundary between monarchists and republicans. His action as liberator of slaves made him a symbol of the benevolence of French values and chimed well in Catholic circles. Last but not least, his reputedly peaceful methods of conquest appealed to the least militarist classes of society, and reflected positively upon the image of the young Republic and its prestige among non-Europeans. In short, this sort of 'African and colonial Boulangism' (comparable to the sudden popularity of General Boulanger in the late 1880s) matched the expectations of those who believed that 'a wounded France' needed those 'individuals who could embody the rebirth of its hopes,' as a French journalist later remarked.[59] Brazza's reputation as a 'pacific conqueror' outlived him and even became a hallmark of the Brazza legend in the interwar years.[60] The peaceful dimension of his legend was fervently defended by his widow, who assiduously defended the image of this 'noble figure of the explorer and the administrator, whose [territorial] conquest did not spill the blood of those whom he had conquered'.[61] By many accounts, Brazza embodied the ideal type of the well-rounded imperial hero whose image was attractive to many constituencies, making him not only a unifying figure but also a powerful promotional tool for many causes. In short, an inherently political animal.

While Brazza was laying the foundations of the French Congo, a few thousand miles further south a young imperialist from Hertfordshire came to 'lead the commercial interests in Cape politics'[62] and used his fortune, gained in diamond mining, to promote the cause of British expansion in southern Africa: Cecil John Rhodes, 'great Victorian, maker and breaker of empires, conspirator and educator',[63] revealed 'himself as a man of consummate political skill'.[64] His achievements make him the British equivalent to Savorgnan de Brazza as a 'direct promoter of imperial expansion', even if he was less consensual than his French counterpart and was an astute political and financial strategist more than a physical hero.

As two of his biographers remarked, Rhodes's interest 'in the wider political scene never flagged'.[65] His ultimate design was to paint large portions of the map red, to propagate the Anglo-Saxon race and to federate the British empire, according to the authors of what has been often considered the 'official' biography of the magnate.[66] In his first confession of faith and will of 1877, Rhodes demonstrated clear political ambitions, since he advocated the 'absorption of the greater portion of the world under [the Anglo-Saxon] rule' and promised to contribute to the fulfilment of this wish.[67] When, later, W. T. Stead sought his views on life and politics, Rhodes just sent him his second confession of faith and will.[68]

Rhodes has been extensively studied and there is no need to dwell in detail upon his political achievements, or on the political consequences of his actions, which are well known.[69] However, some of his most revealing decisions are worth being remembered here. It is Rhodes himself who persuaded in 1887 High Commissioner Sir Hercules Robinson that the territory north of the Limpopo had to be included in the British sphere of influence: he inaugurated his tactic of combining local initiative with official backing in order to extend the British empire in South Africa.[70] The association between the High Commissioner and the diamond magnate was characterized by the Revd John Mackenzie (1835–99) as 'a sort of political and administrative firm'.[71] Even more significantly, Rhodes seized the opportunity to create six new seats in the Cape Parliament and to become a member of this Parliament for Barkly West from 1881. He used this position to voice diamond mining interests, in particular as chairman of the select committee that framed the Diamond Trade Act of 1882. Rhodes rose to become Prime Minister of the Cape Colony from July 1890 until January 1896, thanks to the somewhat surprising support of the Afrikaner Bond, which allowed him to reconcile the opposites and ensured him steady support from the Cape Afrikaners in spite of his English descent. He even secured Afrikaner approval for his scheme for northern expansion at the expense of their kith and kin in the Transvaal. During his premiership, Rhodes showed a contempt for opposition such that he thought it possible, when necessary, to persuade dissenting Members of Parliament by distributing shares of the British South Africa Company to them.[72] Through his shrewd manoeuvring, Rhodes ensured that an unlikely alliance between the Cape Liberals and the Afrikaner Bond worked in power. Rhodes's political power reached its zenith in February 1895, when he was sworn on to the Privy Council on the nomination of Lord Rosebery. Although his prestige was tarnished when his link to the Jameson Raid was proved, he found an opportunity to bounce back with his successful handling of the Ndebele and Shona uprisings of 1896, which won him back part of his respectability. The nomination of the equally enthusiastic imperialist Alfred Milner as British High Commissioner in 1897 also facilitated his rehabilitation.

Although Rhodes regarded certain colonies (such as Southern Rhodesia) as his own, and did not intend to favour direct British imperial annexation of them, his action remained marked by a constant willingness to expand the British empire and what he called in his first will 'the Anglo-Saxon race'. In the last analysis, there is some truth in asserting that 'if Rhodes had never lived, the [1899–1902] Boer War might never have taken place', and South Africa might have not fallen under total British paramountcy.[73] In his last will, Rhodes also endowed the Rhodes Trust to promote the imperial ethos among gifted young scholars, and he left money specifically for political purposes, including the creation of a pro-imperial political party. Following his pivotal contribution to the absorption of the South African subcontinent into the British empire, Rhodes's posthumous legend put the emphasis on his political promotion of imperial expansion and Anglo-Saxon supremacy. He certainly appears as the most vocal and forceful representative of the 'direct promoters of expansion'.

Both Brazza and Rhodes used their popularity, contacts and power to promote formal annexations, exemplifying the type of imperial hero who was fully aware of his political weight and intended to use it to its full potential. In other instances, imperial heroes could be used by politicians to serve their own purposes. The willingness of the hero himself was optional, and they were not actively involved in the processes that gave political value to their reputations. General Gordon exemplified the 'hero used as political argument', even if he himself was far from being a born politician: Winston Churchill once remarked 'there is no doubt that Gordon as a political figure was absolutely hopeless. He was so erratic, capricious, utterly unreliable, his mood changed so often, his temper was abominable, he was frequently drunk.'[74] Paradoxically, an officer who had no interest or talent in politics ended up taking a major stake in the British political scene in the mid-1880s. His case shows the way in which a heroic reputation could serve purposes that the hero himself would have been in no position to promote.

General Gordon's fatal mission to the Sudan was decided by the Gladstone government as a result of the national press campaign sparked by W. T. Stead's interview with Gordon published on the front cover of the *Pall Mall Gazette* on 9 January 1884 under the title

'Chinese Gordon for the Soudan' – a heading that 'became a catch-phrase and also a brand which ignited a forest fire'.[75] The following day, the *Pall Mall Gazette* declared that 'most of the leading papers in town and country reprint the report of our interview with Chinese Gordon, which is the subject of universal comment'.[76] Stead's son later reported his father's flattering opinion of himself when it came to his contribution to Sudanese (and British) politics:

> Since Mordecai the Jew was led in triumph through the streets of Shushan, there surely but seldom has been so sudden an alteration in human fortunes. But yesterday not a minister would even do Gordon the honour of asking his counsel. To-day he is the master of the situation – the virtual Sovereign of the Soudan.[77]

Stead Jr boasted that his father had 'succeeded in compelling the Government to send out General Gordon, believing that it was shameful on our part to proclaim the abandonment of the country and to take no adequate steps to secure the safe retirement of the abandoned garrisons'.[78] W. T. Stead used the already established fame of 'Chinese Gordon', former leader of the 'Ever-Victorious Army', to force Gladstone's hand. He consciously worked towards the blossoming of the new legend of 'Gordon to the Sudan', which became 'Gordon of Khartoum' in the following months and proved to be much more enduring than its 'Chinese' prototype. Although Stead had not yet propounded the 'government by journalism' facet of the 'New Journalism', the case of General Gordon was a clear instance of political use of an existing imperial hero. This use fundamentally reinforced his heroic status and substituted Gordon's link to China with an indelible relation to the Sudan.

Gladstone consequently bowed to public opinion, although his principal private secretary reported that, when he did so, he was unaware of the potential consequences of a decision he played little part in taking:

> The despatch of 'Chinese Gordon' on a mission to the Soudan has been very well received and has for the moment satisfied public opinion. But, notwithstanding all his Soudanese prestige, it is difficult to see what real good he can do. He seems to be a half cracked fatalist; and what can one expect from such a man? The decision about sending him had to be taken in a desperate hurry, for he was just starting on another mission in Africa. It was taken by Lord Hartington, Lord Granville, Lord Northbrook, and Dilke; and Mr. G. had to acquiesce by telegraph knowing next to nothing of the Commisioner or what he is to do.[79]

The outburst of popular optimism generated by the dispatch of General Gordon to the Sudan in January 1884 only temporarily alleviated Gladstone's burden, as it soon appeared that the General's position in Khartoum, besieged by the Mahdists, was increasingly precarious. The defeat and subsequent death of General Hicks at the hands of the Mahdi's men on 5 November 1883 had not generated extreme feelings of grief or political turmoil in Britain, but, predictably, Gordon's fate was much more likely to attract attention. Also, circumstances were different, and Gordon had the potential to become a key political talking point. First, Gladstone had chosen Gordon, and recalled him from administrative retirement, to save a badly compromised situation in the Sudan. Failure to undertake this task properly, or to support him in its implementation, could easily be brandished by Gladstone's political opponents as a proof of the government's ineptitude. Secondly, Gordon enjoyed a fund of sympathy among the public for his fight against the slave trade (although he had also been criticized for being sometimes over-indulgent towards slave traders), for his panache and for his memorable and well-publicized masterminding of the 'Ever Victorious Army' during the Taiping rebellion (i.e. the exceptionally talented 'Chinese Gordon' who had showcased British qualities). Although Sir William MacKinnon remarked that Gordon '[shrank] from public praise and [was] exactly the reverse of Stanley whom by the way he [did] not at all admire', the General was already a public figure in Britain, as has been shown earlier in this chapter.[80] Thirdly, the political situation in Britain was volatile, with the divisive question of electoral reform and, closely linked to it, the burgeoning issue of Home Rule and Land League in Ireland: as Viscount Bryce reflected shortly after the failure of Home Rule, the lowering of the suffrage age in 1884 rendered inevitable the granting of self-government to Ireland.[81] For those who opposed the principle of Irish Home Rule, popular resentment at the way in which the Gordon dossier was handled could be an excellent opportunity to weaken Gladstone. For the Conservatives, 'the Gordon issue [was] a convenient means of getting at Gladstone'.[82] Fourthly, the general election was getting nearer and opposition parties were eager to find electoral arguments. Lastly, the Gladstone Liberal government, which desperately lacked unity, was under constant attack from Salisbury's Tory minority, and was particularly disliked by many of those whose task was to avoid a Gordon débâcle. Gordon himself was no exception; he wrote to his former subordinate Sir Charles Moore Watson:

> I will accept *nothing whatsoever* from Gladstone's Govt. I will not even let them pay my expenses. I will get the King to pay them. I will never put foot in England again but will (DV if I get out) go to Brussels & so on to Congo.[83]

As the situation in Khartoum was deteriorating, Gordon's safety in the besieged city became a question of national importance. His vulnerability almost caused more concern than the situation in the Sudan itself, where British officers or forces had been embattled since Gordon's appointment as Governor-General in the Turco-Egyptian administration in 1877.[84] Between 5 February 1884 and 20 February 1885, ninety-three questions about General Gordon were asked in the House of Lords and House of Commons, compared to 130 about the Sudan. By contrast, the deceased General Hicks was the subject of only six questions during the same period (five times in the Commons and only once in the Lords). As for the Queen's speeches of the period, General Gordon was mentioned on thirteen different occasions, compared to twenty-six for the Sudan. Although the Sudan was mentioned more often than General Gordon (quite understandably), the sheer number of references to Gordon's fate clearly demonstrates the political significance that his perilous situation in the Sudan had come to bear. Naturally, the questions about General Gordon were frequently asked in the Commons by the vocal Conservative, pro-imperialist Ellis Ashmead-Bartlett (who had founded the Patriotic Association in 1877, was the editor of the newspaper *England* and was known for his staunch opposition to the Liberals), and in the Lords by the Tory leader Lord Salisbury.[85] In the wake of the news of the General's death, it was the Conservative Sir Henry Milner who, on 23 February 1885, first proposed to pay a national tribute of honour to General Gordon: fostering the Gordon legend was a worthwhile investment for the opposition.[86]

The ways in which the Tories referred to Gordon and heroized him revealed the political profit they could make out of the government's blunder. Gordon's death was a godsent opportunity for Gladstone's opponents, as he was widely admired and morally immune to attack, and the Prime Minister could be held responsible for his tragic end. When a tragic outcome in Khartoum was still only a likelihood, Queen Victoria 'tremble[d] for General Gordon's safety',[87] and Gordon's qualities were duly praised in the State Opening Speech she read to the Houses:

> The information received from the Soudan includes painful uncertainties; but the energy, courage, and resource conspicuously displayed by General Gordon in the successful defence of Khartoum, deserve my warm recognition.
>
> The advance of my troops to Dongola has for its object the rescue and security of that gallant officer, and of those who have so faithfully co-operated with him.[88]

The respondents to H.M.'s speech further developed the theme of Gordon's heroic status, which laid the ground for his posthumous reputation as a needlessly sacrificed imperial hero. The conservative Henry Strutt, Second Baron Belper, declared that

I need not dwell on the character and career of General Gordon; but I do not believe that there ever was an enterprise which depended more for its success on the personal qualities of one man. The success which General Gordon has attained is owing, not only to his knowledge of the character of the Natives, but also to his own great personal influence and courage.

The following speaker, John Lawrence, Second Baron Lawrence, also a Tory, did not fail to praise General Gordon and argued that he deserved 'the high terms in which my noble Friend [Lord Belper] has spoken of [him]'. His speech was followed by Lord Salisbury's, who delivered in his answer a long hagiography of General Gordon in which he highlighted the government's responsibility should the General be assassinated, paving the way for the future attacks that he would unleash as soon as news of his death reached London. In his own answer for the government, Lord Granville had no choice but to follow the trend and dwell on General Gordon whom he showered with praise. After all, he had been sent out by the government, even if he ultimately became a cause of embarrassment for it. In a few months, Gordon had been turned into a major political subject, less for himself than for the thorny issue of who was to bear the responsibility for his possible loss. Gordon's heroism could not in any way be denied by the government, but the opposition had much more political profit to make out of his heroic reputation. The speeches of the 1884 parliamentary opening session reveal the political trap into which the Gladstone government had fallen unwittingly: it could not help but further celebrate the man whose unfortunate fate was contributing to its political ruin.

The sole responsibility for Gordon's misfortunes could easily be assigned to the government. In an attempt to safeguard his professional *amour-propre* (and at the expense of his former Liberal sympathies),[89] the leader of the Gordon Relief Expedition, Lord Wolseley, wrote shortly after the fall of Khartoum that, when the news of the failure to save Gordon reached London, 'it will make a gentleman living in Downing St. responsible'.[90] The average Briton certainly felt the same. Robin Baily, a Sudanese officer and a great nephew of Sir Samuel Baker, recalled in his memoirs that his father 'was one of those thousands who turned Gladstone's titles of G.O.M. [Grand Old Man] into M.O.G. (murderer of Gordon)'.[91] This opinion was shared by the Queen herself, who did not hesitate to write that 'Mr Gladstone and the Government *have* – the Queen *feels it dreadfully* – Gordon's innocent, noble, heroic blood on their consciences. *No one* who reflects on *how* he was *sent* out, how he was *refused*, can deny it! It is *awful* ... May they *feel* it, and may they be *made to do so.*'[92] Even more damaging to Gladstone's reputation, she sent a telegram *en clair* blaming her prime minister for Gordon's death. Indeed, 'grief and anger were felt throughout Great

Britain' and 'the Queen was so overcome that she fell ill', as a chronicler recalled a few decades later.[93]

In the House, the trauma caused by Gordon's death further weakened Gladstone's already unsteady majority. On 27 February, the Liberal John Morley tabled a vote of censure on the government's action in Egypt and the Sudan, professedly in order 'to call the radical & dissenting conscience, & save their position for the future' rather than to bring down the government.[94] Far from strengthening the Prime Minister, the result highlighted Gladstone's fragile position in the wake of the Khartoum events, as it was rejected by a tiny majority of 302 to 288. Contrary to his habits, the Liberal George Goschen supported this censure motion.[95] William Edward Forster, a Liberal who had been a member of the Gladstone government, finally voted in favour of the motion on the occasion of the same vote.[96] Such unnatural votes show how the death of Gordon overcame traditional allegiances. Another Liberal, Alfred Milner, became an 'imperial patriot' partly because he had been 'angered by the failure to save General Gordon in the Sudan'.[97]

The leader of the Tories saw the political advantage he could gain from Gordon's tragic death, only a few months before the general election of November 1885. Salisbury was reported to have believed that 'thanks to Cabinet dithering in Egypt and over Gordon, the Conservatives might be expected to improve their standing in the House'.[98] Unsurprisingly, the leader of the opposition made full use of the 'Gordon legend' to stir up public opinion against Gladstone, with the obvious intention of turning it into electoral gains. On the occasion of a speech at Dumfries on 21 October 1884, the leader of the opposition expressed clearly what would become his favourite argument over the next few months:

> The one man, the heroic General Gordon, of whose character it is impossible to speak in language of too high encomium – he, in his efforts to do the strange and impossible duty which the Government had imposed on him, placed himself in a position of imminent danger, from which he could not extricate himself. And now [...] we are getting out a great expedition for the purposes of rescuing the man, whom we ought not to have sent out, on a task which was impossible for him to perform, or to save the lives of garrisons who have long been butchered, and to attain no other object whatever, but in this way to remedy the pile of blunders which, one after another, the Government have committed.[99]

Other Tory writers of the period made the most of the Gordon legend and used it as a blatant example of Gladstone's incompetence. By criticizing even the principle of the Gordon Relief Expedition (even before it ultimately failed), they sought to highlight the contrast between the

Prime Minister's supposed amateurish decision making and the exceptional character of Gordon, called 'the truest hero of the nineteenth century' in a book compiling speeches by Lord Salisbury, from which the following extract is taken:

> To help the Government of the Khedive to scuttle out of the Soudan, [the Gladstone government] have selected, with a strange disregard of the fitness of things, the most gallant soldier they can find. They appear to know no other way of retreating from the Soudan than by sending a man whose life has been spent not in retreating, but in advancing, and in striking hard blows against the enemy [...] My impression is that if for such a purpose the employment of an Englishman was necessary at all, there are many other Englishmen who might have been found who would have been just as good for that purpose as General Gordon, and that it was not necessary in order to effect that object to endanger a most valuable life, and to a certain extent to endanger a most untarnished reputation, in performing an act which will certainly reflect no credit upon the government by which it is undertaken.[100]

Not surprisingly, one of the earliest Gordon hagiographers (and a relative of his), who was also a noted Conservative, Alfred Egmont Hake, lectured widely 'on the eve of the general election' on Gordon, and on the failure of the Gladstone government to rescue him.[101] The satirist and journalist Henry Traill (a regular contributor to the *Daily Telegraph*) accused the Liberal majority of 'sacrificing Gordon and tarnishing the national honour'.[102]

The Conservative Edinburgh and London publisher Blackwood and Sons contributed three pamphlets to this wave of Tory attacks: the *Gladstone Almanack*, the *Diary of the Gladstone Government* and the *Egyptian Red Book*, all three based upon satirical diary entries that dedicated much space to General Gordon. The *Diary of the Gladstone Government* thus read for 18 January 1884 'Field-Marshal the G.O.M. reinstated Gen. Gordon because *he* wishes to send him to the Soudan', the italics stressing that Gladstone had to bear sole responsibility for Gordon's death. The 13 May 1884 entry reinforced the accusation: 'General Gordon's abandonment supported by 303 Radicals, who fear they will loose their grasp of place and power, if they vote according to their conscience.' For 26 January 1885, the *Diary* mentioned 'Fall of Khartoum and death of General Gordon after a siege of 320 days' and quoted ironically Gladstone's Home Secretary, Sir W. Vernant Harcourt: 'I say we were *not* too late; and I am entitled to say so!'[103]

Another Blackwood pamphlet, *The Egyptian Red Book*, bore a portrait of General Gordon on its cover, while the preface was an extract from a speech by Colonel Burnaby, in May 1884, which said among other things: 'I think that the Government will, ultimately, but too late, send a relieving force, not because Mr Gladstone wishes it, but because public indignation will compel him, *nolens volens*, to do so; and, little as the Prime Minister may value Gordon, the Prime Minister cares a great deal for Mr Gladstone.' The 17 January 1884 entry stated that 'The G.O.M. recalls Gordon and sends him, *against his wish*, and that of the Egyptian authorities, to save the Gladstone Government'. In another entry Gladstone was accused of forsaking Gordon 'knowingly, willingly, and heartlessly'. Some entries detailed the organizing process of the Gordon Relief expedition while always remaining critical of it. The booklet ended with an extract from the *Adieux* of General Gordon (letter dated 14 December 1884), and a final remark in a box: 'After a year's gallant defence, waiting for succour which never came, Khartoum is betrayed, and General Gordon assassinated.' The authors made the most of this all-powerful argument in politics, that of the 'betrayal' of the country's interests. The pamphlet also featured cartoons depicting Gladstone leading the 'Never-Victorious Army' (an ironic reference to Gordon's famous *Ever Victorious Army*), as a 'Pious Editur' pruning Gordon's Diary, cutting out a despatch called 'Indelebile Disgrace' (sic), or turning his back on an 'Abandoned' Gordon tied to a post, surrounded by a flight of eagles and threatened by a sandstorm.

These three pamphlets enjoyed wide readership, as Blackwood sold steadily most of the 57,976 copies of the *Gladstone Alamanack*, 42,870 copies of the *Egyptian Red Book* and 60,574 copies of the *Diary of the Gladstone Government* printed between March and November 1885.[104] Such works used General Gordon's aura to undermine Gladstone's prestige and popularity, just a few months prior to the general election.

Even more flagrantly, some Tory candidates chose to make the most of the Khartoum disaster and did not hesitate to ask voters in the run-up to the election:

> Who killed General Gordon
> I said Mr Gladstone ...
> Who saw him die
> Not William at the Cri'
> With his laughing eye.[105]

General Gordon's reputation reached a peak in the tumultuous context of the controversy about the extension of franchise. In a mock election conducted in the run-up to the electoral reform in view of testing proportional representation, the hypothetical independent candidate 'General Gordon' won an 'overwhelming victory', although this fact 'upset all calculation'.[106] Such a result demonstrates the depth of General Gordon's political appeal in 1885. British politicians used it to their own advantage, although Gordon himself had never shown an active desire to represent such an influential argument in British politics.[107] The heroic symbols embodied by General Gordon had a potent political value that was used on purpose by Conservative (and even sometimes Liberal) politicians to weaken Gladstone's wavering position during the siege of Khartoum and in its aftermath, when it became clear that the death of Gordon would take on political significance. It was also used as a means of undermining Gladstone's prestige when the Irish Home Rule question was debated.

The Gordon legend did not lose all relevance even after Salisbury had taken office. Describing the process that led him to produce the most famous painting of Gordon's end (see Chapter 3), G. W. Joy provided a detailed account of the political context which drew him to 'do something' with the Gordon legend, against Gladstone and what he embodied:

> I was mildly political in the choice and suggestiveness of my subject, at the time when feeling ran high on the subject of 'Home Rule', so in this picture of Gordon I was desperately in earnest. On no historical or political event have I felt so strongly as on this momentous one. I cannot bring myself to look at it from any point of view but that of a betrayal of all that was highest and best in our national instincts, life and traditions. A betrayal of one of the greatest men we ever possessed; of the anti-slavery cause in the Soudan; as well as of the fooled inhabitants of Khartoum, who had trusted to us, and to our plighted word, to help and protect them.
>
> It was therefore in the genuine hope of doing something, however insignificant, to help on that awakening of the conscience of the nation, that I undertook, with all due reverence, this great subject.[108]

Gordon was set to remain an imperial landmark in the British imagination. In spite of the aversion towards Gordon of the British Consul General in Cairo, the Gordon legend was still influential when the Sirdar Kitchener received approval for his plans for the re-conquest of the Sudan, following the defeat of the Italians at the hands of the Abyssinians in Adowa in 1896.[109] As David Steele remarked in his study of Salisbury's hostility towards Islam in the context of the re-conquest of the Sudan, 'Omdurman [...] avenged the death of Gordon'.[110] The argument was made countless times in the British press in the wake of Kitchener's victory.[111] G. A. Henty argued that 'the long-delayed duty which England owed to one of her noblest sons had been done. [...] The British flag waved over the spot where he disappeared for ever from the sight of his countrymen.'[112] But the British re-conquest of the Sudan 'achieved' even more. The Anglo-Egyptian expedition, and the French Congo–Nile mission that it met in Fashoda in September 1898, gave rise in turn to two new major imperial heroes: Captain Jean-Baptiste Marchand and the Sirdar Horatio Herbert Kitchener, both of whom generated major political consequences.

IMPERIAL HEROES AND DOMESTIC POLITICS

The heroic reputations attached to Marchand and Kitchener are the two case studies whose development is followed in the third part of this book from their inception until they became household names in each country. Discussion here will be limited to their political significance in each country. Although they became famous against the same backdrop of rising Anglo-French confrontation heightened by the Fashoda crisis, their fame fulfilled different political roles: Marchand was another 'hero used as political argument', whilst Kitchener was closer to the 'proconsul turned hero'.

The promotion of the Marchand legend by the nationalist Right upon the return to France of the 'hero of Fashoda' provides an excellent example of a 'hero used as political argument'.[113] Imperial heroes such as Marchand contributed to forcing French nationalists to revise their position about imperial expansion, shifting from outright opposition to 'colonial adventures' to active support to them. Déroulède, who had once claimed that he had lost 'two children' (Alsace and Lorraine) and staunchly refused the 'twenty servants' he was offered instead (the colonies), strongly supported Marchand in 1899.[114] Edouard Drumont, who had in his book *La France juive* vehemently opposed the French occupation of Tunisia (which he argued had been a Jewish manoeuvre), was one of the major supporters of the Marchand legend in 1899 through his newspaper *L'Intransigeant*.[115] Marchand remained a noted figure of the French political scene between 1899 and 1906, and he was regularly courted by some nationalist groups who sought to use his popularity to their own benefit, in the hope that his fame would be a weapon against the government. The 'hero of Fashoda' became a notable player in the French political arena during these years.

By contrast, Kitchener's political role in Britain was less partisan, more technical and more durable. Although he remained throughout his career more akin to a high military commander than a political leader, on several occasions he also played a role in politics – a fact that led Hew Strachan to see in him an example of 'the link between military service and parliamentary career'.[116] His achievements make him rank among the 'proconsuls turned heroes'. First, his tactful handling of his encounter with Marchand did not precipitate a war between England and France. A few years later, on the occasion of the South African war, besides being Roberts's second-in-command for a year, and the supreme commander of the British forces for the rest of the war, he played an important role in the negotiations with the Boers, which led to the peace of Vereeniging. His sensitive political conduct ensured the triumph of his accommodating position over the more radical and more dangerous arguments put forward by Alfred Milner, which could derail the peace process.[117] When Kitchener, promoted to British commander-in-chief in India, disagreed with the Viceroy Lord Curzon, he used, on at least one occasion (24 September 1904), the weapon of resignation to strengthen his position against his rival, making the most of the precarious position of Balfour's unpopular and politically vulnerable Unionist government. With this threat, Kitchener knew that 'the resignation of Britain's most popular serving soldier would have exposed it [Balfour's government] to further attack'.[118]

The most politically significant role Kitchener played was that of Secretary of State for War from 1914 until his death, a post to which he was called following pressing demands formulated in the press. Besides contributing his own personal image to the recruitment campaign, Kitchener was also a leader who kept the French and Russian alliances steady, who set up the mass volunteer forces (the 'Kitchener armies'), and sought to maintain direct control over British forces and strategy for the war. The Kitchener of 1916 exemplified the imperial proconsul turned hero who had become a fully fledged national hero, and who came to play a political role of primary importance in his country.

On the other side of the Channel, another proconsul (arguably the 'last of the great French proconsuls of the nineteenth and early twentieth century')[119] came to hold high national responsibilities as Minister of War during the First World War: Marshal Hubert Lyautey. Having seen the realities of the French colonial empire in Algeria (briefly in February to March 1878, and between 1880 and 1882), Indochina (1894–97) and Madagascar (1897–1902) before being brought to deal indirectly with Moroccan affairs through his postings near the Algero-Moroccan border (as commander of the subdivision of Aïn Sefra and later commander of the division of Oran), Lyautey came to play a major political role through the establishment and implementation of the French protectorate over Morocco. Although a staunch royalist with aristocratic background, he was eager to act within the framework of the Republic and did his best to ensure his nomination as French *Résident-général* when it became clear that Morocco would become a French protectorate.[120] From 1912 until 1925 (with the exception of a few months as Minister of War), Lyautey performed the role of French *Résident-général* and through his action 'gave a Kingdom to the Republic', as one of his recent biographers puts it.[121]

Lyautey's contribution to the political life of France was at least threefold: as an influential colonial administrator who secured more colonies for France, as a widely read theoretician of the social and colonial role of the army and as a politician of national influence, notably with ministerial responsibilities.[122]

IMPERIAL HEROES AND DOMESTIC POLITICS

During his formative years as Gallieni's second-in-command (in Indochina and later in Madagascar), Lyautey gained a thorough understanding of the workings of the French colonial administration and contemplated ways to improve it. Like his mentor, he complained about the heavy burden of bureaucracy and wanted more freedom of action for those men of Gallieni's fibre – 'absolute leader[s], soldier[s] and administrator[s], tough and intelligent' who could not help but complain that 'the French civil servant, general or prefect, was only worried about one thing: general ideas and long-term perspectives'.[123] To overcome the weight of tradition, he used 'the method of an officer who has entered into politics'.[124] Lyautey did his best to apply Gallieni's theory of 'progressive occupation' based upon 'an organization on the march' (*une organisation qui marche*), was adamant that the vanquished had to be treated with respect to become reliable partners (*politique des égards*) and argued that economic penetration was surer than military control.[125] He also stressed that the expansion of areas under French control had to follow the pattern of a 'pool of oil' building upon the practical, medical and commercial benefits that French-administered areas were enjoying, which in turn led more regions to seek the advantages of the *Pax Gallica*.[126] All these ideas formed the cornerstone of Lyautey's action in Morocco between 1912 and 1925. His political role in that country has been amply discussed, in particular by Daniel Rivet's three-volume study of Lyautey's role in the installation of the French protectorate in Morocco – a 'protectorate with a human face'.[127] Lyautey's action contributed to bringing Morocco under French paramountcy in a manner that had no equivalent in the French empire, and was based upon the co-operation between the *forces vives* of Morocco and an elite of administrators and settlers. Lyautey also spread in France his vision that Morocco was 'the most interesting and the most captivating of Muslim countries' and ensured that Morocco had a special status within the French empire, and in French minds.[128] On that account, his political role in Franco-Moroccan relations, and in colonial matters more generally, proved pivotal.

From very early on, Lyautey showed that he had political views to share. Although he was a monarchist, he supported the decision of the Third Republic to make the army a truly national force (by suppressing the complex system of dispensation, conscription by lottery and substitution) and voiced his opinion in an article in the well-read *Revue des deux mondes* under the title *The Social Functions of the Officer under Universal Military Service*.[129] He argued that this scheme would help the army perform a civic role. Informed readers accurately guessed the author of this anonymous letter.[130] A few years later, Lyautey published his views on the colonial role of the army, on the occasion of a lecture at

[165]

the Colonial Union later published in the *Revue des deux mondes* and as a conclusion to the *Letters from Tonking and Madagascar*.[131] With such interventions, Lyautey played a political role – defending the reform of the army, pleading in favour of colonial expansion – that went far beyond what officers usually allowed themselves to say. Perhaps Lyautey's relations with some of the most eminent intellectuals of his time, including the historian Ernest Lavisse, the diplomat and Orientalist Eugène Melchior de Vogüé and the essayist Joseph Chailley, as well as leading politicians such as Albert de Mun, Eugène Etienne or Aristide Briand, helped him feel he was not bound to conform to the traditional cliché of the army as the country's great silent force (*la grande muette*).

Last but not least, Lyautey took a leading part in the ruling of French affairs when he became Minister of War between December 1916 and March 1917 under the premiership of Aristide Briand. This episode was frequently considered a failure: it lasted only eleven weeks and was marked by a deep misunderstanding with the Chambers and the General Headquarters; it also confirmed Lyautey's prejudices and apprehensions regarding Third Republic politicians.[132] Yet it also shows just how powerful a figure the Resident General had become. The Ministry of War of a country at war counts among the most influential positions on offer. The Briand Cabinet did not resist Lyautey's resignation on 14 March 1917 (paradoxically under the protests of the Left), and followed him into retirement two days later. This short episode in the Marshal's life perhaps showed that he lacked the political stamina to confront the pressure of a coalition of deputies opposed to him but, conversely, the fact that 'his departure moved public opinion deeply' and brought the Briand Cabinet down also reveals his political weight in March 1917, largely inherited from his successful handling of Moroccan affairs in the previous five years.[133] Lyautey enjoyed a broad appeal to the French population: he was not only an archetypal 'imperial hero' but also a notable political figure, which is why he seems to have fascinated, but also worried, Third Republic politicians.[134] As we have seen in Chapter 3, he later supported Léon Poirier's effort to produce a popular film on Charles de Foucauld. Launched at the time when the Popular Front arrived in government, this film promoted a traditional and highly mythologized view of heroism and sanctity which appealed particularly to those who fought Léon Blum's policies, whilst at the same time using audiovisual communications strategies similar to that of the Front itself.[135]

A British prototype of Marshal Lyautey, Lord Lugard conceived and implemented in Central, East and West Africa a policy of indirect rule which bore several similarities to the one Lyautey later applied in Morocco. He played a leading role in the establishment of a British protectorate over Uganda, especially through his influential book *The*

IMPERIAL HEROES AND DOMESTIC POLITICS

Rise of Our East-African Empire (1893), which exerted some degree of influence on the government. Like Lyautey, Lord Lugard theorized his conceptions of colonial rule, notably in his famous *The Dual Mandate in Tropical Africa*, first published in 1922, which established him as a leading theoretician of morally right and materially efficient colonial administration. Following his forced retirement from his appointment in Nigeria in 1918, he came to write numerous articles, letters to the press, forewords, lectures, speeches and broadcasts that should have won him fame beyond the circles of the well-informed. He might have been inspired by his wife Flora Shaw, former colonial editor of *The Times*, who once wrote to him that she 'never thought of [her] work exactly as journalism, but rather as active politics without the fame'.[136] Dame Flora Shaw had taken an apprenticeship at the *Pall Mall Gazette* under W. T. Stead and had 'discerned his methods of using the press to achieve political results', and her husband might have contemplated achieving this aim too.[137] Yet, in spite of an impressive list of decorations that reflected recognition from his peers, Lugard never cut a fine figure on the British political scene. If Lyautey, as we have seen above, fascinated large sections of the French public and quickly became the subject of countless biographies and studies, Lugard failed to attract much public attention in Britain. We have seen that Margery Perham's biography of Lord Lugard had been difficult to achieve (thirty years elapsed between the moment Lady Lugard looked for a biographer and when the first volume was published), and left its author highly dissatisfied with its poor commercial result. Lord Lugard remained an excellent, but relatively unknown, colonial administrator who never reached a heroic status in his country. Although he influenced British colonial policies both as a theorizer and as a civil servant, his influence in British politics was no match for Lyautey's on the French political scene.

Ironically, these two fervent advocates of indirect rule resented each other for many years, but they were later used to showcase the political rapprochement between Britain and France. Lyautey had criticized Lugard in his *Lettres du Tonkin* for his mistreatment of French Catholic missionaries in Uganda, and Lugard resented being publicly spoken of so harshly. However, the two were introduced to each other by Austen Chamberlain in 1924 and, in spite of initial prejudices, Lugard was interested in meeting Lyautey as he thought he was 'the only Frenchman who [had] adopted British methods with the native races in Africa'.[138] Lyautey was subsequently awarded in December 1928 the Gold Medal of the African Association by Earl Buxton, with Lord Lugard, Sir Reginald Wingate, Sir Ronald Ross and hundreds of other high civil servants and officers attending. Lord Buxton declared in his speech that:

this function and the bestowal of the Medal is not only intended as a compliment to Marshal Lyautey himself, but through him, to honour the French African Empire.

Further, it would be a gratification to us if we could feel that our gathering to-night would consitute one further link, however tiny, in the chain which helps to strengthen that amity and alliance between France and England, which we all hold so dear.[139]

The figure of Lyautey was obviously used as a means of strengthening the cause of the Franco-British entente, thus exemplifying another political use of imperial heroes.

The increasingly friendly relationship between Lyautey and Lugard allowed the French to set up a scheme to send 'a selected candidate for the French colonial service to Oxford for an academic year' at the expense of the *Fondation Lyautey*, notably so that the future French servant could meet with the young Colonial Office probationers.[140] In October 1931, Lyautey warmly celebrated Lugard at the opening of the Congress of the African International Institute organized in October 1931 as part of the Colonial Exhibition.[141] For his part, Lugard praised Lyautey's role in the Vincennes exhibition, and Lord Buxton wrote the preface to Sonia Howe's biography of Lyautey. Celebrating each other's heroes had become a matter of international politics in the interwar years, probably as a way of alleviating the many episodes of Franco-British tension which marked this period.[142]

By contrast, and as we shall see in more detail in Chapter 6, several books on Marchand and Fashoda were reprinted under the Vichy regime in order to revive Anglophobia and to justify Pétain's collaborationist policy. This recycling process demonstrates that an imperial hero like Marchand still enjoyed a wide popularity forty years after the events that had put him in the limelight, and that his legend had retained enough influence to be used politically during the Second World War.

Imperial heroes had an evident political value that politicians were often eager to use for their benefit. At times, some heroes came to fulfil political roles themselves. Their political weight was significantly amplified by the press, and was used to serve various purposes, the most common being the justification or promotion of imperial expansion or the attempt to damage a government's popularity by making it responsible for a hero's failure to achieve his goal – whether in Khartoum or in Fashoda.

The force of the example was one of the driving reasons behind the political usefulness of heroes. Their deeds set glorious precedents, usually famous to the general public, which could be called to justify many actions or criticisms. When Jules Ferry sought to convince his readers that further colonial conquests were desirable, he made extensive use of the evocative power of colonial heroism:

> this race to the steeple is just five year old, and becomes faster every year, as if it were pushed by its own speed. In the steps of the likes of Livingstone, Barth, Brazza, Stanley and Gerhard Rohlfs, and of the countless known and unknown heroes who have sworn to uncover all the secrets of Equatorial Africa, Germany, Britain and Italy throw themselves speedily from the barren and overheated banks of the Red Sea to the highlands of Central Africa.[143]

The publicity surrounding imperial legends, sustained, as we have seen in Part I, by a variety of new promotional means, could easily be turned into a way of influencing public opinion. This made them useful political tools, even political actors sometimes. Except if we deny political activity the popular resonance it has always had, the political role that many imperial heroes came to play is an important indicator of the depth of popular interest in, and (in many cases) attachment to, imperial heroes.

Notes

1 B. Harrison, *The Transformation of British Politics, 1860–1995* (Oxford, 1996), pp. 55–84.
2 P. D. Marshall, *Celebrity and Power* (1997), p. 203.
3 J. Evans, 'Celebrity, media and history', in J. Evans and D. Hesmondhalgh, *Understanding Media: Inside Celebrity* (Maidenhead, 2005), p. 14.
4 M. Peters, *Pitt and Popularity* (Oxford, 1980).
5 E. Baring (Earl of Cromer), *Modern Egypt*, vol. I (1908), p. 430.
6 P. Cambon, *Correspondance 1870–1924*, vol. II (1940), p. 14.
7 J. Habermas, *L'Espace public* (1978).
8 Baring, *Modern Egypt*, vol. I, p. 435.
9 C. M. Andrew and A. S. Kanya-Forstner, 'The *Groupe Colonial* in the French Chamber of Deputies, 1892–1932', *The Historical Journal*, 17:4 (Dec. 1974), 837–66.
10 J. Marseille, 'La gauche, la droite et le fait colonial en France, des années 1880 aux années 1960', *Vingtième Siècle*, 24 (Oct.–Dec. 1989), 17–28; M. Michel, 'La colonisation', in J.-F. Sirinelli (ed.), *Histoire des droites en France* (1992), pp. 125–63; M. J. Heffernan, 'The French right and the overseas empire', in N. Atkin and F. Tallett (eds), *The Right in France* (2002), pp. 89–113.
11 J. M. MacKenzie, 'David Livingstone and the worldly after-life: imperialism and nationalism in Africa', in J. M. MacKenzie (ed.), *David Livingstone and the Victorian Encounter with Africa* (1996), pp. 201–17.
12 N. Bennett, 'David Livingstone', in R. Rotberg (ed.), *Africa and Its Explorers* (Cambridge, MA, 2nd ed., 1973), p. 59.
13 J. Darwin, 'Imperialism and the Victorians: the dynamics of territorial expansion', *English Historical Review*, June 1997, 623.
14 D. O. Helly, *Livingstone's Legacy* (Athens, OH, 1987), p. 163.
15 A. D. Roberts, 'Livingstone, David (1813–1873)', *ODNB* [Accessed 12 December 2011].
16 NLS, MS 20311, f. 311, MacKinnon to John Kirk, 12 March 1880.
17 NLS, MS 9994, ff. 70–2, Sir John William Gordon, Major General, to an unknown recipient, 6 July 1865.

18 R. Gessi, *Seven Years in the Soudan* (1892), p. 4.
19 R. Davenport-Hines, 'Gordon, Charles George (1833–1885)', *ODNB* [Accessed 12 December 2011].
20 RHL, Waller Papers, Gordon Manuscript, f. 71, Gordon to Horace Waller, 31 January 1877.
21 RHL, Waller Papers, Gordon Manuscript, f. 88, Gordon to Horace Waller, 11 November 1877.
22 On the *Bureaux arabes*, see J. Frémeaux, *Les Bureaux arabes dans l'Algérie de la conquête* (1993).
23 X. de Montclos, *Lavigerie, le Saint-Siège et l'Eglise, 1846–1878* (1965), pp. 365–6.
24 J. D. O'Donnell, *Lavigerie in Tunisia. The Interplay of Imperialist and Missionary* (Athens, GA, 1979).
25 F. Pisani-Ferry, *Jules Ferry et le partage du monde* (1962), p. 254.
26 O'Donnell, *Lavigerie*, p. 90.
27 Letter from Lavigerie to an unknown correspondent, quoted in R. F. Clarke, *Cardinal Lavigerie and the African Slave Trade* (1889), pp. 232–3.
28 A. Hamman (ed.), *Cardinal Lavigerie, écrits d'Afrique* (1966), p. 60.
29 A. Shorter, *Cross and Flag in Africa: The 'White Fathers' during the Colonial Scramble (1892–1914)* (2006), p. 63.
30 J. Tournier, *Le Cardinal Lavigerie et son action politique 1863–1892* (1913), pp. 268–9.
31 C. Lavigerie, *L'Esclavage africain. Conférence sur l'esclavage dans le Haut-Congo faite à Sainte-Gudule de Bruxelles* (Paris and Brussels, 1888), pp. 24–5.
32 Lavigerie, *L'Esclavage*, p. 27.
33 Lavigerie Archives, White Fathers' Generalate, Rome, A17/84 (77), Note by Lavigerie, *L'Œuvre antiesclavagiste*, October 1888. Quoted in F. Renault (trans. J. O'Donohue), *Cardinal Lavigerie, Churchman, Prophet and Missionary* (1994), p. 378.
34 Helly, *Livingstone's Legacy*, p. 327.
35 Renault, *Cardinal Lavigerie*, p. 369.
36 Tournier, *Lavigerie*, p. 225.
37 Lavigerie Archives, White Fathers' Generalate, Rome, A8/1, Memoirs of Chevinesse, secretary to Lavigerie. Quoted in Renault, *Cardinal Lavigerie*, p. 392.
38 O'Donnell, *Lavigerie*, p. 206.
39 J. Martin, *Savorgnan de Brazza, 1852–1905* (2005), pp. 86–7.
40 *Le Rappel*, 19 October 1882, quoted in I. Dion, *Pierre Savorgnan de Brazza. Au cœur du Congo* (Marseille, 2007), p. 56.
41 H. Brunschwig, *Brazza explorateur. Les traités Makoko 1880–1882* (1972), pp. 258–67.
42 R. West, *Brazza of the Congo, European Exploration and Exploitation in French Equatorial Africa* (1972), pp. 91–2.
43 ANOM, Brazza Papers, 16 PA VIII, boxes 1 to 16, albums of press cuttings.
44 ANOM, Brazza Papers, 16 PA VII, box 10, manuscript note from Brazza recounting Ferry's advice to him about the French Congo.
45 N. Ney, *Conférences et lettres de Pierre Savorgnan de Brazza* (1887), p. 173.
46 Anon., *Réception de Monsieur P. Savorgnan de Brazza au grand amphithéâtre de la Sorbonne le 23 juin 1882* (1882), pp. 298–9.
47 C. de Chavannes, *Avec Brazza. Souvenirs de la mission de l'Ouest africain* (1935), p. 11.
48 Report from Brazza to the French Senate, annex to the *Procès-Verbal* of 20 November 1882 session, quoted in C. Coquery-Vidrovitch, *Brazza et la prise de possession du Congo, 1883–1885* (1969), p. 26.
49 ANOM, Brazza Papers, 16 PA III, box 2, Maurice Schwab to PSB, 18 January 1883.
50 ANOM, Brazza Papers, 16 PA III, box 2, A. Rambaud to PSB on card *Revue Bleue, Revue politique et littéraire*, 19 September 18[?].
51 ANOM, Brazza Papers, 16 PA VIII, box 12, the Political Director of the *Moniteur des colonies et des pays de protectorat* to PSB, 22 January 1887.

52 Martin, *Brazza*, pp. 111 and 115.
53 J. Jaurès, *Discours pour l'Alliance française* in Albi, 1884.
54 G. Charmes, 'La politique coloniale', *Revue des deux mondes*, 1 November 1883, 60.
55 ANOM, Brazza Papers, 16 PA VII, box 12, folder *'Lettres reçues et brouillons. Commémorations du souvenir de Brazza'*, draft of a letter from Brazza to the Venerable of the lodge *Alsace-Lorraine*, 23 November 1904.
56 G. Comte, *L'Empire triomphant* (1988), p. 211.
57 Some argue that Brazza's death made this celebration easier, since his philanthropic concerns for the welfare of indigenous populations no longer threatened any established interests in France. For a novelized interpretation, see P. Deville, *Equatoria* (2009), pp. 187–90.
58 ANOM, Brazza Papers, 16 PA VII, box 12, folder *'Lettres reçues et brouillons. Commémorations du souvenir de Brazza'*.
59 AN, Eydoux Papers, 546 AP 1, folder 2, review of H.-P. Eydoux, *Savorgnan de Brazza. Le Conquérant pacifique* by Maurice Reclus, 15 January 1931.
60 See for instance Eydoux, *Savorgnan de Brazza*.
61 AN, Eydoux Papers, 546 AP 1, Comtesse Savorgnan de Brazza to Eydoux, 10 March 1932.
62 D. M. Schreuder, *The Scramble for Southern Africa, 1877–1895* (Cambridge, 1980), p. 191.
63 G. Shepperson, *Cecil John Rhodes: Some Biographical Problems*, Rhodes Commemoration Lecture, Rhodes University, Grahamstown, 29 July 1981.
64 J. Flint, *Cecil Rhodes* (1974), p. 158.
65 J. G. Lockhart and C. M. Woodhouse, *Rhodes* (1963), p. 80.
66 J. C. Williams, introduction to The Royal Commission of Manuscripts, *Report on the Correspondence of Cecil John Rhodes (1853–1902)* (1983), p. 1.
67 Flint, *Rhodes*, appendix, pp. 248–52.
68 S. Marks and S. Trapido, 'Rhodes, Cecil John (1853–1902)', *ODNB* [Accessed 20 December 2005].
69 See in particular R. I. Rotberg, *The Founder: Cecil Rhodes and the Pursuit of Power* (Oxford, 1988)
70 P. Maylam, *The Cult of Rhodes* (Claremont, South Africa, 2005), p. 70.
71 Witwatersrand University Library, Johannesburg, Revd John Mackenzie Papers, Mackenzie to Warren (?), February 1885, quoted in Schreuder, *Scramble*, p. 94.
72 Flint, *Rhodes*, pp. 159–60.
73 Flint, *Rhodes*, pp. xix–xx.
74 R. S. Churchill (ed.), *Winston S. Churchill*, vol. I, companion, part 2 (1967), p. 1017, W. S. Churchill to Lady Churchill, 30 March 1899.
75 R. Jenkins, *Gladstone* (1996), p. 510.
76 *Pall Mall Gazette*, 'Chinese Gordon on the Soudan', 10 January 1884, p. 11.
77 E. W. Stead, *My Father. Personal & Spiritual Reminiscences* (1913), p. 110.
78 Stead, *My Father*, p. 111.
79 D. W. H. Bahlman (ed.), *The Diary of Sir Edward Walter Hamilton 1880–1885* (Oxford, 1972), p. 545 (23 January 1884).
80 NLS, MS 20311, f. 131, William Mac Kinnon to John Kirk, 12 March 1880.
81 H. A. L. Fisher, *James Bryce (Viscount Bryce of Dechmont)*, vol. I (1927), p. 199.
82 R. Shannon, *Gladstone, God and Politics* (2007), p. 352.
83 RHL, Waller Papers, MSS Afr 16, vol. II, f. 276, General Gordon to Watson, 26 November 1884.
84 A. Moore-Harell, *Gordon and the Sudan, Prologue to the Mahdiyya 1877–1880* (2001), provides a good account of Gordon's first experience in the Sudan.
85 A. Thompson, *The Empire Strikes Back* (Harlow, 2005), p. 187.
86 Figures mentioned in this paragraph have been compiled from Hansard, from 5 February 1884 to 23 March 1885.
87 P. Guedalla, *The Queen and Mr Gladstone* (1933), vol. II (1880–1898), p. 259 (9 February 1884).

USES

88 Hansard, vol. CCXCIII, 23 October 1884 to 17 November 1884, Column 3, Queen's speech (23 October 1884).
89 A. Preston (ed.), *In Relief of Gordon: Lord Wolseley's Campaign Journal of the Khartoum Relief Expedition* (1967), pp. xxxix, 80, 136.
90 MECA, Wolseley Papers, GB 165-0305, ff. 21-2, letter from Wolseley to H. R. Hopkins, 2 March 1885.
91 SAD, Baily Papers, 533/4/29-30, 'Anecdotes about the Sudan'.
92 G. E. Buckle (ed.), *The Letters of Queen Victoria* (1928), second series, third volume p. 608.
93 W. Steed, 'Book of the Month: Queen Victoria's Letters', *Review of Reviews*, 457 (15 Feb.–15 March 1928), 115–28.
94 City Library, York, Hickleton Manuscripts, A4.51, Stansfeld to Halifax, 22 February 1885. Quoted in A. Jones, *The Politics of Reform* (Cambridge, 1972), p. 117.
95 T. J. Spinner Jr, 'Goschen, George Joachim, first Viscount Goschen (1831–1907)', *ODNB* [Accessed 18 December 2006].
96 A. Warren, 'Forster, William Edward (1818–1886)', *ODNB* [Accessed 20 December 2006].
97 C. Newbury, 'Milner, Alfred, Viscount Milner (1854–1925)', *ODNB* [Accessed 18 December 2006].
98 Jones, *Politics of Reform*, p. 143.
99 P. H. Bagenal, *The Tory Policy of the Marquis of Salisbury* (Edinburgh and London, 1885), p. 57.
100 F. S. Pulling, *The Life and Speeches of the Marquis of Salisbury* (1885), pp. 181–2.
101 C. Camporesi, 'Hake, Alfred Egmont (1849–1916)', *ODNB* [Accessed 5 October 2010].
102 H. D. Traill, *The Marquis of Salisbury* (1892), p. 189.
103 Anon., *A Diary of the Gladstone Government* (Edinburgh, 1885).
104 NLS, Blackwood Papers, MS 30862, Publication ledger 1881–1889, f. 436.
105 De Ricci and Barttelot election poster, 1885. Quoted in Jones, *Politics of Reform*, p. 117. 'Cri' is probably the then new Criterion Theatre in London.
106 Jones, *Politics of Reform*, p. 98.
107 Beyond MacKinnon's already cited appraisal in 1880, Gordon's sister also wrote to Horace Waller that 'My brother quite rightly to my mind wishes to withdraw from the world and I am sure he will find peace and rest in seeking for things unseen rather than in the world's' (RHL, Waller Papers, vol. II, f. 259, Augusta Gordon to Horace Waller, 11 May 1883).
108 G. W. Joy, *The Work of George W. Joy, with an Autobiographical Sketch* (1904), pp. 20–1.
109 A good proof of Cromer's antipathy towards the Gordon legend was when he asked Churchill 'not to pander to the popular belief on [General Gordon]' in his book *The River War* (Churchill, Winston S. Churchill, vol. I, companion, part 2, p. 1017, W. S. Churchill to Lady Churchill, 30 March 1899).
110 D. Steele, 'Lord Salisbury and the "False Religion" of Islam', in E. M. Spiers (ed.), *Sudan. The Reconquest Reappraised* (1998), p. 12.
111 Countless references to Kitchener as General Gordon's avenger were made in the press: see for instance *Pall Mall Gazette*, 5 September 1898, p. 7; *The Times*, 8 September 1898, p. 10; *Illustrated London News*, 10 and 17 September 1898, pp. 377–9 and 411.
112 G. A. Henty, *With Kitchener in the Soudan* (1903), p. 245.
113 See Chapter 6 below, as well as B. Sèbe, 'From Thoissey to the capital via Fashoda: Major Marchand, partisan icon of the Right in Paris', in J. Wardhaugh (ed.), *Paris and the Right in the Twentieth Century* (Cambridge, 2006), pp. 18–42.
114 AN, F/7/15981/1, Police records of the *SG*, file '*Notes de police 1899–1906*', 12 December 1904.
115 E. Drumont, *La France juive* (1887), pp. 476–82.
116 H. Strachan, *The Politics of the British Army* (Oxford, 1997), p. 32.

117 D. Judd and K. Surridge, *The Boer War* (2002), pp. 287–97.
118 K. Neilson, 'Kitchener, Horatio Herbert, Earl Kitchener of Khartoum (1850–1916)', *ODNB* [Accessed 13 August 2005].
119 B. Singer and J. Langdon, *Cultured Force* (London and Madison, 2004), p. 181.
120 D. Rivet, *Lyautey et l'institution du protectorat français au Maroc, 1912–1925*, vol. I (1996), p. 150.
121 A. Tessier, *Lyautey* (2004), pp. 262–311.
122 R. Postal, *Présence de Lyautey* (1946), p. 110.
123 H. Lyautey to his sister, 9 February 1895, in H. Lyautey, *Lettres du Tonkin et de Madagascar* (1920), pp. 122–3.
124 Tessier, *Lyautey*, p. 444.
125 W. A. Hoisington, *Lyautey and the French Conquest of Morocco* (New York, 1995), pp. 1–20.
126 P. Doury, *Lyautey, un Saharien atypique* (2002), p. 117.
127 Rivet, *Lyautey*, 3 vols.
128 Rivet, *Lyautey*, vol. III, pp. 311–22.
129 H. Lyautey, 'Du rôle social de l'officier dans le service universel', *Revue des deux mondes*, 15 March 1891.
130 J. Benoist-Méchin, *Lyautey ou le rêve immolé* (Lausanne, 1966), pp. 21–2.
131 H. Lyautey, *Du rôle colonial de l'armée* (1900) in H. Lyautey, *Lettres du Tonkin et de Madagascar* (1920), pp. 629–53.
132 W. D'Ormesson, *Auprès de Lyautey* (1963), p. 102.
133 S. E. Howe, *Marshal Lyautey* (1931), p. 245.
134 Tessier, *Lyautey*, p. 237.
135 On the use of the mass media and audiovisual propaganda material by the Popular Front, see S. Dell, *The Image of the Popular Front. The Masses and the Media in Interwar France* (Basingstoke, 2007).
136 RHL, Perham Papers, 309/1, f. 25, Lady Flora Shaw to Sir Frederick Lugard, 13 November 1904.
137 H. Callaway and D. O. Helly, 'Journalism as active politics: Flora Shaw, *The Times* and South Africa', in D. Lowry (ed.), *The South African War Reapparaised* (Manchester, 2000), p. 51.
138 RHL, MSS Lugard, 2/6, ff. 37–8, Austen Chamberlain to Lord Lugard and Lugard to Chamberlain, 31 January and 3 February 1924.
139 RHL, MSS Lugard, 12/2, f. 13, speech reported in *The African World*, 8 December 1928.
140 RHL, MSS Lugard, 12/2, f. 6 , from H. Vischner to L. Lugard, 23 June 1936.
141 RHL, MSS Lugard, 14/9, ff. 63–4, Note by Lord Lugard and letter from Lyautey to Lugard, 6 February 1931.
142 M. Cornick, '*Faut-il réduire l'Angleterre en esclavage?* French Anglophobia in 1935', *Franco-British Studies*, 14 (January 1993), 3–17; R. Boyce, 'Behind the façade of the *Entente Cordiale* after the Great War', in A. Capet, *Britain, France and the Entente Cordiale since 1904* (Basingstoke, 2006), pp. 41–63.
143 J. Ferry, *Le Tonkin et la Mère-Patrie* (1890).

CHAPTER 5

Cross-Channel *entente*? The values embodied by imperial heroes

'In all epochs of the world's history, we shall find the Great Man to have been the indispensable saviour of his epoch', argued Thomas Carlyle in the first of his famous early Victorian lectures on heroes and hero-worship.[1] If we are to give any credit to this contemporary appraisal (after all, Carlyle exerted enormous influence upon Victorian minds), imperial heroes should have been seen, at least at the time when they were celebrated, as inspirers capable of playing a pivotal role in society, as trailblazers and moral, patriotic and religious examples. To the public of the two countries, their stories exemplified a set of values which matched the dominant mindset of the time, and their promotion was regarded as desirable. Most of the time, they were seen as epitomizing the civilizing enterprise, national grandeur and courage that advocates of imperialism expected to see displayed on the world stage through colonial expansion. Although the role of the colonial experience in the shaping of modern European national identities has long been undervalued, its central place has now been recognized.[2] Ultimately, the success of imperial heroes, fostered by the social, cultural and technological improvements of the Industrial Revolution (as we have seen in the previous chapters), was sustained by the fact that they embodied values which resonated in their societies at the time when they became heroes. Their reputations, which fuelled feelings of European superiority over indigenous populations and cultures, matched racial prejudices that gained the upper hand in Europe towards the end of the nineteenth century (in stark contrast to the triumph of philanthropic ideals in the early nineteenth century).[3] Conversely, their exemplarity could have been a good reason for a variety of hero-makers to support their legends, in an attempt either to promote their convictions under the mantle of edifying stories or to re-ignite beliefs they feared could be caught in a downward spiral.

The rise of imperial heroes occurred in the two countries against a backdrop which viewed favourably lessons taught by, and learnt through, exemplary historical figures (especially from the past), who were considered to be a reliable moral compass. Cicero's concept of *'Historia Magistra Vitae'* (history is the teacher of life) was particularly popular among educational thinkers: the recourse to history was seen as a means of learning from the past in order to emulate the best that earlier generations had offered, and to ensure that the most glorious moments were remembered from generation to generation. For instance, upon reviewing a new biography of Brazza, the monthly *L'Afrique française* argued that

> Such a biography should be spread assiduously among young people. It would help them understand the kind of dedication that France inspired in the past, and the nobility of soul which exists in some men.[4]

In Britain, national coherence and convictions crystallized frequently around heroes throughout a period that resorted to history as a way of understanding its present and preparing its future, notably under the influence of Carlyle and Ruskin.[5] Victorian interest in heroes was such that Walter Houghton's study of the Victorian age, with half a century of hindsight, dedicated a significant thirty-six-page chapter to 'hero-worship', which he presented as a 'nineteenth century phenomenon'.[6] In France, Christian Amalvi has demonstrated that a *'culte des grands hommes'* (cult of the Great Men) took shape from the Restoration onwards, resulting from a tradition initiated in the second half of the eighteenth century. In this last stage of the Enlightenment, it became fashionable to celebrate virtuous men who had bestowed upon humankind the benefit of knowledge and progress – one clear instance of such celebration being Laurent-Pierre Béranger's *La Morale en action par l'histoire* (Morality in action through history), published in 1783.[7] The celebration of Great Men and the concept of *'pédagogie par le grand homme'* (pedagogy through the Great Man) have been analysed from various angles, whether statues or schoolbooks, which all demonstrate the depth of French attachment to heroic figures.[8] More generally, Great Men played a pivotal role in French history and helped to entrench the popular belief in the *homme providentiel* who stood above political parties – which made the concept particularly suspicious to Third Republic politicians who saw in it a constant threat to a predominantly parliamentary regime.[9]

The edifying value of great lives was acknowledged very early on and was until the second half of the twentieth century a recurrent feature of educational strategies, ever since Plutarch undertook to teach history through biography in his *Lives*, which implied that great men could serve as models for imitation. The edifying power (*'pouvoir édificateur'*) of these exemplary lives was reinforced by the teaching of biographical details and myths to wide sections of the population. This was particularly true in the case of educational books or schoolbooks, as nearly all theoreticians of education (except Rousseau) have underlined the pedagogical value of Great Men as exemplary models to be given to children.[10] A good example of the strength of such a belief is given by Samuel Smiles's decision to feature a portrait of David Livingstone on the frontispiece of his best-selling book *Self-Help*, following the explorer's death.[11] The social, technological and commercial changes discussed earlier in this book extended the scope of this trend which also greatly benefited from the universalization of education and the concomitant development of an ever wider offer of written texts. This coincided in Britain with a 'Boswellian' interest in the detail of exemplary lives, typical of Victorian times, which generated further interest in biographies and ensured the persistence of heroic reputations throughout the life of most of Victorian Britons, from school to retirement.[12]

Beyond the common attributes displayed by heroes, which put to the forefront the notion of 'sacrifice' above and beyond the call of duty, and insisted upon their exceptional talents, imperial heroes presented a number of particularities which, taken together, made them a special type.[13] Because 'New Imperialism' was primarily about conquest, many of them shared some traits with the broader and more permanent category of the 'military hero' that had been so popular since the Napoleonic wars – and best represented by Wolfe, Nelson and Wellington, or Napoleon, Ney or Murat. Yet, beyond military ability (when applicable), imperial heroes also had to display highly specialized qualities, such as the capacity to lead or convert indigenous populations and inspire in them respect or awe for the conquering Europeans; the capacity to display, at least in appearance, superior moral values (including religious fervour, fairness or even in certain circumstances forgiveness); and the intelligence and empathy necessary to win local support from populations who might be intolerant of foreign interference. Most of the time, this meant that they had to be apparently endowed with charismatic qualities, in the Weberian sense: in other words, possessing 'a certain quality of an individual personality by virtue of which [the hero] is set apart from ordinary men and treated as endowed with supernatural, superhuman or at least superficially exceptional qualities'.[14] Their much-praised ability to display the highest levels of self-discipline was not only a way of generating admirative local support but it was also perfectly in keeping with dominant conceptions, especially prevalent in literary representations of masculinity.[15] The moral exemplarity of imperial heroes (often vividly reflected in sheer physical strength or, on the contrary, in self-restraint) cannot be separated from both the rise of nationalism linked to the development of nation-states and the quest for universalism of late-nineteenth-century Europe that was inherent to the concept of 'civilizing mission' underlying colonial expansion, and which Gary Wilder has argued was inherent to French republicanism.[16] The French Revolution, and especially the *déclaration des droits de l'homme*, clearly had universalist ambitions.[17] Even after the Restoration, Victor Hugo famously claimed that 'enlightened nations' would have to 'enlighten obscure nations' and that 'to educate mankind [was] Europe's mission'.[18] In Britain, imperial heroes matched the assumptions of the Whig interpretation of history that stressed the British fight for liberal freedom under the universal rule of law, and therefore made the British elite more self-confident about its world role.[19] At a more grassroots level, they reinforced the self-assigned European duty to shape the world in its image in order to spread progress. Eric Savarèse has shown the pivotal role played by school textbooks of the colonial era in promoting the vision of colonial history as an epic stressing the great deeds of colonial heroes, while native populations were left in the shadow.[20] These roles also tend to explain why imperial heroes proved to be so predominantly male, in a society that associated activity (conquest and progress) with manliness, and favoured a passive image of women confined to the role of mothers or, at best, nurses.[21]

This chapter considers primarily the moral meanings given to the heroic *reputations* of imperial heroes by their promoters, more than their actual moral achievements. Geoffrey Cubitt has described the process through which certain individuals are allocated 'imputed meanings and symbolic significance' that 'makes them the object of some kind of collective emotional investment', before adding that their lives are 'imaginatively reconstructed and rendered significant'.[22] This translation between the real lives and the 'heroic reputations' that develop out of them gives room for adding a special meaning to these destinies (*'destins'*). Contrary to today's celebrities, who bear 'no moral connection with moral elevation', the way heroic reputations took shape clearly reflected the requirement to fulfil an ethical agenda.[23] The ideological underpinnings of any heroization did not reflect real life as much as an attempt to alter its course in the future.[24]

Heroes' relatives or hero-makers were well aware throughout the period of the importance of this translation, and were very often actively involved in it. General Gordon's sister Henrietta once confided to Horace Waller, a major contributor to the posthumous legends of Livingstone and Gordon, as we saw earlier, that she considered that '[General Gordon's] Soudan letters were not well selected, in my opinion much would have been better left out'.[25] Indeed, several letters cast doubt upon Gordon's sanity and soundness of judgement when he was stranded in Khartoum and it was partly for that reason that Gladstone insisted that the government should not undertake the pruning office.[26] Understandably, his sister feared the letters, which were 'opinionated, egocentric, manipulative, and self-righteous' as his *Dictionary of National Biography* entry states, would damage his reputation and threaten the future of his legend.[27]

Events in the life of a hero also had to match the vision of the hero projected by his admirers. When Margery Perham wrote Lord Lugard's biography, his brother Edward Lugard ensured that the two-volume comprehensive biography did not mention his first love with an American divorcée named Celia, and that the corresponding series of love poems archived with the rest of the papers did not come to light. Edward Lugard also wrote in a preamble to the archives a statement under the title 'The Man as a Brother', which was expressly addressed to 'The Biographers of Lord Lugard' and intended to depict his brother under the best possible light.[28]

Heroes themselves realized the importance of posterity, and some of them allegedly orchestrated the image they wanted to leave behind them. One obvious case was Marshal Lyautey, who was so conscious of his posterity and sought so methodically to leave the best image of himself that he compiled throughout his life a voluminous personal archive, in which he meticulously assembled all articles, documents and letters that were related to himself in some way. He was reported as still ordering it the day before he died.[29] Sylvain Venayre has shown that the same happened with some famous adventurers of our period, such as Henry de Monfreid, who carefully polished his own image in his travel accounts, to enhance his posthumous image.[30]

Two major sequences have to be distinguished over the period 1870–1939, with the First World War as turning point. Imperial heroes of the forty-five years preceding the Great War contributed to the ethos advocated by the promoters of New Imperialism, and their reputations were significantly influenced by fashionable Social Darwinian approaches exacerbated by European racial assumptions, an increasingly competitive national self-assertion as well as muscular forms of masculinity (often in stark contrast with everyday practices and customs).[31] This was the moment when the Victorian ideal of heroes reached its full momentum, with imperial figures such as Gordon, Wolseley, Roberts and Kitchener regularly lionized in Britain. This phase came to an end with the disappearance of African territory available for conquest in 1912, and was abruptly halted in September 1914. By diverting all resources, media attention and hopes to the Western Front, the Great War caused a significant evolution in the way in which Africa and Africans were perceived by their white rulers.[32] The role and perception of imperial heroes concomitantly changed. First, imperial heroes did not stand a chance of remaining at all noticed in the press unless they performed an active role during the War. Those imperial heroes who did remain in the limelight, such as Gallieni or Marchand, did so because they led their men on the front, and it was worth reporting. Secondly, they faced the danger of being overtaken by concurrent reputations attached to heroes of the Great War, such as Pétain (the hero of Verdun) or Joffre (the winner of the battle of the Marne). Even Kitchener's reputation as a hero of the First World War tended to overshadow his pre-existing fame as an imperial hero. His being featured on the well-known 'great poster' (as Margot Asquith put it), which did not bear his name, and played only on the symbolic value of his face, does testify to prewar celebrity. Yet, as the poster became a powerful icon, the prewar colonial past of the hero tended to become second to the wartime figure.[33] This shift in heroic traditions related to all heroes, including, for instance, Captain Scott.[34] The war severed the pre-1914 cultural and social patterns (especially in France), and the place and role of imperial heroes in the two countries therefore changed, in particular because the place of the colonies in society evolved, and heroes were celebrated as the founding fathers of a system which became increasingly valued as the worldwide standing of the two countries was threatened.[35] The last part of this chapter considers in more detail this shift towards the celebration of a bygone age.

Victorian and Edwardian Britain had apparently little in common with Third Republic France, and it could be argued that comparing the incomparable is artificial. After all, a contemporary theoretician of the British empire, J. R. Seeley, once wrote of 'a gulf which seemed as unbridgeable as that moral gulf which separates an Englishman from a Frenchman'.[36] Indeed, imperial matters very often caused disagreement between the two countries, occasionally pushing them to the brink of open confrontation, and mutual distaste was not uncommon. Yet, because of this harsh competition, the values embodied by imperial heroes in Britain and in France presented common features and often paralleled each other. It is acknowledged that Franco-British and Anglo-French antagonism have played a pivotal role in national identity making on each side of the Channel.[37] All in all, this is a story of competitive emulation more than outright repulsion, and drawing a sharp moral distinction between the two countries on the subject of imperial heroes would be a perilous as well as an artificial task.

The late nineteenth century was propitious to hero-worship in Britain, not only because, as discussed earlier, the socio-economic context made hero-worship easier and more efficient but also because there was a distinct search for moral inspiration at a time when accelerated industrialization and, above all, religious uncertainty threatened established beliefs, as Walter Houghton argued:

> To the Victorians, a hero [...] was certain to be a man of the highest moral stature, and therefore of enormous importance to a period in which the alarming increase of both the commercial spirit and religious doubt made moral inspiration a primary need.[38]

This quest for moral examples contributed to the success of several heroic reputations of the period – especially that of David Livingstone. One of his contemporary biographers ended his preface hoping that 'the lessons [this book] is intended to convey, may be deeply impressed upon the minds and hearts of those who read it'.[39] A more modern biographer of Livingstone's remarked that '[Victorian Britain] took him to his heart because he embodied all the ingredients of heroism that it idealizes – rugged simplicity, a victory against odds, dedication to a cause, plus a patina of piety that stirred the emotions'.[40]

In the mid-1880s, General Gordon equally encapsulated deeply Victorian values, and the Tories did not have a monopoly when it came to praising their moral resonance among the British public. In the wake of the fall of Khartoum, Gladstone pronounced a posthumous moral eulogy in response to his Liberal colleague John Morley in the Commons:

> [The Right hon. gentleman, Mr John Morley] stated that General Gordon had devoted his life, and all that makes life valuable, to his Sovereign and to the country. Sir, he might have enlarged that eulogium, for the life of General Gordon was not limited even to those great objects. It was devoted to his Sovereign, to his country, and likewise to the world. General Gordon's sympathies were not limited by race, or colour, or religion. In point of fact, he seems to have deemed it his special honour to devote his energies and to risk his existence on behalf of those with whom he had no other tie than that of human sympathy. General Gordon was a hero, and permit me to say he was still more – he was a hero among heroes. For there have been men who have obtained and deserved the praise of heroism whose heroism was manifested chiefly on the field of battle or in other conflicts, and who, when examined in the tenour of their personal lives, were not in all respects heroic; but if you take the case of this man, pursue him into privacy, investigate his heart and his mind, you will find that he proposed to himself not any ideal of wealth and power, or even fame, but to do good was the object he proposed to himself in his whole life, and for that one object it was his one desire to spend his existence. Such is the man we have lost – a loss great, indeed; but he is not all lost, for such examples are fruitful in the future, and I

trust there will grow from the contemplation of that character and those deeds other men who in future time may emulate his noble and most Christian example.[41]

Gladstone's words are revealing on two accounts. First, they were pronounced by the Prime Minister who was widely held responsible for Gordon's death, and who had the least interest in promoting the legend of the 'Hero of Khartoum' (although he had to show extra deference to Gordon's qualities as he was responsible for his despatch to Khartoum). This was actually very much in line with the position the liberal press had adopted throughout the Sudan crisis, showing respect towards Gordon's heroic qualities whilst trying to downplay the emotion stirred by his loss.[42] Secondly, this eulogy skilfully combined several levels of argumentation that reveal the qualities an idealized imperial hero had to display in 1885 to be 'a hero among heroes'. Patriotism, fidelity to the Sovereign, universality regardless of 'race, colour or religion' and the charitable desire 'to do good' were the cornerstones; but Gordon's personal asceticism that went hand in hand with setting a 'Christian example' were equally important. Gladstone also paid particular attention to the 'exemplarity' of Gordon for future generations. Christianity, universality and an exceptional selflessness surpassed the mere heroism of the usual military hero on the battlefield. On many accounts, the Gordon legend was a vast moral programme which was widely publicized by a variety of books, pamphlets and newspaper articles, the output of which reached an unparalleled peak in 1885.[43] Gladstone's celebration of the General is all the more remarkable as Gordon was obviously an ideal 'symbol of the rightness and righteousness of imperialism' for the advocates of New Imperialism who precisely had to overcome the Prime Minister's doctrinal reluctance to British imperial expansion.[44] Gladstone's speech shows that the edifying value of the Gordon legend had to be praised even by those who would have benefited politically from the weakening of his reputation.

This pattern of 'exemplarity' applied in varying degrees to all other imperial heroes, as it was one of the major roles heroes were expected to fulfil. Stanley was presented in the same light in the opening paragraph of a biography published in 1890 by a writer who established for his own benefit a symbolic line of heroic descent on the title page through the statement 'by the author of *"The Life of General Gordon"'*:

> All nations honour their heroes: and the world at large claims Stanley, and gives him almost unanimous applause. He is a hero, not chiefly because he has fought battles, but because he has faced tremendous dangers for the rescue of others, and has coveted for himself neither emoluments nor fame. He has proved himself a genius by his painstaking work, and a

brave man as well by his true courage as by his gentleness. He has never known what cowardice is, and has not hesitated to stand to his post when ninety-nine men out of a hundred would have fled.[45]

Once again, Stanley's heroism was not only due to military prowess (which was the basis for previous military legends) and intrepidity, but owed a lot to his supposed altruism and unselfishness, even at the cost of gross inaccuracy. Stanley's journey to find Livingstone for the *New York Herald* did not exactly confirm that he 'coveted neither emoluments nor fame', and his 'gentleness' was not so unanimously praised in the wake of the Emin Pasha relief expedition, which had just taken place. For all its flaws, such an *incipit* reflected an idealized vision of Stanley, intent to promoting a set of values that went far beyond sheer strength, and put the emphasis on moral qualities such as courage, dauntlessness, selflessness, and the use of his exceptional abilities to 'rescue [...] others', as the author put it.[46]

It is hardly surprising therefore that imperial heroes were used to serve a strict moral agenda in children's literature, as their example was expected to teach a certain set of moral values and practices.[47] Several studies have demonstrated how boys' literature (periodicals and adventure tales alike) promoted imperial enthusiasm, and their findings can be extended to imperial heroes.[48] The names of Kitchener, Buller and Roberts were featured in the titles of three of George Henty's very popular children's books.[49] Although Henty's heroes are typically young adolescent boys, and great imperial figures feature in the background, the fact that they bore titles mentioning military heroes served 'one of Henty's frankly acknowledged aims', which was 'to teach British boys how to behave'.[50] Constant references to the pantheon of British imperial heroes allowed Henty to promote his enthusiasm for colonial expansion, his deep belief in British moral superiority and his interpretation of the colonies as lands of opportunities able to bestow prosperity, physical strength and moral rectitude upon their conquerors.[51] Children's education was of primary importance in perpetuating those qualities most valued by Englishmen of the time, and which the historian Emil Reich argued were acquired thanks to strength of character and will: 'The Englishman's idea is that the world is ruled by character, by will, and in order to secure himself that domination, he appplies himself to the development of those qualities.'[52] Such qualities could be conveniently taught in juvenile literature using the example of imperial heroes: as we have seen, many authors (including Henty) used them to serve an edifying purpose at the time of the 'democratization of manliness'.[53] Henty himself claimed for himself this formative role when he declared 'I know that very many boys have joined the cadets and afterwards gone into the army through reading my stories'.[54] Young readers could be persuaded that great imperial figures such as Cecil Rhodes combined exceptional talent as empire-builders and social conscience.[55]

On the other side of the Channel, school textbooks of the Third Republic included chapters that taught children to love the values embodied by imperial heroes (as we will see later) while the production of cheap biographies popularized the idea of a 'France overseas'. In his study of the 'immaterial pantheons of national memory', Christian Amalvi argued that after 1870 a form of consensus towards a 'national Pantheon' appeared among authors of popular literature. Among the dead heroes featured in popular biographies which he analysed, six (notably seamen) were linked to the first colonial empire, totalling forty-one books: Duguay-Trouin (seventeen biographies), Duquesne (ten), Montcalm (six), Dupleix (four), La Pérouse (four).[56] Although they were far from the top two national heroes (Napoleon with 205 biographies and Joan of Arc with 191), they attest to a steady interest in colonial history that made living imperial heroes (*de facto* excluded from Amalvi's 'Pantheon' as they were still alive) a potential good source of exemplary lives, as we shall see in this chapter.

Among the various values that could be exemplified through imperial heroes, three stood out between 1870 and 1914. First, they spurred the taste for exploration, the cult of progress (see for instance how Hugo or Beaudelaire supported the linearity of time) and the belief in the 'civilizing mission' that frequently went along with heartfelt admiration for the entrepreneur, characteristic of the era of New Imperialism. Secondly, in certain cases, these heroes played the role of religious examples, not only spiritually but also in concrete terms in their struggle with other religions (especially Islam) or with paganism. Thirdly, with the 'age of empire', imperial heroes (especially in their military version) intrinsically embodied patriotic and nationalist values.[57]

As Robert Cornevin has demonstrated, explorers who served as examples to young Europeans in the 1870s had operated in Africa in the majority of cases.[58] Although Asia was the breeding ground of several military heroes, very few heroes of exploration gained their fame following action on this continent. *Terrae incognitae* were located mostly in Africa and it is hardly surprising that exploration proved a key value in the legends attached to imperial heroes who acted in Africa.

As we have seen in the first chapter, geographical societies were leading promoters of geographical knowledge, the imperial project and those who served these causes, and as such they lay at the nexus between exploration, imperial expansion and heroism. A major channel of recognition and promotion of the work done by explorers, they institutionalized the intrinsic qualities of exploration and promoted the values on which the developing geographical science was based. The *Société de géographie* sought to promote the moral value of exploration through its famous medals, which were inevitably accompanied by a *discours de réception* where the intrinsic value of exploration and geography was as much praised as the achievements of the recipient. Besides, the *Bulletins* of French geographical societies, in Paris and in the provinces, were eager to publicize the deeds of 'our great Africans', which went along with a celebration of Western science, geographical methods and imperial expansion.[59] In Britain, the ethos of the Royal Geographical Society is reflected by the case of its President from the 1850s until the 1870s, Sir Roderick Murchison, whose 'concerns with empire and geography were so intertwined, that it is difficult to say where one ended and the other began'.[60] More generally, scholars in the field of geography's history have shown the close links between geographical knowledge and imperialism (and even between geography and war).[61] In such context, explorers could easily be used to promote the cause of imperial geography and colonial expansion – Felix Driver argued that Murchison did not hesitate to make full use of the 'sensationalism' surrounding African exploration.[62] David N. Livingstone's work made a case for a history of geography that would consider more closely the links between geographical texts and 'contexts'.[63] A similar approach to the imperial heroes promoted by members of the Royal Geographical Society and other geographical societies highlights the values and beliefs that the societies sought to propagate through these exemplary individuals, and how these reputations partook of the wider trend of imperial heroes: it is certainly not a coincidence if it has been remarked that 'some of the obligatory adjectives preceding the noun *explorer*' were '*intrepid, heroic, courageous*'.[64]

A librarian at the RGS published in January 1890 in the *Contemporary Review* an article entitled 'What Stanley has done for the map of Africa'. The summary of the explorer's contribution to African geography includes a celebration of the courage, endurance and explorational acumen displayed by the man who 'entered [Central Africa] as a newspaper correspondent to find and succour Livingstone, and came out burning with the fever of African exploration'. Two maps compared European knowledge of the interior of Africa 'before' and 'after' Stanley, the former being nearly blank and the latter bursting with details.[65] Although Stanley's fame stemmed mainly from his own articles, or articles on him, in the popular press, pieces such as J. S. Keltie's published in prestigious reviews like the *Contemporary Review* gave Stanley a moral clout that only a third party could grant him. Similarly, the support lent to Henri Duveyrier by the Paris *Société de géographie* (and particularly by its Secretary General, Charles Maunoir) compensated for the relative lack of governmental support for the explorer, and it spread his reputation as a tactful negotiator and an eminent specialist of Saharan African affairs, which was widely publicized in various newspapers in the late 1860s and 1870s – especially when he arranged for a Franco-Tuareg treaty of trade and friendship to be signed.[66] Through the promotion of such achievements, geographical societies publicized the benefits bestowed by exploration.

Recognition fostered by geographical societies or circles could go beyond journal or newspaper articles. An ambitious 'Stanley and African exhibition' was set up in London's Victoria Gallery (Regent Street) shortly after it became known in London that Stanley had successfully completed his crossing of Africa. Through Stanley, the organizers (many of whom had close links with the Royal Geographical Society) sought to promote the idea of the European domination of Africa due to the efficiency, intellectual value and moral standards of white men such as Stanley. As Felix Driver remarked, the exhibition was primarily 'devoted to the accomplishments of British men in Africa (especially explorers, missionaries, traders and hunters)': these imperial heroes were used to popularize a set of values that justified imperial expansion, and especially the opening up and conquest of the 'Dark Continent'.[67] Imperial heroes were also regularly featured in specific pavilions of universal or colonial exhibitions, where they were presented as the founders of a highly successful imperial epic.[68] The theatricalization of their overseas action suited very well the commodification of culture which unfolded in the period.[69]

This instance of *mise en scène* of a hero with pedagogical undertones is far from isolated. Waller wrote proudly to Livingstone after seeing the explorer's statue at the Royal Academy:

> You were exhibited in the Royal Academy this year, clad in knicker bockers, gaiters, a huge revolver strapped around your abdomen and a sword by your side – o' you did look so beautiful! and I need not say so, natural![70]

In Waller's eyes, the 'huge revolver' and the sword did not seem to contradict the religious role the missionary had to perform. The 'beauty' of the heroic statue reflected the pureness of his soul, while his weapons were just tools to exert his right of conquest and duty to spread civilization. Yet Waller was right in that this statue encapsulated Livingstone's ideas: he relentlessly advocated European intervention in Africa in order (supposedly) to raise the living standards of Africans through free trade (through exports of raw material), an improvement that would in turn open African hearts to the message of Christian salvation.[71] David Livingstone's 'legacy', as Dorothy Helly put it, included a belief in Britain's civilizing mission that may even have influenced Joseph Chamberlain's justification of the annexation of Uganda on the grounds of a 'manifest destiny' in 1894.[72]

In France, the *mission civilisatrice* was, quite famously, a pivotal aspect of Third Republic expansionism, and it was a recurrent theme in the literature dedicated to imperial figures. Bugeaud and Lyautey embodied the old myth of France as a righteous soldier defending the world against the oppression and barbarity of ignorance, which was largely used by colonial propagandists to promote the ideal concept of the empire builder (*'le bâtisseur d'empire'*). It was not a coincidence that Bugeaud's motto was *Ense et Aratro* ('With sword and plough'). This concept was particularly popular among journalists and authors of school textbooks who were eager to present manly, good and magnanimous imperial heroes who knew how to make the most of newly conquered territories (in particular through the concept of *'mise en valeur'*).[73] Lyautey liked to claim that 'my enemies of to-day will be my collaborators of to-morrow and the places which I take at the point of the bayonet must be turned into market places'.[74] Lyautey biographies constantly praised his strategy to conquer new territories by moderate force while paving the way for future co-operation and development, which were supposedly conducive to indigenous admiration for, and gratitude towards, the colonizer for the beneficial implementation of *Pax Gallica*.[75] As Amalvi remarked, colonial heroes made it a 'sacrilege' to refuse the 'happiness' brought by the tricolour.[76]

Most of the time, schoolbook authors represented colonial campaigns as a conflict between good and evil. They resorted to highly symbolic and Manichean scenes, especially when targeting a young audience. Engravings showing Cardinal Lavigerie buying out African slaves in order to liberate them were common; the questions asked below the image were designed to lead the child to understand the gratitude the slaves felt towards their liberator.[77] One of the key images featured in schoolbooks represented Brazza freeing slaves in the Congo.[78] In one instance, a secondary school textbook illustrated the French expansion under the Republic with four engravings. The top left image featured the slaughter of the Flatters mission in 1881, in an attempt to disqualify morally the local inhabitants for attacking the peaceful soldier-explorer and his column. The second image, top right, showed Brazza welcomed by King Makoko who 'wanted to give the Congo to France', according to the caption. The third illustration represented the victorious attack of Fuzhou by Admiral Courbet during the campaigns against China in 1884–85. The fourth and last image of the series, at the bottom right, showed the capture of the Dahomean king Behanzin by Colonel Dodds, with a revealing caption: 'He captures King Behanzin and puts an end to all the ever-growing number of human sacrifices that the negro despot liked to perform.'[79] Thus multiple facets of the colonial hero are shown: he falls victim of the 'savagery' of the indigenous populations (Flatters), performs a civilizing role, making local rulers understand the benefit of co-operation with Europeans (Brazza), or fights successfully the forces of ignorance and cannibalism (Courbet and Dodds).

The 'Marchand legend' was also promoted to the young generations. Gabriel Galland's *Une poignée de héros: la mission Marchand à travers l'Afrique* intended to teach children the virtues of French character – duty, honour and patriotism – through Marchand's example. In the typical patriotic discourse prevalent under the Third Republic, the author wanted his reader to be ready to die for his motherland, and to learn from Marchand how to value devotion and the spirit of sacrifice.[80] Galland's work thereby turned Marchand into an edifying example for young French boys and girls. The theme of imperial heroes easily and vividly conveyed to the children an evocative, albeit simplistic, message that they could easily visualize. This goes a long way towards explaining their popularity in school textbooks intending to spread the message of the 'civilizing mission' to generations of State school pupils. British school textbooks played a pivotal role in the promotion of imperial heroes from the 1890s onwards, when free primary education increased the ideological impact of such texts.[81] For instance, in the sixth volume of her 1890 textbook, Miss Yonge described Gordon as the prototype of the Christian warrior, and praised the 'spirit that sustained him and made his death a victory of the soul and his name one that will live for ever more'.[82] Gordon's exemplarity was clearly stressed for consumption by young minds.

British propagandists could use a type of hero peculiar to the British Isles to embody the economic development that they argued went along imperial expansion: the figure of the individual entrepreneur was a singularly British aspect of the civilizing mission. To a large extent, it also tended to epitomize the 'heroic imperialist', combining political clout, business acumen and military abilities. Cecil Rhodes and Sir George Goldie and their personal South and West African empires were the most telling examples offered to imperial apologists. Goldie has never aroused much interest (seemingly because he tried to escape public attention), and very few books or biographies have dealt with him.[83] By contrast, Cecil Rhodes was much more prominent in his own lifetime and performed many political roles, and accounts of his life were extensively used by his admirers to promote various values. Rhodes exemplifies the potential for over-interpretation of a hero's real life into a projected life, in a context when historical facts of conquest were 'rearranged, dramatised and mythologised almost as soon as they happened' in an attempt to epitomize the triumph of civilization over barbarism.[84] The Janus-like Rhodes legend caused intense admiration among some, and deep contempt and criticism among others. Advocates of the 'chauvinistic approval' school were naturally those most intent on praising Rhodes as an exemplary figure.[85]

In his detailed study of the *Cult of Rhodes*, Paul Maylam has summed up the essential characteristics of the heroic Rhodes so eagerly promoted by his former associates, who, in what appeared to be an attempt to counter the attacks of his already numerous contemporary critics, became what Maylam called his 'hagiographers'. The term refers particularly to his former associates and admirers, such as the former *Fortnightly Review* assistant editor John Verschoyle, the MP James Rochfort Maguire and a few others who knew him very well, such as Howard Hensman, Thomas Fuller, Lewis Michell, Philip Jourdan, Ian Colvin, Gordon Le Sueur, Vere Stent, J. G. MacDonald and Herbert Baker.[86] On the basis of their personal recollections, and their own admiration for their hero, they depicted him as a visionary and a man of ideas, whose foresight had allowed Britain to claim the lion's share in southern Africa, and therefore to spread British values and culture in this part of the world. In an attempt to exempt him from the probable criticism that he was only a contemptible materialist, hagiographers emphasized that he was not interested in money itself, but only in the power it gave him to carry out his projects: one of the most controversial aspects of his personality was thereby turned into a quality. For his hagiographers, Rhodes was 'selfless, driven by a sense of duty and service towards Britain and southern Africa, and by a concern for the welfare of others'.[87] Besides, they became increasingly willing to shape an image of Rhodes as a friend of the Africans in order to dismiss the accusations of racism that came to be voiced as beliefs in Social Darwinism were losing strength and starting to come under fire. They also stressed Rhodes's qualities as a man of action endowed with a strong personality (an argument they used to excuse the gross mistake of the Jameson Raid), to such an extent that Sidney Low, editor of the *St James Gazette*, wrote that 'a belief in Rhodes became a substitute for religion'[88] and that Rudyard Kipling is said to have described him in 1898 as 'the greatest of living men'.[89] Maguire, who wrote under the revealing pseudonym of 'Imperialist', saw in Rhodes a personality combining unique qualities:

> [The Colonists of Rhodesia], like the Cape Dutchmen, have felt the charm of greatness of ideas combined with simplicity of tastes; have come to

know his large nature and perfect frankness and manliness; and men who once believed in Rhodes from their belief in Jameson, now know their great man and believe in him for himself. The free unconventional life of a young country suited one who needs no trappings of office or title to enhance his greatness, who loves reality and hates ceremony and show.[90]

To the eyes of his hagiographers, who retained the upper hand well until the 1930s, Cecil Rhodes exemplified entrepreneurship, vision, strength, leadership and devotion to Britain and the British Empire, all values they judged highly commendable and that they sought to spread among British society through numerous hagiographical works.

The hagiographers even went beyond praising the qualities of their hero. By turning potentially criticizable actions into further proofs of Rhodes's personal value as a faithful friend and a man of honour, they revealed the mechanisms of the hagiographic process. In his chapter on the consequences of the Jameson Raid, one such author claimed that

[Rhodes] was actually far more concerned for Jameson than for himself; and he seems to have guided his immediate action, especially with regard to the High Commissioner's Proclamation, by a strong feeling of sympathy for his friend which made him anxious to give him every possible chance to avoid the impending failure. A less large and generous nature would have taken care to safeguard himself, but Mr. Rhodes thought only of standing by his impetuous comrade, of not making the situation worse for his old friend by disowning him.[91]

The inappropriateness of the Jameson Raid was therefore presented under a much more favourable light that saved both the reputation and the moral value of the entrepreneur.

The Victorian era praised the work of another type of imperial entrepreneur, but of a religious nature this time: the missionary. The wave of New Imperialism coincided with the acme of British Protestant missionary activity, as a result of internal, metropolitan factors as well as those linked to the development of colonial rule (with which missionaries had ambiguous relations).[92] Founded in 1796, the London Missionary Society led a missionary impulse that was geared towards both foreign evangelization and action directed at Britain's own ostensibly heathen working classes, often promoting what has been termed 'missionary celebrity'.[93] Missionary heroes represented an excellent interface between the two sides of missionary activities. Consequently, missionary societies were anxious to censor through complex systems of patronage and control the accounts published by their envoys, in order to convey a convincing message to Christian readers.[94] The public consumption of material promoting its 'most famous missionary son',

David Livingstone, studied earlier in this book, has shown the profound appeal of his legend in Britain.[95] Dorothy Helly has analysed the way in which Horace Waller pruned the *Last Journals* of the missionary, taking out in particular all racial or sexual remarks in order to deliver as pure an image as possible, which would strenthen his exemplarity.[96] All these initiatives shared the aim of presenting to the public an idealized, highly religious image of Livingstone which the title of his own first popular account, *Missionary Travels and Researches in South Africa*, had clearly claimed for him as early as 1857. The real or idealized path he opened proved exceptionally influential: it was a guiding principle of missionary work in southern Africa, not least through the naming of missions after him, and his life was prominently featured in all the Victorian books of heroes, making him one of the most celebrated embodiments of Victorian ideals.[97] The religious dimension of his commitment was always underlined, as was clearly shown by numerous biographies that referred to him, in a typically biblical vein, as a good and faithful servant of the Lord (an example being H. G. Adams's 1867 biography mentioned earlier) or by his epitaph in Westminster Abbey, the first lines of which stated 'For thirty years his life was spent in an unwearied effort to evangelize / The native races'. The author of a book on Livingstone, Gordon and Patteson, published by the Society for Promoting Christian Knowledge, went even further: he linked these 'Three Martyrs of the Nineteenth Century' (two of whom are central to this book) to the theories of Social Darwinism, making them religious examples as well as proofs of the theory of the 'survival of the fittest', thus oddly combining in the same movement religious, imperial and evolutionary considerations:

> Here are three men inspired, through historical Christianity and the Eternal Spirit, to rise entirely above the ordinary aims of the world, so inwardly convinced of the truth of the old Faith, so steeped in its light, that death to each of them was but the last of countless acts of sacrifice which they thought no sacrifice for the joy of love which inspired them. ... Here are three hearts glowing with a passion to succour and to save ... .
>
> And again, if we come to a narrower national horizon, our England, our 'Greater Britain', is said by some to be verging towards decline, false to her old ideals, capable only of selfish aims and vacillating efforts as of decrepid old age. But here are three of her sons with a romantic, boyish love of enterprise, keen as in the days of Drake and Raleigh and the old explorers; and with a chivalrous care for the weak and oppressed such as King Arthur might have craved for his Round Table. ...
>
> And, moreover, these lives are no anachronisms, no mere exceptional abnormal survivals of obsolete forms, but essentially normal 'survival of the fittest'.[98]

This extract by Elizabeth Rundle Charles (1828–96), who acknowledged her authorship indirectly through a reference to her very successful *Chronicles of the Schönberg-Cotta Family*, frequently uses the notion of 'sacrifice' that proved so pivotal to many imperial heroes, in particular when they bore religious meanings. Gananath Obeyesekere has demonstrated the potency of 'apotheoses' in Christian cultures of those who died violent deaths.[99] Gordon's violent end at the hand of the Mahdi's army played a highly symbolic role in promoting his image as a selfless officer invested with quasi mystical religious powers. G. W. Joy clearly underlined this religious dimension in his representation of Gordon's assassination:

> It was, he said 'truly one of the most pathetic sights in all history. Stern determination, not unmixed with scorn, is in his whole bearing. One cannot help being reminded of that other scene in dark Gethsemane, the most momentous and tragic the world has ever witnessed, and of the words: – "Whom seek ye?"'[100]

The sacrifice of the hero's life was a singularly powerful symbol of his devotion to the cause, self-sacrifice being closely associated with altruism: a biographer of Livingstone's remarked that 'like all true heroes, instead of toiling for himself, he [Livingstone] gave his services to God and mankind'.[101] A violent and 'sacrificial' end was a powerful heroic marker in Victorian Britain, contrary to the late twentieth century, when it lost some of its value in societies that increasingly see death as a taboo.[102]

Death appeared all the more sacrificial as imperial heroes usually performed their deeds in non-Christian territories. Christian martyrs, such as General Gordon or Charles de Foucauld (the latter initiated the 'Association for the Growth of the Missionary Spirit'),[103] embodied the fight against Islam which was sometimes openly advocated in missionary circles. Their deaths were seen as a form of victory: 'it was not just as a moral victory but as a victory of the will'.[104] G. W. Joy (he again) lamented that 'To have had his warnings and advice rejected by his own countrymen until too late, and to be slain by those he came to succour and set free – such was Gordon's fate.'[105] The epilogue of the Gordon chapter in the afore-mentioned book by E.R. Charles argued that the hero of Khartoum had made it 'impossible to forget that every Christian life is a warfare to the end, because the Church is still militant here below, an army of conquest against stronghold after stronghold of iniquity and wrong'.[106] The theme of the fight between the enlightened Christian Gordon and the obscure, vicious and fanatical Muslim Mahdi quickly became a cliché linked to the General.[107] The combination of the religious and military roles of a hero, and the need to repel forcefully Muslim challenges, were clearly implied in the book *Heroes of Our Empire*, which included a chapter on 'General Gordon. The Christian Soldier and Hero'.[108] Still, in 1910, Protestant pioneers who gathered in Edinburgh were urged to 'throw a strong missionary force right across the centre of Africa to bar the advance of the Moslem and to carry the Gospel northwards'.[109] The belief that the European conquest of Africa had the duty to counter Muslim expansionism was also widely spread (although not universally) among sympathizers of the French colonial army.[110]

Once the Sudan had been re-conquered in 1898, Gordon came to represent the final triumph of Christianity in Khartoum, to such an extent that he seemed almost a local saint to the British expatriates and was extensively remembered in the newly built Westernized city, which seemed literally to revolve around his legend: the Gordon statue was located in Khartoum's main square, on Gordon Avenue. Gordon played the role of the spiritual founding father of colonial Khartoum. Significantly, Khartoum Cathedral had been designed to remind worshippers of the religious meanings of the Gordon legend, as stated on the occasion of the consecration of the Cathedral, on the twenty-seventh anniversary of Gordon's death (1912):

> Preaching on Consecration Day from the text 'Greater love hath no man than this, that a man lay down his life for his friends', he [the Bishop of London] passed from Gordon's self-sacrifice to the sacrifice of God, and earnestly urged all, the Administrator or Official in his office or his distant Province, the soldier at his post, to take strength from the thought of 'God, as his comrade', to be true to all that made Gordon great, and so be a living witness to Gordon's God.[111]

A further twenty-three years later, on the occasion of the fiftieth anniversary of the death of Gordon, in a sermon in Khartoum Cathedral, the Canon of Westminster Abbey referred to 'that spiritual legacy which Gordon has bequeathed to the Sudan'.[112] Even after the Second World War, for the thirty-fifth anniversary of the Cathedral's consecration, it was remembered that 'the Cathedral was built by the gifts of rich and poor alike as a fitting memorial of Charles George Gordon, and as a worthy monument of the Christian Faith'.[113] Another author of the same period claimed that 'out of the death of General Gordon sprang the first seeds of an English Cathedral in Khartoum, for, through his martyrdom, peace and security were established'.[114] Gordon was remembered in several places and through several means in the Khartoum cathedral, notably with a Gordon chapel, a Gordon altar, a Gordon lectern, a Gordon east window, a Gordon west window, a Gordon sanctuary lamp and a Gordon memorial inscription.[115] The inscription for the west wall of the Gordon Chapel best summarized the religious meaning that the Gordon legend had been invested with: 'Praise God / For Charles George Gordon / The Servant of Jesus-Christ / Whose labour was not in vain / in the Lord'.[116]

Naturally, such religious fervour for the imagined and idealized Gordon presented him holier than he was. His supposed freedom from ostentation and pride, notably claimed by Tennyson on the epitaph he wrote for St Paul's Cathedral ('O never proud in life lie down in pride') and his 'passionate love and desire to serve the oppressed people of the Sudan' praised in religious sermons[117] was not always so evident in his private letters:

> 3 years ago I gave you a memo of my ideas of what ought to be done to establish a sort of Hudson Bay Company in Africa. Are you prepared to carry this out? If so I will be inclined to help as far as I can. I do not like Belgians, I could not dispute with Kings. I must be King of the territory as far as appts [appointments] go. Would Kirk [James Kirk] get the concession? That is the most important point. I do not believe in Kirk. I think he would never be content with a passive part. Waller thinks otherwise.[118]

This private exchange with MacKinnon shows the gulf between the projected, polished image of Gordon as a religious example and patron saint of Khartoum, and his real personality which was much more complex and not devoid of defects (such as pride or manoeuvring). However, these were glossed over to fit the religious requirements of the Gordon legend.

In France, the perception of some imperial heroes as religious examples was less easily possible as the Third Republic maintained tense relations with Rome and anti-clericalism remained rife and constantly developing until it culminated in the separation between State and Church in 1905.[119] Overt association between Republican nationalism and religion was therefore not common, except perhaps when France claimed its duty to protect Christian minorities, as was the case in the Ottoman empire where France projected a 'Christian image' that was not in keeping with its anti-clerical domestic policies.[120] In Africa, missionaries rarely worked in harmony with the representatives of the Third Republic, especially since, for practical reasons, the colonial administration was reluctant to interfere in religious matters whenever Muslims were involved.[121] Cardinal Lavigerie allegedly embarrassed French authorities in Algeria with his zealous proselytism, but he remained a popular figure in Republican France for his fight against slavery, as noted earlier. In the eyes of French Catholics, he was even more: being based in a predominantly Muslim territory, he was permanently performing a 'divine mission'.[122] Besides having contributed to the reconciliation of the Republic and the clergy thanks to the famous 'toast of Algiers' in 1890 (which paved the way for the rapprochement formalized in Pope Leo XIII's encyclical *Au milieu des sollicitudes*), he was remembered for consecrating the cathedral of *Notre Dame d'Afrique* in Algiers in 1872 and for creating the *Fondation des Pères Blancs* in 1868 and the *Sœurs Missionnaires d'Afrique* in 1869, in both cases with the overt intention to convert North and black Africa to Christianity. An imposing statue representing Cardinal Lavigerie was displayed on the esplanade in front of *Notre Dame d'Afrique* in Algiers, attesting the importance of the Cardinal as a religious hero of French (but not Republican) Catholicism in Africa. Naturally, he also inspired generations of missionaries who became Little Brothers and Little Sisters, to whom he served as a religious example. Some Catholic authors felt that the French missionary epic was underplayed in Republican France, and endeavoured to celebrate their memory in books such as Valérien Groffier's *Héros trop oubliés de notre épopée coloniale*, an ode to missionary work published just three years after the separation of Church and State.[123]

If imperial heroes illustrated a variety of real or supposed qualities (such as civilizing powers, entrepreneurship and religious exemplarity, as we have just seen), they all had at least one common denominator: they served to reinforce and comfort the patriotic beliefs of their fellow countrymen in an age of triumphant nationalism all over Europe.[124] They quickly became almost universal national references which made them constitutive elements of 'banal nationalism', which were just 'near the surface of contemporary life'.[125] Patriotism crossed party lines in both countries: in Britain, it proved to be a radical ideal before becoming a favourite theme of the right, and in France it repeatedly played a unifying role, whether during the Revolutionary wars or the Great War.[126] Unsurprisingly, imperial heroes of this period are inseparable from national beliefs. As a direct consequence, military commanders were clearly over-represented. In a world where violent conquest was still tolerated and even encouraged to further national status, male heroes were the norm, whilst heroines were confined to a more allegorical than exemplary role, and women served the nation as procreators rather than conquerors.[127]

In Britain, the military hero of empire was cherished by the Victorians who admired his chivalric and Christian virtues revealed by the colonial enterprise.[128] Clearly, this category pre-existed and survived the Victorian era: some officers had become heroized during the Napoleonic wars, and others gained similar status later as a consequence of the First World War, without direct connection with the Empire. Yet the military hero in its imperial variant became the dominant form of military heroism between 1870 and 1914, under the influence of the wave of New Imperialism that swept over Europe. John MacKenzie has demonstrated how military activity and, whenever possible, victories sustained interest in imperial expansion in the late Victorian period.[129]

Officers who had become military heroes became role models the public turned to. The name of 'Kitchener' became in the early twentieth century a common reference to the world of the military. When G. K. Chesterton wrote his *Miscellany of Men* in 1912, he did not hesitate to compare William Morris and Lord Kitchener, remarking that, unlike Morris, 'Lord Kitchener does not fail if he is underpaid, but only if he is defeated'.[130] The military imperial hero reinforced beliefs in the country's superiority, and his martial values inspired many to follow the same path and serve the glory of the country. MacKenzie was right when he argued that 'War was an essential part of the foundation and growth of the Empire, and was therefore the source of British greatness'.[131] It is therefore not surprising that military heroes inspired the public to emulate them and quickly formed part of the 'moral training' of the youth. Their examplarity was even used by the groups and interests lobbying in favour of imperial expansion to promote the ideology of colonial imperialism within official circles, which were initially reluctant to embark upon full-scale imperial expansion (as shown on the occasion of the British re-conquest of the Sudan, delayed until 1896). Those who 'lionised Stanley in 1890, Lugard in 1892–3, Rhodes in 1894–5 and Kitchener in 1898–9' even reached the Liberal Party, the leadership of which had been denied to the two anti-imperialists Sir William Harcourt and John Morley.[132] By renewing and perpetuating the successful genre of the military hero (in a society that long perceived itself to be less militaristic than its continental counterparts),[133] British imperial heroes maintained and promoted a set of martial values that were closely associated with British national ideals.[134] Consequently, a very high standard of behaviour was expected from them, and their halo could be significantly damaged if they did not comply with the idealized chivalric rules of war, especially in the rare cases when opponents were white (as was the case when the British public disapproved of Kitchener's concentration camps for Boer women and children).[135] However, racial prejudices prevented from applying the same principles to indigenous populations, and the violence that surrounded military operations did not damage in any way heroic reputations which, on the contrary, effectively sanitized and glamorized colonial violence.

In France, colonial expansion and military activism were also closely intertwined.[136] Most of the imperial heroes of the period were officers of either the army or the navy: Marchand of course, but also Brazza,

Table 11 'The most illustrious Frenchmen of the nineteenth century': Nationwide poll carried out by *Le Petit Parisien*, 11 January 1907

Rank	Name	No. of votes
1	Louis Pasteur	1,338,425
2	Victor Hugo	1,227,103
3	Léon Gambetta	1,155,672
4	Napoléon 1	1,118,044
5	Auguste Thiers	1,039,453
6	Lazare Carnot	950,772
7	Pierre Curie	851,107
8	A. Dumas Sr	850,602
9	Docteur Roux	603,941
10	A. Parmentier	498,863
11	Louis Ampère	452,460
12	Pierre de Brazza	344,515
13	Emile Zola	334,747
14	A. de Lamartine	298,892
15	Sarah Bernhard	198,742
16	Waldeck-Rousseau	170,421
17	Marshal MacMahon	132,420
18	Sadi Carnot	123,394
19	Eugène Chevreul	122,084
20	Chateaubriand	119,487

Gallieni, Lyautey or Laperrine. Their victories, widely publicized in the full-colour engravings of the *Supplément* to the *Petit Journal* as we have seen in Chapter 3, compensated for the low national self-esteem following the defeat of 1870. However, as shown in Table 11, the French were less prone than the British to associate closely military prowess and national achievements.

Although this poll about French heroes of the nineteenth century could include heroes of the Napoleonic wars, Napoleon was the only military character of those wars still dear to the public. Another of his contemporaries was ranked tenth, but Antoine Parmentier had been a pharmacist and an agronomist. None of the great marshals of the Empire, such as Soult, Ney or Davout, qualified. On the contrary, scientists, writers, poets and politicians seemed in high esteem. Brazza, ranked twelfth, was the only imperial hero of the list, but outnumbered eminent figures of the time such as Zola, Lamartine, Chateaubriand, Ferdinand de Lesseps (21st), Michelet (22nd) and Jules Verne (25th). Marchand had probably not qualified because he had become famous too late, in 1898–99, to be a true nineteenth-century *homme célèbre*. Judging from the predominance of intellectuals in the list, Brazza's

20 Brazza (with the pith helmet, on the right) supervises the freeing of slaves. Interpretation by Riou, *Tour du Monde*, second semester, 1888

charisma and achievements had probably counted more than his *faits d'armes* to qualify him among the greatest Frenchmen. Brazza, who was popularized from 1888 onwards as a liberator of slaves following engravings by Riou in *Le Tour du monde*, appealed to the public as he embodied a form of strength that had more to do with persuasion and attractiveness than sheer force (Figure 20).[137] The public admired Brazza for his tactful conquest of the Congo and his skilful handling of relations with the local populations. Sympathetic articles appeared in the press when he met adverse conditions. This applied even to his private life: when his five-year-old son Jacques died, no fewer than forty-four newspapers announced his bereavement.[138] Brazza's patriotic value was also acknowledged by the various rewards the French government voted for himself and his family, including a pension of 10,000 francs in 1902 as a reward from the nation.[139]

Upon Major Marchand's return to France in 1899 after the Fashoda showdown, the *Figaro* journalist George Duruy lyrically called his readers to welcome this 'pure embodiment of military honour':

> Here comes at last, after the gloomy string of sombre days, a pure day, a day beaming with joy which will soon rise ... Soldiers and citizens

of France, you can prepare the laurels as if you were waiting for your brother![140]

The patriotic value of imperial heroes was clearly asserted when in 1909 a committee presided by the leading imperialist Eugène Etienne and based in the *Hôtel de la Dépêche coloniale* was set up in order to raise funds for a monument celebrating the heroes of French colonial expansion: explorers, politicians, soldiers, civil servants.[141] Although the military dimension of their achievements did not count as much as in their British counterparts, French imperial heroes conveyed and personified an important patriotic message.

Naturally, the values attributed to imperial heroes as representatives of national qualities led them to become, in some instances, vectors of acutely nationalist views, in particular when the Franco-British relationship was confrontational and nationalism led to Anglophobic or Francophobic feelings – which tended to have reciprocal effects.[142] Chauvinistic Anglophobia remained a significant feature of the French press until 1904, and the image of the Englishman suffered greatly in French public opinion as a consequence of colonial competition.[143] Authors who chose to celebrate the merits of colonial heroes were often not devoid of Anglophobic feelings. Paul d'Ivoi, author of the encyclopaedic account of the Marchand mission, was a well-known author of children's books, including the allegedly Anglophobic novel *Sergent Simplet* which was written when France and Britain were competing for Madagascar, Siam and the Sudan.[144] Even when the brothers Jérôme and Jean Tharaud chose to write a novel about Kipling, their primary purpose was to denounce the voracity of British imperialism.[145] Their novel included an epigraph vehemently criticizing Cecil Rhodes, who had died shortly before the work went into print.[146] The British press also let loose at times overtly Francophobic feelings, in particular when the two countries competed for the same African territory. Jingoism was particularly evident in Britain on the occasion of the Fashoda confrontation, as the combination between the jubilation brought about by the avenging of Gordon, the resentment at what was seen as a French usurpation and the admiration for the British martial values embodied by Lord Kitchener unleashed violent Francophobic reactions in the press and in public opinion.[147] For instance, the *Illustrated London News* argued that 'the Marchand Expedition exists to-day by virtue of the prowess of the British arms; a fact our neighbours should digest with humility', a statement that grossly underplayed the mission's own resources.[148] While the heroism of Marchand's crossing of Africa was sometimes acknowledged, as by *The Times* on 11 October 1898, the crushing superiority of Lord Kitchener and his Anglo-Egyptian troops comforted jingoist feelings in Britain and the Sirdar was seen as the embodiment of the British superiority over the French.

The signing of the Entente Cordiale helped to diminish the potential use of imperial heroes as anti-French or anti-British arguments, yet the old prejudices of public opinion in the two countries did not disappear overnight. Although it has been argued that the Fashoda incident was quickly forgotten on the two sides of the Channel, the old confrontational frame of mind was still found until the First World War.[149] Anxious to evaluate the reception of their representatives among their French allies, an observer from the British Embassy in Paris commented for his colleagues in London that the exceptional qualities displayed by Lord Kitchener contributed to enhancing his popularity in France during the Great War:

> I do not suppose that there is anyone, who has been so cordially disliked here as Lord Kitchener, yet it is perfectly true that he is the only Englishman now, whether soldier or civilian, who has anything like a place in Frenchmen's affection. They think a great deal of him and appear entirely to have forgotten the memories of Fashoda. It is difficult to account for this, but there is no doubt something in the magnetism of his personality and as far as I can see no one on our side seems to have that quality, or the art of appealing to Frenchmen's imagination. [...] Lord Kitchener, however, though once very unpopular, is now the only Englishman to whom Frenchmen look up with trust and respect.[150]

Similarly, post-1904 British accounts of the Fashoda incident tended to stress the 'civilizing goal' of the Marchand mission, and went as far as to acknowledge in the friendliest manner Marchand's heroic qualities, even in books dedicated to Kitchener.[151] Kitchener even became the epitome of Franco-British co-operation in a wartime postcard (Figure 21).

By giving an unprecedented place to colonial troops in the defence of the mother country, and by putting to the forefront metropolitan defence (as opposed to imperial warfare in the previous decades), the First World War changed the ways in which the great deeds of imperial heroes could inspire their compatriots. During these four years, a feeling of urgency and uncertainty shook the tranquil self-assurance that had prevailed beforehand. The long-term benefits of the European civilizing mission or religious proselytism disappeared from the public arena as more pressing issues, such as the possible German invasion of Paris in the autumn 1914, replaced them. Consequently, great battles of the War created new heroic reputations, such as those attached to Pétain and Nivelle following Verdun. In these troubled times, some prominent imperial heroes still embodied values that sustained the war effort and helped the public believe in the final victory of their country.

21 Fashoda revisited: wartime postcard with Kitchener's portrait adorned by the Union Jack and the tricolour

Kitchener's military record during the Sudan campaign, followed by his successful handling of the 1902 peace negotiations that ended the South African war (which compensated for his earlier tactical errors and mistreatment of Boer women and children), won him a long-lasting popularity that made him a perfect saviour figure. Significantly, Herbert Asquith decided to appoint Kitchener as Secretary of State for War (instead of Richard Haldane who had previously held the post) under pressure from the press – in particular from Charles À Court Repington's writings in *The Times*. The success of the mass volunteer force (also known as the 'Kitchener armies') was due in large part to Kitchener's personal appeal for volunteers, which was conveyed through the famous poster. Even if the quality of both the design and the slogan might have contributed to the impact of the campaign, the reputation of Kitchener, and the exemplary value of his career and achievements, played a major role in convincing potential recruits to join the volunteer army. The military, patriotic and personal values embodied by Kitchener contributed to the success of this recruitment campaign, and Kitchener himself represented a case of an imperial hero whose exemplarity was used and amplified in the context of the Great War.

In France, although Lyautey can be seen as a sort of *alter ego* to Kitchener in his capacity as Minister of War under the premiership of Aristide Briand, the French Resident General in Morocco had less impact on the course of the War: his time as Minister of War did not exceed eleven weeks, from December 1916 to April 1917. Disliking parliamentary control in times of war and frustrated at being denied the role of supreme commander, he resigned after failing to deliver a speech to the French Assembly owing to the outcry of the deputies present.[152] Gallieni, who had conquered territories for France in the Western Sudan, Senegal, Tonkin and Madagascar, had also come to play a prominent role during the War shortly before Lyautey: having been appointed governor of Paris and commandant of the armies of Paris, he conducted the plan of the 'Taxis of the Marne' (which considerably expanded his fame) in September 1914, and became Minister of War from October 1915 until March 1916. The President of the Council, Briand, wrote to him 'you cannot imagine your popularity [...]. Your glorious role in September 1914 had given you universal popularity.'[153] Although there was no Gallic equivalent to Kitchener, several French military heroes of the Great War had a notable colonial background that could not fail to be mentioned in the documents celebrating their wartime heroic deeds. In the list of the seven *Heroes of 1914–1918* presented to the pupils of a postwar intermediate primary course, one of the three Marshals featured had had extensive colonial experience (Joffre), as did three of the four heroic generals depicted (Gallieni, Gouraud and Mangin).[154] The war offered Marchand the opportunity to join the army again, and he served as a general at the head of an African regiment. When Marchand was wounded by shrapnel on the occasion of the battle of Champagne in September 1915, *Le Matin* referred to him as 'the most popular of our African heroes' and stated that he was 'too famous' for readers to be reminded of his deeds. A meeting between Kitchener and Marchand a few days before the accident was described as the best symbol of the 'entente cordiale that saved the world from the invasion of the Barbarians'. The articled ended: 'Marchand was one of the jewels of France, and one of her motives for pride. France is now leaning with emotion and hope over his bed and his sufferings.'[155] A few weeks later, as the newspaper announced Marchand's convalescence, it quoted with undisguised satisfaction the General's remark: 'one is allowed to die, but not to fall ill'.[156] When his second in command on the Congo–Nile mission, Captain Baratier, was killed in action in October 1917, all the 227 articles that appeared in the French press about his death between October 1917 and January 1918 mentioned the heroic figure of Marchand.[157] *Je sais tout* mourned 'a fallen hero' whilst *Le Vétéran* argued that he 'awoke memories of heroism and glory'.[158] Twenty-one other articles appeared in the international press, including in the United States, Italy, Switzerland, Greece and Chile. Baratier's posthumous glory resulted from a combination of a glorious past shared with an imperial hero, and a heroic death in a European war. The Great War gave some French imperial heroes the opportunities to confirm and expand their reputations, provided they demonstrated outstanding qualities on European battlefields as well.

However, imperial heroes who did not intervene on the Front (such as Brazza, who had died a decade earlier) temporarily lost pre-eminence to the benefit of new, war-related, legends. The landscape of heroism had changed, and the imperial heroes who did not or could not contribute to the war effort were less prominently featured, as the values they embodied were less in keeping with the circumstances.

In Britain and in France, the First World War deeply altered the conditions in which moral and exemplary messages could be passed on to the public, especially as 'fiction, together with visual illustrations and popular films, played an important role as part of the unofficial propaganda effort to mobilize the nation'.[159] New major figures emerged during these four years and could potentially replace the old imperial legends that had been so influential in earlier decades. Lieutenant Colonel F. S. Brereton played the role of the Henty of the Great War, with novels such as *With French at the Front* (1915), *With Joffre at Verdun* (1916), *Under Haig in Flanders* (1917) and *With the Allies to the Rhine* (1919), vividly describing the heroic deeds of 'the thin khaki line of heroes, the cool, calm, cheery sons of Empire'.[160] In France, new popular books appeared about Great War heroes, such as Henri Lavedan's *Le Général Joffre* (1915), Emile Hinzelin's *Foch ...* (1918), René Puaux's *Foch, sa vie, sa doctrine, son œuvre, la foi en la victoire* (1918), Raymond Recouly's *Foch, le vainqueur de la guerre* (1919), Gabriel Mermeix's *Fragments d'histoire, 1914–19* (eight volumes between 1919 and 1926) and Baron André de Maricourt's *Foch, une lignée, une tradition, un caractère* (1920). These works favoured the appearance of a new style of military hero (best exemplified by Marshal Pétain) that left less room for military heroes of the colonies, and contributed to altering the values that the latter came to embody in the interwar years.

The results of the 1919 French general election clearly showed the prestige of war veterans. Voters elected a nationalist 'sky-blue Chamber', a reference to the fact that a majority of parliamentarians were either war veterans or supporters of French military interests. With the dramatic increase in the number of stories of military heroism during the Great War, imperial heroes could no longer embody modern exemplary values: the new hero was definitely the *poilu* who had stood in the trenches, rather than the officer who had led his Senegalese soldiers to victory in the African wilderness.

However, the interwar survival or revival of reputations attached to imperial heroes was eased by a fresh upsurge of interest in the concept of 'Greater France' (particularly attractive in a country decimated by the conflict), and by the appeal of the African wilderness that formed the background to these legends.[161] Following four years of a full-scale war that left very few families untouched, the public craved new exotic horizons and popular literature 'increased the public's appetite for colonial escapism'.[162] Imperial heroes were joined by a new generation of adventurers. Historicizing the concept of 'adventurer', Sylvain Venayre borrowed the concept of 'hypostase' from Reinhard Koselleck, who had noted that the ideas of Art, Concept and Progress were singularized and given a universal meaning at the turn of the nineteenth century, to argue that the idea of 'adventure' followed the same transformation at the turn of the twentieth.[163] Venayre also quantified the success of this movement that gained its true momentum after the Great War: the number of adventure accounts appearing in the 1920s and 1930s equalled those published between 1850 and 1920.[164] Because heroes were pathfinders, role models and symbolic links between the known (Europe) and the unknown (Africa), the image of imperial heroes was influenced by the rise to fame of the 'adventurer', and the values they embodied were altered in consequence. The interwar taste for purity, solitude and moral endurance paved the way for new legends in which the call of the desert was potent. The image of Charles de Foucauld blending in with his Tuareg friends echoed that of Thomas Edward Lawrence in Arab dress and advising Faysal during the Versailles conference.[165] Both exemplified the perfect integration of the European hero among his target population, and his capacity to learn local languages and to become a respected adviser to local rulers. Such features, combined with the more traditional quality represented by the strength of individual will, ensured the success of these new heroic reputations.[166]

Charles de Foucauld popularized a new ideal of religious charity from the moment the first large-scale biography was published by the patriotic and religious writer René Bazin (upon the invitation of the leading scholar of Islam, and an admirer of Foucauld's, Louis Massignon), who concluded his biography by imploring 'Lord Jesus Christ' to 'Give part of Thy riches to the poor of Islam, and forgive the nations of the baptized their inveterate love of money' as a reward to Brother Charles who had 'died at his work'.[167] Even in religious circles, the emphasis was not so much on conversion (an idea that had been abandoned, and did not fit Foucauld, who had never converted anyone) but on peaceful co-existence and friendship with the local populations. This is why his death was forcefully attributed to the Sanusiyya Muslim brotherhood, which was presented in French literature and colonial circles as the hereditary enemy of France.[168] Biographers insisted that Foucauld's assassination was due not to Muslims but to a marginal, albeit well-known, enemy.[169] His legend combined the heroic appeal of martyrdom with the Christian ideal of a simple, Biblical, life in a poor country. His example and prescriptions were subsequently followed by generations of Little Brothers and Sisters of Jesus, and his life attracted many other biographers, who, as Dominique Casajus has observed, turned him into one of the most popular imperial heroes after the Great War, to such an extent that his reputation joined the pantheon of France's colonial epic.[170]

The Great War cast serious doubts on the beneficence of Western values, which had remained uncontested until mechanized slaughters on European battlefields brought widespread scepticism on the impact of European beliefs and technology (best exemplified by the poems of Sigfried Sassoon and by Paul Valéry's concern about the death of civilizations). These shifts influenced the ways in which prewar imperial heroes were perceived. The Great War traumatized the whole of French society, and it changed British culture irremediably.[171] Comparing pre- and postwar textbooks is edifying. The 1913 edition of Ernest Lavisse's schoolbook ended with 'France is a great country that has brave soldiers to defend her, and scientists that do good to the rest of the world'.[172] In 1928, the same textbook included a last chapter on 'General thoughts', in which Lavisse revealingly wrote:

> But you will not be as arrogant as the Germans used to be. You will not want to dominate or humiliate other peoples. You know that war is a terrible curse. You will detest, you will loathe war.[173]

This *'montée de l'idéal genevois'*, this belief in the principles defended by the newly created League of Nations, cast doubt upon the sometimes aggressively patriotic imperial heroes of the prewar years. The War precipitated a moral and intellectual crisis that deeply influenced colonial developments, as the symbolic 'virginity' of conquered or conquerable territories struck audiences and re-shaped the European frame of mind.[174]

In several instances, beliefs that had been commonly held were shaken. From the short but intense life of the Saharan hero Ernest Psichari, the public forgot his nationalist fervour but retained the image of a young man denouncing the mistreatment of indigenous populations in Chad and Mauritania, of the spiritual thinker eager to promote religious tolerance, and the philosopher who advocated intelligence against violence.[175] Lytton Strachey's description of General Gordon as a mad, insubordinate individual with a noted taste for alcohol, published in *Eminent Victorians* just six months before the end of the Great War, offered a provocative re-appraisal of the Gordon legend among intellectuals.[176] It spread a more critical vision that had been initiated discreetly by Lord Cromer in his 1908 *Modern Egypt*, and which deprived Gordon of most of the values with which he had been previously credited.[177]

This tendency was reversed, however, in the 1930s, when popular imperialism reached its widest audience in both Britain and France, notably through the success of colonial exhibitions, popular literature about Black Africa and the Sahara, and imperial films: this was the period which I have called elsewhere the 'climax of self-confident popular imperialism'.[178] The success of these forms of popular exoticism also coincided with the increasingly threatening German menace, leading Britain and France to look back triumphantly to their heroic years of imperialism with more satisfaction and pride. Crucially, most of the imperial heroes were either already dead or were dying one after the other, and some felt it their duty to revive colonial legends of the past. Among them was the Paris-based publisher Larose, who explicitly stated in the authors' contracts for his series *Médaillons coloniaux*:

> Colonial history, it has been noted on many occasions, is very often a history of the 'individual' .... We are starting this series of the *Médaillons coloniaux* in order to raise awareness of these 'heroes' of colonial history. They will be depicted life-like, with the detail of their existence, and under the real features of their character, and we hope that [these books] will contribute to make one of the most moving achievements of our homeland appealing to French people.[179]

The shift from contemporary celebration to retrospective admiration explains why this period was also marked by the re-appearance of hagiographic works. In the 1930s, Cecil Rhodes was still the object of hagiographical biographies that could include a chapter grandiloquently entitled 'An example to mankind'.[180] In this decade, representations of David Livingstone (on the occasion of the centenary of his ordination) remained highly moralizing and in keeping with the prewar heroic canons, as shown in the following extract:

> Among the great missionaries of the nineteenth century no name ranks higher than that of David Livingstone. Not only is his fame in all the Churches, but also far beyond their borders. He is one of our national heroes, whose memory is honoured by multitudes who own no Church allegiance. He was a great explorer, who did more than any other to 'blaze the trail' in the interior of the Dark Continent, and in that respect his labours and achievements were of national and international importance. He made contributions to geographical and ethnological knowledge the value of which was gratefully acknowledged by the learned societies of the civilised world.[181]

The canons of the Gordon legend came back to their original shape in many cases too. On the occasion of a public lecture at the Jerusalem Young Men's Christian Association on 26 January 1935 to celebrate Gordon Anniversary Sunday, Humphrey Ernest Bowman (1879–1965) remembered Gordon in a very traditional manner that borrowed most of its structure and argument from prewar rhetoric about the religious, military and patriotic values taught by his exemplary life:

> Thus Gordon's memory lives in the two institutions which bear his name, the College in Khartoum, and the Boys' Home in Woking. And we, who are assembled here to pay a tribute to his memory today, may well regard Gordon with reverence and with pride: a soldier who never took a life if he could spare it, a Christian who, as far as is humanly possible, lived the life of Christ, a public servant, who put honour and duty before all else – one who lived and died a very gallant English gentleman.[182]

In France, Catholic propagandists discussed at length, and with great satisfaction, the 'heroic virtues' of the life and death of Charles de Foucauld, using Pope Benedict XIV's concept of 'heroic degree of the [Christian] virtues' to demonstrate the relevance of the beatification of the hermit of the Sahara, a process which had formally started in 1927.

Religious circles were not the only ones to find imperial heroes useful in the 1930s. Growing uncertainties on the international arena also favoured recourse to old and reassuring myths that confirmed the strength and stamina of the two declining powers who had to cling to their past achievements. This was particularly true in France, where the weak and pathologically unstable parliamentarian Third Republic became a major cause of concern as Germany regained strength. France also had to face economic recession, a deterioration of the job market and a weakening of domestic demand as well as an international crisis threatening the world order inherited from Versailles.[183] As the empire increasingly appeared as a valuable asset, imperial heroes regained the popularity that had been monopolized by Great War heroes in the previous decade. When the French navy launched a new cruiser named after Brazza, the opening speech of the launching ceremony, given in the presence of the 'elite of Bordeaux and elsewhere', revived the old prewar hagiography:

> The *Savorgnan de Brazza* battleship will soon take to far-flung seas this name that is in itself a programme and a symbol, as it means conquest of people and land through gentleness and kindness, detestation of violence and bloodshed, triumph of benevolent and generous subtlety over cynical treachery and brutality.[184]

Brazza's high moral values were put to the fore to revive his prestige, glossing over his unpopularity among many officials of the Ministries

22 Posthumous celebrations reviving heroic reputations: the transfer of the remains of Marshal Lyautey from Nancy to Morocco. *L'Illustration*, 2 November 1935

of the Navy and the Colonies, who resented his foreign origin and his success.[185] The passing of years had turned Brazza into an icon equally palatable to the two rivals, the Navy and the Colonies, which was a significant achievement.

Occasionally, the passing away of the last surviving imperial heroes offered an opportunity to give a new lease of life to their reputations. This was particularly the case with Marchand's and Lyautey's deaths in the same year, 1934. *L'Illustration* dedicated several pages to each funeral, accompanied with photographs of each stage of the national ceremony highlighting popular fervour for these highly symbolic events. A few months later, special coverage was given to the ceremony of the transfer of Marshal Lyautey's remains from his native Lorraine to Morocco, in an attempt to convey the pomp and circumstance surrounding the farewell to one of France's greatest imperial proconsul (Figure 22).

Imperial heroes provided powerful symbols to two countries in need of reassurance, and film-makers seized the opportunities offered by the improvement of cinematographic techniques to contribute to the hagiographical wave of the 1930s, not only to secure financial benefits (as we saw in Chapter 3) but also to convey the exemplary value of these heroes to their public. The evocative potential of films with soundtracks was used to promote openly the values that had been attributed to empire builders before the War. The 1924 film on Livingstone had been designed, according to the organizer of the *Livingstone Film Expedition*, not only 'to revive the memory of the great missionary, Dr. Livingstone' but also to 'stimulate interest in missionary work and enterprise' and to 'revisualize for the present generation one of the finest Christian characters of the Victorian era'.[186] The description of the film project clearly stated that 'The British Missionary Societies and the leaders of the Churches are most enthusiastic on the subject' and that it would be 'widely used in the Churches and Schools and will appeal to all lovers of Missionary enterprise'.[187] The London Missionary Society agreed to support the initiative since it deemed the film would 'prove of the deepest interest to all those supporters of missionary work who know the work of David Livingstone'.[188] Apparently the Livingstone legend was being actively promoted in 1925 for educational and missionary purposes, and the figure of David Livingstone was still used to teach moral and religious values. Not surprisingly, the first screening took place at the Albert Hall under the auspices of the Forward Movement of the Congregational Union, and the proceeds were 'to go in support of the half-million fund which Congregationalists are raising for missionary and other purposes'.[189]

A similar edifying role was assigned by Léon Poirier to his film *L'Appel du silence*: the epigraph of the book in which he explained how he would produce this film mentioned 'the development of the country through the development of consciences', while the opening citation by Marshal Lyautey argued that 'not only is it good to make this film, but in the present circumstances, it is urgent to produce it'.[190] Poirier evoked in his memoirs a 'patrimony of heroism of which we are the direct heirs and which we need to transmit untouched to the next generation'.[191] The film's closing scene depicted Laperrine's burial next to Charles de Foucauld in Tamanrasset in 1920, with an officer remarking 'From now on, the soldier of Faith and the soldier of France shall be on watch side by side, at the outpost of civilization'. Foucauld's religious exemplarity was associated with outstanding patriotic, moral and civilizing values that bore similarities to pre-1914 representations of imperial heroes. Curiously, as Paul Pandolfi has remarked, Foucauld's scientific contributions in grammar, linguistics and what would be called today ethnography, which were numerous, remained completely ignored in the film.[192]

When the same film-maker submitted to Brazza's widow, Thérèse de Chambrun, the proposal for a feature film on her husband, he suggested they called it 'Brazza, heroic colonial officer' and showed clear patriotic concerns in the typical vein of the hagiographic and nationalist works. The proposal concluded:

> And now, after the 1914 war, during which the Congo faithfully provided men and wealth to our endangered motherland, now that Brazza's achievements are complete and have brought more justice and more human progress, white blanks have disappeared from Africa and the French empire defies rivals.[193]

Although the usual argument about the usefulness of colonies had been updated with the experience of the war, the rhetoric remained unchanged compared with pre-1914 arguments: exploration, justice, human progress and defence of the 'endangered motherland' were still potent values illustrated *en majesté* by imperial heroes. The epigraph to the book of dialogues of the film *Brazza* read, quite limpidly: 'Brazza, simple page of the history of our empire, dedicated to France and to those who love it'.[194] For his part, a journalist noted in 1940 with evident satisfaction: '*Brazza* [...] celebrates the colonial genius of France in a simple and moving way.'[195]

This chapter has argued so far that imperial heroes could be used to promote a set of religious, moral or patriotic values to the British and French public. However, this view should be moderated on two accounts. First, the polished and attractive legends discussed here were not universal, and in some cases counter-legends or controversies arose: the limits of the 'exemplarity' of imperial heroes should not be under-estimated. Secondly, these heroes present scholars with a mostly Eurocentric conception of heroism and heroic values, as the impact of these 'exemplary lives' on the local populations was limited, while local African conceptions of heroism had no real influence on the shaping of those reputations.

The determination and ability to go above and beyond the call of duty is often seen as a hallmark of out-of-the-ordinary characters. As a result, the hero's real or supposed achievements had to meet high expectations, and criticisms quickly arose if imperial heroes failed to represent the high standards that were usually attributed to them or which they had been endowed with in the past. Hence, when the Flatters mission was ambushed in 1881 by a group of Tuareg warriors, the explorer Henri Duveyrier, once fêted throughout the Parisian establishment for his daring exploration of the *Tassili* and his careful observation of the mores of the Tuaregs, was suddenly accused of delivering a misleading, unrealistically friendly image of the inhabitants of the desert.[196] He subsequently became an object of calumny to such an extent that his suicide in 1892 (itself a consequence of his falling into disrepute) remained almost unnoticed and that his posthumous reputation as an explorer never regained its pre-1881 levels.[197]

In Britain, one of the most obvious cases of controversial heroism of the Victorian period was Henry Morton Stanley. Keltie's praise of Stanley's contribution to the geographical knowledge of Africa, mentioned earlier in the chapter, did not reflect the opinion of all the Fellows of the Royal Geographical Society. As Felix Driver has shown, Stanley's reputation was dubbed 'sensationalism' by a significant fraction of the RGS Fellows, while his claimed philanthropic pretensions and his exploration methods (which included the use of violence) were a subject of controversy, and even mockery.[198] Stanley was also the object of repeated attacks from the geographical and liberal London establishment (particularly the pinnacle of philanthropy, Exeter Hall) on several occasions, notably in 1876, when rumours spread about the use of violence on his second expedition, raising concerns about the humanitarian value of his work, and again in 1890–91, when philanthropists and anti-slavery supporters claimed that the Emin Pasha relief expedition had been a mere smokescreen for the extension of the influence of both the British East Africa Company and Leopold II. Stanley was also accused of using violence against African villages, and of turning a blind eye to the practice of slavery.[199] Imperial heroes could be in danger of losing their status if reports about their activities demonstrated that they failed to put into practice the ideals of progress, moral highness and acuity of judgement openly advocated by geographical societies, philanthropic associations and the defenders of the 'civilizing mission'. Should these breaches remain unknown or unpublicized, the hero's reputation generally remained safe.

The pivotal importance of representation (which was open to processes of selection and elimination) engendered bitter battles about the content of heroic reputations. In spite of the efforts of his hahiographers, the figure of Cecil Rhodes proved even more controversial than Stanley's. Several critical voices appeared during his lifetime and some hostile articles or essays appeared both before and after his death.[200] Naturally, his hagiographers did all that was in their power to ensure that Rhodes's dominant image as an empire builder, successful capitalist and patriotic politician did not suffer from the development of a more critical perception among a fraction of the British public that put his integrity into question. They succeeded in keeping the critical view in a minority until well after the Second World War: the arguments of the 'debunkers', as Maylam calls them, did not completely replace the hagiographical ones until the late 1960s.[201]

These examples show the importance attached to the high moral, intellectual, religious and patriotic values encapsulated by imperial heroes. If the image of a hero suddenly failed to demonstrate the value(s) he had been celebrated for, and if this failure was publicized enough, being either criticized or forgotten became almost unavoidable. The big-game hunter, explorer and Rhodesian pioneer Frederick Courtenay Selous was a case in point: having enjoyed immense celebrity in his lifetime, he was subsequently forgotten because of his moral evasiveness and his opposition to the South African war (a position deemed unacceptable for a British imperial hero).[202]

Lastly, the values exemplified by the heroic reputations studied in this book largely reflected what Europeans expected from their heroes, more than any intrinsic heroic value that would have a universal appeal, including among local populations. Europeans were prone to universalizing their own beliefs regardless of their actual reception among indigenous populations, exactly as 'the most striking aspect of the British image of Africa in the early nineteenth century was its variance from the African reality', and imperial heroes are no exception to this.[203] Gananath Obeyesekere demonstrated a similar phenomenon of discrepancy in the eighteenth-century conquest of the Pacific: the myth according to which Hawaiians deified Captain Cook as their long-awaited god Lono was in fact a European construction, 'attributing to the native the belief that the European was a god', as had been the case for Columbus and Cortés.[204] A similar situation may have arisen when biographers and other hero-makers tried to persuade themselves about the effects of 'their' heroes upon local populations. For instance, General Gordon was frequently described as having magnetic powers over his Chinese soldiers or the Sudanese population, although he knew no Chinese and no Arabic. When Lady Lugard paid a compliment to her husband for the civilizing effect of his action, she did it in a very Eurocentric way: 'You have added your articulate idea to the ideas which govern the world. The natives have gained a new conception of modern civilization. You have opened the door and civilization must do the rest.'[205] Dominique Casajus has shown how long-term processes of misinterpretation (on the part of biographers) of Tuareg reactions to Foucauld's role in the Hoggar mountains resulted as much from the tweaked terms of the dialogue as from the prevalence of preconceived views on local reactions to the Christian hermit: mutual miscomprehension prevented the development of any genuine interpretation of indigenous views on Charles de Foucauld.[206] The Eurocentric nature of the criteria used to evaluate the actions of imperial heroes, as well as the unequal power relations established

M. de Brazza rassurant le jeune garçon qui vient de tirer sur lui. — Dessin de Riou, d'après les indications de l'auteur.

23   Brazza 'reassuring a young boy who had just shot him', by Riou, *Tour du monde*, second semester, 1888

through their very action, proved an unsurpassable obstacle to any judgement of the views of local populations on the colonizer's Great Men: when indigenous feelings were portrayed, it was invariably to celebrate the benevolence of the imperial hero and his moral superiority. The hero's standing was further enhanced by the prevalence of well-established myths about Africans propagated through literary production.[207] Riou's depiction of Brazza reassuring a boy who had just shot at him illustrates this tranquil and paternalistic righteousness (Figure 23). Indigenous populations certainly featured outside the civilized world in the European vision of the world at that moment, yet they were indispensable elements of the *décor* without which the hero lost all significance: in popular imagination, they were destined to be the recipiendaries of the benefits that heroes sought to bestow on them sometimes at the price of their own lives. Although this idealized vision was scarcely confirmed by events on the ground, it had a potent influence on popular visions of empire in Europe.[208]

Because they had dared to leave their homeland to represent, or expand the possessions of, their country or religion in an environment that was judged hostile and in need of civilization, imperial heroes could easily be used to demonstrate the worth of moral, religious, or patriotic values heralded as testaments of superiority over other cultures. After all, it is probably not a coincidence if Carlyle produced, besides his influential theory about the place of heroes among humankind, a profoundly racist pamphlet entirely in keeping with the development of forms of discrimination based upon supposed biological foundations.[209]

Imperial heroes constituted a new and successful type of *Magistrae Vitae*, used to teach and illustrate highly regarded qualities at a time of unprecedented optimism in Western Europe. Léon Poirier, the main cinematographic French hero-maker of the interwar years, lyrically described the Belle Epoque as the moment when 'mankind, multiplying tenfold its faculties through the force of its genius, saw new and limitless horizons open up. Mankind sees itself as the master of the universe.'[210] Judged by the standards of their own time, often considered the personification of either the ideal imperial type or at least a noble and notable aspect of it, heroic figures of the empire constituted, willingly or unwillingly, convenient symbolic standard-bearers. Because their reputations survived several ideological shifts (the most notable one being the Great War), the values which imperial heroes embodied varied over time. The type of medium used to promote their reputation, the author who praised their 'exemplarity' and the target market also notably influenced the shape that their legends took.[211] Technical innovations could sometimes lead to the revival of old-style approaches, with the cinema unexpectedly giving in the 1930s a new lease of life to the old hagiographic material and style of the nineteenth century. By contrast, the fact that they represented *Christianity* (rather than Catholicism or Protestantism), and *civilization* (rather than Frenchness or English or British values) ensured a relative homogeneity of argumentation on both sides of the Channel: the religious and intellectual arguments that these heroes conveyed drew a sort of 'cross-Channel entente' in spite of the Franco-British competition that prevailed until at least 1904.

These heroes established a tradition of high imperial behaviour which was valued by the hero-makers and the European public alike, and formed an integral part of the hero-making phenomenon surrounding these imperial legends. The edifying message of a heroic reputation was one of the main keys to its success, and gave it social meaning, respectability and pertinence in societies that dreaded moral and political decline above anything else. Moral messages gave heroic reputations their substance, and helped hero-makers justify their contribution to the making of national legends. But how did these legends come into being in the first place? This is precisely what the following two chapters seek to analyse, following the patient 'path to heroism' of the two figures of Jean-Baptiste Marchand and Horatio Kitchener.

Notes

1 T. Carlyle, *On Heroes and Hero-Worship* (1841), Lecture I, p. 13.
2 See for instance S. Gikandi, *Maps of Englishness: Writing Identity in the Culture of Colonialism* (New York, 1996); N. Bancel, P. Blanchard and F. Vergès (eds), *La République coloniale* (2006); H. Lebovics, *True France: The Wars over Cultural Identity, 1900–1945* (1992); A. Conklin, *A Mission to Civilize* (Stanford, CA, 1997); G. Wilder, *The French Imperial Nation-State* (Chicago, 2005).
3 On the vast subject of French and British views on race, see for instance J. N. Pieterse, *White on Black: Images of Africa and Blacks in Western Popular Culture* (New Haven, 1992); P. B. Rich, *Race and Empire in British Politics* (Cambridge, 1990); C. Reynaud-Paligot, *La République raciale. Paradigme racial et idéologie républicaine 1860–1930* (2006) and *Races, racisme et antiracisme dans les années 1930* (2007); D. S. Hale, *Races on Display* (Bloomington, IN, 2008); S. Peabody and T. Stovall (eds), *The Color of Liberty: Histories of Race in France* (Durham, NC, and London), 2003).
4 *L'Afrique française*, April 1932.
5 A. Dwight Culler, *The Victorian Mirror of History* (New Haven and London), 1985.
6 W. E. Houghton, *The Victorian Frame of Mind* (1957, repr. 1979), p. 305.
7 C. Amalvi, 'L'exemple des grands hommes de l'histoire de France à l'école et au foyer (1814–1914)', in 'Le grand homme', *Romantisme*, 100 (1998), 93.
8 See in particular M. Agulhon, 'La "statuomanie" et l'histoire', *Ethnologie française*, 8:2–3 (1978), 145–72 and M. Agulhon, 'Nouveaux propos sur les statues de "grands hommes" au XIXe siècle', in 'Le grand homme', *Romantisme*, 100 (1998), 11–16; C. Amalvi, *Les Héros de l'histoire de France. Recherche iconographique sur le Panthéon scolaire de la Troisième République* (1979).
9 P. Serna, *La République des girouettes, 1789–1815 et au-delà. Une anomalie politique: la France de l'extrême centre* (Seyssel, 2005), pp. 542–4.
10 Amalvi, *Héros de l'histoire de France*, p. 25.
11 J. M. Mackenzie, 'The iconography of the exemplary life: the case of David Livingstone', in G. Cubitt and A. Warren (eds), *Heroic Reputations and Exemplary Lives* (Manchester, 2000), p. 92.
12 Houghton, *Victorian Frame of Mind*, p. 305.
13 On common heroic attributes, see A. Muxel, 'Les héros des jeunes Français. Vers un humanisme politique réconciliateur', in P. Centlivres, D. Fabre and F. Zonabend (eds), *La Fabrique des héros* (1998), p. 95.
14 M. Weber, *Economy and Society*, ed. G. Roth and C. Wittich (Berkeley, CA, 1968), p. 241.
15 J. E. Adams, *Dandies and Desert Saints: Styles of Victorian Manhood* (Ithaca, NY, 1995).
16 On the nineteenth-century quest for universalism and its echoes in the colonial context, see for instance J. T. Johnson, 'Searching for common ground: ethical traditions and the interface with international law', in D. S. Browning, *Universalism vs Relativism* (Plymouth, 2006), pp. 93–118; Conklin, *Mission to Civilize*; Wilder, *French Imperial Nation-State*; or K. Nicolaidis, 'The "Clash of Universalisms"', unpublished article (2006).
17 C. Fauré, *Les Déclarations des droits de l'homme de 1789* (1988), p. 22.
18 V. Hugo, *Le Rhin* (1842).
19 E. Perreau-Saussine, 'Quentin Skinner in context', *Review of Politics*, 69 (2007), pp. 106–22.

20 E. Savarèse, *Histoire coloniale et immigration. Une invention de l'étranger* (Biarritz, 2000).
21 G. Dawson, *Soldier Heroes* (1994), and G. L. Mosse, *The Image of Man* (Oxford, 1996), p. 13.
22 G. Cubitt, 'Introduction', in Cubitt and Warren, *Heroic Reputations*, p. 3.
23 C. Rojek, *Celebrity* (2001), p. 61.
24 G. Duby, *Les Trois Ordres ou l'imaginaire du féodalisme* (1978), p. 20.
25 RHL, Waller Papers, Gordon Manuscript, f. 260, Henrietta Gordon [Gordon's sister] to Horace Waller, 11 May 1883.
26 H. C. G. Matthew, *The Gladstone Diaries*, vol. XI (Oxford, 1990), p. 311, Gladstone to Lord Hartington, 22 March 1885.
27 R. Davenport-Hines, 'Gordon, Charles George (1833–1885)', *ODNB* [Accessed 10 November 2005].
28 RHL, Lugard Papers, box 3, files 1 and 10.
29 P. Lyautey, *Lyautey l'Africain* (1953), p. vi, and A. Tessier, *Lyautey* (2004), pp. 443–5.
30 S. Venayre, *La Gloire de l'aventure* (2002), pp. 100–5.
31 G. N. Sanderson, 'Partition and the Ideology of Imperialism', in R. Oliver and G. N. Sanderson (eds), *The Cambridge History of Africa*, vol. 6 (Cambridge, 1985), pp. 156–7; J. Tosh, *Man's Place: Masculinity and the Middle-Class Home in Victorian England* (1999).
32 A. Roberts, 'The imperial mind', in A. Roberts (ed.), *The Cambridge History of Africa*, vol. 7 (Cambridge, 1986), pp. 41–3.
33 K. Surridge, 'More than a great poster: Lord Kitchener and the image of the military hero', *Historical Research*, 74 (2001), 298–313. However, Kitchener's reputation as an imperial hero has remained vivid to this day; see for instance K. Kwarteng, *Ghosts of Empire. Britain's Legacies in the Modern World* (2011), pp. 211–33.
34 M. Jones, *The Last Great Quest. Captain Scott's Antarctic Sacrifice* (Oxford, 2003), p. 270.
35 For Britain, see R. Holland, 'The British Empire and the Great War', in Wm R. Louis and J. M. Brown (eds), *The Oxford History of the British Empire*, vol. IV (Oxford, 1999), pp. 114–37. For France, see E. Deroo, 'Mourir: L'appel à l'Empire', in P. Blanchard, S. Lemaire and N. Bancel (eds), *Culture coloniale en France* (2008), pp. 163–72 or B. Sèbe, 'Exalting imperial grandeur', in J. M. MacKenzie (ed.), *European Empires and the People* (Manchester, 2011), pp. 34–42.
36 J. R. Seeley, *The Expansion of England* (1891), p. 297.
37 M. Cornick, 'The myth of perfidious Albion and French national identity', in D. Dutton (ed.), *Statecraft and Diplomacy in the Twentieth Century: Essays Presented to P. M. H. Bell* (Liverpool, 1995), pp. 7–33.
38 Houghton, *Victorian Frame of Mind*, p. 316.
39 H. G. Adams, *The Weaver-Boy who Became a Missionary: Being the Story of the Life and Labours of David Livingstone* (1867), p. xviii.
40 C. Northcott, *David Livingstone: His Triumph, Decline and Fall* (1973), p. 50.
41 Hansard, vol. CCXCIV, 18 Nov. 1884 to 3 Mar. 1885, Col. 1080, Gladstone, during a Notice of Motion on Egypt and the Soudan, 23 February 1885.
42 K. E. Hendrickson, *Making Saints: Religion and the Public Image of the British Army, 1809–1885* (Madison, NJ, 1998), p. 176.
43 R. Hill, 'The Gordon literature', *The Durham University Journal*, XLVI:3 (June 1955), 97–103.
44 D. H. Johnson, 'The death of Gordon: a Victorian myth', *Journal of Imperial and Commonwealth History*, 10:3 (1982), 301.
45 E. Hope, *Stanley and Africa* (1890).
46 For a good appraisal of Stanley's rise to fame orchestrated by himself, see F. McLynn, *Stanley, The Making of an African Explorer* (1989).
47 S. Hannabuss, 'Ballantyne's message of Empire', in J. Richards (ed.), *Imperialism and Juvenile Literature* (Manchester, 1989), pp. 54–71.

48 In particular, P. A. Dunae, 'New Grub Street for Boys' in Richards (ed.), *Imperialism and Juvenile Literature*, pp. 12–33, as well as L. James, 'Tom Brown's imperialistic sons', *Victorian Studies*, 27 (1973), 89–99; P. Howarth, *Play Up and Play the Game* (1973); P. A. Dunae, 'Boys' literature and the idea of race, 1870–1900', *Wascana Review*, 12:1 (1977), 84–107; P. A. Dunae, 'Boys' literature and the idea of empire, 1870–1914', *Victorian Studies*, 24 (1980), 105–21; J. M. MacKenzie, *Propaganda and Empire* (Manchester, 1984); J. Bristow, *Empire Boys: Adventures in a Man's World* (1991). For a comparative study of the French and British cases, see M. Cornick, 'Representations of Britain and British colonialism in French adventure fiction, 1870–1914', *French Cultural Studies*, 17:2 (June 2006), 137–54.
49 *With Buller in Natal* (1901), *With Roberts to Pretoria* (1902) and *With Kitchener in the Soudan* (1903).
50 J. Richards, 'With Henty to Africa', in Richards (ed.), *Imperialism and Juvenile Literature*, p. 75.
51 M. K. Logan, *Narrating Henty* (1999), pp. 81–3.
52 E. Reich, *Success among Nations* (1904), p. 99.
53 K. Boyd, *Manliness and The Boy's Story Paper in Britain: A Cultural History 1855–1940* (2003), pp. 70–99.
54 Quoted in G. Arnold, *Hold Fast for England: G. A. Henty, Imperialist Boys' Writer* (1980), p. 63.
55 K. Castle, *Britannia's Children: Reading Colonialism through Children's Books* (Manchester, 2006), p. 114.
56 Amalvi, 'L'exemple des grands hommes', 100–1.
57 E. Hobsbawm, *The Age of Empire* (1987).
58 R. Cornevin, 'Numa Broc et les explorations africaines', in N. Broc, *Dictionnaire illustré des explorateurs français du XIXe siècle, Afrique* (1988), p. xi.
59 Broc, *Dictionnaire illustré*, p. xix.
60 F. Driver, *Geography Militant: Cultures of Exploration and Empire* (Oxford, 2000), p. 42.
61 Notably A. Godlewska and N. Smith (eds), *Geography and Empire* (Oxford, 1994); M. Bell, R. A. Butlin and M. J. Heffernan (eds), *Geography and Imperialism: 1820–1940* (Manchester, 1995); Y. Lacoste, *La Géographie, ça sert d'abord à faire la guerre* (1976).
62 Driver, *Geography Militant*, p. 129.
63 D. N. Livingstone, *The Geographical Tradition: Episodes in the History of a Contexted Enterprise* (Oxford, 1992).
64 J. Fabian, *Out of Our Minds: Reason and Madness in the Exploration of Central Africa* (Berkeley, CA, 2000), p. 5.
65 J. S. Keltie, 'What Stanley has done for the map of Africa', *Contemporary Review*, January 1890, reproduced in *Science*, 15:364. (24 Jan., 1890), pp. 50–5.
66 E. Mambre, 'Henri Duveyrier, Explorateur du Sahara (1840–1892)' (Maîtrise thesis, University of Aix-en-Provence, France), pp. 105–18 and 142.
67 Driver, *Geography Militant*, pp. 146–69, and 'Geography, empire and visualisation: making representation', *Royal Holloway Research Papers General Series* (1994), pp. 8–9.
68 On colonial and universal exhibitions, see P. Greenhalgh, *Ephemeral Vistas: The Expositions Universelles, Great Exhibitions and World's Fairs, 1851–1939* (Manchester, 1988), and P. Ory, *Les Expositions universelles* (1982).
69 T. Richards, *The Commodity Culture of Victorian England: Advertising and Spectacle, 1851–1914* (1990).
70 RHL, Waller Papers, MSS. Afr. S. 16, I/B, f. 219, Waller to Livingstone, 25 October 1869.
71 D. O. Helly, *Livingstone's Legacy* (Athens, OH, 1987), ch. 7.
72 T. Jeal, *Livingstone* (1973), p. 382.
73 Savarèse, *Histoire coloniale*, p. 93.
74 RHL, MSS Lugard, 12/2, f. 10, Note on conversation at luncheon given to Marshal Lyautey.

75 For instance, A. Paluel-Marmont, *Lyautey* (1934), pp. 72–88, or A. Maurois, *Lyautey* (1931), pp. 207–18.
76 Amalvi, *Héros de l'histoire de France*, p. 240.
77 This scene is featured in J. Guiraud, *Histoire de France, cours préparatoire* (1914).
78 G. Bourdé and H. Martin, *Les Ecoles historiques* (1983), p. 161.
79 L. Brossolette, *Histoire de France, cours préparatoire* (1907).
80 See in particular J. and M. Ozouf, 'Le thème du patriotisme dans les manuels primaires', *Le mouvement social*, 49 (Oct. – Dec. 1964), 5–31.
81 MacKenzie, *Propaganda and Empire*, pp. 174–97.
82 C. M. Yonge, *Westminster Reading Books*, vol. 6 (1890), p. 255.
83 Apart from D. Wellesley, *Sir George Goldie, Founder of Nigeria* (1934), D. Wellington, *Sir George Goldie, Founder of Nigeria: A Memoir* (1934), J. E. Flint, *Sir George Goldie and the Making of Nigeria* (Oxford, 1960).
84 R. H. MacDonald, *The Language of Empire* (Manchester, 1994), p. 113.
85 R. A. MacFarlane, 'Historiography of selected works on Cecil John Rhodes (1853–1902)', *History in Africa*, 34 (2007), 437–46. MacFarlane distinguishes between two schools of interpretation of Rhodes's action: 'chauvinistic approval' and 'utter vilification'.
86 Vindex [pseudonym of F. Verschoyle], *Cecil Rhodes, His Political Life and Speeches* (1900); Imperialist [pseudonym of J. R. Maguire], *Cecil Rhodes: A Biography and Appreciation* (1897); H. Hensman, *Cecil Rhodes: A Study of a Career* (Edinburgh and London, 1901); T. E. Fuller, *The Right Honourable Cecil John Rhodes: A Monograph and a Reminiscence* (1910); L. Michell, *The Life of the Rt. Hon. Cecil John Rhodes 1853–1902* (1913); P. Jourdan, *Cecil John Rhodes: His Private Life* (1911); I. Colvin, *Cecil John Rhodes 1853–1902* (1913); G. LeSueur, *Cecil Rhodes: The Man and His Work* (1913); V. Stent, *A Personal Record of Some Incidents in the Life of Cecil Rhodes* (Cape Town, 1925); J. G. MacDonald, *Rhodes: A Life* (1927); H. Baker, *Cecil Rhodes: By His Architect* (Oxford, 1934).
87 P. Maylam, *The Cult of Rhodes* (Claremont, South Africa, 2005), pp. 4–6.
88 Quoted in A. Thomas, *Rhodes* (1996), p. 7.
89 Hensman, *Rhodes*, p. 73.
90 Imperialist [Maguire], *Rhodes*, p. 218.
91 Imperialist [Maguire], *Rhodes*, p. 159.
92 See for instance B. Stanley, *The Bible and the Flag: Protestant Missions and British Imperialism in the Nineteenth and Twentieth Centuries* (Leicester, 1990); J. S. Dharmarah, *Colonialism and Christian Mission: Postcolonial Reflections* (Delhi, 1993); A. Porter, *Religion versus Empire? British Protestant Missionaries and Overseas Expansion, 1700–1914* (2004).
93 A. Johnston, 'British missionary publishing, missionary celebrity, and empire', *Nineteenth Century Prose*, 32:2 (2005), 20–47.
94 G. Griffith, '"Trained to tell the Truth": Missionaries, Converts and Narration', in N. Etherington (ed.), *Missions and Empire* (Oxford, 2005), pp. 153–72.
95 S. Thorne, *Congregational Missions and the Making of an Imperial Culture in Nineteenth-Century England* (Stanford, 1999), p. 89.
96 Helly, *Livingstone's Legacy*.
97 J. M. MacKenzie, 'David Livingstone and the worldly after-life: imperialism and nationalism in Africa', in J. M. MacKenzie (ed.), *David Livingstone and the Victorian Encounter with Africa* (1996), pp. 201–17.
98 E. R. Charles, *Three Martyrs of the Nineteenth Century* (1886), pp. vi–ix.
99 G. Obeyesekere, *The Apotheosis of Captain Cook. European Mythmaking in the Pacific* (Princeton, 1992), p. 124.
100 G. W. Joy, *The Work of George W. Joy, with an Autobiographical Sketch* (1904), p. 22.
101 Article in the *North British Review*, quoted in H. G. Adams, *The Weaver-Boy*, p. 317.

102 Muxel, 'Les héros des jeunes Français', p. 96.
103 R. Bazin, *Charles de Foucauld, Hermit and Explorer* (Engl. trans., 1923), p. 355.
104 K. Tidrick, *Empire and the English Character* (1990), p. 46.
105 Joy, *Work of G. W. Joy*, p. 22.
106 Charles, *Three Martyrs*, p. 286.
107 Hendrickson, *Making Saints*, pp. 122–42.
108 G. B. Smith, *Heroes of Our Empire* (1909).
109 G. Robson, *World Missionary Conference, 1910: Report of Commission I* (Edinburgh, n.d.), p. 406, quoted in R. Gray, 'Christianity', in A. D. Roberts (ed.), *The Cambridge History of Africa*, vol. 7 (Cambridge, 1986), p. 143.
110 J.-C. Jauffret, 'Les armes de la plus grande France', in G. Pedroncini (ed.), *Histoire militaire de la France*, vol. 3 (1992), p. 63.
111 *Sudan Church Notes*, 15 February 1912.
112 SAD, E. C. L. Flavell Papers, 304/5/35, Gordon Memorial Sermon preached on the Fiftieth Anniversary of the death of Charles George Gordon, Sunday evening 27 January 1935.
113 Leaflet *Gordon Anniversary Sunday*, Sunday 25 January 1948, p. 7.
114 A. Morris Gelsthorpe, *Introducing the Diocese of the Sudan* (1946), p. 6.
115 SAD, 830/8, file 'Khartoum Cathedral', record of expenses related to the building of the Cathedral.
116 *Sudan Church Notes*, 15 September 1915.
117 SAD, G. W. Bell Papers, 700/6/36, Gordon Memorial Sermon by Revd Canon C. Gordon, Sunday evening 25 January 1931.
118 NLS, MS 20311, f. 119, C. G. Gordon to MacKinnon, 5 February 1880.
119 R. Rémond, *L'Anticléricalisme en France de 1815 à nos jours* (new ed. 1999).
120 H. Laurens, 'La projection chrétienne de l'Europe industrielle sur les provinces arabes de l'Empire ottoman', in P. J. Luizard (ed.), *Le Choc colonial et l'islam* (2006), pp. 39–55.
121 J. Frémeaux, *La France et l'Islam depuis 1789* (1991). On the relationship between missionaries and the Third Republic, see J. P. Daughton, *An Empire Divided, Religion, Republicanism, and the Making of French Colonialism, 1880–1914* (Oxford, 2006), pp. 25–55 and 227–59.
122 A. Ruscio, *Le Credo de l'homme blanc* (Brussels, 2002), p. 115.
123 V. Groffier, *Héros trop oubliés de notre épopée coloniale* (1908).
124 See in particular Hobsbawm, *Age of Empire*, ch. 6.
125 M. Billig, *Banal Nationalism* (1995).
126 J. Parry, *The Politics of Patriotism* (Cambridge, 2006); H. Cunningham, 'The language of patriotism 1750–1914', *History Workshop Journal*, 12 (1981), 8–33; J. Lestocquoy, *Histoire du patriotisme en France* (1968); R. Girardet, *Le Nationalisme français (1871–1914)* (1966); P. Darriulat, *Les Patriotes. La gauche républicaine et la nation 1830–1870* (2001).
127 Mosse, *Image of Man*, p. 176. See also J. Sharpe, *Allegories of Empire: The Figure of Woman in the Colonial Text* (Minneapolis, 1993); V. Ware, *Beyond the Pale: White Women, Racism and History* (1992).
128 J. M. MacKenzie, 'Heroic Myths of Empire', in J. M. MacKenzie (ed.), *Popular Imperialism and the Military* (Manchester, 1992), pp. 109–38; Cubitt and Warren, *Heroic Reputations*; M. Girouard, *The Return to Camelot: Chivalry and the English Gentleman* (New Haven, 1981), pp. 219–30.
129 MacKenzie, *Popular Imperialism and the Military*.
130 G. K. Chesterton, *A Miscellany of Men* (1912), p. 215.
131 MacKenzie, *Propaganda and Empire*, p. 189.
132 Sanderson, 'Partition', p. 155.
133 A. Summers, 'Militarism in Britain before the Great War', *History Workshop*, 2 (1976), 105.
134 Dawson, *Soldier Heroes*, pp. 1–2.
135 G. Searle, '"National efficiency" and the "lessons" of the War', in D. Omissi (ed.), *The Impact of the South African War* (Basingstoke, 2002), p. 202.

136　This close relation is particularly evident in the case of the French Sudan; see A. S. Kanya-Forstner, *The Conquest of the Western Sudan* (Cambridge, 1969).
137　J. Martin, *Savorgnan de Brazza, 1852–1905* (2005), p. 221.
138　ANOM, Brazza Papers, PA 16 (VIII), box 2.
139　C. de Chavannes, *Le Congo français* (1937), p. 376.
140　*Le Figaro*, 28 May 1899.
141　*Le Petit Parisien*, 31 October 1909.
142　M. Cornick, 'Les problèmes de la perception réciproque de la France et de l'Angleterre au seuil du XXe siècle', in M.-M. Belzoni et al. (eds), *Images des peuples et histoire des relations internationales du XVIe siècle à nous jours* (2008), pp. 239–52.
143　M. E. Carroll, *French Public Opinion and Foreign Affairs, 1870–1914* (New York, 1931); A. Barblan, *L'Image de l'Anglais en France pendant les querelles coloniales (1882–1904)* (Bern, 1974); J. Guiffan, *Histoire de l'anglophobie en France* (Dinan, 2004), pp. 137–48.
144　On d'Ivoi and Anglophobia, see Cornick, 'Representations of Britain'.
145　J. and J. Tharaud, 'Dingley, l'illustre écrivain', *Les Cahiers de la quinzaine*, April 1902. The story was re-issued as a Goncourt award-winning book in 1906.
146　M. Leymarie, 'Jérôme et Jean Tharaud, écrivains et journalistes. Des années de formation à la notoriété, une marche au conformisme' (Ph.D. thesis, *Institut d'études politiques de Paris*, 1994), pp. 279 and 290.
147　M. Hugodot, 'L'opinion publique anglaise et l'affaire de Fachoda', *Revue d'histoire des colonies*, XLIV (1957), 114–37.
148　*Illustrated London News*, No. 3101, Vol. CXIII (24 September 1898), p. 431.
149　On the situation in Britain: Hugodot, 'L'opinion publique anglaise'; in France: G. N. Sanderson, *England, Europe and the Upper Nile* (Edinburgh, 1965), p. 372.
150　PRO 30/57, piece 57, WH 42, British Embassy, Paris, 24 August 1915, from H. L. Lewis.
151　For example, see W. Jerrold, *Earl Kitchener of Khartoum* (1915), pp. 150–4; H. F. B. Wheeler, *Lord Kitchener* (1916), pp. 138–9, E. Protheroe, *Lord Kitchener* (1916), p. 226.
152　W. d'Ormesson, *Auprès de Lyautey* (1963), pp. 100–1.
153　P. Lyautey, *Gallieni* (1959), p. 279.
154　Gauthier-Deschamps, *Cours moyen d'histoire de France* (1923).
155　*Le Matin*, 29 September 1915.
156　*Le Matin*, 12 November 1915.
157　AN, Baratier Papers, 99 AP 3.
158　*Je sais tout*, 15 January 1918; *Le Vétéran*, 1 November 1917.
159　M. Paris, *Warrior Nation. Images of War in British Popular Culture, 1850–2000* (2000), p. 112.
160　F. S. Brereton, *With French at the Front* (1915), pp. 10–11.
161　C.-R. Ageron, 'Les colonies devant l'opinion publique française (1919–1939)', *Revue française d'histoire d'outre-mer*, 77:286 (1990), 31–73; G. Wilder, 'Framing Greater France between the wars', *Journal of Historical Sociology*, 14:2 (2001), 198–225.
162　M. Thomas, *The French Empire between the Wars* (Manchester, 2005), p. 195.
163　Venayre, *Gloire de l'aventure*, p. 107. On the concept of 'hypostase', see R. Koselleck, *Geschichtliche Grundbegriffe*, vol. II (Stuttgart, 1975), pp. 384–90.
164　Venayre, *Gloire de l'aventure*, p. 112.
165　For an appraisal of Foucauld's and Lawrence's relationship with the desert, see C. Jordis, *L'Aventure du désert* (2009).
166　MacKenzie, 'Heroic myths', pp. 109–38.
167　Bazin, *Charles de Foucauld*, p. 354.
168　J.-L. Triaud, *La Légende noire de la Sanûsiyya*, vol. II (1995), pp. 803–9.
169　The epigraph of Charles de Foucauld's tomb in Tamanrasset reads: 'Died for France on 1 December 1916, assassinated in Tamanrasset by the Senussists' (quoted in G. Gorée, *La Vérité sur l'assassinat du Père de Foucauld* (Rabat, 1941), p. 125).

170 Among the most important biographies of the period (after Bazin's) are S. E. Howe, *Les Héros du Sahara* (1931); E.-F. Gautier, *Figures de conquêtes coloniales. Trois héros. Le Général Laperrine – Le Père de Foucauld – Prince de la Paix* (1931); P. Lesourd, *La Vraie Figure du Père de Foucauld* (1933); H. Rossi-Gallieni, *L'Ermite du désert. Quatre images de la vie de Charles de Foucauld* (1933); J.-M. Bouteloup, *L'Appel du désert. Vie et martyre du Père Charles de Foucauld* (1936); G. Gorrée, *Sur les traces de Charles de Foucauld* (1936); R. Hérisson, *Avec le Père de Foucauld et le général Laperrine* (1937); M. André, *L'Ermite du grand désert. Le Père Charles de Foucauld* (1938); C.-M. Robert, *L'Ermite du Hoggar. La vie au désert de Charles de Foucauld* (1938); L. Baudiment, *En plein désert. Avec le Père de Foucauld* (1939); G. Gorée, *Les Amitiés sahariennes du Père du Foucauld* (1940). For an appraisal of Foucauld's posthumous reputation, see. D. Casajus, *Charles de Foucauld, moine et savant* (2009), pp. 13–30.
171 On the impact of the Great War on values and beliefs, see for instance P. Fussell, *The Great War and Modern Memory* (Oxford, 1975 and 2000).
172 E. Lavisse, *Histoire de France, cours élémentaire* (1913), p. 180.
173 E. Lavisse, *Histoire de France, cours élémentaire* (1928), p. 182.
174 M. Roux, *Le Désert de sable. Le Sahara dans l'imaginaire des Français (1900–1994)* (1996), p. 34.
175 F. Neau-Dufour, *Ernest Psichari. L'ordre et l'errance* (2001), pp. 302–12.
176 L. Strachey, *Eminent Victorians* (repr. Oxford, 2003), pp. 171–243.
177 E. Baring (Earl of Cromer), *Modern Egypt*, vol. I (1908), pp. 417–78.
178 Sèbe, 'Exalting imperial grandeur'.
179 AN, 546 AP 1, folder 2, contract between Henri-Paul Eydoux and Editions Larose for the book *Savorgnan de Brazza. Le conquérant pacifique*.
180 MacDonald, *Rhodes*, pp. 374–80.
181 NLS, MS 20318, f. 32, 'David Livingstone: Centenary of Great Missionary's Ordination', *The Life of Faith*, 20 November 1940, 643.
182 MECA, Bowman Papers, GB 165-0034, BM 2/5, ff. 46 and 47. The transcript of the lecture was published in a Diocesan magazine of the Anglican Church in Jerusalem and throughout the Holy Land, Transjordan, Syria and Cyprus.
183 R. Rémond, *Notre siècle* (1991), p. 127.
184 ANOM, Brazza Papers, PA 16 VII, box 12, folder '*Lancement de l'Aviso Savorgnan de Brazza*' (18 June 1931).
185 Martin, *Brazza*, pp. 19 and 195.
186 NLS, MS 7875, f. 122, J. Aubrey Rees (Livingstone Film Expedition) to W. Smith Nicol, 10 November 1923, and f. 149, J. Aubrey Rees (Livingstone Film Expedition) to W. Smith Nicol, 29 March 1924.
187 NLS, MS 7875, f. 124, description of the Livingstone Film project on letterhead 'The Livingstone Film Expedition'.
188 NLS, MS 7875, f. 150, N. Bitton, Home Secretary to the London Missionary Society, to J. Aubrey Rees, 26 March 1924.
189 NLS, MS 20318, f. 26, *Weekly Gazette*, 24 January 1925.
190 L. Poirier, *Pourquoi et comment je vais réaliser L'Appel du Silence* (Paris and Tours, 1935), pp. 3–5.
191 L. Poirier, *24 images à la seconde* (1953), p. 245.
192 P. Pandolfi, review of D. Casajus, *Chants touaregs*, in *Cahier d'études africaines*, 40:157 (2000), pp. 145–8. On Foucauld's scientific achievements, see A. Chatelard, 'Charles de Foucauld linguiste ou le savant malgré lui', *Etudes et documents berbères*, 12 (1995), 145–77.
193 ANOM, Brazza Papers, PA VII, box 10, Léon Poirier to Thérèse de Brazza, undated.
194 L. Poirier, *Brazza ou l'Epopée du Congo* (Tours, 1940).
195 *Cinémonde*, 14 February 1940.
196 D. Casajus, *Henri Duveyrier. Un Saint-Simonien au désert* (2007), pp. 202–10 and 260–2.
197 Mambre, 'Henri Duveyrier', pp. 120–40.

198 Driver, *Geography Militant*, pp. 117–45.
199 F. Driver, 'Henry Morton Stanley and his critics: Geography, exploration and empire', *Past and Present*, 133 (1991), 134–66.
200 Although the first real attempt at debunking the Rhodes legend did not happen until long after his death: W. Plomer, *Cecil Rhodes* (1933), closely followed by G. E. S. Green, *Rhodes Goes North* (1936).
201 Maylam, *Rhodes*, p. 6.
202 Tidrick, *Empire and the English Character*, pp. 48–87.
203 P. Curtin, *The Image of Africa. British Ideas and Action, 1780–1850* (Madison, 1964), p. 479.
204 Obeyesekere, *Apotheosis of Captain Cook*, p. 8.
205 RHL, Perham Papers 309/1, f. 31, Lady Lugard to Lord Lugard, 11 April 1905.
206 Casajus, *Foucauld*, pp. 87–99.
207 L. Fanoudh-Siefer, *Le Mythe du Nègre et de l'Afrique noire dans la littérature française de 1800 à la 2e guerre mondiale* (1968), and W. B. Cohen, *The French Encounter with Africans. White Response to Blacks, 1530–1880* (Bloomington and London, 1980).
208 On the representation of indigenous populations as sitting beyond the boundaries of civilization, see B. Taithe, *The Killer Trail* (Oxford, 2009), conclusion.
209 T. Carlyle, 'The Nigger question', *Fraser's Magazine for Town and Country*, XL (February 1849).
210 Poirier, *24 images*, p. 235.
211 This phenomenon is charted very convincingly in Captain Scott's case in Jones, *Last Great Quest*.

PART III

Case studies

CHAPTER 6

The creation of the Marchand legend, 1895–1906

'It is always good to know how a hero is made. I remember, as if it were yesterday, the first time I saw Jean-Baptiste Marchand.'[1] The journalist, monarchist and renowned writer Léon Daudet (the son of Alphonse Daudet, the famous author of *Tartarin de Tarascon* and the *Letters from My Windmill*) could not have offered a better introduction to this chapter and the next one. Daudet and many other 'hero-makers' succeeded through their patient work in turning an expedition leader into a national hero. These two chapters intend to follow step by step the development of two exemplary heroic legends, on the basis of the advancement of their military career and the reporting that was made of it by a coterie of acquaintances, friends or interested parties. They show the making of an imperial hero from behind the scenes, revealing not only the role that the heroes themselves could play in the promotion of their own legends but also the production process of works that succeeded in establishing heroic legends.

Posterity has retained the polite but frosty meeting in Fashoda (now Kodok), on 19 September 1898, between Major Jean-Baptiste Marchand and the Sirdar Kitchener, then commander-in-chief of the Anglo-Egyptian Expeditionary Force to the Sudan. Marchand was at the centre of the most symbolic and perilous event of the Franco-British confrontation in the upper Nile (and even in Africa), and has been mentioned since then in countless studies of modern European imperialism or diplomacy. This historic meeting propelled Marchand to the pinnacle of celebrity in France. Yet the political context, and the concerted efforts of a variety of interests and players, made him for a few months far more than the mere 'hero of Fashoda' who went down into history: he was soon turned into an icon of the nationalist, anti-Dreyfusard and anti-parliamentarian right. In a country torn apart by the Dreyfus affair, the anti-Dreyfusards saw in Marchand the embodiment of the

CASE STUDIES

righteousness of the army, setting an example against what they considered to be *the* counter-example *par excellence,* Captain Dreyfus.[2] His hagiographers depicted him as a selfless providential man who had not sought this rise to fame. Yet this idealized interpretation hardly resists any analysis of Marchand's career since his early years. Networks of patronage, various commercial and political interests that his reaching an iconic status might have served, nationalist attempts to find a providential man and his own possible tendency to self-promotion allowed him to become for a time a prominent figure of French political life and one of the most successful imperial heroes of the period.

Marchand is still remembered today in his hometown of Thoissey (thirty miles north of Lyon) with a statue whose plinth reads 'To Major Marchand, Hero of Fashoda and the Great War, 1863–1934'. Almost eighty years after his death, this is a considerable achievement for the eldest son of a carpenter. Honours were not a family tradition. Leaving school aged fourteen to become a clerk for the local solicitor, with few qualifications, he joined the French navy on 17 September 1883 as a second-class sailor.[3] He worked hard to enter the military school of Saint-Maixent, a respectable alternative to the more prestigious but more aristocratic Saint-Cyr. His promotion to sub-lieutenant in March 1887 marked the beginning of a glorious career, during which he would climb to the rank of general after a series of African campaigns, a mission in China during the Boxer rebellion and noted action during the First World War.

Marchand's first distinction (*Chevalier* of the Legion of Honour) came when he was still a sub-lieutenant, after he was wounded in Senegal and a glowing report was sent by Louis Archinard (then Colonel Commander of the French Sudan). Whilst still in the field in the Western Sudan, the young *sous-lieutenant* expressed his deep gratitude to his mentor for this recognition of his military achievement.[4] Marchand had quickly managed to attract the favourable attention of this Polytechnician, who is considered the architect of the French conquest of the Sudan and in whom Lyautey saw the master of French colonial development together with Gallieni. This was the beginning of an early collaboration between Marchand and Archinard, with the latter supporting the former throughout the early years of his career, trying to provide him with the official honours he undeniably coveted. They retained epistolary contact and weaved close socio-professional relations.[5] Writing to Archinard, Marchand suggested his own promotion to the rank of Officer of the Legion of Honour 'because he had no chief to advocate his case'.[6] Eager to climb the military ladder, the young officer did not hesitate to ask for the powerful patronage of Archinard, an 'undisputed commander of the colonial troops'.[7]

At the same time as Archinard facilitated Marchand's ascension in the military hierarchy, politicians also backed up applications for promotion in the Legion of Honour or even in the army. Just four months before becoming Finance minister, the Radical deputy and future President of the Republic (1931–32) Paul Doumer personally supervised the progress of Marchand's promotion in the Legion of Honour.[8] The Republican (but formerly a staunch Boulangist) René Le Hérissé, an influential member of the *Groupe colonial*, strongly supported Marchand's promotion. Revealingly, he replied to the grateful Captain 'you owe your distinction only to yourself and to your exceptional deeds. My intercession has merely avoided an injustice and on that account I am most happy.'[9] Emile Chautemps, Minister of the Colonies, also wrote to Marchand personally to inform him of the successful outcome of the process: a further proof of the Major's powerful connections.[10]

The ambitious Marchand honed them through assiduous letter-writing in spite of his ceaseless African missions. His early successes in the Sudan and the Ivory Coast allowed him to join the circles of influential officers with powerful ministerial connections. He was closely in contact with some leading officers with strong colonial links, such as Victor Largeau (who conquered Chad between 1902 and 1915), Emile Hourst (remembered for his campaigns in the Niger area and in China), Gustave Binger (Lieutenant Governor of the Ivory Coast in 1893 and head of the African Affairs department of the Ministry of the Colonies in 1896) and Charles Mangin (a Saint-Cyrian who became one of the most influential French officers during the first two decades of the twentieth century, working with Lyautey and Nivelle).[11]

It was a reception given by Mangin's brother-in-law that allowed Marchand to be introduced to Hanotaux, the future Minister for Foreign Affairs to whom he would submit the Congo–Nile project.[12] In the summer of 1895, Marchand met Hanotaux again, this time in the lounge of his physician Louis Ménard (well known in Sudanese circles), and submitted his plan for a *Mission du Congo-Nil*.[13] Marchand's connections with influential colonial officers, who sometimes enjoyed direct contact with the *Quai d'Orsay* or the *Pavillon de Flore*, proved useful when he endeavoured to organize his own mission, the one that would strengthen and expand his nascent heroic reputation already recognized by membership of the *Légion d'honneur* and his being admitted in exclusive circles.

During his occasional stays in Paris, Marchand never omitted to liaise with societies or individuals likely to provide useful contacts. Pascal Venier has shown how Gallieni and Lyautey used such visits to the mother country to promote the cause of the overseas territories they were representing; in Marchand's case his agenda was less to further the cause of a new French overseas territory than to promote his own case as a successful colonial officer.[14] As early as 1893, Marchand approached the *Comité de l'Afrique française* (launched in 1890) and met its influential founder the Prince d'Arenberg. He also joined the *Société de Géographie de Paris*, proposed by none other than Gustave Binger and the Society's permanent secretary Charles Maunoir.[15] He was quickly co-opted to this highly reputable Parisian institution (the resonance of which expanded dramatically over the period, as we have seen in Chapter 1): Maunoir intended to make the Society's President publicly acknowledge Marchand's attendance to the general assembly, should he be able to come.[16] Marchand expanded his links with geographical societies when he represented the Ministry of the Colonies at the Congress of Geographical Societies held in Bordeaux (1–7 August 1895).[17] He favourably impressed the host society (*Société de géographie commerciale de Bordeaux*, founded in 1874), and then remained in contact with the *Société de géographie de Toulouse*, the *Société de géographie de l'est* from Nancy, and the *Société de géographie commerciale de Saint-Nazaire*, which all wanted him to lecture to their members.[18] These connections helped Marchand when time came to lobby for his Congo–Nile mission, as was subtly implied by the *Société de géographie commerciale* when preparing the invitation cards for a lecture given by Marchand:

> I am convinced that you are placing a high trump into the cards of the Minister of the Colonies, and that this trump will come at the only favourable moment. You owe this to us, which I would thank you to understand.[19]

During the decisive summer of 1895, the restless Marchand corresponded regularly with Auguste Terrier, a journalist at the *Journal des débats* and the general secretary of the *Comité de l'Afrique française*. Although Terrier had entered into contact with Marchand almost by accident, they soon became friends and Terrier offered to publish an article by the explorer on the question of African slavery in the influential bulletin of the *Comité*. Terrier also gave Marchand a few books to help him design his exploration projects.[20] Terrier, who enjoyed a network of powerful contacts among colonially minded lobbyists, was to prove a reliable intermediary when Marchand left France for Africa: he kept him informed of controversies or governmental changes which were likely to influence the outcome of his mission.

Backed by the *coloniaux*, Marchand also appealed to those who wished to expand French influence more generally. The *Alliance française*'s head office in Paris invited him to join its propaganda committee and to give a series of lectures to schoolchildren and their parents. It was suggested he intermingle in these talks his own exploration recollections and 'economic and political considerations on the need to spread the French language'.[21] Marchand was already renowned before the Congo–Nile mission had even begun.

When in Paris, Marchand also made useful contacts with two important categories of opinion-makers: publishers and journalists. Among them was H. Méhier de Mathuisieulx, a friend from the early days in Toulon, turned a geographer and an engineer, and who then worked for the bookseller-publisher Hachette and for Elisée Reclus's *Géographie universelle*. Méhier, who acknowledged that he 'was not short of contacts in the world of the press', was to be an unconditional supporter of the man whom he called 'his Buddha'.[22] A writer of military stories who dedicated some of his works to episodes of the Hundred Years' War, Captain Paul Paimblant du Rouil contacted Marchand in 1895 so as to include his biography in his book on 'soldier-explorers'. He asked him for a portrait, preferably dressed 'as an explorer', undoubtedly because Marchand had to fit in the mould of his reputation.[23] Emile Cère, from the Political Department of the *Petit Journal*, avowed his fascination with Marchand's dauntlessness. After a victory at Thiassalé (Ivory Coast), Cère wrote lyrically that he deeply admired Marchand and that he was sure he would soon be showered with praise.[24] Cère, who was to become a deputy for the *Jura* area (supporting the moderate Republican Waldeck-Rousseau) and was also in contact with the future *généralissime* Joseph Joffre, was enthusiastic again in March and May 1894: he wished Marchand 'new triumphs' and hoped that crowds would line the platform when he returned (an insightful premonition).[25] *Le Petit Journal* echoed Marchand's discovery of the Bandama and Ba-Pi rivers, in the Niger region, on 24 May 1895. Roughly at the same time, Marchand corresponded with A. Henry from *L'Eclair* (about a report on Marchand's exploration of the Baule river), with *L'Illustration* (for an account of the 'Kong column', led by Monteil but which Marchand had joined) and with E. Bourgeois from *Le Tour du monde*, three reputable newspapers with high levels of circulation.[26] Bourgeois offered to contribute significantly to the nascent 'Marchand legend': he wrote that he 'would very much like to let [his] public read the often heroic account of [Marchand's] deeds'. Bourgeois even discussed the financial side of his offer: he offered FF. 113 (approximately £235 today) for every set of twelve pages published in *Le Tour du monde*, plus royalties of 5 per cent of the retail price (FF. 20, £40 today) for a prospective book collecting the series of articles. Bourgeois's proposals were never implemented, but the journalist and the Captain remained on cordial terms; Bourgeois still hoped that they would collaborate at some point in the future.[27] The Captain seems to have been quite a gifted networker, but probably not an especially talented writer: he frequently failed to submit the papers he was asked to write. However, he maintained good relations with journalists, who were then likely to become influential supporters when the time came to celebrate the 'heroic Marchand'. In lieu of papers *by* Marchand, they got the licence to produce articles *on* him. For instance, *A travers le monde* (a geographical illustrated linked to *Le Tour du monde*) published a piece (with introductory portrait of the officer wearing the statutory kepi) entitled *'la question du Transnigérien; missions du Capitaine Marchand'*.[28] The lead announced a complete report on this mission in a forthcoming issue of *Le Tour du monde*.

There are some reasons to take issue with the analysis of G. N. Sanderson, for whom Marchand was still in 1895 'a mere junior officer on leave from Africa' who 'cut no figure whatever in the political society of Paris': Marchand seemed more an already promising officer who enjoyed powerful contacts with journalists, biographers, learned societies, respected senior officers and, above all, a variety of politicians of various leanings.[29] His relentless attempts to join elite circles indicate that Marchand created a network able to provide the social mobility he longed for: as Wesseling fittingly remarked, he 'had a certain elegance, ambition and relations. He was undeniably patriot, but money, promotions and prestige were also of great importance to his eyes.'[30] He was probably not the only young officer vying for the attention of Parisian decision makers (for instance, Bertrand Taithe has shown that Voulet and Chanoine were quite good at it), but he was certainly among the most effective lobbyists.[31]

An innocent exchange between Marchand and his future third-in-command, Albert Baratier, shows that he sought primarily to organize a famous expedition, but its aim and purpose remained hazy:

> Dear Friend,
> What's new? Will we go and look for Flatters, or will we go up the Ubangui? ... See you, and good luck with your efforts to convince these always too timorous authorities which govern us.[32]

This undated letter, written in the years 1895–1896 according to the archivist, explains why Marchand had been able in the 1890s to give information on Flatters to a journalist of *L'Eclair*.[33] Given that Marchand informed Hanotaux of his desire to 'dedicate himself to the cause of French Central Africa' on 18 July 1895, Baratier's question is all the more surprising since this alternative project had hardly anything to do with the future Congo–Nile mission.[34] Major Paul Flatters had led two missions in 1880 and 1881, hoping to gather geographical knowledge and conclude local alliances in view of the building of a trans-Saharan railway linking Algeria to the French Sudan. The second Flatters mission was attacked by Tuareg warriors, who slaughtered the majority of its *spahis*, and no French officer survived. This disaster stopped all attempts to conquer the Sahara for the following twenty years. Hence, in 1895, to 'go and look for Flatters' – as Baratier put it bluntly – implied obviously to find Flatters's remains and, in all likelihood, to punish the Tuaregs. This promised to be a glorious feat, the success of which would have undoubtedly attracted much public attention. Only a very enterprising Captain could toy with two highly ambitious projects at the same time, and this goes a long way towards demonstrating Marchand's commitment to establishing his own reputation as a talented expedition leader and a distinguished Frenchman.

The Captain's indomitable ambition finally found a convenient outlet in the race for the upper Nile. France and Britain had been struggling for political, economic and cultural influence over Egypt since 1798. After the British had imposed in 1882 what they claimed was a 'temporary' occupation, France sought to re-open the Egyptian question. For such purpose, the Nile Valley seemed ideal from 1885 owards. Some French colonials believed it was possible to blackmail the British with the Sudan and particularly the Nile basin – a prospect which was feared in England, notably by Sir Ellis Ashmead-Bartlett, who reported to the House of Commons the late Samuel Baker's view that 'any European Power holding the upper Nile would hold Egypt at its mercy'.[35] Brazza had ordered his subordinate Victor Liotard to occupy the Ubangui River as early as 1891 as a first step towards the Nile, and, in April 1893, Delcassé, then under-secretary for the Colonies, requested an expedition to the upper Nile as early as possible. In January, the Polytechnician Victor Prompt had demonstrated in a lecture at the *Institut Egyptien* in Cairo (and privately to his friend President Sadi Carnot) that damming the Nile at Fashoda would give France the opportunity to exert control over the Nile waters and, thus, to blackmail the British out of Egypt. In May 1893, Carnot ordered the thirty-eight-year old Captain Monteil to occupy Fashoda. The project aborted in 1894, victim of Belgian activity in the area, of the Anglo-Belgian agreement, and above all of a warning from the British ambassador on 29 June. However, the idea was taken up by the *Comité de l'Afrique française* and the *Groupe colonial* in 1895, and their lobbying was so efficient that the Liotard mission left the Congo with the goal of occupying Fashoda, just a few months before Sir Edward Grey declared famously in the House of Commons, on 28 March 1895, that any French encroachment on the Nile basin would be seen as 'an unfriendly act' by Britain, which provoked a firm answer from the Minister of the Colonies André Lebon.

Meanwhile, Marchand, then on leave, did his best to convince a somewhat inconsistent French 'official mind' that his project of *Mission Congo–Nil* submitted on 11 September 1895 was practicable and worthy. Acute governmental instability made the task difficult: France saw no fewer than three governments between January 1895 and April 1896. In his unpublished memoirs, Baratier recognized that the mission was all Marchand's idea, that he had fought nearly a year for it and that the result was a *tour de force* of which only Marchand was capable. Perhaps too emphatically, he argued that the mission entirely changed the course of French foreign policy, directing it against England without Germany's neutral benevolence, and making acceptable the risks of this new line of conduct.[36] Contrary to what some eminent observers believed at the time (notably Brazza's private secretary),[37] Marchand did not conceal the implications of his mission: he recognized in a note that the 'extension up to the Nile of French influence ... can create at some point an incident in international politics'.[38] This was not the most desirable prospect for French diplomats: the Franco-Russian alliance appeared as a stop-gap measure while Franco-British relations had been tense in spring 1895, and both sides were trying to arrange a rapprochement.[39] Although aged only thirty-one, Marchand was bold enough to attempt to bend – perhaps even alter – the balance of international relations. The conqueror of the Congo (from where Marchand was due to set out), Brazza, had not even been consulted: Marchand carried out his grand designs alone.[40]

From the outset, the project that came to be known as the 'Marchand mission' enjoyed powerful patronage. It was formally ordered by the new Minister for Foreign Affairs, the scientist Marcellin Berthelot, on 30 November 1895. In reality, the decision had been taken by his predecessor Hanotaux. Facing Hanotaux's reluctance (justified by his desire to appease Franco-British relations), Marchand had counted on the support of political leaders and journalists who hailed from diverse backgrounds to get his project through.[41] Marchand himself later recalled that he had known 'Brisson, Loubet, Bourgeois' in their capacity as '*Présidents du Conseil* around 1892, 93, 95'.[42] Marchand's personal relations in the highest spheres thus seem to have been instrumental in forcing through the Congo–Nile project. They also helped him overcome the opposition from some of his colleagues, who were jealous of his quick rise to fame. Among them, Parfait-Louis Monteil still resented the cancellation of his own mission (similar to Marchand's) and bluntly warned the young Captain that he could easily 'cut the wings of his ambition' and suggested he behaved with 'more reserve'.⁴³ Monteil's threat proved totally ineffective on the dashing officer.

The mission started from Loango in July 1896 and endeavoured to carry six hundred tons of equipment and supplies to Brazzaville, five hundred kilometres inland. In the process, the relationship between Brazza and Marchand deteriorated signifantly: the extra burden that the mission imposed on the colony of the Congo ultimately cost Brazza his post as *commissaire général du gouvernment*, through the combination of negative feedback from Marchand to the ministers and a scathing press campaign against the founder of the French Congo which saw a short-lived but dramatic volte-face in the opinion about Brazza conveyed by the French press.⁴⁴ The mission covered a further two thousand kilometres through the valleys of the Congo, Ubangui, M'Bomou and Sueh rivers, crossed the Bahr el Ghazal swamps and reached the former Turkish post of Fashoda on 10 July 1898, immediately setting out to rebuild it. The French party successfully repelled a Dervish attack on 25 August, and had no choice but to 'greet in the name of France' Kitchener and his flotilla of five steamers to Fashoda, on 19 September 1898, just seventeen days after Kitchener's crushing of the Mahdists in Omdurman.⁴⁵

While he was between Loango and Fashoda, Marchand was not yet a household name. In Europe, the fate of the mission remained uncertain after it had left Brazzaville. The French government preferred to leave it unnoticed so as to avoid suspicions from foreign competitors, particularly the British. The *Bulletin du comité de l'Afrique française* mentioned in just six lines, in February 1896, that the Ministry of Marine had ordered Captain Marchand to the upper Ubangui.⁴⁶ Journalists did not crowd the pier when Marchand and his officers embarked for the French Congo.

The only exception was the illustrator Charles Castellani, sent on a self-financing basis by the newspaper *L'Illustration*. Castellani, also known as *Le Panoramiste*, intended to sketch the mission and Central Africa itself but was soon sent back for repeatedly disregarding Marchand's orders. This short-lived experience allowed Castellani to publish as early as 1898 an account of his journey, in which he downplayed his misconduct and portrayed himself as a friend of Marchand's. He dedicated the book to 'Captain Marchand and [his] glorious companions of the mission', adding 'I have one sole desire, which is to clasp them in my arms, safe and sound, covered with laurel and flowers'.⁴⁷ Although inaccurate and fanciful, Castellani's account emphatically praised Marchand and his men (presumably out of self-interest). Castellani inspired deep contempt in Marchand, who once sardonically asked Baratier whether *Vers le Nil français* (the title of

CASE STUDIES

Castellani's book) was bound to become *'Dans le Nil??'* or *'Dans le Grand Marais???'* as a result of an 'occult intervention'.[48]

Once the mission had disappeared into the African jungle, its achievements had hardly any opportunity to be publicized in the French press. Newspapers such as *Le Temps* often had no choice but to translate reports from the British press on the progress of the French expedition.[49] Only exceptionally did the press echo the progress of the mission. In 1896–97, personal letters which officers sent to their relatives leaked into the press when the mission was still within reach of French bases in the Congo. Their sometimes candid testimonies exposed the fact that the mission was not as 'humanitarian' as it pretended to be, and they embarrassed the French government. By contrast, several rumours, some of them coming from Belgium, declared the mission destroyed or slaughtered.[50] Lastly, a few echoes extracted from the English press reminded the French that a handful of their compatriots were going their way through Africa, and that the prospect of a French advance towards the Nile was perceived as 'an unfriendly act' on the other side of the Channel.

When the crisis between Britain and France about Fashoda finally broke out, the English press had been showing for months deep concerns about Kitchener being overtaken by his Gallic rival.[51] As early as June 1897, British nervousness about the mission had been reported to Marchand whilst he was in the field.[52] The British eagerness to avenge Gordon, and prevalent jingoistic feelings, exacerbated hostility towards any potential French competitor. By contrast, the French paid little attention to the fate of their expedition, as the pressing issue of the moment was more the Dreyfus affair, particularly after Colonel Henry's confession and suicide (30–1 August 1898) and the call for revision launched by Mme Dreyfus (3 September).[53] Some specialist papers, such as *La Quinzaine coloniale*, *Le Correspondant*, *Le Voltaire* and *L'Eclair*, had discussed in the previous months the humanitarian goals and value of the mission when it supposedly reached Fashoda, but their audience had remained limited. The popular *Le Petit Parisien* did not dedicate much space to Marchand until 13 September 1898, when the large article *'La Mission Marchand'* was published on the second page, followed on 16 September by an editorial by Jean Frollo (pseudonym of the former Boulangist deputy and scientist Charles-Ange Laisant). When the news of the meeting with Kitchener was publicized, the French press reacted initially with caution, discovering with relative surprise the violent accusations of the British press, and generally calling for a friendly but firm response from the French government. As French diplomats tentatively tried to initiate negotiations with their British counterparts, for whom any negotiation started with an immediate French withdrawal from Fashoda, the French press adopted different lines of argumentation. Moderate newspapers such as *Le Matin, Le Journal des débats, Le Petit Parisien* or *Le Temps* acknowledged that the situation was tense but hoped that two civilized nations would find the wisdom to devise a workable solution. They also stressed the futility of Fashoda to France, especially because, as *Le Petit Parisien* pointed out, 'France cannot desire to direct towards the Nile, i.e. towards British hands, the products of [its] territories'.[54] On the contrary, the interest of the French nationalist press in the Fashoda crisis increased as Delcassé's position became more hazardous. *Le Petit Journal, L'Instransigeant, Le Gaulois* or *L'Eclair* attacked both Britain for trying to prevent France from reaping the rewards of the Marchand expedition and Delcassé for bending to the supposedly unacceptable British demands of withdrawal.[55] Delcassé was a particularly easy target; the nationalist and anti-Dreyfusist Rochefort did not hesitate to declare that 'The Dreyfusard newspapers, unofficial and even official mouthpieces of the Ministry of Treason, unanimously encourage [Delcassé] to back down and they congratulate him for his cowardice in response to the provocations of England'.[56] The ultimate goal was to make Marchand an expiatory victim of a weak Republic undermined by the Jews and the Masons, and to glorify the role of the army at a moment when the re-opening of the Dreyfus case seemed to threaten its prestige. After this turning point, Marchand was no longer merely the name of a mission but also a leader, potentially a national hero, who could be portrayed as betrayed by corrupt politicians.

Marchand subsequently became the focus of the nationalist press. Juliette Adam argued in *La Nouvelle Revue* (an Anglophobic and Germanophobic monthly she had founded in 1879) that Marchand was 'the complete expression of [the French] race' and 'France's standard bearer'.[57] When Baratier travelled to France and Marchand later reported on the situation at Fashoda in Cairo, French public opinion became inflamed. On 26 October 1898, Baratier was welcomed on the station platform by large crowds:

> When the train stops, I put my head through the carriage door, the platform is packed with people, some are shouting, there is a powerful surge, the guards cannot cope, the crowd gets squashed against my carriage, I want to get off, I am seized, some people embrace me, I am lifted up, and carried up to the reserved lounge before I have even realised what is happening. There, M. Etienne, on behalf of [the Committee for] French Africa, Colonel Monteil, who else …? – I cannot remember, give speeches.[58]

CASE STUDIES

Following his three-day stay in Paris, Baratier was dismayed at Delcassé's final decision to withdraw, but found solace in the enthusiasm of the crowds for Marchand and him. Meeting Marchand in Ismailia on 4 November, both immediately went to Cairo. There, Marchand was welcomed by the *Cercle français*, and by numerous fellow countrymen. Cogordan, the *agent diplomatique français* in Cairo, reported that

> To sum up, our fellow countryman has given an excellent impression here, not only among French expatriates – of whom he was the idol, but also among locals, foreigners and even Englishmen.[59]

The French government's decision to recall Marchand in early December 1898, a little more than a month after a major strike had paralysed the country, sounded like treason to the nationalists and anti-Dreyfusards. The withdrawal from Fashoda was irrevocable, but the fate of the Congo–Nile mission, and the personality of its leader, increasingly appealed to the public. The Fashoda climbdown launched the Marchand legend.

Having received clear withdrawal orders, Marchand and Baratier left Cairo for Fashoda on 13 November. The mission was spared the humiliation of being repatriated from the Nile on British steamers, and instead was ordered to reach Djibouti, via Abyssinia. As it headed eastwards, the French press lost interest in Fashoda, especially because of the secrecy of officials once the decision to withdraw had been taken. Arguably, French public opinion also lost interest in the matter and by January 'resentment at the surrender ... had indeed died down to a surprising degree'.[60]

Prime Minister Charles Dupuy, a moderate Republican, soon had to face another crisis. The scandalous circumstances of Félix Faure's death (from over-exertion in the arms of his mistress on 16 February 1899), coupled with the struggle between Dreyfusards and Anti-Dreyfusards which still raged, further weakened the government. The arrival of the Marchand Mission in Addis Ababa, a supposedly friendly capital, was featured in many French newspapers. *Le Temps*, known to reflect governmental positions, used this news to celebrate the final vanishing of internal divisions in France.[61] Fashoda was being quietly forgotten, unlike the burgeoning 'hero of Fashoda'. Celebrating Marchand's return to France seemed unavoidable, yet it could give a good opportunity to the Anti-Dreyfusards and militarists to strengthen their case. Public interest shifted from '*La Mission Marchand*' to Marchand himself – i.e. from the function to the man. The political turmoil of the moment made this potential messiah, this prospective saviour of society, all the more attractive to forces close to the army: as Sanderson argued, 'there was plenty to be made of Marchand as the gallant soldier who had defied perfidious Albion, only to be basely betrayed by politicians sold to the Jews'.[62] All the ingredients were united to turn Marchand into a possible national hero, and certainly a partisan icon.

Whilst the government could not shun honouring Marchand upon his return to France, official celebrations had to avoid turning him into a potential putschist. Governmental ingratitude was politically impossible, but any potential manoeuvre by Marchand or his friends to cash in on his popularity had to be carefully checked. Three months earlier, Paul Déroulède had unsuccessfully tried a *coup* which ended farcically, and the spectre of General Boulanger was still very fresh after little more than a decade. The government had to play a close game.

Once it had reached Djibouti, the whole of the mission, including the Senegalese *tirailleurs*, boarded the cruiser *D'Assas* and headed for Toulon. In spite of governmental concerns, Marchand's return made the headlines, especially thanks to the numerous ceremonies that were organized in several French cities, which marked the blossoming (and climax) of an exceptionally powerful nationalist legend.

Having landed in Toulon on 30 May 1899, Marchand was immediately invited to lunch on board the squadron flagship *Brennus* and to have formal dinner at the *préfecture*. Admiral La Jaille solemnly presented him with the medal of Commander of the Legion of Honour, which was also a means of re-asserting his link with, and allegiance to, the State.[63] The Major also visited the Town Hall and answered questions from journalists on the occasion of a reception at the *Grand Hôtel*.[64] According to *Le Figaro* dated 1 June, five thousand people gathered at Toulon's railway station to cheer him when he headed for Paris. *Le Siècle* reported that his train also carried 'his officers, the deputies, the delegations and the journalists', showing the various professional activities of Marchand's most eminent supporters. The Senegalese *tirailleurs* stayed in Toulon under the direction of Captain Mangin, presumably in an attempt to deter any nationalist coup supported by this small but well-disciplined force. Large crowds greeted the train in Marseilles, where Marchand was invited to have lunch with some fellow officers and veterans. In Avignon, Lyon, Mâcon, Dijon and Laroche, delegations waited for the train to show their enthusiasm for Marchand, sometimes right in the middle of the night. The train finally reached Paris's *Gare de Lyon* in the early morning of 1 June, giving rise to displays of popular enthusiasm and professional solidarity. For example, the *Conseil d'administration du cercle des armées* offered to accommodate Marchand and his officers during their stay in Paris.[65]

The welcoming committee at the station included numerous high-ranking civil servants or influential individuals. In stark contrast with the mission's low-key departure, its return was paradoxically covered with laurels in spite of its failure to secure an outlet on the Nile for France. Among those present were representatives of the ministries of the Navy, War and Colonies, the secretaries of the *Société de géographie de Paris* and the *Société de géographie commerciale*, the leading colonial figures Brazza and Gouraud, the Prince Henri d'Orléans, leading literary figures such as the members of the French Academy François Coppée and Jules Lemaître, politicians such as the former Boulangist Lucien Millevoye and 'all the nationalist deputies and those of the anti-Dreyfusard *Groupe de défense nationale*', according to *Le Siècle*.[66] This composition of this spontaneous committee reflected the political groups where the Marchand legend took hold: nationalists, Orléanists, anti-Dreyfusards in general and of course colonial supporters. Marchand was fêted while the prospect of the re-opening of the Dreyfus affair was looming (the *Cour de cassation* invalidated the 1894 judgement on 3 June), and just the day after Paul Déroulède and Marcel Habert (co-founders of the *Ligue des patriotes*, of which Coppée and Lemaître were members) had been acquitted at the trial following their attempted *coup* on the occasion of the funeral of President Faure.

The 'Marchand day' started at the *Gare de Lyon* (Figure 24). From there, the procession reached the Ministry of Navy, where the officers had lunch with Minister Lockroy, to whom Marchand was ultimately responsible. In the afternoon, the party crossed the *Champs-Elysées* to visit President Loubet at the Elysée Palace, which was guarded by roadblocks. Marchand and his officers then reached the Interior Ministry (Place Beauvau) to meet the new Premier, Charles Dupuy. Continuing on the other bank of the Seine, they were cheered by large crowds gathering in front of the National Assembly, stopped at the Ministry for Foreign Affairs to meet briefly Théophile Delcassé, and reached the Ministry of War, where they spent twenty minutes. At the *Pavillon de Flore*, they met the Minister of the Colonies, Antoine Guillain. The procession paid an unplanned (and unsuccessful) visit to the Governor of Paris and former Minister of War, General Zurlinden. The last part of the programme led the party to the *Cercle militaire*, near the *Place de l'Opéra*, where Marchand had a celebratory dinner with numerous eminent officers after addressing the crowds from the balcony, from where he re-stated his allegiance to the regime (see *Le Petit Parisien*, 11 June 1899, Figure 5).[67]

This itinerary reflected the government's willingness to remain in control of the 'Marchand legend' and avoid it being hijacked by the nationalists: the 'official' celebrations staged at five ministerial headquarters and at the Elysée Palace showed due recognition of

Marchand's achievements, yet roadblocks around the Elysée were set up just in case to prevent any Boulanger or Déroulède-style attempt. Support for Marchand was likely to be drawn from nationalists and/or anti-Dreyfusards, as was testified by slogans such as 'Long live Marchand! Long live the Army!' or 'Long live the Army! Long live Marchand! Down with the traitors!' which were regularly heard that day. The itinerary avoided all the working-class areas of Paris, as well as the main Parisian areas where spontaneous support for a nationalist uprising could be expected. Marchand himself seemed willing to calm the atmosphere: he shouted on several occasions, notably from the balcony of the *Cercle militaire*, 'Let us unite for the fatherland! Long live France! Long live the Republic!'[68]

However, the political situation in Paris remained tense in the following days. On 5 June, Baron Cristiani attacked with his cane the new President Loubet because of his pro-Dreyfusard leanings. On 12 June, Prime Minister Dupuy resigned, 'swept away by the nationalist crisis'.[69] However, ten days later, the new Waldeck-Rousseau government judged that Marchand was no longer a threat to the Republic and invited the mission's officers, sub-officers and infantrymen to parade at Longchamp for Bastille Day. This invitation reinforced the Marchand legend: the explorer was officially granted heroic status, crowning a skilful campaign which had begun even before his return to France.

These displays of popularity resulted from some effective groundwork undertaken by some deputies and admirers, led by the deputy Le Hérissé, whilst the mission was still in Africa. Le Hérissé was not a newcomer on the political arena: a deputy in Ille-et-Vilaine since 1886, he undertook the political direction of the newspaper *La Cocarde* in 1887, and had supported Boulanger's programme '*Révision-Constituante-Référendum*' in 1889. A friend and powerful supporter of Marchand's since the very beginning, he was one of the most influential members of the *Groupe colonial*. He submitted to the National Assembly a legislative proposal on 1 February 1899 aiming to give a 'national reward' to 'the men who were part of the Marchand Mission on the upper Nile'. The proposal, supported by 200 deputies (out of 585), officialized a terminological shift: it used the term 'Marchand mission' instead of the more neutral 'Congo–Nile mission', standard in official documents. Marchand's name had become more important than the mission itself.[70] With the name of its signatories made public, this text reveals a troubled political landscape crystallized around the heroic man. Although, arguably, the initial impulse came primarily from the nationalists and the *coloniaux*, support for Marchand seemed to overcome political divisions. United in their admiration for Marchand were Orléanists such as Prince de Broglie, colonial lobbyists

24 Paris celebrates the heroic Marchand, 'The very latest favourite of France'. *Black and White*, 10 June 1899

like Etienne, a political figure of the Left, and nationalists such as Le Hérissé. More broadly, the alliance between Le Hérissé, a former Boulangist, and Etienne, leader of the colonial group and a Republican of the Left ('Républicain de gauche'), reflects the progressive shift of the nationalists who, in 1899, no longer saw *La Plus Grande France* as the antithesis of *La Revanche*: Marchand greatly helped them reassess their position. While the two hundred deputies who supported the motion were far fewer than the 482 who voted the credits for the Congo–Nile mission, they represented a substantial fraction of the National Assembly and show that Marchand was supported by a strong body of elected representatives, far beyond the ranks of the nationalists who counted only eighteen representatives.[71]

Local celebrations of Marchand completed the political picture: numerous town councils, mayors and regional counsellors were eager to express their admiration for the leader of the mission. The Ministry of the Colonies and the Ministry of the Navy received numerous letters expressing their formal congratulations. The most significant came from the prefects of the Gard and the Ain departments, the General Councils of the departments of Loir-et-Cher, Finistère, Oran (Algeria) and Constantine (Algeria), the town councils of Pommerit-le-Vicomte, Tourcoing, Nantes, Carcassone and Blidah (Algeria).[72] Algiers even counted a *Comité algérien des admirateurs de la mission Marchand*.[73]

Not only was Marchand admired by elected representatives, but the press also prominently featured him in May and June 1899 (although some newspapers, such as the Socialist *Le Cri du peuple*, blacked Marchand for political reasons). Indeed, a newspaper's appraisal of Marchand depended upon its position on the Dreyfus affair. The length of the article, as well as the chronicler's point of view, varied according to the political tendency of the newspaper and its opinion about *L'Affaire*. Engravings enhanced the impact of the articles most openly in favour of Marchand. The French newspaper world differed from the British in being more partisan and offering more titles, a fact which influenced significantly the making of the Marchand legend. Editors and journalists used newspapers more overtly as political tools in order to shape public opinion, which is why few titles remained strictly neutral about Marchand.

Among those who tried not to inflate media interest in Marchand, the moderate Republican *Le Temps*, close on principle to governmental views, dedicated as little space as possible to the Major. It announced Marchand's promotion to the rank of Commander of the *Légion d'honneur* with only twenty lines, quoting directly from the *Journal officiel*.[74] A two-page special supplement on 'La Mission Marchand'

CASE STUDIES

was issued on 28 May – it would have been difficult to avoid it, but it stressed that the withdrawal was a 'painful but wise decision of the French government' and that the officers had indeed understood 'the superior interest of the country'.[75] The conservative and Dreyfusard *Le Figaro* said nothing on Marchand in the week from 20 to 27 May, but published a laudatory article by a professor at the *Ecole polytechnique*, George Duruy. However, his article clearly warned Marchand about a potential misuse of his popularity:

> Keep away of the tempting evil spirits. Ask them what they did with the weak blue-eyed adventurer whom they seduced [Général Boulanger] in the same way they will undoubtedly try to seduce you. Let them know that you are a soldier, and that alone is enough.

Although it was opposed to the re-opening of the Dreyfus case, *Le Petit Parisien* supported the government and cautiously handled the Marchand hot potato. A hardliner at the beginning of the Fashoda crisis, it softened its position when it became clear that chauvinistic imprecations could lead to a disastrous war. The newspaper subsequently adopted the governmental line, downplaying the interest of Fashoda for France and arguing that withdrawing was not shameful *per se*. It reported Marchand's return along the same line, depicting Marchand as a good military commander faithful to the government. The journalist thus underlined that the 'Marchand day' was a success as it proved that the country was 'devoted to the Republic, followed its government in the current circumstances, and asked for nothing more than being governed'.[76] *Le Siècle*, founded by the Radical Ledru-Rollin in 1832, remained rather neutral in its account of the ceremonies. However, it betrayed its scepticism about Marchand when it published under the title 'Impressions of a friend' a series of extracts from Charles Castellani's book about cases of misconduct of Marchand's officers in Africa, and the clumsiness of Marchand himself in the African swamps.[77] The profoundly Dreyfusard *L'Aurore* tried to counter actively the Marchand legend. Beyond defending the Republic, the newspaper sought to crush an icon of the Anti-Dreyfusards. The 29 May edition dedicated two front-page columns to an attack on Marchand by the anti-militarist lawyer, writer, journalist and lampoonist Urbain Gohier. The journalist, who had authored *The Army against the Nation* and had been sued for it in 1898, claimed that Marchand had confronted France with the painful dilemma of a humiliating climbdown or an unwinnable war. *L'Aurore* continued its campaign over the summer, with articles such as 'Marchand, the jackdaw dressed in peacock's feathers', while the socialist press did its best to undermine the Marchand legend, with ironic pieces like 'Marchand's achievements'.[78]

THE CREATION OF THE MARCHAND LEGEND

At the other end of the spectrum, the anti-Dreyfusard *L'Intransigeant*, founded by Henri Rochefort in 1880 to defend radical-socialist theses, which had ferociously opposed Jules Ferry's policies, largely warmed public opinion up before the *D'Assas* berthed at Toulon.[79] As early as 22 May, the newspaper announced on its front page the return of Marchand, detailing his deeds and violently criticizing the government for omitting Fashoda in the decree of promotion to the rank of Commander of the Legion of Honour. On its second page, the newspaper praised the weekly *Le Drapeau* for publishing an extended report from Georges Thiébaud, 'special delegate of the *Ligue des patriotes* and *Le Drapeau*'. Founded in 1882 by Déroulède, Naquet and Rochefort, the *Ligue des Patriotes* had been dissolved by the French governement for staunchly supporting the Boulangist movement, and had just been revived in 1899 under the name of *Ligue de la patrie française*. On 3 June, *L'Intransigeant*'s account of Marchand's arrival in Paris was openly partisan; the headlines read 'Major Marchand in Paris. Those who failed to attend'. As provocative as usual, Rochefort asserted that all the Dreyfusards had chosen to abstain, even 'those who had challenged Marchand to a duel while he was away'. Another strong anti-Dreyfusard newspaper, the popular *Le Petit Journal*, supported the Marchand legend after having been Anglophobic during the Fashoda crisis (it published the famous engraving assimilating France to Little Red Riding Hood with a 'Fashoda' loaf of bread for the English Wolf in bed).[80] Unlike *Le Petit Parisien*'s, its position remained unchanged. Its 21 May edition reported a lecture on Marchand given by a member of Déroulède's *Ligue de la patrie française*. On 28 May, it dedicated two columns on the front page to the mission, claiming (rather grandly) that its members 'had sacrificed their lives for their homeland'.[81] On 2 June, Marchand's old friend Ernest Judet, the *Petit Journal*'s director since 1892, stressed the weaknesses of the French government, praised the union between the French people and its army, and saw in Marchand the proof of this union maintained 'in spite of the parliamentarian mistakes, misappropriation of public funds, and iniquities'. As we have seen in Chapter 3, several weekly illustrated supplements to *Le Petit Journal* also carried full-page illustrations depicting Marchand's heroic deeds. *Le Petit Journal* was well placed to promote the Marchand legend actively, given its high print-runs throughout the period (e.g. 1,060,750 copies printed on 29 May). Among other pro-Marchand titles, the well-educated, noble or bourgeois audience of *Le Gaulois* could read on 2 June warm praise of Marchand by the famous poet and Academician François Coppée. Initially tempted to call for the re-opening of the Dreyfus case even before Zola had published his *J'accuse*, Coppée lacked the courage to uphold his views and became

CASE STUDIES

anti-Dreyfusard.[82] He advocated close cooperation between Marchand and Déroulède to attack the government. The Monarchist and conservative *Gaulois* undeniably used – and contributed to – Marchand's heroic status to make its case against Dreyfus. Satirical newspapers published cartoons that pointed out the awkwardness of the situation. On 1 June, *Le Charivari* depicted on its front page a lonely Marchand walking off the station, leaving a large crowd behind him. The end of the caption ironically read 'In front of the English haughtiness / He proved the French value / Very plainly because he was always Marching!' On 3 June, the newspaper was ironical about the government's reaction, stating 'They would rather like to put him straight into the Pantheon', implying that Dupuy and Delcassé would have preferred to see Marchand dead rather than alive. This cartoon summarized accurately the government's cruel dilemma. The sheer extent of the coverage in the French press of Marchand's return confirms that he had genuinely reached a heroic status in France, as very few newspapers failed to echo his return, whilst most of the best-selling titles covered the subject extensively.

As we have seen in Chapters 2 and 3, this infatuation of the press with Marchand was echoed by a sustained rhythm of production of books, serialized accounts and other cultural products, such as songs, cabarets and *images d'Epinal* (Figure 25), making the 'Marchand legend' one of the best-selling heroic reputations of the French empire, which remained for long in the 'hagiographical domain', as Marc Michel noted.[83] Serialized accounts such as Michel Morphy's *Le Commandant Marchand* epitomized the nationalist, anti-parliamentary, anti-Republican and frequently anti-Semite tone of most of the Marchand hagiography. Chapter 2 demonstrated how the biographical and hagiographical works which followed the media frenzy of May to June 1899 turned Marchand into a 'publishing phenomenon', even capable of inspiring poets.[84] Only a consistently hot public market can explain such a sustained output of cultural artefacts relating to the Major.

Yet press publicity and commercial success were only the tip of the iceberg. Above all, they reflected the fact that Marchand was supported by influential admirers, whose views had been relayed in the press. These hero-makers of the shadows reveal the key role of informal aspects of a successful hero-making campaign, especially because many of Marchand's supporters enjoyed fame and possessed extended networks to promote his reputation. Captain Paimblant du Rouil, who introduced himself as 'Major Marchand's biographer', wrote to the President of the Republic, the Premier and the appropriate ministers to make sure that 'Marchand will be celebrated in France the same

25 *Image d'Epinal* representing Marchand as 'France's hope' (ca. 1898)

way Kitchener was rewarded in England'.[85] As seen at the beginning of the chapter, Marchand was also a close friend of the renowned writer Léon Daudet. A prominent figure in fashionable Parisian life, Daudet counted among his friends politicians, artists, writers, composers and women leading the most fashionable *salons* of Paris. In his highly successful 1917 autobiographical account *Salons et Journaux* (first print run: 17,050), Daudet dedicated a dozen pages to his first encounter and later meetings with Marchand.[86] In his later book *Les Universaux*, Daudet mentioned that he liked to wander in the streets of Paris with his friends Marchand and the erudite poet Paul Mariéton, a founder of the *Félibrige*.[87] Daudet admired Marchand, and Marchand seemed very affectionate towards him. He performed (with the nationalist and anti-Semite journalist Edouard Drumont) the role of witness for the writer's wedding on 3 March 1903.[88] Through his close friendship with Daudet, Marchand had access to a vast network of politically or culturally influential individuals.

Some of Marchand's friends or admirers organized direct promotional events. In October 1898, a lawyer lectured the Students' Association of Marseille on 'Marchand and Fashoda', praising Marchand as a man and as a commander endowed with exceptional qualities.[89] In the run-up to the official ceremonies, on 20 May 1899, a lecture on Marchand held at the *Société d'horticulture* was presided over by François Coppée, and included speeches by the nationalist leader Maurice Barrès, the President of the civil Chamber of the Court of Appeal Jules Quesnay de Beaurepaire, the intellectual and artist Jean-Louis Forain, the future nationalist deputy of Paris Gabriel Syveton, and the ubiquitous Le Hérissé. Coppée delivered a vibrant patriotic speech in which he quoted Shakespeare – 'That day we will triumphantly carry you in our hearts' – and repeated 'Long Live Marchand! Long Live the Army!' The lecture was said to have attracted an audience of more than 1,500.[90] A member of the French Academy since 1884, and a leading figure in nationalist circles as a founder and honorary president of the *Ligue de la patrie française*, Coppée became a close and influential friend of Marchand's in the following months, visiting him several times when he enjoyed a few days of rest in Barbizon in September 1899, under the close scrutiny of the *Sûreté générale* (*SG*). The poet was so famous that the spy who observed him stated his astonishment and admiration in his report.[91] The nationalist and anti-Semite journalist Edouard Drumont had high ambitions for his new hero: he saw in Marchand the man who would bring back the monarchy.[92] In his eyes, Marchand could be the long-awaited successor to the Marquis de Morès (who died in the Sahara in 1893), whom he had compared to Boulanger in his funeral oration a few years earlier: 'Morès dreamed, like Boulanger, to free this country that is drowning itself in the parliamentary mud, and to replace with the healthy activity of life this regime that exhales an odour of corruption and putrefaction that asphyxiates France.'[93] Drumont undoubtedly thought the same of Marchand. In these troubled political times,

THE CREATION OF THE MARCHAND LEGEND

agitators were hoping to cash in on Marchand's newly acquired reputation: as posited by Max Weber and, later, S. N. Eisenstadt, instability and uncertainty were excellent breeding grounds for charismatic figures, whose appeal could be used to support a call for a more orderly, or stable society.[94]

But Marchand did not limit his appeal to daydreaming nationalists. Contrary to what could have been assumed given the nationalist and militaristic content of the Marchand legend, it enjoyed the support of many influential personalities coming from the artistic world rather than a purely military or religious environment. Out of the sixty-five signatories of a statement of support for Marchand published by *Le Petit Journal* on 28 May, only two were top military men, and one was a priest. The rest were writers, artists and composers. Writers proved the most supportive group, with twenty-five signatories, including three members of the French Academy: Frédéric Mistral, future Nobel Literature Prize winner in 1904, Paul Adam, naturalist, symbolist and then social novelist, and Horace Bertin, one of the most famous Provençal writers. Supporters were also recruited among poets, with the famous Juliette Adam (also a journalist, and a personal friend of Flaubert and Pierre Loti), Georges de Lys or Léon Dierx, elected 'prince of the poets' after the death of Mallarmé in 1898. Other supporters included the economist (and theoretician of colonization) Paul Leroy-Beaulieu; the Director of the *Comédie-française* Jules Claretie; famous artists such as the sculptor Auguste Rodin; established politicians (the nationalist leader Maurice Barrès, the former Foreign Office minister Gabriel Hanotaux) and well-known composers (Jules Massenet, author of twenty-five operas, or Vincent d'Indy, founder of the *Schola Cantorum*). The 'Marchand legend' was not only able to gather powerful supporters but it also seemed to appeal to artistic and literary circles, crossing boundaries to recruit beyond the nationalist and anti-Dreyfusard movements. The same names appeared on a list of Marchand's supporters published in two issues of the *Revue Illustrée*, which dealt extensively with the figure of Marchand, including a extensive list of his supporters ornamented with dozens of laudative quotations, a eulogy ('Portrait of a hero') and an analysis of the lines of Marchand's palm by a chiromancer.[95] Such an anecdotal approach betrays a commodification of Marchand's image, which contributed to, and reflected, a shift of popular interest from the soldier-explorer to the man and his special abilities. A further proof of this speedy heroization came when the 1899 generation of Saint-Cyriens was christened after him ('*promotion Marchand*'), an honour that had never before been granted to an officer still alive.[96] In just one year, Paris christened two of the streets of its sixteenth arrondissement after Marchand: after the

Rue de la Mission Marchand in 1900 came the Rue du Commandant Marchand in 1901.

Yet the ceremonies in the *province* organized on the occasion of Marchand's return to France reveal that his fame clearly extended beyond Paris, which suggests that 'popular imperialism' in France was not exclusive to the capital: attachment to the empire was also present in the *province*.[97] Celebrations took place (with or without the municipality's consent) in large or medium-sized cities, and even in villages. Beyond the official ceremonies in Paris, Marseille, Toulon, Nantes, Vittel, Remiremont, Cette or Thoissey all had their special events to celebrate Marchand's return.[98] When he travelled through France, outbursts of popular joy regularly welcomed him, as was the case when he went to Saint-Malo in June 1899, and was spontaneously greeted by hundreds of supporters at each station where his train stopped (he was welcomed by more than two thousand people at Rennes railway station alone).[99] In Marseille, the *Société patriotique et philanthropique des anciens militaires des corps de la Marine* lavishly honoured Marchand (who belonged to the navy): they offered a medal and a 156-page book to each officer and indeed to their chief, in order to pay their 'homage of admiration to the heroes of the Marchand column'. Production costs were covered by sixty-six benefactors, among whom were twenty businessmen, thirty-two traders or owners of private businesses and six unemployed (the rest coming from a variety of backgrounds).[100] The mixed socio-professional background of the sponsors tended to indicate that Marchand attracted supporters with various political leanings.

In the highly divisive context of the Dreyfus affair, Marchand's popularity was particularly attractive to the anti-Dreyfusards, the militarists and the nationalist elements looking for a rallying figure. Governmental services were all the more aware of this potential threat to the political stability of the country since an earlier bout of instability linked to the Fashoda crisis had probably induced the Salisbury government to send war orders to the Mediterranean fleet, on 26 October 1898.[101] Unsurprisingly, Marchand was put under surveillance upon his return to France. The government of a weakened Republic, facing the anger of the nationalist, anti-Semitic, anti-Masonic, anti-Dreyfusist and anti-parliamentarian *ligueurs*, was particularly worried at the prospect of Marchand being turned into their 'providential man', a new and this time successful General Boulanger. The comparison is all the more accurate as one of Marchand's staunchest supporters, Georges Thiébaud, had played a major role in the launching of *Boulangisme*. One informer wrote:

> Thiébaud [from the *Ligue des Patriotes*] really believes that he has found his providential man in Major Marchand. He does not want to let him

go, and wants to make out of him what he once made out of Boulanger. When listening to him, one would believe that the safety of France is in the hands of the 'hero of Fashoda' (sic). ... This is at least what appeared from a meeting we had with Thiébaud himself, on the occasion of which he talked of nothing but his hero.[102]

Under such circumstances, Marchand represented a potential threat to national stability which the government did its best to contain. Various reports written by *Sûreté générale* informants provide a detailed picture of Marchand's potential influence in various political and social milieux, which was far greater than had been previously acknowledged. In spite of limited charismatic qualities, Marchand's popularity was so established that he was persuaded to run as a nationalist candidate between 1904 and 1906. These reports sounding out various layers of French society show the depth, extent and potential of the Marchand legend in the 1900s.

Marchand's return put informers on alert: they reported as early as 27 May that all orders regarding Marchand's celebrations by nationalist and anti-Semitic groups and leagues had been issued by Déroulède (one of the most serious threats to the Republic), and that on the occasion of Marchand's arrival in Paris the *Ligue des Patriotes* had planned to distribute in the streets a hundred thousand copies of photographs of Marchand and Baratier, and of a letter from Coppée to Déroulède. Another informer reported that representatives of the *Ligue des patriotes*, the *Jeunesse antisémite et nationaliste*, the *Ligue Antisémitique* and the *Parti républicain socialiste français* (Rochefortiste, i.e. following the ideas of Henri Rochefort, founder of *L'Intransigeant* and another former Boulangist) had met to organize demonstrations 'planned for the three affairs: trial of Déroulède, trial of Dreyfus and arrival of Major Marchand' – the worst combination governmental spies could think of.[103] The leader of the *Ligue antisémitique*, and editor of the newspaper *L'Anti-Juif*, Jules Guérin, was thought to be contemplating kidnapping Marchand in order to 'carry him in triumph'. The same informer feared, on 1 June, that Déroulède had planned to whip up the crowd in front of the *Cercle militaire*, and to lead it to the Elysée in an attempt to re-enact his 23 February attempted *coup*, hoping to be more successful this time. On 31 May, the *plébiscitaires* and *Bonapartistes* were reported to be actively preparing a 'patriotic demonstration', with the support of the Head of the Napoleonic *Maison impériale* 'Prince Victor'. Both groups felt concerned about government measures taken to preserve order.

It transpired from *La Libre Parole* that the nationalists had actually shifted their hopes from one colonial hero to another in May 1899. Following the lack of enthusiasm of the crowds for Gallieni (back from Madagascar earlier in May), they transferred all their hopes to

Marchand: 'At the *Libre Parole* headquarters, all hopes are resting on Marchand and, from what they say, they will try to stir the crowd the day the Major dines at the *Cercle militaire*.'[104] In the editorial offices of revisionist newspapers such as *L'Aurore* and *Le Journal du Peuple*, there were palpable anxieties that the nationalists, anti-Semites and *ligueurs*, made more 'audacious' by the official ceremonies, would attack their headquarters during the celebrations. *L'Aurore* was particularly fearful of a dictatorship after it was reported that Georges Thiébaut had said 'This man [Marchand] is of the stuff conquerors are made of. He is an unexpected opportunity. If we do not seize it, we will be [rude word meaning 'lost'] for long.'[105]

Marchand's opponents, mostly Dreyfusists, had made elaborate plans for a counter-attack. Marc Michel noted that the anti-nationalist *Le Petit Bleu de Paris* reported that some crowds shouted '*Vive Gamelle!*' at Marchand supporters, but concerted steps to counter the nationalists had remained hitherto ignored.[106] Yet, the threat to the Republicans embodied by Marchand was felt not only at governmental level as seen above but also among the socialists and Leftist revolutionaries:

> We learnt yesterday at the *Journal du peuple* that in numerous groups, notably among the *Coalition révolutionnaire* and in various socialist circles in Saint-Ouen and Saint-Denis, arrangements were being actively made in view of responding to the demonstrations the nationalists are preparing on the occasion of Major Marchand's return. ... It is almost certain that demonstrations of this type will be organized in Saint-Ouen and Saint-Denis.[107]

Informers gathered that the *révolutionnaires* (notably at the *Journal du Peuple*) were expecting noisy demonstrations in front of the *Journal*'s headquarters and were getting ready to answer them should they actually happen, in particular because they feared the *Préfecture de Police* would abstain from reacting against Déroulède and Habert (a fear the police informer disagreed with). The *révolutionnaires* were also considering sending some groups to whistle their disapproval should the *patriotes* shout any praise of the Army.[108]

Marchand's obvious lack of interest in a *coup* (as it appeared when he addressed crowds from the balcony of the *Cercle militaire*) did not lift all suspicions. When, in September 1899, Marchand and Baratier rented a house together in Barbizon, some forty miles south of Paris, they remained under close surveillance by a full-time spy (who asked for five or six more inspectors 'just about enough to do the job').[109] The episode of *La Villa Fougères* shows Marchand's enduring popularity among nationalist circles, and how the government kept fearing his political influence, especially when the Ministry of the Interior gathered on 10

August 1899 that Marchand had finally yielded to the nationalists' solicitations, promising 'in the most formal manner his most serious and most devoted support to this party':

> He would even be ready, if deemed necessary, to resign from his commission as officer, but the nationalist party, which does not really know how it can use his support, prefers to see him stay in the Army, because he would lose all his prestige in the country if he left it. The nationalist party would greatly prefer, and seems to wish, that Marchand should be the object of some sort of disciplinary sanction from the government, which would then be put to full use politically.[110]

Another cause for concern was the number and calibre of influential visitors who came to Barbizon to meet Marchand: beyond the influential Judet (who stayed two nights), Drumont and Coppée, informers reported social interaction with the former commander of the Cavalry School of Saumur, General Rottwiller and numerous officers of the *Ecole d'application de Fontainebleau*, as well as the Irish nationalist Maud Gonne, who had just ended her relationship with Lucien Millevoye, Nationalist-Republican deputy for Paris, and the editor-in-chief of the nationalist newspaper *La Patrie*. Millevoye had been a chief adviser to General Boulanger, and one of the main contributors to the 1889 Boulangist *Programme de Tours*. Governmental suspicions towards these visits ran high as President Loubet pardoned Captain Dreyfus (19 September 1899), bypassing the Rennes verdict.

Endowed with such popularity, Marchand's political journey outlived the turbulences stirred by the Fashoda incident. His lectures remained highly popular and politically sensitive in the following years, and occasionally gave rise to celebrations. A self-described 'Masonic' informer reported that a patriotic demonstration in support of Marchand was planned for 10 January 1900 (more than seven months after the 'Marchand day'), at the *Trocadéro*, on the occasion of a lecture organized by the *Société de géographie* in the *Salle du Trocadéro*. Prince Henri d'Orléans was one of the announced VIPs, and it was expected that, rather than being scientific, the conference would be an indictment of the government, the Minister for Foreign Affairs and their colonial policy.[111]

In spite of initial fears, the post-Fashoda Marchand seemed to conform to the rules of *La Grande Muette*. After a few months of rest, he resumed his military life and was sent to China. However, the news of Marchand's resignation from the army broke in the press in the spring of 1904. Having been unable to take up his new posting in the French Sudan because of an illness, he was subsequently ordered to Indochina, in spite of his request to be sent to Russia as an attaché to General Kouropatkine, busy in Manchuria with the Russo-Japanese war. Premier Emile Combes and the Minister for War General André had been worried by the international influence of Marchand, whose contacts in Russia included the Tsar himself. Marchand resigned, arousing speculations about the true motive of his decision, and leading some newspapers, such as the radical-socialist and anticlerical *La Lanterne* (founded by the already mentioned Rochefort before he became a nationalist), to speculate about a political manoeuvre.[112] Marchand's resignation reportedly delighted the nationalists and especially the '*plébiscitaires-bonapartistes*' who hoped they would make him 'their man'. Apparently Marchand never intended to take up their offer, and another informant noted that 'in nationalist circles, it is increasingly felt that Marchand is very boring and very empty' and that he was 'perceived as an ill and unbalanced person'. A few months later, another informant reported that Marchand had told his close friends that he did not intend to enter politics: the Marchand threat seemed to recede out of the hero's own wishes.[113] In addition, *Le Figaro* was reportedly dissatisfied with the lacklustre nature of a series of articles on his experience in Fashoda which he had started to publish in its pages in August 1904: the legend did not seem to hold water.

Yet the run-up to the 1906 general election showed that Marchand's popularity had not entirely waned. The sheer number of constituencies where he was considered a suitable candidate (and a potential winner) reveals the extent of his reputation and credibility, at least in nationalist circles. As in the case of General Boulanger ten years earlier, the prevalence in the constituency of the ideas he was representing seemed more important than his local networks.[114] As early as May 1904, informers learnt that Marchand was considering becoming a candidate in the fourteenth arrondissement of Paris as a substitute for the nationalist Dr Dubois. Arguing that success was far from guaranteed, Jules Lemaître talked him out of the idea at the end of May 1904. In November 1904, rumours established that Marchand intended to run for deputy as the *Patrie française*'s representative in the working-class district of Montreuil-sous-Bois, where the 'independent Republican, socialist and patriot' Charles Hémard was being impeached.[115] Once again, Marchand declined. In December 1904, Marchand was suggested by Henri Rochefort as a potential candidate for the second arrondissement of Paris, where he could try to replace the recently deceased nationalist deputy Gabriel Syveton, one of the hopes of French nationalists and a founder of the *Ligue de la patrie française*, who had died just before the opening of his trial. The prospect was 'widely discussed in the corridors of the Chamber', as it did not necessarily suit the interests of the mainstream nationalists, who saw Marchand as the candidate of radical dissenters. Paul Doumer (who had followed Marchand since the early days of his career, as seen earlier in this chapter) strongly supported Marchand's candidacy, but was reportedly embarrassed that Rochefort backed the same candidate. In any case, Marchand was not to run officially as a nationalist. Other informers reported that Déroulède, Hoilhan (general secretary of the *Patrie Française*), General Jacquey and Jules Lemaître strongly supported Marchand, as did Thiébaud, who saw in Marchand 'the Napoleon he had long been searching for to save France, which was so weakened'.[116] Marchand finally stepped down only to become a potential candidate in the constituency of Pontoise (Seine-et-Oise department), in place of Roger Ballu who had beaten the Radical Emile-Théodore Aimond in 1902 and did not intend to run again. Marchand's supporters also imagined he could be a candidate in the fourteenth arrondissement, against the Republican Adolphe Messimy. The prospects of a victory against Messimy being slim, and Major Driant having been chosen in the meantime to succeed Ballu, Marchand officially became in January 1906 an official candidate in the twentieth arrondissement of Belleville–St Fargeau (upon invitation of the *Comité socialiste-patriote*). This made him the rival among the Right of Count Castillon de Saint-Victor, a staunch monarchist. The predicted bitter contest between Marchand (who could count only on the support of the *Patrie française*) and monarchist supporters just shows how divided anti-governmental forces could be. A day later, he was reported as being considered by the nationalists 'a useless and arrogant person who has been helped by the circumstances of an African expedition and who has since seen himself as the mainspring of France'. Beyond such reservations among his own natural, if not formal, camp, the obvious obstacle for Marchand was the socialist Edouard Vaillant, who had held the seat since 1893. Observers believed Marchand faced the prospect of an 'appalling failure'.[117] By early February, Marchand seemed to have changed his mind once again: he had apparently chosen to run for MP in the tenth arrondissement. It was soon predicted that the militants would only reluctantly support him, as they preferred another candidate, one M. Girou, to succeed Gabriel Bonvalot, whom they no longer wanted as their candidate. In a striking parallel with Marchand, the explorer of Central Asia Bonvalot had been sent to Ethiopia in 1897 to prepare the ground for the Marchand mission. Disappointed by the turn of events, he came back to France and joined the nationalist party. Despite this fitting precedent, local supporters tended to consider Marchand 'a sick man, rather unhinged'.[118] Marchand's indecisiveness had badly damaged his image, even in the nationalist camp.

Marchand finally did run in the tenth arrondissement. He centred his campaign on the establishment of the 'family-based proportional vote', which he saw as the only way of maintaining the unity of households. He obtained 7,230 votes in the first round, while 5,464 went to the socialist Groussier (a mechanic and engineer, who had held the seat between 1893 and 1902, until Bonvalot beat him) and 2,344 to the radical-socialist Monteux.[119] This was a good result for Marchand given that he was competing in a working-class district which was not traditionally a nationalist stronghold in spite of the Bonvalot precedent. Groussier won the second round of the election on 20 May, with 7,540 votes against 7,114 for Marchand. The *Dictionnaire des parlementaires français* remarked that Groussier 'had had to face a significant challenge in the person of Major Marchand, the hero of Fashoda', and that the campaign had been 'tough'.[120] The very day Marchand was beaten, Rochefort reportedly wanted to turn Marchand into one of the 'ornamental representatives' of his small *Parti socialiste-patriote*.[121] The idea was never implemented, and Marchand never ran for an election in Paris again. He was elected in 1913 only as a *conseiller général* for the *canton* of Sumène, in the Gard department, where his wife owned an estate.[122]

Although Marchand's political ambitions at national level were obviously shattered by his failure to secure a seat at the National Assembly between 1904 and 1906, his legend remained powerful in the following decades. In 1910, he was still an inescapable reference (alongside the civilizing mission) when *Pathé Frères* presented a new film on hunting in Africa:

> As they lodged their bullets in the hard carapace of the crocodiles or in the thick skin of hippopotami, the hunters reached, in the middle of the Shilluk tribe, the famous little village of Fashoda, where they found still intact the memory of Marchand and the love of the French, who had freed once and for all the nice blacks from the greedy pursuits of slave traders.[123]

Following his retirement from his short-lived political life, Marchand did not disappear entirely from the public sphere. He produced for his friend Ernest Judet, who had bought the newspaper *L'Eclair* in 1905, a series of articles on a wide variety of subjects, including astronomy, the relationship between land and sea, and diplomatic warfare. He also authored biographical articles on Jules Ferry and his former boss Théophile Delcassé.[124]

After the Great War, the appearance of new military heroes such as Pétain and Foch proved somewhat detrimental to the 'Marchand legend'. Symptomatically, the print run of Baratier's *Vers le Nil*, published after the war, was just one-fourth that of the prewar *Au Congo*. Not only did Marchand's achievements look more modest after the horror of the trenches, but the unprecedented scale of the conflict had been detrimental to the belief in the civilizing mission. The trend was reversed in only a few years, when the exoticism of Africa and Africans conquered the French public and popular imperialism reached its climax in France.[125] As the appeal of these mysterious territories increased (best exemplified by the rising 'Saharomania' described in Chapter 2), readers' curiosity about those who had conquered large swathes of Africa for France increased, and Marchand was an inescapable reference. He featured prominently in the pavilion dedicated to imperial conquerors at the *Musée des Colonies*, set up on the occasion of the colonial exhibition of Vincennes.

Marchand's military achievements during the Great War (notably during the battle of Verdun and the capture of Koblenz) remained overshadowed by the Congo–Nile mission: he remained the 'hero of Fashoda' and, unlike Kitchener, his First World War *faits d'armes* did not supersede his colonial pedigree. He spent the last fifteen years of his life as a respectable man bearing a name that seemingly still helped to sell books. In 1923, he prefaced a book by Count Arnauld Doria, *Héros obscurs*, whose title offered quite fittingly a reflection upon the coming and going of glory. In 1930, a book by Hippolyte Roy about the 'romantic and heroic life of Doctor Charles Cuny, explorer (1811–1858)' featured a preface by Marchand, who was introduced on the title page as the 'Head in 1898 of the Congo–Nile mission'.[126] Shortly before his death, he wrote a preface for a children's book of the *Bibliothèque des écoles et des familles* on the French conquest of Chad.[127]

When Marchand died in January 1934, *Le Monde colonial illustré* asked with indignation 'Where are today the people of Paris whose hearts were so stirred in 1900? Where is the Minister of War? Where is the Minister of the Colonies? Where is the Minister of Navy? They have all left Marchand to leave this world alone.'[128] Such a statement could cast doubt upon the prevalence of the Marchand legend in the 1930s. Yet, if it is true that Marchand did not get a state funeral, and no minister attended the ceremony, he did get a 'solemn funeral' in the prestigious chapel *Saint-Louis des Invalides*, with eminent generals (including Pétain) in attendance, and a speech by General Weygand. *L'Illustration* of 27 January 1934 dedicated four illustrated pages to *Marchand l'Africain*, described as 'an exceptional moment of the French soul' who made the journalist regret that the French were 'usually afraid of those who emulate enthusiasm'. In Britain,

The Times mentioned in its two-column obituary that Marchand had been 'enshrined as the "Hero of Fashoda" in the loving memory of his enthusiastic countrymen'.[129] Shortly afterwards, a *Comité pour l'érection d'un monument au général Marchand* was set up, with its headquarters at the *Société de géographie de Paris*, which thus retained its place as one of the institutions where heroic reputations were made and maintained.[130] In 1935, the Paris town council started to discuss the project of a memorial to the 'Marchand mission' opposite to the new *Musée des colonies*.[131] Above all, the extensive biography published by Jacques Delebecque only two years after this funeral helped to keep the Marchand legend alive. In typical hagiographical vein, Delebecque tried to give the best image of the hero he called 'a valiant knight', 'a crusader', 'a blade of pure steel' or even 'an apostle', combining the chivalric and religious parallels that characterized nineteenth-century British imperial heroes like Gordon.[132] Delebecque emphasized that Marchand was not embarrassed by worldly preoccupations, writing that 'Everyone agrees about Marchand's absolute unselfishness. He has never been preoccupied at all with the "vile metal". ... But this selflessness went far beyond the mere contempt of money.'[133] In reality, Marchand's emolument as chief of the Congo–Nile mission was 15,000 francs per year, the equivalent of the income of a *Directeur des affaires politiques* in a ministry.[134] Delebecque's 254-page opus came too late to generate a commercial frenzy about his topic, but it enjoyed significant echo even across the Channel, where *The National Review* discussed it in April 1937.[135] In September 1937, another notable biography of Marchand (223 pages) was issued by the renowned publisher Mame, which suggests that the 'hero of Fashoda' was still a subject of interest to the public.[136]

The Second World War offered the Marchand legend a new lease of life when the Vichy government sought to arouse Anglophobic feelings among the French public to justify its collaborationist policy. In the wake of Mers-el-Kebir, old arguments from the Fashoda crisis were readily unearthed, such as Déroulède's statement 'I have seen well how Marchand disliked the English much more than the Germans'.[137] The endearment of nostalgic nationalists with their ephemeral hero was not new: as early as 1933, a small book on Marchand entitled *Qui Vive? ... France! ... La mission Marchand, 1895–1899* clearly echoed the slogan of Déroulède's *Ligue des patriotes-plébiscitaires*, '*Qui Vive? France! Quand même*'.[138] Following the military collapse of May to June 1940, and with the collaborationist government trying to improve French morale by promoting a cult of national heroes (from Joan of Arc to Pétain, with a marked preference for the Anglophobic ones), the Marchand legend was revitalized. Baratier's third part of his account of the mission, from Fort-Desaix to Fashoda, was re-issued in 1941 under the revealing title *Fachoda. Souvenirs de la mission Marchand* (Baratier's other books never mentioned Fashoda). The famous publisher Grasset made at least two printings. In 1942, Fayard reprinted Baratier's *A travers l'Afrique*. The same year, a biography of Marchand inaugurated a series of books that was intended, according to its publisher, to introduce French people to 'the great men of their country' so that 'they could be proud of their past and be confident in the future of their country'. Pierre Croidy's *Marchand, le héros de Fachoda* sometimes reflected upon the French situation of the moment, in particular when the author ventured that 'like all great men, like all great captains, and great leaders, he trusted his lucky star and let Destiny decide'.[139] In the paragraphs dedicated to the Marchand celebrations of May to June 1899, the author praised the nationalists and vilified Dreyfusists, Republicans and the government of the time. Apart from these lyrical or political digressions, the text followed the plan of, and at times openly plagiarized, Delebecque's biography. The book was duly approved by the Vichy censors.[140] Future titles announced in this series included Henri de Bournazel (for July 1942), Jean-Baptiste Charcot, Ernest Psichari, Cardinal Lavigerie, Admiral Courbet, Louis Pasteur, and Father Charles de Foucauld: in line with the preoccupation of the Vichy regime with the French empire (especially in Africa), explorers and conquerors of Africa outnumbered all other types of hero.[141] The member of the Goncourt Academy and Femina prize-winner Roland Dorgelès also evoked at length Marchand (alongside Brazza, Mangin and a few other empire builders) in his 1941 opus, *Sous le casque blanc*.[142] The Marchand legend was even revived in far-flung corners of the French empire: in 1943, a book about 'the heroic career of Marchand' was published in Hanoi.[143] This series of books was, to a certain extent, the swansong of the Marchand legend, as such a high output of biographies has never happened again since then.

Marchand was not completely forgotten after the war, however, as the efforts of the above-mentioned *Comité pour l'érection d'un monument au général Marchand* finally bore fruit. On 1 July 1949, President Auriol inaugurated a monument to Marchand opposite the entrance of the *Musée de la France d'Outre-Mer* in Paris. Marchand was no longer an icon of the nationalists, and the President of the Committee was the eminent Paul Reynaud, who had been a faithful servant of the Third Republic, former President of the Council and former minister of the Colonies. Owing to the postwar warming of Franco-British relations, one of the last two surviving British officers of the Fashoda confrontation, Admiral Sir Walter Cowan, former Major of one of the steamers, was invited to give a speech on the occasion of the opening ceremony.[144] Marchand had ceased to be an icon of the Anglophobes, and remained simply a famous colonial hero. Fifteen years after *Le Monde colonial illustré* had complained about the ingratitude of the French public, the Marchand legend was still well alive, albeit no longer charged with any major political significance.

The Marchand legend proved to be one of the most enduring heroic reputations of the so-called 'second' French colonial empire. It owed its initial success and subsequent longevity to the circumstances surrounding the Fashoda crisis as much as to the networks of patronage and influential supporters that spread it through various means. In the summer of 1899, anti-Republican and anti-Dreyfusard politicians perceived the appeal of such a 'saviour' at a moment when France was divided, weakened and unsure about its future. The combination of colonialist and nationalist support (which revealed a significant change in nationalist positions vis-à-vis colonial expansion) brought this imperial figure to the forefront of the French political scene. Marchand hitherto became part of the tactic of nationalist elements to monopolise all symbols of national grandeur ('from Joan of Arc to Marchand, from the patriots of 1789 to Gambetta'), in order to prevent political opponents from cashing in on them.[145] It is therefore hardly surprising that he was perceived for more than half a decade as a potentially powerful leader of the anti-Parliamentarian Right, by both the government and the *ligueurs* and other anti-parliamentarian supporters. Marchand's desire to preserve the unity of the Republic explains why he ultimately refused to instigate a *coup*.

Chapters 2 and 3 demonstrated that the commercial opportunities opened by Marchand's sudden popularity following Fashoda further entrenched the legend as journalists, writers and publishers were attracted by the opportunity for success. By contrast, this case study chapter has followed the development and impact of networks of patronage which first allowed a future imperial hero to obtain a commission that would distinguish him from his colleagues, and then ensured his nationwide promotion and invested it with political meaning, before lapsing into the more consensual, and mostly apolitical, mould of the 'imperial hero' after 1906.

The commercial appeal of Marchand's popularity can still be perceived in today's flea markets, which frequently offer Marchand memorabilia such as plates, bonbon dishes, portraits, or other commemorative objects and collectibles (Figure 26). Naturally, Marchand is always shown at his best and larger than life. The frequent label 'hero of Fashoda' which ornaments these items reminds buyers that Marchand

THE CREATION OF THE MARCHAND LEGEND

26 'Marchandise': collectible cards produced by *Chocolats Cémoi* and *Félix Potin* shops.

was celebrated not for a victory but instead for a painful setback. Ironically, the same event launched another heroic reputation on the other side of the Channel, which is analysed from a complementary angle in the following chapter.

Notes

1   L. Daudet, *Salons et journaux* (1932), p. 157.
2   J.-P. Rioux, *Nationalisme et conservatisme. La Ligue de la patrie française 1899–1904* (1977), p. 38.
3   AN, LH/1729/36 (*Légion d'honneur* record), état de service established in Saint-Louis, Senegal, July 1890.
4   AN, LH/1729/36 (*Légion d'honneur* record), form dated 12 September 1889. For Marchand's expression of gratitude to Archinard, see ANOM, Private Papers, Archinard Papers, 60 APC/1 Marchand to Archinard, 3 November 1889.
5   AN, 231 Mi, Marchand Papers, box 2, file 6: Archinard to Marchand, 3 August 1891 (about the latter's promotion); Lieutenant-Colonel Bonnier to Marchand, 17 September 1892 (about Archinard's invitation to have dinner when all three would be in Paris).
6   AN, 231 Mi, Marchand Papers, box 9, file 11, letter No. 28, letter to Archinard thought to date from 1894–95.
7   H. Wesseling, *Le Partage de l'Afrique* (French trans., 1991), p. 470.
8   AN, 231 Mi, Marchand Papers, box 2, file 10, f. 38, Paul Doumer to Marchand, 12 July 1895.
9   AN, 231 Mi, Marchand Papers, box 2, file 10, f. 52, René Le Hérissé to Marchand, 17 July 1895
10 AN, 231 Mi, Marchand Papers, box 2, file 10, f. 40, Emile Chautemps, 13 July 1895. Chautemps, a senator and Minister of the Colonies, was the father of Camille Chautemps, a leading Radical politician.
11 AN, 231 Mi, Marchand Papers, box 1, file 6, and box 2, file 6.
12 G. Hanotaux, *Le Général Mangin* (1935), p. 1.
13 Wesseling, *Partage*, p. 471.

CASE STUDIES

14 P. Venier, 'A campaign of colonial propaganda: Gallieni, Lyautey and the defence of the military regime in Madagascar, May 1899 to July 1900', in T. Chafer and A. Sackur (eds), *Promoting the Colonial Idea* (2002), pp. 29–39.
15 AN, 231 Mi, Marchand Papers, box 2, file 6, notification of admission dated 9 January 1893.
16 AN, 231 Mi, Marchand Papers, box 2, file 10, f. 27, Maunoir to Marchand, 18 July 1895.
17 AN, 231 Mi, Marchand Papers, box 2, file 10, f. 63, Ministry of Colonies to Marchand, 22 July 1895.
18 AN, 231 Mi, Marchand Papers, box 2, file 10, ff. 80, 82, 134 and 140, August–November 1895.
19 AN, 231 Mi, Marchand Papers, box 2, file 10, f. 112, *Société de géographie commerciale*, Paris, to Marchand, undated but probably autumn 1895.
20 AN, 231 Mi, Marchand Papers, box 2, file 1, ff. 14, 19 and 47, Terrier to Marchand, June 1895–February 1896.
21 AN, 231 Mi, Marchand Papers, box 2, file 10, f. 142, *Alliance Française* to Marchand, 20 November 1895, and box 2, file 1, f. 13, 23 January 1896.
22 AN, 231 Mi, Marchand Papers, box 2, file 1, f. 61, undated (spring 1896), and box 2, file 3, f. 95, 5 April 1900.
23 AN, 231 Mi, Marchand Papers, box 2, file 10, f. 156, Paimblant du Rouil to Marchand, 14 December 1895.
24 AN, 231 Mi, Marchand Papers, box 2, file 7, Emile Cère to Marchand, 15 September 1893.
25 AN, 231 Mi, Marchand Papers, box 2, file 7, Cère to Marchand, 8 March and 2 May 1894.
26 AN, 231 Mi, box 2, file 10, f. 58, Henry to Marchand, 20 July 1895 and box 2, file 1, f. 26, *L'Illustration* to Marchand, 25 February 1896.
27 AN, 231 Mi, box 2, file 10, ff. 54 and 79, file 1, f. 12, Bourgeois to Marchand, July 1895 to January 1896.
28 *A travers le monde*, No. 38 (21 September 1895).
29 G. N. Sanderson, *England, Europe and the Upper Nile* (Edinburgh, 1965), p. 271.
30 Wesseling, *Partage*, p. 470.
31 B. Taithe, *The Killer Trail* (Oxford, 2009), pp. 90–2.
32 AN, 231 Mi, Marchand Papers, box 2, file 10, f. 72, Baratier to Marchand, undated.
33 AN, 231 Mi, Marchand Papers, box 2, file 6, f. 30, R. Aubry to Marchand, dated 189[?].
34 AN, 99 AP, Baratier Papers, box 1, file Landeroin 1896, f. 3, p. 1.
35 Hansard (Commons), 4th Series, vol. XXXII, 28 March 1895, c. 391.
36 AN, 99 AP, Baratier Papers, box 2, notebook entitled '*La Mission Marchand de l'Atlantique à la Mer Rouge, Loango-Fachoda-Djibouti, 10 mai 1896–29 mai 1899*', p. 5.
37 C. de Chavannes, *Le Congo français* (1937), p. 360.
38 ANOM, Missions, box 42, '*Note analytique complémentaire du projet de mission au Nil dressé par le capitaine Marchand*', dated 11 September 1895.
39 M. Michel, *La Mission Marchand* (1972), p. 27.
40 Chavannes, *Congo*, p. 360.
41 Michel, *Mission Marchand*, p. 36.
42 AN, 99 AP, Baratier Papers, box 4, Marchand to Mme J. Delorme-Jules Simon, undated.
43 AN, 231 Mi, Marchand Papers, box 2, file 10, f. 110, Monteil to Marchand, 17 October 1895.
44 M. Michel, 'Autour de la mission Marchand: le rappel de Brazza en 1897', *Cahiers d'études africaines*, 7:25 (1967), 152–85.
45 Expression used by Marchand in his letter to Kitchener, 19 September 1898. A. Baratier, *Fachoda. Souvenirs de la Mission Marchand* (1941), pp. 142–3.
46 R. Arié, 'L'opinion publique en France et l'affaire de Fachoda', *Revue d'histoire des colonies*, XLI (1954), 329–67.

THE CREATION OF THE MARCHAND LEGEND

47 C. Castellani, *Vers le Nil français* (1898), p. I.
48 AN, 99 AP, Baratier Papers, box 4, Marchand to Baratier from Beijing, undated but surely written on 10 July 1901.
49 J. F. V. Keiger, 'Omdurman, Fashoda and Franco-British Relations', in E. M. Spiers (ed.), *Sudan: The Reconquest Reappraised* (1998), p. 167.
50 ANOM, Afrique III, 35a, folder 2.
51 ANOM, Afrique III, 35b, report from the French ambassador in London, 12 January 1898. The review of the English press which Marchand possessed in his papers (AN, 231 Mi, 8 notebooks entitled *La Presse anglaise au sujet du conflit de Fachoda*, by C. Fidel, *licencié en droit*) includes a press cutting from the *Daily Telegraph* dated 25 August 1898 (well before the Fachoda encounter) in which Marchand is expressly cited.
52 AN, 231 Mi, Box 2, File 2, M. Terray to Marchand, 9 June 1897.
53 On the Dreyfus affair, see R. Harris, *The Man on Devil's Island: Alfred Dreyfus and the Affair that Divided France* (2010).
54 *Le Petit Parisien*, 30 October 1898.
55 For an analysis of the British and French public opinions, see Arié, 'L'opinion publique en France', and M. Hugodot, 'L'opinion publique anglaise et l'affaire de Fachoda', *Revue d'histoire des colonies*, XLIV (1957), 114–37, and C. R. Ageron, *France coloniale ou parti colonial?* (1978), pp. 175–87.
56 *L'Intransigeant*, 22 October 1898.
57 Arié, 'L'opinion publique en France'.
58 Baratier, *Fachoda*, p. 205.
59 ANOM, Afrique III, 34a, dispatch from Cogordan to the Minister for Foreign Affairs, 21 November 1898.
60 Sanderson, *Upper Nile*, p. 372.
61 *Le Temps*, 21 April 1899 ('*En Ethiopie*').
62 Sanderson, *Upper Nile*, p. 373.
63 AN, '*Légion d'honneur*' files, LH/1729/36.
64 *L'Intransigeant*, 28 May 1899.
65 ANOM, Afrique III, 35 c.
66 *Le Siècle*, 1 June 1899.
67 For a fuller account of the Marchand day, see B. Sèbe, 'From Thoissey to the capital via Fashoda: Major Marchand, partisan icon of the Right in Paris', in J. Wardhaugh (ed.), *Paris and the Right in the Twentieth Century* (Cambridge, 2006), pp. 18–42.
68 *Le Petit Journal*, 2 June 1899.
69 J.-M. Mayeur, *La vie politique sous la Troisième République 1870–1940* (1984), p. 181.
70 *Chambre des Députés, Septième Législature, session de 1899, Annexe N° 695 au procès verbal de la séance du 1er février 1899.*
71 Some of the deputies who voted the credits for the mission on 8 December 1896 deeply believed its claimed scientific and peaceful aims. In particular, the Socialists who voted for it had no idea, or at least claimed to have no idea, of its international implications (Jean Jaurès in *La Petite République*, 13 November 1898).
72 ANOM, Afrique III, 35 c, various reports.
73 ANOM, Afrique III, 35 a, telegram from Broussais, President of the *Conseil général d'Alger*, 18 April 1899.
74 *Le Temps*, 21 May 1899.
75 *Le Temps*, 28 May 1899.
76 *Le Petit Journal*, 3 June 1899.
77 *Le Siècle*, 1 June 1899.
78 *L'Aurore*, 26 July 1900; *La Petite République socialiste*, 25 July 1900.
79 F. Pisani-Ferry, *Jules Ferry et le partage du monde* (1962), p. 254.
80 *Le Petit Journal*, 20 November 1898.
81 *Le Petit Journal*, 28 May 1899.
82 R. de Livois, *Histoire de la presse française*, vol. II (1965), p. 350.
83 Michel, *Mission Marchand*, p. 8.

CASE STUDIES

84 J. Grégoire (lyrics and music), *'Dédié aux Membres de la Mission Congo-Nil' - Le Commandant Marchand - Retour au Pays* (Châtillon sur Chalaronne, 1899); G. d'Aizenay (signed *'Par un Patriote'*), *Salut à Marchand!... Marchand et Kitchener à Fachoda* (Cusset, 1899).
85 ANOM, Afrique III, 35 a, f. 33.
86 E. Mas, *Léon Daudet, son œuvre* (1928), p. 84; Daudet, *Salons*, pp. 157–70.
87 Quoted in E. Vatré, *Léon Daudet ou le libre réactionnaire* (1987), p. 250.
88 J.-N. Marque, *Léon Daudet* (1971), p. 71.
89 R. Teisseire, *Marchand et Fachoda. Conférence faite à l'association des étudiants de Marseille le 26 octobre 1898* (Marseille, 1898).
90 *Le Petit Journal*, 21 May 1899.
91 AN, F/7/15981/1, Police records of the *SG*, file *'Notes de police 1899–1906'*, folder *'Commandant Marchand à Barbizon: septembre et octobre 1899'*, report dated 19 September 1899.
92 Marque, *Daudet*, p. 74.
93 E. Drumont, *Les Héros et les pitres* (1900), quoted in M. Winock, *Edouard Drumont et Cie* (1982), p. 61.
94 S. N. Eisenstadt (ed.), *Max Weber on Charisma and Institution Building* (Chicago, 1968), p. 329.
95 *Revue Illustrée*, 1 January 1900 (No 2) and 15 January 1900 (No. 3).
96 SAD, PK 1637 [MARCHAND], P. Reynaud, leaflet *Au Commandant Marchand, chef de la Mission Congo-Nil, et aux membres de l'expédition* (1949), p. 12.
97 On popular imperialism in the provinces, see O. Georg, 'The French Provinces and "Greater France"', in Chafer and Sackur (eds), *Promoting the Colonial Idea*, pp. 82–101; R.-C. Grondin, 'L'Empire palimpseste: l'exemple des années trente dans le Limousin', *French Colonial History*, 7 (2006), 165–80; Grondin, 'La colonie en province: diffusion et réception du fait colonial en Corrèze et en Haute-Vienne', Ph.D. thesis, University Paris 1-Panthéon-Sorbonne, 2007; E. Godin, 'Provincial elites and the Empire: the case of Rennes (1880–1905)', *French History*, 21:1 (March 2007), 65–84.
98 AN, F/7/15981/1, Police records of the *SG*, file *'Manifestations en province au retour du commandant Marchand'*, various reports.
99 AN, F/7/15981/1, Police records of the *SG*, file *'Manifestations ...'*, folder *'Cdt Marchand à St-Malo, St-Servan, Rennes - 11 juin 1899'*, various reports dated 17 June 1899.
100 Anon., *Livre d'or offert à chacun des membres de la mission Marchand* (Marseille, 1899).
101 Robinson, *Africa*, p. 375.
102 AN, F/7/15981/1, Police records of the *SG*, file *'Notes ...'*, Report from M898, 'Thiébaud et Marchand', 4 July 1899.
103 AN, F/7/15981/1, Police records of the *SG*, file *'Manifestations ...'*, report from the informer 'Berlin', 27 May 1899.
104 AN, F/7/15981/1, Police records of the *SG*, file *'Manifestations ...'*, report from the informer 'Jean', 29 May 1899.
105 AN, F/7/15981/1, Police records of the *SG*, file *'Notes ...'*, Report from M669, *'Ce qu'on dit de l'arrivée de Marchand chez les révisionnistes'*, 18 May 1899.
106 Michel, *Mission Marchand*, p. 241.
107 AN, F/7/15981/1, Police records of the *SG*, file *'Manifestations ...'*, report from the informer 'Albert', 27 May 1899.
108 AN, F/7/15981/1, file *'Notes ...'*, report from M732, 'Nationalistes et anarchistes à l'arrivée de Marchand', 30 May 1899 and file *'Manifestations ...'*, report from 'Mr Albert au Journal du Peuple', 16 May 1899.
109 AN, F/7/15981/1, Police records of the *SG*, file *'Direction de la SG: 4e Bureau'*, report from M. Tomps to the director of the *SG*, 19 September 1899.
110 AN, F/7/15981/1, Police records of the *SG*, file *'Commandant Marchand à Barbizon: septembre et octobre 1899'*, letter from the Ministry of Interior to the *SG*, 10 August 1899.

THE CREATION OF THE MARCHAND LEGEND

111 AN, F/7/15981/1, Police records of the SG, file 'Notes ...', Report from A.971, 'Rapport', 5 December 1899.
112 *La Lanterne*, 13 April 1904.
113 AN, F/7/15981/1, Police records of the SG, file 'Notes ...': report from 'Metz', 27 April 1904; 20 May 1904; 20 June 1904.
114 Boulanger had been a successful candidate in five departments (Dordogne and Nord in April 1888, Charente inférieure, Somme and Nord again in August 1888), and in Paris (January 1889). Multiple candidacies were forbidden in 1889, in an attempt to decapitate the Boulangist movement.
115 J. Jolly, *Dictionnaire des parlementaires français* (1960), p. 1950.
116 AN, F/7/15981/1, Police records of the SG, file 'Notes ...', 12 and 13 December 1904.
117 AN, F/7/15981/1, Police records of the SG, file 'Notes ...', 24 and 25 January 1906.
118 AN, F/7/15981/1, Police records of the SG, file 'Notes ...', 4 and 13 February 1906.
119 J. Delebecque, *Vie du général Marchand* (1936), p. 207.
120 Jolly, *Dictionnaire des parlementaires*, p. 1893.
121 AN, F/7/15981/1, Police records of the SG, file 'Notes ...', 25 January 1906.
122 Delebecque, *Marchand*, p. 211.
123 Pathé Archives, PRO-P-497 M6, booklet *Les Grands Films Pathé Frères: voyage et grandes chasses en Afrique* (ca. 1910), p. 8.
124 Delebecque, *Marchand*, p. 209.
125 B. Sèbe, 'Exalting imperial grandeur', in J. M. MacKenzie (ed.), *European Empires and the People* (Manchester, 2011), pp. 35–42.
126 H. Roy, *La Vie héroïque et romantique du docteur Charles Cuny, explorateur (1811–1858)* (1930), p. XIII.
127 Y. de Coppet, *Au pays du Tchad* (Coulommiers, 1934).
128 *Le Monde colonial illustré*, No. 126, February 1934.
129 *The Times*, 15 January 1934.
130 SAD, 764/9/18, *Médecin Général inspecteur* J. Emily to Mr A. G. Pawson, dated 18 March 1935.
131 Archives de la Ville de Paris, Fonds Debuisson, Direction des affaires culturelles de la Ville de Paris, conservation des œuvres d'art religieuses et civiles, dossier Marchand, VM92.
132 M. Girouard, *The Return to Camelot: Chivalry and the English Gentleman* (New Haven, 1981), pp. 219–30.
133 Delebecque, *Marchand*, p. 10.
134 Michel, *Mission Marchand*, p. 34.
135 SAD, 244/6/56 and 57.
136 J. Maigret, *Marchand l'Africain* ... (Tours, 1937).
137 P. Déroulède, *Qui vive? France! Quand même* (1910), p. 97.
138 F. Léonnec, *Qui Vive?... France!... La mission Marchand, 1895–1899* (1933). The eight-page booklet, which included the statutes of the *Ligue des patriotes-plébiscitaires*, was entitled *'Qui vive? France? Quand-même'*.
139 P. Croidys, *Marchand, le héros de Fachoda* (1942), p. 32.
140 Authorisation of publication No. 10.613 delivered by the French State authorities in Vichy.
141 R. Ginio, *French Colonialism Unmasked* (Lincoln, NE, 2006), pp. 11–22.
142 R. Dorgelès, *Sous le casque blanc* (1941).
143 A. Acard, *La Carrière héroïque de Marchand* (Hanoi, 1943).
144 SAD, PK 1637 [MARCHAND], W. Cowan, leaflet *Au Commandant Marchand, chef de la Mission Congo-Nil, et aux membres de l'expédition* (1949), pp. 16–19.
145 Rioux, *Nationalisme et conservatisme*, p. 44.

CHAPTER 7

George Warrington Steevens, Blackwood Publishers and the making of *With Kitchener to Khartoum*

Following the careful study of the birth and development of the 'Marchand legend', which has shown how a powerful network of patronage and a variety of friends and admirers in the press and the political and literary worlds ensured the success of an imperial hero among various sections of the French public, the present case study illustrates another crucial aspect of hero-making: the role of commercial interest alongside ideological convictions. To that purpose, this chapter follows the process through which a war correspondent following the Anglo-Egyptian expeditionary force for the London *Daily Mail*, George Warrington Steevens, his wife Christina and his Scottish and pro-imperial publisher William Blackwood III consciously used, and contributed to, the fame of Lord Horatio Herbert Kitchener in the months following the battle of Omdurman (2 September 1898).

Steevens's book *With Kitchener to Khartoum* detailed the Sudan Campaign from March 1898 (British advance on Berber) until the recapture of Khartoum (2 September). The latter event was unanimously celebrated in the British press as the avenging of General Gordon's death, and as a consequence *With Kitchener to Khartoum* was marketed as patriotic writing. However, the correspondence between the author, his wife and his publisher reveal other intentions that, albeit not incompatible with sincere patriotic purposes, may explain the process in less altruistic terms. Private exchanges between the author and his publisher reveal the impact of commercial interest on the publishing process that led to the celebration of the 'brain of the Egyptian army'.[1]

With Kitchener to Khartoum was the first book on Kitchener's action to become a nationwide best-seller and it established the 'Kitchener legend'. The present chapter shows step-by-step the publishing process that turned Steevens's *Daily Mail* chronicles into a commercial success. The strategies implemented sometimes bluntly by both Steevens and Blackwood demonstrate how self-interest played a large part in the popularization of imperial heroes and how hero-makers could devise sophisticated methods to promote 'their hero' at the same time as their own work.

With Kitchener to Khartoum compiled Steevens's reports from the Sudan in the *Daily Mail*, the leading imperialist mass-circulation newspaper.[2] Although the last chapter on the battle of Omdurman was written specially for the book, most of the chapters had already been published in the columns of the London newspaper. R. T. Stearn describes the book as an 'instant history' of the campaign.[3] Presumably many buyers had already read Steevens's reports in the press, or at least had heard about them. Yet the release of these writings in book form ensured them greater longevity: unlike newspapers, books are generally not disposed of, increasing in the present case the lifespan of Steevens's reports.

Steevens's volume was the first to mention Kitchener's name in its title, pioneering a genre that he would contribute to making successful. It was the first to exploit to its full potential what could be made of Kitchener as a hero, which earlier works had not done. Kitchener himself had published some articles and a book aimed primarily at learned circles.[4] In 1897, the *Daily Chronicle* correspondent focused in his *Study of the Soudan War of 1896* more on the military proceedings and the scenery than on the Sirdar himself.[5] A year later, the *Daily Telegraph* correspondent Bennet Burleigh published a book on the Anglo-Egyptian campaign two months before Steevens's, but it did not mention Kitchener's name in its title, nor did he dedicate any specific chapter to the Sirdar, and ended with the battle of Atbara (8 April 1898), symbolically far less important than Omdurman.[6] Another account of the Sudan campaign stressing the role of the Sirdar was written by the *Pioneer*'s special war correspondent under the title *With the Sirdar to Omdurman*, but the impact of this short work (87 pages) published in Allahabad, United Provinces (now Uttar Pradesh), on the British public remained limited.[7] *With Kitchener's Army*, by the expeditionary force's chaplain, was published two years after Steevens's account, as was the first ever Kitchener biography.[8] G. A. Henty's children's book *With Kitchener in the Soudan*, the title of which shows a striking resemblance to Steevens's (which was itself admittedly Hentyesque),[9] was not published until 1902.[10] Steevens's book was the first to use the story of the re-conquest of the Sudan to celebrate the name of the 'man of destiny' (as Steevens put it) who directed the Anglo-Egyptian forces. Not only was this book the first to celebrate the name of Kitchener but it also proved to be one of the most successful – perhaps the most

CASE STUDIES

successful – of all books dedicated to Kitchener, with almost 240,000 copies sold in just two years, as we have seen in Chapter 2. The title, timing, content and immediate success justify the appraisal made by a later biographer:

> It was by the work of a very brilliant newspaper correspondent, the late G. W. Steevens, that the name of Kitchener became suddenly familiar to British democracy, and it was by the work of the same writer that the Kitchener legend took possession of the public mind.[11]

This account failed to mention the uproar caused, in Parliament and in the press, by the violence of Kitchener's armies in the aftermath of the battle of Omdurman, and by the desecration of the Mahdi's tomb (which moved even the Queen herself). Steevens's book, which glossed over these vengeful practices which 'savour[ed] too much of the Middle Ages' (to quote Victoria herself), overshadowed more critical reports published in the *Manchester Guardian* or the *Contemporary Review*, and established durably the legend surrounding Gordon's avenger.[12]

With Kitchener to Khartoum owed its success to three main factors: a subject appealing to the public's taste, a war correspondent turned author who enjoyed renown as a consequence of his contributions to the daily press and a publisher who was in a position to promote and distribute the new book efficiently. As announced by the title, the book put the emphasis on the Sirdar Kitchener, created Baron of Khartoum and Aspall, awarded many honours and lionized by the British public as a consequence of his victorious conduct of the Sudan campaign of 1896–98. The book's author, George Warrington Steevens, was 'for a few years at the end of the nineteenth century probably the best-known and most eulogized, and possibly the most influential, British journalist'.[13] The publisher, Blackwood and Sons, was a Scottish firm founded in Edinburgh in 1804 (a London office opened in 1840), reputedly conservative and imperialist. The interaction of these three factors goes a long way towards explaining why the *Oxford Dictionary of National Biography* can argue that Steevens's book 'particularly helped to form the popular image of Kitchener'.[14]

Horatio Herbert Kitchener was appointed Sirdar (Commander-in-Chief) of the Egyptian Army in April 1892, having already acquired extensive experience of desert warfare as part of the ill-fated Gordon relief expedition under General Wolseley (September 1884 to July 1885) and in the Khedive's service for six years. Like Marchand, the new Sirdar was already a well-connected officer, who never failed to visit influential friends at their country houses when on leave in England. Aged forty-four, he received a knighthood for his services in Egypt. During the first four years of his sirdarship, he fought to gain official support to his project of reconquest of the Sudan. Then a Brigadier-General under Foreign Office control (rather than the War Office), he had to overcome Salisbury's reluctance at organizing a new 'Nile Campaign'. The Prime Minister knew that unsuccessful overseas campaigns could easily throw a government out of power: Disraeli lost his premiership as a consequence of the Zulu War, and Gladstone resigned over the failure of Gordon's expedition. Kitchener's victory at Dongola in September 1896 was a positive development, and the Sirdar was authorized to advance further south, building a railway in order to carry troops and supplies across the Egyptian and Sudanese deserts.

When Kitchener ordered his men to march south of Berber, he was still little known to the general public. The spectacular crushing of the Mahdi's army at Omdurman changed the situation and brought him national fame, especially thanks to the war artists and war correspondents who vividly reported the victory to the British public. Up to then, the army's slow advance failed to attract much public interest.[15] In the spring 1898, the British press was more interested in the Spanish–American war than on the Sirdar's preparations against the Khalifa. In spite of the presence of war artists such as Henry Seppings Wright for the *Illustrated London News*, Charles Seldon for *Black and White* and Henry Pearse for the *Graphic*, visual coverage of the Nile campaign in the British press remained low key.[16]

War correspondents showed more interest in the campaign than war artists, some of them spending the whole three years alongside the expeditionary force – but their reports did not make the headlines of their newspapers immediately. As events unfolded, newspaper interest increased and, in the end, around thirty journalists covered Kitchener's campaign. Some were prominent war correspondents, such as Bennet Burleigh for the *Daily Telegraph*, Charlie Williams for the *Daily Chronicle*, Francis Scudamore for the *Daily News* and E. F. Knight for *The Times*. The *Daily Mail* initially sent a former army officer, A. Dacrot, to report, but they substituted him in December 1897 with George Warrington Steevens, who quickly 'gained a high reputation and raised the status of the *Mail*'.[17] *With Kitchener to Khartoum* originated from this commission.

Steevens's background influenced his careeer as a war correspondent and a writer. Born in 1869 in Sydenham, Kent, and the son of a bank clerk, he was educated at the City of London School and at Balliol College, Oxford, where his intellectual talents quickly earned him the nickname of 'the Balliol prodigy'.[18] At the time, the brilliant student felt attracted to Radical ideas, frequented the National Liberal Club, supported the Liberal candidate for Oxford and helped Sir Montague

Edward Browning's Gladstonian campaign in East Worcestershire against Austen Chamberlain.[19] Having gained firsts in Oxford in classical moderations and *literae humaniores* and a London BA with 'highest honours', Steevens was offered in 1893 a fellowship at Pembroke College, Oxford. He also spent some time at Cambridge, editing a weekly periodical, the *Cambridge Observer*. Concomitantly, W. E. Henley invited him to become a contributor to the *National Observer*. Journalism proved more attractive to Steevens than academia and he left Oxford for London where Harry Cust, editor of the Tory *Pall Mall Gazette*, offered him a position. There the journalist Lincoln Springfield 'took Steevens under his wing in order to introduce him to a few of the finer things Fleet Street had to offer', a patronage that would have a beneficial influence when time came to promote *With Kitchener to Khartoum*.[20]

In August 1894, Steevens married a much older widow, Christina Rogerson, of whom Steevens 'always said that she had been the making of his career'.[21] This last point, reported by the author of *Who's Who*, is confirmed by the extensive correspondence between Christina Steevens and William Blackwood relating to the publishing of her husband's works, which is discussed later.

Following his resignation from the *Pall Mall Gazette* in 1895 due to an editorial conflict, Steevens joined the staff of the *Daily Mail* almost immediately after its creation by Viscount Northcliffe in May 1896. The newspaper editor Ralph Blumenfeld remembered that Alfred Harmsworth

> deliberately converted the newspaper into a daily topical magazine. He got this idea from the French press, from Emile Zola and Henri Rochefort of *L'Intransigeant*. [...] Wherever possible the News too was written up as 'story', in order to attract the public by its human appeal. He introduced the descriptive 'sketch'writer everywhere. For example, Kitchener went to Khartum. With him went young G. W. Steevens.[22]

Bearing in mind the *Pall Mall Gazette*'s emphasis on interviews, inherited from W. T. Stead (who had left it in 1890 to found the *Review of Reviews*), Steevens was indeed an ideal choice for Harmsworth's project.

Beyond the *Daily Mail*, Steevens tried his hand at publishing books, following a first attempt during the gap between his resignation from the *Pall Mall Gazette* and his hiring by the *Daily Mail*. His first book, published by Methuen, advocated the strengthening of the British navy to face the rise of new industrial powers such as Japan, Belgium or the United States.[23] Steevens never worked again with Methuen; on the recommendation of the novelist Margaret Oliphant, the widow of the author, traveller and mystic Laurence Oliphant, he approached in April 1896 William Blackwood (known as William Blackwood III in the firm's history), editor of *Blackwood's Magazine* ('*Maga*'), chairman of Blackwood's and Sons Ltd and the grand-nephew of the founder of the family business, William Blackwood I. Mrs Oliphant, who was writing at the time the first two volumes of the official history of the firm, *Annals of a Publishing House*, was apparently a good friend of Christina Rogerson/Steevens.[24] Further to his first meeting with Steevens, Blackwood jotted down that he was 'married to Mrs Oliphant's friend Mrs Rogerson' (thus acknowledging Christina Steevens's role from the outset) and that the young journalist looked 'a clever and self-confident man + has been on the sub editor staff of Pall Mall Gazette under Mr Cust'.[25] His experience with the Conservative daily from Northumberland Street could only be an advantage in the eyes of the 'High Tory' Edinburgh publisher.[26]

Steevens subsequently submitted an article to W. Blackwood (presumably the article 'A naval utopia', published in *Maga* vol. 159, June 1896), and promised he would later send another one on 'The Customs of the Matabele'. A shrewd businessman eager to find new trends, Blackwood pencilled on Steevens's covering letter 'I am hearing that *New Review* has increased its circulation greatly since its Transvaal articles appeared.'[27] Trading in a highly competitive environment, Blackwood showed a distinct commercial preoccupation when making editorial choices. Confident of Steevens's potential, he asked him to suggest 'any article on foreign affairs or other subjects', prompting Steevens to publish in *Maga* two articles in July and October 1896.[28] After the *Daily Mail* sent Steevens to the USA as their special correspondent for two months in July 1896, *Maga* featured an article on 'The [American] presidential election as I saw it' in December. This journey also gave birth to the first Steevens book with the Edinburgh firm, *The Land of the Dollar*. Launched in January 1897, this work sold relatively well: 1,225 copies in the first four months.[29] Although Blackwood invested in advertising (£50 4s 11d), the financial results remained rather poor for its author with only £56.11 royalties.[30] Although *The Land of the Dollar* was far from being a best-seller, Blackwood viewed Steevens's work favourably and several more articles appeared in *Maga*. Blackwood published an account by Steevens of the Graeco-Turkish war in October 1897. With no more than 322 copies sold in its first month, and a mere 47 more ordered in the following two months, *With the Conquering Turk* was disappointing.[31] Steevens did not manage to attract much attention to his work, and neither was he famous in his professional environment: H. W. Nevinson remembered that he had 'hardly heard his name' when he first met the new *Daily Mail* correspondent in Greece.[32]

By contrast, Blackwood was a well-established and pre-eminent firm with a prestigious literary record including John Wilson, Thomas De Quincey, George Eliot, the explorer John Hanning Speke, Anthony Trollope and Laurence and Margaret Oliphant. The London office of the Edinburgh company ensured swift access to the literary, journalistic and political circles of the capital. The combination of a journalist full of potential and a famous publishing house certainly increased the possibilities of success, but the team needed a suitable subject. Found almost by chance, the Sudan campaign and Kitchener fitted the bill even beyond expectations.

In December 1897, the *Daily Mail* suddenly sent Steevens to Egypt. Knowing little about his commission but expecting to 'be back before the end of January [1898]', he did not anticipate much public interest in his venture:

> I know of nothing about a march to Khartum, except that something is being kept exceedingly dark. I will remember about Wingate. But our mission is merely a series of articles on Egypt generally and especially Britain's task there. No way of heartening up a public a little.[33]

The correspondence between George and Christina Steevens and Blackwood shows that no book was initially planned from his Middle-Eastern wanderings, let alone anything on Kitchener's advance in the Sudan.[34] Some military operations near the Sudan were suspected, but, when Steevens started to think about a book, its likely tone seemed more along the lines of an Alfred Milner in *England in Egypt*. This angle was later confirmed when Christina Steevens suggested *How We Govern Egypt* and *What We Are Doing in Egypt* as possible titles for the book they had finally decided to publish.[35]

Steevens's literary plans evolved as the political and military situation changed on the ground. While he was following Kitchener's preparations for war, his wife and Blackwood became increasingly busy organizing the publishing of his *Daily Mail* chronicles in book form: Blackwood had read them with 'the greatest interest & delight' and judged them 'vivid, realistic & correct', and Mrs Steevens noted with evident pleasure that they were 'much talked about in the Clubs & Literary circles'.[36]

By mid-January 1897, Blackwood anticipated that Steevens would follow Kitchener 'up the Nile', adding that 'the advance coming just at this time is most fortunate for him'. He suggested to Christina that the *Diary of a Sun-Seeker* (the title of Steeven's regular contribution to the *Daily Mail* from Egypt) should be published as a 'companion volume' to the *Land of the Dollar*.[37] From a commercial point of view, launching a new volume on a topical subject was a good means of relaunching the older *Land of the Dollar*. Mrs Steevens eagerly accepted this offer, and went further: on 21 January 1898 she suggested a first book on Egypt followed by an account of the fall of Khartoum the following autumn.[38] Mrs Steevens later referred to the second project as *How we took (or failed to take) Khartoum*, before suggesting turning it into *Gordon Avenged or How We Took Khartoum*.[39] Finally, they chose to look towards the future rather than the past, and retained in the title the name of Kitchener instead of Gordon. The *Diary of a Sun-Seeker* became *Egypt in 1898*, while *How We Took Khartoum* was transformed into *With Kitchener to Khartoum*. Arguably, *With Kitchener to Khartoum* was a somewhat accidental sequel to the *Diary of a Sun-Seeker*.

From the early stages of the negotiation, Christina Steevens tried to enhance financial terms by referring to '4 applications from publishers', whilst recognizing that her husband had requested she 'must give Mr Blackwood first choice, tho' of course [she] must take the best terms [she] can get.'[40] Given the poor results of *With the Conquering Turk*, Blackwood offered for the *Diary* a smaller sum on account (£50), but with the same royalty percentage (16 2/3 per cent). He insisted that, if the first of the two books did well, he would be 'very willing to increase the sum to account for the second one', adding that 'the second one, if the material was prepared and handed to us without delay, should have a ready sale'.[41] Finally, the advance on royalties was increased to £100, but Blackwood simply did not want to 'bind himself' for the 'Khartoum book'.[42]

Blackwood and Christina Steevens proceeded with the publishing of *Egypt in 1898*. Throughout the whole process, success was a recurrent concern. For instance, Blackwood suggested including illustrations as 'it might help the volume to be more popular with the lower middle class readers who are so fond of pictures'. In an attempt to combine self-interest with patriotism, he claimed that 'it is in view of what you told me Lord Salisbury said about educating the people of England as to what we had done for Egypt that illustrations seem to me desirable'.[43] In May 1898, the first 1,050 copies were printed and £33.7.10 was spent on advertising.[44] The book was slow to take off. In July 1898, Blackwood wrote to Steevens:

> I hope your Egypt book will take a fresh start in sales when the tourists begin to visit that interesting country & we must see what can be done to push the sale next October. So far sales have been poor & disappointing which I can't make out as the book is so readable, amusing & instructive in small space.[45]

In the end, the book sold well (865 copies in four months), although it remained far from being a best-seller.[46]

CASE STUDIES

If *Egypt in 1898* had been a relatively simple publishing endeavour, *With Kitchener to Khartoum* proved much more laborious. Back in May 1898, as Blackwood was launching *Egypt in 1898*, he was already negotiating for *How We Took Khartoum*. In April 1898, he had agreed with Steevens that it was necessary to have 'the volume published as soon after the fall of Khartoum [as possible]'.[47] A stiff negotiation ensued between Blackwood and Christina Steevens, who tried to force through the best possible deal:

> Are you inclined to offer for the book or are you satisfied with *Egypt* [in 1898]? You know how we both feel about publishing with you, but we (you & we also) must consider the financial side as well.[48]

As the negotiation seemed bogged down for a couple of months, she pointed out that 'we have many asking for it [the book] but have spoken to no-one awaiting an answer from you'.[49] Blackwood finally decided to publish the book on the Sudanese campaign, and revised his terms to Steevens's advantage: the author received a royalty of 20 per cent of the book's selling price and a sum of £150 paid in advance of royalties. The American rights were reserved to the author.[50]

From the outset, Blackwood considered that the book would sell better if it was the first to deal with its subject. Steevens agreed, even suggesting that he would deserve an advance of £200 'if it [the book] is published before any other eye-witness', even suggesting to 'make the terms conditional on that'.[51] A race against the clock, driven only by commercial reasons, ensued. In May 1898, Mrs Steevens announced to Blackwood that her husband proposed 'working on the Khartoum book while at home so as to make efforts to get it out *before anyone else* – a great point must be made of this'. She also mentioned the possibility of telegraphing the last chapter in the hours following the fall of Khartoum, 'by arrangement with Mr Harmsworth as to expense'.[52] As anxious as Mrs Steevens to reap the benefits of being first in the (literary) field, Blackwood explicitly asked Steevens to keep his project secret:'take care your brother correspondents do not know that the work is as well in advance & what arrangements have been made for early publication after fall of Khartoum'.[53] In another letter, Blackwood reiterated his concern, referring explicitly to one of Steevens's colleagues, the *Daily Telegraph* correspondent Bennet Burleigh: 'I trust Burleigh will not get out a new edition of his book continuing the narrative to Omdurman before Steevens' volume.'[54] Quite understandably, Blackwood feared that a follow-up to *Sirdar and Khalifa*, detailing the military operations undertaken between Atbara and Omdurman, would spoil the novelty of Steevens's book. He therefore followed closely developments in the Sudan, showing remarkable foresight when he wrote to Christina

Steevens: 'events on the Nile are marching rapidly. I shall not be the least surprised if Khartoum falls before Saturday. We are driving on with the printing of the book.[55] Whereas the battle of Omdurman took place on 2 September, and the Gordon Memorial service was subsequently held on 4 September, Blackwood had *With Kitchener to Khartoum* almost entirely printed on 6 September (save the last chapter describing the battle of Omdurman, as he was still awaiting Steevens's account, expected to be telegraphed). Steevens failed to wire his account in due time, and Blackwood openly expressed his concern and annoyance:

> It was Mr Steevens' intention to telegraph such an account when you made the arrangement for the book & we had on the 6th everything printed ready for the binders except it [the last chapter] & the recapitulatory chapter which is all in type & ready for press & the machines waiting. The bookbinder has the cases all made ready for the sheets of the volume so it is *no fault of ours* that the work is not ready for publication next week. Had we received the descriptive account of the battle on Tuesday or even yesterday as the 'Daily Mail' & 'Standard' had, we could have had the complete book in the hands of the binders this evening.[56]

Finally, Steevens preferred to rush back to London and hand in to his publisher his account of the battle immediately after his return home, much to the dismay of Blackwood who had the first 225 pages of the book already printed, but could not launch the volume on the market: 'After receiving the distinct instruction from Mr Steevens I have now stopped the printing of the concluding sheets & will wait further instructions from him & yourself. It is very unfortunate.'[57] The book was published on Monday 3 October, with a preliminary note stating that 'it has been thought better to delay the publication of this book a week, and produce the final chapters in a fuller form'.[58] The first edition (1,050 copies) had been sold twice even before publication, with 2,119 orders in the books.[59] This was only the beginning of a resounding commercial success, which would see Blackwood sell 236,762 copies of *With Kitchener to Khartoum* in a year and half (as we have seen in Chapter 2): the first book revolving around the figure of Kitchener met with exceptional popular acclaim. Reflecting on 'the advantage of novelty' that his best-seller had enjoyed, Blackwood noted retrospectively that *'Kitchener to Khartoum* [had] had the great advantage of being the only book on the market for at least three months of its publication'.[60]

Blackwood's modest appraisal of his success downplayed other key factors which he carefully looked after during the launching period. In the publishing industry, marketing and distribution are cornerstones. Success stems from good press coverage, word of mouth and an efficient distribution network that will ensure a good visibility to the book as well as swift replenishments. None of these aspects was neglected when *With Kitchener to Khartoum* was launched.

Obviously, the press is the most straightforward way of promoting a new book. For the reasons that we saw in Chapter 1, journalists already had considerable leverage in 1898: an article in the press could sell thousands of copies. Fully aware of the power of the press (after all, her husband was a journalist), Christina Steevens did her best to ensure the most efficient campaign, confiding to Blackwood 'I have written to every-one I can think of to review the book *quickly*'.[61] Blackwood also drew heavily upon his network of friends, acquaintances and colleagues, occasionally arranging meetings between his author and leading journalists. He arranged for Charles A. Cooper, editor of the *Scotsman*, to have lunch with Steevens at the exclusive New Club when the war correspondent came to Edinburgh. Blackwood also made the most of his contacts in London, such as Frederick Greenwood who was a former editor of the *Cornhill Magazine*, as well as the first and deeply influential editor of the *Pall Mall Gazette* (from its first edition in 1865 until 1880) and the founder and editor of the *St James's Gazette* until 1890. Greenwood enjoyed a wide network of friends in Conservative circles. Blackwood wrote him a revealing letter detailing his declared intentions behind *With Kitchener to Khartoum*:

> Kitchener & those who have helped him are I think worthy of all the praise we can give them & I would like you to speak out about those men, Cromer, Kitchener, Wingate & the others who strong in mind & purpose have saved the honour of England.
>
> What a contrast to the poltrons who brought such humiliation upon us thirteen years ago. I do not envy them their feelings now & history is certainly taking it out of that old villain Gladstone's reputation. I would like all those who by their foresight, endurance, courage, capacity & skill have materially aided in the great work to come in for special mention & the transport & railway heads too. With this view I am sending you a set of the sheets of G. W. Steevens' volume 'With Kitchener to Khartoum' which we hope to publish in a few days. In his narrative you will I think find sketched most of those who have borne the heat of the day, the years of patient preparation & the thankless drudgery. Don't hesitate to quote from Steevens anything specially interesting, picturesque, or telling, if you think it would heighten the effect of what you say. He brings Egypt & the Sudan before me to the very life & as I saw it & have often wished to see it brought before the public.[62]

This letter seems a profession of faith with its summary of Blackwood's official beliefs and intentions: anti-Gladstonian, Conservative, imperialist and a keen promoter of those 'who have saved the honour of England'. The tone is markedly different from the letters to the

Steevens: *With Kitchener to Khartoum* is presented here as a contribution to the celebration of Kitchener and his collaborators, rather than as a purely commercial venture. The only hint at Blackwood's real intentions was the suggestion to quote from Steevens's work, which is a good means of acknowledging the existence of his latest book and possibly generating sales. Greenwood followed Blackwood's recommendation and highly praised Kitchener's and Steevens's respective achievements in his October 1898 *Looker On* chronicle. Blackwood expressed his great satisfaction:

> I am so glad you thought as highly of Steevens' forthcoming book & you have brought out splendidly all I wished said about the Sirdar's great achievement & the men who have so brilliantly worked under him these last 10 years.[63]

Steevens anxiously scrutinized reviews of his book. Ten days after the book launch, he wrote to Blackwood that press cuttings were 'very satisfactory', especially in the *Scotsman* (which was hardly surprising after his meeting with Cooper), the *Dundee Advertiser* and the *Irish Times*. He also noted reviews in the *Leeds Mercury*, *Athenaeum*, *Outlook* and *The Times*. Although he seemed slightly disappointed with the latter, he remained confident it could not do them much harm. In spite of Blackwood's extensive connections, being published by an Edinburgh-based firm remained probably a handicap, as Steevens noted that 'the provincial papers of course do us better than the London [ones]'.[64] Mrs Steevens was equally concerned with the issue of press coverage and its commercial implications, once reflecting to Blackwood that 'Saturday's *Spectator* was splendid & will help the sale, I feel sure, this week'.[65]

Blackwood made every effort to secure articles and features in the first place, before turning his sights to advertisement. He did not buy any advertising space for this book before 1899, when he invested £203 4s 3d, probably in order to prolong the book's life beyond the Christmas period.[66]

To amplify the echo of his press campaign, Blackwood assiduously whetted the appetite of influential individuals likely to publicize the book in the learned circles. To the historian Charles Grant Robertson, attached to the prestigious All Souls and Exeter Colleges in Oxford, he wrote:

> [Steevens] came straight home from Khartum to rewrite & extend the telegraphic accounts of his doings with Kitchener & it is a brilliant piece of work. Will you order it from your library & wake up Oxford men about it?[67]

Blackwood also knew prominent politicians, such as Alexander Hugh Bruce, sixth Lord Balfour of Burleigh, 'the most outstanding figure in the public life of Scotland', to whom he introduced Steevens.[68]

'[Balfour] at once ordered a copy [of *With Kitchener to Khartoum*], and said he was going to Balmoral next week as Minister in Attendance & would call the Queen's attention to it.' Blackwood was pleased that the book would be 'brought directly to the notice of Her Majesty'.[69] Further to Mrs Steevens's suggestion, a complimentary copy had been sent to Queen Victoria, and she rejoiced that the sovereign's attention would be drawn to it. Not only did the *Standard* report the Queen's thanks, but Blackwood published the 'Queen's acceptance & thanks' in the hope to uphold sales.[70] Steevens believed that 'the paragraph about the Queen should do good'.[71]

Although Steevens only rarely used public events to promote his book (he was often invited to do so according to Christina Steevens), he agreed to lecture at Aldershot in November 1898, which he presumably saw as a good means of being introduced to influential officers, especially as his lecture was 'favourably received and praised as "admirable, interesting and valuable"'.[72]

While Blackwood was fostering demand for his new best-seller through contacts with journalists and influential connections, he also had to make sure that it would be available from the shelves of libraries and retail booksellers. Writing directly to the main booksellers, he recognized that it was a 'thing he very rarely [did]', but he was 'so delighted with the book and the pains W. Steevens took with it that [he] ventured on the unusual step'.[73] Before the book was realeased, he contacted W. Faux, Head of the Library department of the booksellers W. H. Smith and Son, deploying a sales pitch which had hardly anything in common with the views he exchanged privately with Steevens in the run-up to the book's launch:

> I think you know I am immensely interested in the future of Egypt & have watched all the Sirdar's operations with the greatest attention & satisfaction. On Monday next we hope to publish that able writer Mr G. W. Steevens' narrative of Kitchener's campaigns from the commencement of this year & with this I have the pleasure of sending you an early copy, your acceptance of which will give me much pleasure. ... The work is one in which I think your firm will have a special interest & pleasure in taking up as I feel it is quite out of the common work of War correspondents. Indeed the contents of this book I consider very high class literature. If you can see your way to helping its sale at the Library & the Bookstalls I shall feel much obliged.[74]

The letter shrewdly merged the publisher's own interest with those of his nation, and used patriotic reasons to justify what was primarily a commercial endeavour.

Mudie, the leading firm in the distribution and supply of literature through its network of circulating libraries, which exerted a significant influence upon book sales, also received a personalized promotional letter. Jingoist feelings were not exacerbated in this philanthropic organisation, and Blackwood adapted his discourse accordingly:

> Will you give me the pleasure of accepting a special early copy of G W Steevens' brilliant narrative of Kitchener's last two campaigns. It is literature in the highest sense of the word and ought to receive a hearty reception from the reading public with which your house has so close and old a connection. ... The plans of Omdurman battle were drawn for him [Steevens] by one of the Generals commanding a division actively engaged, and may be relied upon for accuracy as also the earlier ones and maps which Colonel Wingate gave him, and he was one of the few men Wingate and Kitchener [illegible word – perhaps 'spoke'] to at all freely.
>
> Hope you will have a success with the book both for the author's sake and my own.[75]

As he had done for W. H. Smith, Blackwood pointed out to Mudie that he was publishing a literary work rather than a mere journalistic account born out of opportunism. Then he somewhat shifted his line of argumentation (compared to W. H. Smith) and toned down his nationalist arguments. Instead, he emphasized the documentary interest of the maps. Each covering letter accompanying a 'special early copy' was adapted to the supposed beliefs and inclinations of the addressee.

These two examples show that Blackwood pulled out all the stops in order to promote his new book among distributors and booksellers. Mudie did buy 'steadily in fifteen' for its circulating libraries; however, W. H. Smith did not 'come to the scratch as [Blackwood] should have ... expected'. Blackwood hoped that 'they may yet have a run on them for the book to force them to buy more freely' after the ceremonies granting Kitchener the freedom of the city of London (4 November). On the other hand, Simpkins, Hamilton & Co, wholesale booksellers in London, made two large orders for 500 copies each at the end of October.[76] More generally, the book was widely distributed in bookshops all over the United Kingdom throughout the winter of 1898. Blackwood reported that 'the booksellers are making special efforts to push the book in every way', adding 'I think that sales will keep up well until Xmas'.[77] Christina Steevens reported at the end of November that 'I hear "With K to K" is to be much run as a Xmas book for boys', and again three weeks later, 'I hear from London "the book" is selling rapidly as a Xmas gift'.[78] On one occasion, she complained that two big West End shops at which she asked for copies of *With Kitchener to Khartoum* replied that the title was sold out. To this grievance, Blackwood replied that his 'representative has been calling on the booksellers daily and keeping the book constantly before them'.[79] She also resented the absence of her husband's books at W. H. Smith to such an extent that she rudely mentioned in retaliation that 'several publishers have already asked for George's next book'. Slightly upset, Blackwood pencilled on the letter 'a most ungrateful woman!'[80]

A cheap popular sixpenny edition, launched in March 1899, ensured Steevens's enduring presence in British bookshops, an idea first suggested by Steevens but only implemented when Blackwood judged it advisable to bring Steevens's work 'within the reach of buyers of cheap literature'. The publisher anticipated it 'would greatly stimulate the patriotic feeling stirred up in the country over [the] Egyptian campaigns'.[81] On his own admission, he hoped the sixpenny edition would tend 'to popularise Mr Steevens' writings'.[82] And so it did. An undergraduate student at Clare College, Cambridge, remarked: 'when I went out yesterday I saw copies [of the sixpenny edition] in the windows of all the booksellers'.[83] Blackwood noted that 'I feel sure the issue of the sixpenny edition, large as it was, must have added to the reputation of the work and its author, and helped sustain the interest in the volume'.[84] The book's popularity expanded even beyond the British Isles. As Steevens was on his way back from India, he wrote to Blackwood that

> It seems we are to congratulate ourselves more than ever on the success of *Kitchener to Khartoum*; I saw it everywhere in India & people slumbered over it on every steamer. The cheap edition was a splendid idea.[85]

The book was in demand in Canada, where the Copp Clark Company of Toronto ordered 600 copies, while in Bombay Thacker & Company bought quantities on 'special terms' in order to 'push it'.[86] Blackwood and Steevens were even victims of their success, witnessing helplessly the launch of a 'pirate' edition of *With Kitchener to Khartoum* in the United States made out of the letters published in the *Daily Mail*, which was even widely advertised in American railway stations as 'With Kitchener to Khartoum'.[87]

Print-runs and press-cuttings put the decisive contribution of Steevens's book to the establishment of the 'Kitchener legend' beyond doubt. Blackwood's correspondence reveals the means he used to promote his future best-seller, actioning powerful promotional mechanisms through networks of literary, political and commercial pratronage. Publisher and author implemented their intentions, superbly encapsulated by Blackwood's words upon the book's release: 'We shall hit the nail on the head this time.'[88]

Steevens hoped that this book would establish him as a talented writer, while Blackwood attempted to resume publishing best-sellers after two decades of relatively poor performance.[89] The correspondence between William Blackwood and the Steevenses reveals a clear desire to produce a successful book – a 'coup', as Blackwood put it.[90] Blackwood's comments on their literary triumph reveal an almost cynical quest for gain and success. He declared to Steevens that 'it is a real pleasure to me to have got a book from you *at last* that the public will buy', adding that it would probably 'induce them to take to your excellent volume on *Egypt in 1898*'.[91] A week later, Blackwood raised the matter again: 'I am awfully pleased over [the success of the book] for both our sakes & that the public are at last recognising your literary promises'.[92] Blackwood's comments underline the fact that Steevens's previous books had been quite difficult to sell, but he was also expressing a clear commercial and pecuniary satisfaction. Steevens echoed these preoccupations with a merry 'Excellent! We seem to have got something they will buy at last.'[93]

This recurring concern with commercial value is perfectly in keeping with what we have seen concerning the making of *With Kitchener to Khartoum*, from the inclusion of illustrations to the constant wish to be first on the market immediately after Khartoum's fall and the marketing strategies behind the sixpenny edition. Blackwood was running a business, albeit a literary one, and he was preoccupied with selling as many copies of Steevens's books as he could. As a direct consequence, he welcomed any event that would sustain public interest in Egypt and the Sudan. In particular, the longer the Fashoda crisis lasted, the happier Blackwood was. At the end of September, he remarked that 'It is fortunate that the Fashoda matter has cropped up to maintain some interest in Egypt when in these days foreign politics & campaigns are old in a week'.[94] A bit disappointed by the volatile taste of his contemporaries, Blackwood did not realize that the change he was complaining about (the ephemerality of the public's tastes) had actually boosted his own publishing success. As lines of communication improved, more events could be reported, shortening the lifespan of each piece of news, but in turn the potential public expanded, creating new customers for books dealing with topical subjects. In mid-October, Blackwood believed that the 'Fashoda business is great good luck for us as it keeps Egypt in front of the China mess'.[95] Indeed, the Boxer rebellion potentially threatened the popularity of Steevens's book, as it could have thrown the re-conquest of the Sudan into oblivion and, with it, Kitchener.

The promotional campaign Blackwood undertook built mostly upon the fame Kitchener enjoyed in British newspapers as a result of his victorious Sudan campaign, but it also expanded and consolidated it: *With Kitchener to Khartoum* transferred the Kitchener legend from newspaper to book form. In the process, a possibly ephemeral glory was turned into an enduring legend. Unlike newspapers, which are short-lived by

CASE STUDIES

nature, books tend to remain permanently on bookshelves, ready to be read again long after they were produced. This difference explains why *With Kitchener to Khartoum* was so pivotal in the development and consolidation of the image of Kitchener as an imperial hero. But what did the hero-makers Steevens and Blackwood, whose action was decisive as we have just seen, get out of it?

The well-established Edinburgh firm had already shown in the past that it was capable of publishing best-sellers by George Eliot, Mackay (*Outlines of Geography*: 58,965 copies in the 1880s) or the *Educational Series* (781,904 copies in the early 1890s).[96] With the sale of these 236,762 copies, Steevens's book generated an overall profit of £6,785 12s 11d, which was approximately the equivalent of £550,000 in 2002.[97] This obviously profitable title also re-asserted in the British publishing industry Blackwood's capacity to publish highly successful books. Because of its strong impact on the British public, the title and content of this best-seller contributed to enhancing the publisher's reputation and alter its lists, where literary works became overshadowed by colonial or imperialist content.

If *With Kitchener to Khartoum* confirmed Blackwood's flair, it had a much deeper impact on its author's career, greatly expanding Steevens's renown in literary and journalistic circles, and establishing his fame among the general public. Fellow journalist Nevinson remarked that Steevens's 'great success had been his account of the Egyptian campaign, *With Kitchener to Khartoum*, a book of enormous sale'.[98] Major Fitzroy Gardner remarked that Steevens had made 'a great reputation by his descriptive dispatches to the *Daily Mail* in the second Egyptian campaign' and that 'his book *With Kitchener to Khartoum* is of course almost a classic'.[99]

Not only did the Sudan campaign gave Steevens the opportunity to launch his literary career, but it allowed him to make a name for himself among British officers, in spite of their generally poor opinion of war correspondents in general. The future Earl Douglas Haig, still a young officer, aptly described to his wife the general contempt of officers towards war correspondents (and their remit), save Steevens:

> I think my letters ... have shown you the class of 'creature' which represents the Press in this part of the world. ... The idea of coming as a Correspondent is absurd. Briefly my reasons are first: the Sirdar has no intention of having a thorough criticism of his methods. So the correspondents are kept entirely by themselves and only allowed to see in the report what he chooses. Secondly the class of correspondent here is very low indeed (only 1 man, Stevens [sic] of Daily Mail at all *educated* as a gentleman), that I should be sorry to have to live, mess and spend long days in company with such. Thirdly, the work performed by a newspaper

correspondent is most degrading: they can't tell the whole truth, even if they want to do so. The British Public likes to read sensational news, and the best war correspondent is he, who can tell the most thrilling lies. ... The B.P. [British Public] would not be satisfied until they read about the fallout pipers![100]

Kitchener's second-in-command, Sir Reginald Wingate, wrote appreciative comments on Steevens to Blackwood, to whom he confided that 'if all press correspondents were like him, the duties of a censor would be less onerous'. He considered Steevens an 'accomplished writer' and 'a charming fellow', to such an extent that he sent 'a line to thank him for his excellent book which is in every respect one of the best done pieces of work [he had] ever seen'.[101] Steevens's celebration of the 'Sudan Machine' in *With Kitchener to Khartoum* could only enhance his reputation among these influential circles. The only, but notable, exception was Queen Victoria, acknowledged to be 'annoyed' by this 'rather inhuman portrait of the Sirdar as "the Sudan machine"',[102] but the concept of clockwork organizer was later echoed by G. A. Henty when he celebrated the 'marvelous campaign – marvelous in the perfection of its organization, marvelous in the completeness of its success'.[103]

Kitchener himself held Steevens in high esteem, which was remarkable given his heartfelt animosity towards war correspondents (whom he once collectively addressed as 'drunken swabs'). He expressed deep regret at the loss of the famous *Daily Mail* correspondent during the siege of Ladysmith in the course of the Boer War (15 January 1900), and requested that the other *Daily Mail* correspondent covering the campaign should call in to express his 'great regret':

> I was anxious to tell you how very sorry I was to hear of the death of Mr Steevens. He was with me in the Sudan, and, of course, I saw a great deal of him and knew him well. He was such a clever and able man. He did his work as correspondent so brilliantly, and he never gave the slightest trouble – I wish all correspondents were like him. I suppose they will try to follow in his footsteps. I am sure & I hope they will. He was a model correspondent, the best I have ever known, and I should like you say how greatly grieved I am at his death.[104]

One of Kitchener's biographers noted that Steevens was one of the two correspondents who enjoyed 'favouritism' during the Sudanese campaign.[105]

Steevens's good relations with high-ranking officers were indeed a great advantage when it came to accessing major sources of information. When Steevens sailed to India for his next assignment after the Sudanese campaign, he happened to travel in the same steamer as the newly appointed viceroy of India, Lord Curzon, who, in Steevens's

CASE STUDIES

own account, 'most cordially welcomed' him and 'made him one of his party' during the journey.[106] Authorship of a best-seller and support for the imperial ethos ensured that Steevens was welcomed by his potential informers, facilitating snowballing techniques and easing his introduction into these exclusive circles.

Beyond improving Steevens's personal prestige, *With Kitchener to Khartoum* also greatly enhanced his financial situation. Although the scale of the profits generated by the book could not have been foreseen from the outset, royalties represented a direct reward to the author who contributed successfully to the development of a heroic reputation. Neither George nor Christina Steevens could rely upon private means, and for that reason financial issues mattered. Christina Steevens once avowed to Grant Richards, a friend of her husband's and a journalist at the *Strand*, that 'funds are so low that I must perforce do the best I can for him [G. W. Steevens]'.[107]

Whilst her husband was away in the Sudan, Mrs Steevens faced financial hardship, even soliciting an advance on royalties on the forthcoming *Egypt in 1898*:

> I am exceedingly sorry to trouble you - but I hear from George & he counts on my receiving money from you to pay Insurances & rents which are due to-morrow (Lady day).
> Can you let me have the £100 for the Egypt book? It would help greatly at this moment.[108]

In September 1898, Mrs Steevens was anxious to 'secure a good American price for the book', as 'of course, [she] was disappointed at the falling off of the English price'.[109] She was probably referring to the diminution of the advance on royalties from £200 to £150 decided in September 1898: the sum of £50 was of great importance to the Steevenses' fragile budget.[110] Later, although the success of *With Kitchener to Khartoum* had already brought some financial benefits, Christina Steevens still complained about her financial situation, asking Blackwood 'Ought we not be getting some money from America?' before adding 'December is an expensive month & it would be very welcome'.[111] Mrs Steevens was certainly relieved to learn shortly afterwards that the balance of royalties was £1,901, 6s and 7d, the purchasing power of which was roughly similar to that of £152,000 in 2002.[112] At the beginning of February 1899, Mrs Steevenses noted that it had been 'a most satisfactory business so far & midsummer may show further fruits'.[113] The Steevenses later declared that they intended to 'buy a small house' with the royalties earned from *With Kitchener to Khartoum*.[114] Although journalism provided a stream of income, the Steevenses considerably improved their financial position through their contribution to the Kitchener legend, which proved a sound bet from this perspective.

The Steevenses also enjoyed longer-term benefits, notably because they had more leverage on publishers during royalties negotiation. Whilst Steevens was reporting from India, collecting information for *In India*, his wife proved to be a talented negotiator, managing after intense bargaining to double the advance on royalties (now paid on the first 5,000 copies), and to increase the percentage from 20 to 25 per cent of the published price.[115] Being successful significantly benefited Steevens's bargaining position: reflecting on the fact that 'the India book [would] not be the same sort of success', he believed that 'still with "K. to K." to take off from it ought to do well enough'.[116]

Other clues indicate that *With Kitchener to Khartoum* made Steevens's financial demands expand. In October 1897, when discussing with Grant Richards the possibility of writing together a book on John King, they considered how they would share profits in the following situations: 'profits up to £500', 'from £500 to £750', 'from 750 to £1,000' and 'if the profits exceed £1,000'. However, the project dragged on and Steevens's expectations had increased to £2,000 by April 1899. A month later, Steevens squeezed Richards out of the plan and asked for no less than £2,000 on account of royalties for 'all the rights, serial & book, British and American' concerning this long-planned project.[117]

Following the success of *With Kitchener to Khartoum*, the Steevenses hired in the spring 1899 a literary agent, James Brand Pinker (1863–1922), who later represented the likes of Joseph Conrad, Arnold Bennett, Stephen Crane, John Galsworthy, James Joyce and H. G. Wells.[118] Negotiating the terms of a projected new book on London, Pinker managed to increase the amount of the advance on royalties to £1,000.[119] Blackwood had been reluctant to bestow such largesse, but he confided to his American colleague Dodd that 'having cultivated Mr Steevens for so many years [he] was reluctant to let him go although there was the prospect of not doing more than covering one's expenses'.[120] The financial negotiation about another book, *From Capetown to Ladysmith*, even became so tense that Christina Steevens learnt through the firm's literary adviser, David Storrar Meldrum, that 'Mr Blackwood will not make an alternative proposal because he thinks that it would be merely used as a lever against another publisher'.[121] By all accounts, *With Kitchener to Khartoum* greatly enhanced the Steevenses' financial position as it earned its author considerable royalties and allowed him to increase his demands on his publisher (percentage and advance on royalties).

Posterity was the last parameter which Steevens may have considered in his quest for success. Siding with, and writing on, a character

CASE STUDIES

who is seemingly making history is a good means of ensuring one's own place in history. This seems confirmed by the fact that Steevens's name has hardly been cited outside of works dedicated to Kitchener. Although he was briefly evoked in the memoirs of some of his contemporaries such as Fitzroy Gardner, Douglas Sladen, Grant Allen, Winston Churchill and H. G. Wells, his memory quickly became 'little regarded'.[122] Whilst it is symptomatic that no biography of George Warrington Steevens has been published to date, authors of books on Kitchener ensured that Steevens came down to posterity. In his *Lord Kitchener of Khartoum* published in the 'Bijou Biographies' series, W. F. Aitken quoted several paragraphs from the 'graphic pages of Mr G. W. Steevens' absorbing volume'.[123] The same year, H. G. Groser recognized in his biography of Lord Kitchener (the first to be written), that 'the scenes in Omdurman have been too vividly presented in the pages of Mr. G. W. Steevens' book to warrant description here'.[124] W. Jerrold quoted from Steevens as early as pp. 8–9 of his biography of Kitchener, and described *With Kitchener to Khartoum* as a work 'of rare excellence' alongside W. Churchill's *River War*.[125] H. Begbie, author of the popular books *The London Girl, Closed Doors* and biographies of Baden-Powell and Edward Grey, clearly acknowledged Steevens's role as a promoter of the Kitchener legend:

> In a series of very dramatic and sometimes brilliant articles, which appeared in a popular London newspaper, George Steevens described the famous march to Khartoum, filling the grey commercial atmosphere of London with the rich colours of the East, with the exciting adventure of war, and with the still more exciting sensation of anxiety. And, like a wise story-teller, Steevens gave his readers a hero in this brave tale of adventure. In one brief article he thrust Kitchener before the roused attention of the British public and made not only the title of 'The Sirdar' but the personality of this particular Sirdar a permanent possession of the British mind.[126]

In his biography of Lord Kitchener, E. S. Grew mentioned Steevens three times, quoting twice from *With Kitchener to Khartoum*.[127] However, Steevens's name failed to appears in G. Arthur's three-volume biography.[128] In the mid-twentieth century, Steevens's name appeared twice in P. Magnus's classic biography of Kitchener.[129] Later in the century, Steevens was quoted once and cited twice in a biography of Kitchener by a military history writer, while *With Kitchener to Khartoum* was described as 'a classic best seller' by the author of *Kitchener: Architect of Victory*.[130] The popular writer J. Pollock cites Steevens several times in his biography of Kitchener up to the Boer War, as does the author of a story of the battle of Omdurman.[131]

Steevens was also repeatedly cited in more recent scholarly works dedicated to British operations in the Sudan or to popular imperialism.[132] In 1990, two British and American publishers jointly reprinted *With Kitchener to Khartoum*, showing that they believed there was a still a potential market for it.[133] A recent historian of the *Daily Mail* went as far as to state that Steevens had 'created the myth of Lord Kitchener's invincibility as a leader of men'.[134] Discussing Kitchener's image as a military hero, Keith Surridge remarked that 'Kitchener's prestige soared as a result [of the victory of Omdurman], helped in this instance by the gushing tributes of the *Daily Mail* correspondent G. W. Steevens'.[135] Although Steevens's posthumous reputations suffered heavily from his premature death, *With Kitchener to Khartoum* secured him durable fame as the first promoter of the Kitchener legend, saving his name from total oblivion. Had he been able to produce more works of the magnitude of *With Kitchener to Khartoum*, he might have confirmed his promising status. What remains beyond doubt is that his hero-making enterprise of the years 1896–1899 launched his reputation in earnest.

This micro-history of the role of George and Christina Steevens and William Blackwood in the making of the Kitchener legend exemplifies the mechanics of hero-making towards the end of the nineteenth century, when the world had already witnessed the rise of print capitalism. The trio formed by Steevens in the Sudan, Mrs Steevens in London and Blackwood in Edinburgh gradually realized how profitable the nascent 'Kitchener legend' could prove for their new book dealing with the Sudan campaign. Their major contribution to the long-term popularization of Kitchener stemmed primarily from a quest for commercial success, elegantly covered up by patriotic reasons for promotional purposes. Kitchener's newly acquired reputation served their literary ambition and economic interests, and they intended to benefit from, and contribute to, a snowballing effect. What was initially designed to be an account of the Sudan campaign became *nolens volens* a celebration of Kitchener as it became apparent that such an approach would benefit the sales strategy.

The correspondence behind *With Kitchener to Khartoum* shows that hero-makers did not necessarily expect to be directly rewarded by the hero they were promoting, or by any other constituted body associated with him, but that they could be recompensed merely by commercial success. As he was making the most of what could have been otherwise a passing glory, Steevens generated further interest in the celebrated individual and, in so doing, he durably established the legend. Tellingly, following the success of *With Kitchener to Khartoum*, Mrs

CASE STUDIES

Steevens suggested *With Curzon to India* as the title for her husband's next book.[136] To George and Christina Steevens, hero-making seemed definitely a worthwhile role, and their papers throw light upon an often ignored but crucial aspect of the process through which, to quote André Malraux, a life became a destiny.

Notes

1   G. W. Steevens, *With Kitchener to Khartoum* (Edinburgh and London, 1898), p. 54.
2   M. Engle, *Tickle the Public. 100 Years of the Popular Press* (1996), pp. 75–8.
3   R. T. Stearn, 'War correspondents and colonial war, c. 1870–1900', in J. M. MacKenzie (ed.), *Popular Imperialism and the Military* (Manchester, 1992), p. 157.
4   H. H. Kitchener, *Photographs of Biblical Sites* (1876).
5   A. Hilliard Atteridge, *Toward Khartoum* (1897).
6   B. Burleigh, *Sirdar and Khalifa* (1898).
7   Anon., *With the Sirdar to Omdurman. Letters from the Pioneer's Special War Correspondent* (Allahabad, 1898). The work was attributed to the 'Special War Correspondent of *The Allahabad Press*' (see H. F. B. Wheeler, *Lord Kitchener* (1916), p. 96).
8   O. S. Watkins, *With Kitchener's Army* (1900), and H. G. Groser, *Lord Kitchener. The Story of his Life* (1901).
9   J. Richards, 'Popular imperialism and the image of the army in juvenile literature', in Mac Kenzie (ed.), *Popular Imperialism and the Military*, p. 82.
10 G. A. Henty, *With Kitchener in the Soudan. A Story of Atbara and Omdurman* (1902).
11 H. Begbie, *Kitchener, Organiser of Victory* (1915), ch. VI.
12 R. Owen, *Lord Cromer. Victorian Imperialist, Edwardian Proconsul* (Oxford, 2004), pp. 301–2.
13 R. T. Stearn, 'G. W. Steevens and the Message of Empire', *Journal of Imperial and Commonwealth History*, 17 (1988–89), 210.
14 K. Neilson, 'Kitchener, Horatio Herbert, Earl Kitchener of Khartoum (1850–1916)', *ODNB* [Accessed 15 April 2006].
15 P. Magnus, *Kitchener, Portrait of an Imperialist* (1958), p. 103.
16 P. Harrigton, 'Images and Perceptions: Visualising the Sudan Campaign', in E. M. Spiers (ed.), *Sudan: The Reconquest Reappraised* (1998), pp. 84–5.
17 H. Cecil, 'British Correspondents and the Sudan Campaign of 1896–98', in Spiers, *Sudan: The Reconquest Reappraised*, pp. 102 and 104.
18 Sidney Lee, 'Steevens, George Warrington (1869–1900)', rev. Roger T. Stearn, *ODNB* [Accessed 15 April 2006].
19 Stearn, 'Steevens', 212.
20 S. J. Taylor, *The Great Outsiders. Northcliffe, Rothermere and the* Daily Mail (1996), p. 27.
21 D. Sladen, *Twenty Years of My Life* (1915), p. 318.
22 R. D. Blumenfeld, *The Press in My Time* (1933), p. 127.
23 G. W. Steevens, *Naval Policy* (1896).
24 NLS, MS 4667, ff. 8 & 9, Christina Steevens to WB, 19 and 22 February 1897.
25 NLS, MS 4652, f. 220, GWS to WB, 29 April 1896.
26 D. Finkelstein, *The House of Blackwood* (University Park, PA, 2002), p. 98.
27 NLS, MS 4652, f. 221, GWS to WB, 8 May 1896.
28 NLS, MS 4652, ff. 237 and 239, GWS to WB, 20 June & 2 July 1896. The two articles were 'The apotheosis of Russia' and 'Arbitration in theory and practice'.
29 NLS, MS 30864, Sales ledger, p. 395.
30 NLS, MS 30385, PLB, p. 368, WB to CS, 4 February 1898.

31 NLS, MS 30864, Sales ledger, p. 396.
32 H. W. Nevinson, *Fire of Life* (1935), p. 66.
33 NLS, MS 4667, f. 91, GWS to WB, 8 December 1897.
34 NLS, MS 30385, PLB, p. 250, WB to CS, 3 December 1897.
35 NLS, MS 4682, f. 5, CS to WB, 30 January 1898.
36 NLS, MS 30385, PLB, p. 306, WB to CS, 20 January 1898; MS 4682, f. 3, CS to WB, 21 January 1898.
37 NLS, MS 30385, PLB, p. 306, WB to CS, 20 January 1898.
38 NLS, MS 4682, f. 3, CS to WB, 21 January 1898.
39 NLS, MS 4682, f. 5, CS to WB, 30 January 1898; f. 25, CS to WB, 1 June 1898.
40 NLS, MS 4682, f. 3, CS to WB, 21 January 1898.
41 NLS, MS 30385, PLB, p. 344, WB to CS, 1 February 1898.
42 NLS, MS 30385, PLB, pp. 347–348, WB to CS, 3 February 1898.
43 NLS, MS 30385, PLB, p. 455, WB to CS, 14 March 1898.
44 NLS, MS 30864, Sales ledger, p. 398.
45 NLS, MS 30386, PLB, p. 26, WB to GWS, 5 July 1898.
46 NLS, MS 30864, Sales ledger, p. 398.
47 NLS, MS 30385, PLB, p. 531, WB to CS, 16 April 1898.
48 NLS, MS 4682, f. 44, CS to WB, 12 [no month, probably April] 1898.
49 NLS, MS 4682, f. 23, CS to WB, 18 May 1898.
50 NLS, MS 30385, PLB, p. 526, Blackwood & Co. to CS, 24 May 1898.
51 NLS, MS 4682, f. 67, GWS to WB, 12 May 1898.
52 NLS, MS 4882, f. 21, CS to WB, 6 May 1898.
53 NLS, MS 30386, PLB, p. 26, WB to GWS, 5 July 1898.
54 NLS, MS 30386, PLB, p. 193, WB to CS, 21 September 1898.
55 NLS, MS 30386, PLB, p. 149, WB to CS, 29 August 1898.
56 NLS, MS 30386, PLB, p. 172, WB to CS, 8 September 1898.
57 NLS, MS 30386, PLB, p. 184, WB to CS, 13 September 1898.
58 NLS, MS 30386, PLB, p. 207, WB to GWS, 28 September 1898; Steevens, *With Kitchener*, p. VIII.
59 NLS, MS 30386, PLB, p. 228, WB to GWS, 3 October 1898.
60 NLS, MS 30386, PLB, p. 460, WB to CS, 4 January 1899.
61 NLS, MS 4682, f. 27, CS to WB, 30 September 1898.
62 NLS, MS 30386, PLB, p. 174, WB to Frederick Greenwood, 6 September 1898.
63 NLS, MS 30386, PLB, p. 188, WB to Frederick Greenwood, 19 September 1898.
64 NLS, MS 4682, f. 77, GWS to WB, 10 October 1898.
65 NLS, MS 4682, f. 48, CS to WB, 17 [no month, most probably October] 1898.
66 NLS, MS 30864, Sales ledger, p. 188.
67 NLS, MS 30386, PLB, p. 218, WB to Robertson, 30 September 1898.
68 W. F. Gray, 'Bruce, Alexander Hugh (1849–1921)', rev. H.C.G. Matthew, *ODNB* [Accessed 6 May 2006].
69 NLS, MS 30386, PLB, p. 219, WB to CS, 29 September 1898.
70 *The Standard*, 7 October 1898 and NLS, MS 30386, PLB, p. 240, WB to CS, 5 October 1898.
71 NLS, MS 4682, f. 75, GWS to WB, 7 October 1898.
72 NLS, MS 4682, f. 48, CS to WB, 17 [no month, certainly October] 1898; MS 30386, PLB, p. 281, WB to GWS, 26 October 1898; and Stearn, 'Steevens', p. 213.
73 NLS, MS 30386, PLB, p. 220, WB to CS, 29 September 1898.
74 NLS, MS 30386, PLB, p. 460, WB to W. Faux, 29 September 1898.
75 NLS, MS 30386, PLB, p. 221, WB to Mudie, 29 September 1898.
76 NLS, MS 30386, PLB, p. 281, WB to GWS, 26 October 1898.
77 NLS, MS 30386, PLB, pp. 329–30, WB to GWS, 9 December 1898.
78 NLS, MS 4682, ff. 36 and 54, CS to WB, 26 November and 20 December 1898.
79 NLS, MS 30386, PLB, p. 412, WB to CS, 29 December 1898.
80 NLS, MS 4682, f. 29, CS to WB, 8 October 1898.
81 NLS, MS 30386, PLB, pp. 464–5, WB to CS, 12 January 1899.
82 NLS, MS 30387, PLB, p. 166, WB to CS, 10 August 1899.

CASE STUDIES

83 NLS, MS 30069, Henry T. A. Dashwood (on Clare College letterhead) to WB, Cambridge, 11 March 1899.
84 NLS, MS 30387, PLB, pp. 52–3, WB to CS, 15 May 1899.
85 NLS, MS 4695, f. 52, GWS to WB, 19 April 1899.
86 NLS, MS 30386, PLB, pp. 397–8, WB to CS, 31 January 1899; MS 30387, PLB, pp. 24–5, WB to GWS, 25 April 1899.
87 NLS, MS 30386, PLB, p. 275, WB to GWS, 20 October 1898.
88 NLS, MS 30386, PLB, p. 220, WB to CS, 29 September 1898.
89 Finkelstein, *House of Blackwood*, p. 105.
90 NLS, MS 30386, PLB, p. 411, WB to CS, 29 December 1898.
91 NLS, MS 30386, PLB, p. 245, WB to GWS, 7 October 1898 (my italics).
92 NLS, MS 30386, PLB, p. 258, WB to GWS, 7 October 1898.
93 NLS, MS 4682, f. 73, GWS to WB, 1 October 1898.
94 NLS, MS 30386, PLB, p. 193, WB to CS, 21 September 1898.
95 NLS, MS 30386, PLB, p. 259, WB to GWS, 15 October 1898.
96 Finkelstein, *House of Blackwood*, Appendix 1: pp. 159–64.
97 NLS, MS 30864, Sales ledger, ff. 188 and 347. G. Allen, 'Inflation: the Value of the Pound 1750–2002', House of Commons Library, Economics Policy and Statistics Section, 11 November 2003, www.parliament.uk/commons/ lib/research/rp2003/ rp03-082.pdf [Accessed 10 November 2005].
98 Nevinson, *Fire of Life*, p. 100.
99 G. Gardner, *More Reminiscences of an Old Bohemian* (ca. 1913), p. 116.
100 NLS, MS 28002, f. 133, Douglas Haig to Henrietta Haig, 5 June 1898.
101 NLS, MS 4684, f. 156, F. R. Wingate to WB, 23 October 1898.
102 J. Pollock, *Kitchener, the Road to Omdurman* (1998), p. 153, quoting V. Mallet, *Life with Queen Victoria* (1968), p. 142.
103 Henty, *With Kitchener in the Soudan*, p. vi.
104 V. Blackburn, 'The last chapter', in G. W. Steevens, *From Capetown to Ladysmith* (1900), p. 178.
105 Magnus, *Kitchener*, p. 134.
106 NLS, MS 4682, f. 36, CS to WB, 20 December 1898.
107 PCL, 61/6/24/12, CS to Grant Richards, 22nd [no date, presumably summer 1898].
108 NLS, MS 4682, f. 16, CS to WB, 24 March 1898.
109 NLS, MS 4682, f. 27, CS to WB, 30 September 1898.
110 NLS, MS 4682, f. 25, CS to WB, 1 June 1898; MS 30386, PLB, p. 207, WB to GWS, 28 September 1898.
111 NLS, MS 4682, f. 54, CS to WB, 26 [no month, probably November] 1898.
112 NLS, MS 30386, PLB, pp. 397–398, WB to CS, 31 January 1899; Allen, 'Value of the Pound'.
113 NLS, MS 4665, f. 9, CS to WB, 5 February 1899.
114 NLS, MS 4665, f. 33, CS to WB, 9 August 1899.
115 NLS, MS 30386, PLB, p. 547, WB to CS, 8 February 1899.
116 NLS, MS 4695, f. 53, GWS to WB, 19 April 1899.
117 PCL, 61/6/24/3, 8 and 10, GWS to Grant Richards, 11 October 1897, 28 April 1899 and 11 May 1899.
118 Finkelstein, *House of Blackwood*, p. 146.
119 NLS, MS 30387, PLB, p. 102, WB to J. B. Pinker, 19 June 1899.
120 NLS, MS 30387, PLB, p. 106, WB to Mr Dodd, 22 June 1899.
121 NLS, MS 4695, f 42, CS to WB, 9 December 1899.
122 Stearn, 'Steevens', 210.
123 W. F. Aitken, *Lord Kitchener of Khartoum and of Aspall* (1901), p. 57.
124 Groser, *Lord Kitchener*, p. 190.
125 W. Jerrold, *Earl Kitchener of Khartoum* (1915), p. 136.
126 Begbie, *Kitchener*, ch. VI.
127 E. S. Grew, *Field-Marshal Kitchener. His Life and Work for the Empire*, vol. I (1916), pp. 207, 237 and 240.

128 G. Arthur, *Life of Lord Kitchener* (1920).
129 Magnus, *Kitchener*, pp. 94 and 134.
130 P. Warner, *Kitchener, the Man Behind the Legend* (1985), pp. 43–4, 82 and 98; G. H. Cassar, *Kitchener: Architect of Victory* (1977), p. 178. Steevens is also cited pp. 80, 95 & 352.
131 Pollock, *Kitchener*, pp. 121–2, 126, 135, 153 and 248 (footnote); P. Ziegler, *Omdurman* (1973), pp. 86, 134, 166, 195 and 203.
132 For instance, Spiers, *Sudan*, pp. 5, 86, 104, 106–7, 112, 114–15 and 123, or MacKenzie (ed.), *Popular Imperialism*, pp. 15, 16, 44–5, 82, 129, 139, 141, 148, 149, 157.
133 Greenhill Books, London, and Presidio Press, California.
134 Taylor, *Great Outsiders*, p. 174.
135 K. Surridge, 'More than a great poster: Lord Kitchener and the image of the military hero', *Historical Research*, 74 (2001), 301.
136 NLS, MS 4682, f. 4, CS to WB, 9 January 1899. The book was finally entitled *In India*, probably because neither Steevens nor Blackwood liked Curzon (Blackwood papers, MS 30387, PLB, pp. 24–5, WB to GWS, 25 April 1899).

CONCLUSION

Inspired by John Darwin's call to 'reconstruct more fully the functioning and interaction of [the] bridgeheads at home and abroad' which, in his view, would allow historians to 'explain properly the erratic, unpredictable, tentative, opportunistic but ultimately insatiable progress of Victorian imperialism', this book has attempted to uncover the mechanisms and structures that permitted the translation of meritorious lives spent abroad into imperial 'heroic reputations', in other words to turn a handful of 'men on the spot' into significant national figures.[1] The variety of manuscript and other sources used to document these processes have shown how a successful imperial hero resulted from the convergence of political, moral, religious and commercial interests, which very often mattered more than the actual series of events on the ground.

Household names become so evident with the passing of time that it is easy to forget how their status was first mediated to the public through a variety of channels, the combination of which reinforced each other, giving rise to the durable reputations which ultimately remained entrenched in popular imagination. Retracing the genesis and development of several heroic reputations linked to the expansion of Britain and France in Africa has highlighted the changing conditions that made possible their success and their rise to commercial success over seven decades. Evidence suggests that the numerous occurrences of spontaneous expressions of popular enthusiasm towards imperial heroes owed much of their momentum to conscious promotional attempts undertaken by a variety of admirers, biographers and politicians who had specific interests to serve through their attempt at hero-making.

The concept of 'hero-makers' is pivotal in reflecting the variety of stakeholders who contributed, individually or in groups, and for various reasons, to the development of heroic myths linked to the empire at a time when the media became a fundamental structural component of heroizing processes, which directly led to the 'commodification' of imperial heroes. These intermediaries played a pivotal role in publicizing actions which, in their view, deserved the admiration of their compatriots: in a study of discourse production like this one, it is quite fitting that story-tellers and narrative producers are given due credit. They illustrate vividly the pivotal contribution of the 'commercial bourgeoisie' to popular culture, dictated by capitalist interest and, often, ideological considerations: as Raymond Williams observed, 'the main source of ... "popular culture" lies outside the working class altogether'.[2] The hero-makers discussed in this book demonstrate that this statement is equally true in the narrower field of 'popular imperialism'. These hero-makers, the majority of whom came from outside the working classes (with a few notable exceptions, such as Stanley), proved to be a vital conduit for the development of heroic reputations of empire in popular culture, even if their involvement could occasionally be fortuitous. Steevens's role as a self-conscious hero-maker is beyond doubt, as is that of Charles Maunoir or Roderick Murchison. This is not to say either that all contributors to heroic legends were active imperialists: when Robert Darène was selected to play Brazza in Léon Poirier's film, physical resemblance was the primary criterion, and the actor recognizes that he did not invest his role in the film with any particular edifying mission or propaganda effort.[3]

The imaginary maps of the average British and French person underwent dramatic changes between the mid-nineteenth century and the Second World War: not only because of the expansion of common geographical knowledge but also as a result of the dramatic changes in systems of production of meaning which diversified and expanded like never before in human history: the period covered here saw the appearance of many new ways of conveying messages of an increasingly varied nature (written texts, images, sounds and audiovisual material). Arguably, imperial heroes were among the first instances of 'mediated personae' and, as such, the prevalence and survival of their reputations relied upon a subtle alchemy between various components, which allowed the multiple locations of imperial heroism to reach a critical mass.[4]

Being cultural constructions in keeping with the beliefs and aspirations of a community of people at a certain time of history, heroic legends are heavily influenced by the context in which they develop. It is no coincidence that no heroine is featured in this book. Although I have written elsewhere about female explorers of, or travellers to, Africa, none of these female characters reached the level of fame that would warrant the qualifier of 'heroine', along the lines drawn for its male counterparts in the introduction to this book.[5] Florence Nightingale could cut a figure in the late Victorian period because her commitments were in keeping with the dominant values of femininity at the time (putting the emphasis on homely chores and, occasionally, nursing), but the dominant social structures left no space for a female explorer or empire builder: even Mary Kingsley supported the policy of exclusion of women from membership of the Royal Geographical Society.[6]

Late nineteenth-century imperial heroes rose to prominence in the era of the second Industrial Revolution, and its cohort of technical innovations which made the advent of the mass-media possible, at the very moment when the wave of 'New Imperialism' took place, pushed forward by technological advancement and increased international rivalry. The combination of these two processes – the Industrial Revolution and the 'New Imperialism' – led to the appearance of a new type of hero, the imperial hero, which was as much an engine producing imperial sentiment as a mirror reflecting popular interest in overseas conquest and, consequently, in the empire. The mutual interaction between consumers and producers, with the latter trying to anticipate or cater for the former's tastes, secured a firm place for imperial heroes in the ever-evolving 'popular culture' of Britain and France from the second half of the nineteenth century onwards. The rise of the mass-media led producers to engineer strategies to reach wider audiences than in the past, and to adapt to mentalities and conducts which changed rapidly under the influence of new laws of education and enfranchisement, which increased the influence of public opinion on the running of the country.[7] The success or failure of imperial heroes could represent valuable political arguments as they appealed to the public's imagination at a moment when public opinion became more important than ever before.

Because their constant quest to expand their readership led them to search for common denominators, the mass-media fostered the appearance of a 'popular culture' that attenuated class lines (especially in Britain) and reshaped the contours and practices of popular culture. It is beyond doubt that technological developments influence the way in which a population is educated, writes, communicates and ultimately thinks.[8] The synthetic approach adopted in this book has demonstrated that imperial heroes appealed across various classes and diverse political sensibilities, and as such demonstrates the place of imperialism at various levels of the social stratification – what Andrew Thompson called 'imperialism as a broad church'.[9] In France, in the highly divisive context of the Third Republic, imperial heroes initially spearheaded pro-colonial propaganda efforts, but they took on a more universal and consensual meaning after the First World War. In both countries, some heroes (such as Rhodes or Marchand) appealed to particular constituencies, while others proved more consensual (like Kitchener or Brazza), but they all contributed to the propagation of an imperial ideal.

The development of the reputation attached to Major Marchand reveals the intertwining of these various interests over a period of more than a decade, during which political and military patrons, admirers,

CONCLUSION

journalists, authors and other artists all played a role, first in helping the future hero to organize the expedition that would win him fame, and later in promoting his achievements to the public. It also throws light upon the eminently politicized environment of fin-de-siècle France which, against the backdrop of the Dreyfus affair, brought to the forefront discussions about the role and place of the army both in the metropole and abroad.[10] In Britain, the strategies devised by G. W. Steevens and W. Blackwood III to promote the best-seller *With Kitchener to Khartoum* reveal that commercial and ideological interest went hand in hand in the making of the Kitchener legend. This case study, which shows print capitalism at work in shaping heroic reputations not only out of altruism but also out of self-interest, is a clear indicator of the increasing impact of the mass-media, which clearly fostered the emergence of the heroes of 'New Imperialism'. Imperial heroes allowed pro-imperial propagandists to boost not only patriotic attachment to their cause, but also their own profits, and this was an appealing argument at the time of 'print-capitalism', which witnessed the appearance of an 'economy of celebrity' which has never ceased to develop since then.[11]

The above-mentioned technical and political reasons should not overshadow the morally edifying value of imperial heroes at a time when British and French societies underwent profound moral, religious and practical changes linked to the advent of a society based upon industrial production, trade and shrinking spiritual confidence. Arguably, heroes are particularly important to groups in distress, and several imperial reputations tend to confirm this trait: the heroization of General Gordon reflected a British feeling of weakness after the Mahdist victory over the Anglo-Egyptian army under an apparently pacifist Gladstone government, while the Marchand celebrations compensated for the humiliation of the withdrawal from Fashoda, and offered an excellent opportunity to the nationalists to attack a weakened Republican regime.[12] Over the *longue durée*, imperial heroes served to exemplify different sets of values, and their use as edifying stories contributed to sustaining their long-term fame, obviously illustrated, for instance, by their being commonly featured in school textbooks.

The contrast between the proactive and self-seeking Marchand and the austere Kitchener, much less inclined towards self-promotion in the press, reveals clear differences in each hero's level of personal involvement in his legend (though both cultivated relationships with the powerful, but for different ends). At least some of the cases considered in this book were not insensitive to the appeal of fame and posterity. Marshal Lyautey was conscious of his posterity and sought to leave the best image of himself, as shown by his voluminous personal archive, in which he meticulously assembled all articles, documents and letters that were more or less in accordance with his own persona.[13] Although this trait is not uncommon among public figures, it appears here more clearly than in any previous study, notably thanks to the extensive use of private correspondence which provides much richer evidence than the final, printed product offered for public consumption at the time.

Notable differences between official narratives of heroism and the situation which transpired from behind-the-scenes documents are made even more striking by the fact that the textual material which made the flesh of the cultural products discussed in this book was rarely a model of subtlety. These texts provided one-sided accounts which very often verged on the hagiographic, with limited literary ambition – if any at all. Narratives were often flatly descriptive. Tales of imperial heroism tell us very different stories from, for instance, the elaborate literary dilemmas about identity and exoticism identified by Charles Forsdick in French travel-writing accounts.[14] After all, hero-makers were not necessarily talented writers (though some were), and these apologists of muscular imperialism provided an often crude celebration of the civilizing mission through the prism of their heroes, and definitely an outdated vision of the world and of what Europeans could achieve in it. But the very existence of such an abundant textual corpus requires examination of what made its existence possible in the first place.

Britain and France offer an excellent parallel view of the phenomenon of mass-mediatized 'imperial heroes' at the time when Europe seemed intent upon swallowing the rest of the world. Although royalist British and the French, those 'children of the Revolution' who squabbled over what to do with the legacy of Louis XVI's beheading, might not have looked like a natural match,[15] in the late nineteenth century these two countries were an obvious choice given that they ruled the two most important empires of the age and endeavoured to colonize Africa at approximately the same time. They also highlight significant similarities and differences in the political, cultural and religious backgrounds against which such heroic reputations rose. Hero-makers certainly used comparable means to promote imperial myths on each side of the Channel, notably because of the similarity of the technological and, to a certain extent, commercial and political developments that took place synchronously in these two countries which traditionally looked towards each other (acrimoniously or admiringly). In some cases, British and French hero-makers were on the same wavelength. For instance, the ability to co-operate with local rulers, and to bring them under European control (preferably without the use of force), was equally appreciated in both countries, and taken as a proof of the overwhelming power of these heroes on indigenous populations. Yet promotional strategies were largely shaped according to local dominant beliefs: Protestantism, loyalty to the Queen (or King after 1901) and martial valour were prerequisites in Britain; the criteria were less obvious in France, where conflicting allegiances to Catholicism, the Republic, Bonapartism, the monarchy or the 'imperial duty' of France split up potential audiences in a more tormented Third Republic long traumatized by the defeat inflicted by Prussia. Over the period, the French public appeared as more fragmented, whilst British audiences, traditionally divided along class lines, appeared as more homogeneous with the rise of a powerful commercialized culture. Chastity was generally not as valued in France as it was in Britain (although French Catholics were naturally inclined to praise it). The case studies of Kitchener and Marchand reveal profoundly different circumstances in Britain and in France at the turn of the twentieth century. French officers had to lobby much more actively than their British counterparts to advance their careers through colonial activity. On the other hand, interaction between the press and the publishing world was much more systematic in Britain than in France: if British war correspondents routinely published accounts of their observations in book form, the scarcity of French *grands reporters* on African battlefields prevented this situation from arising in France. British advances in telegraphic cabling were indeed of precious help when it came to transmitting urgent reports, and French inferiority in this domain hampered the Gallic press. The concept of 'print capitalism' is applicable to the context of the two countries: if print-runs reveal how far the French book trade for imperial heroes lagged behind the British, popular newspapers carrying tales of imperial heroism regularly passed the million mark in both countries. The contrast between the similarity of the physical means of promotion on the one hand (whether books, illustrated newspapers or films), and the domestic conditions of their use on the other, demonstrates the agency of consumers who, far from being passive recipients of blind propaganda material, had the last word through their control of the strings of the purse: it is ultimately buyers' willingness to spend some of their spare cash in this type of material, which made the development of heroic reputations of empire possible over the years. Without this flow of material which recycled and further disseminated tales of dedication and heroism, there would not have been much left of these legends. We should therefore contextualize the power and influence of print capitalism: the relationship between producers and consumers appears much more dynamic than in Adorno and Horkeimer's model of the culture industry, with clear occurrences of reciprocal influence.[16] The buying public did not *have* to buy the material manufacturers offered them about imperial heroes, but the very existence of this material (and its success, in most cases) did help to promote heroic reputations of empire.

The large networks of patronage and promotion which sustained these legends of empire, and the success of the popular material produced about imperial heroes, demonstrate conclusively the existence of popular interest in heroic actions linked to the empire. As such, this book validates John MacKenzie's concept of 'popular imperialism' and subsequent efforts, by authors in the present series, as well as the likes of Catherine Hall, Antoinette Burton, Ann-Laura Stoler, Frederick Cooper and others, to analyse the complex interaction between metropolitan and overseas cultures, and to demonstrate the central place of empire in European identity building. This book adds a new dimension to the equation when it reveals the capitalist drive that lay behind the cultural industry which promoted the imperial idea. Producers of material on colonial heroes not only sought to serve the cause of the empire (and some of them may have not had this explicitly in mind) but they also intended to line their pockets with often substantial fortunes – as seen in the case of William Blackwood and G. W. Steevens.

This preoccupation with profit, typical of a commercial setting, directly leads to the correlated question of the popular success of this material, which turns out to be much more than a mere question of reception. The very existence of an extended corpus of works on a subject like imperial heroes reveals the existence of an adequate market encouraging more players to join the field. The heroes themselves might not have been enchanted to be turned into cultural commodities, but the evidence gathered in this book suggests that this was the case. Indeed, the best-selling figures registered for many books on imperial heroes, and the 'blockbuster' status of some films dedicated to their careers, demonstrate the popular appeal of these tales of empire across large sections of the population. The wide coverage of imperial heroes in the press showed uncontested cross-class appeal which tends to invalidate claims that the idea of empire did not appeal beyond the elites and had only a superficial impact on British and French cultures, which has been running from J. A. Hobson to the present day.[17] It is certainly true that imperial heroes brought more than the empire with them (exoticism, escapism, exemplarity and a reassuring feeling of superiority spring to mind), but their place at the core of the imperial edifice remains beyond doubt. 'Popular imperialism' was primarily a mindset, and it was not exclusive of other feelings or interests. We have seen on several occasions in this book, from Roderick Muchison to Charles Maunier, that geographical curiosity could go hand in hand

CONCLUSION

with imperial promotion, and they did not necessarily have to be mutually exclusive. The same applies to larger-than-life imperial heroes, who could satisfy various interests of the public at the same time because of their 'structured polysemy'.[18]

Unless we reduce imperial sentiment to such a narrow definition that it becomes meaningless (e.g. that popular imperialism was nothing else than *active* support), there is no reason to entertain doubts about the imperial meaning with which the heroes studied in this book were invested. This appears to be equally true on both sides of the Channel. Although the French public took longer than the British to show interest in imperial subjects, talking of 'French popular imperialism' in the late nineteenth and early twentieth centuries is perfectly legitimate. The Great War, which was as much a war for empire as a war of empires,[19] appeared as a turning point in the history of 'popular imperialism', with imperial heroes taking even greater significance in the interwar years, when popular celebrations of the empire became enshrined with new meanings as the world became more uncertain for both Britain and France – by then, unlikely allies. Imperial heroes played major political and moral roles in the context of 'New Imperialism' but, later in the period, they were turned into promotional instruments serving the celebration of the imperial idea, especially during the interwar 'apotheosis of Greater France'.[20] This evolution of the meaning and relevance of imperial heroes ensured their growing success over the period, as it allowed their reputations to adapt to the profound changes that affected Britain and France between 1870 and 1939 and which offered unprecedented opportunities for successful large-scale hero-worship. The example of imperial heroes, which show us vividly one of the multiple symbolic paths to modernity that the metropoles followed, provide a potent confirmation of Etienne Balibar's view that 'every modern nation is a product of colonization'.[21] The modalities of this mediated form of interaction with imperial peoples and spaces throws lights on fundamental processes in the formation of European national identities.

The primary purpose of this book has been to deliver a quantitative and qualitative appraisal of metropolitan cultures of empire, through the prism of imperial heroes. Its ambition has been neither to judge the content of these reputations nor to condone them. Looking primarily at the socio-political background and commercial success of metropolitan *representations* of heroes means that there is hardly any place for the suffering of the colonized or the atrocities that some of these heroes ordered or supervised, usually as an integral part of the action for which they were praised.[22] The documents discussed here told the public only one side of the story. Indigenous populations were in the background, absent, criticized or infantilized, and were never given the opportunity to give their own account of events. Only now are we starting to uncover the other side of the story, with, for instance, a recent attempt to investigate the role of Gordon's opponent in 1884-5, the Mahdi, as a charismatic leader.[23]

The framework for this book has been dictated by the emergence of a 'new regime of heroism' linked to imperial expansion, which contributed to altering the 'shared culture of meanings' in the British and French metropoles.[24] It ought to be said that the development of a distinct strand of 'imperial hero' is not mutually exclusive with other forms of heroism over the period, such as for instance the engineer and inventor seen as heroes, though arguably 'neither inventor nor engineer could compete for attention with the explorer – the quintessential hero of late nineteenth-century imperialism'.[25] The contours of the object of study were clearly defined by this heroic dimension, and, as a result, European villains have scarcely appeared. One obvious reason was that they tended to be quickly forgotten once they had fallen from their pedestal, and they quickly left the realm of popular culture to remain known only to specialists or anti-imperial propagandists (who generally met very limited success, as shown by the case of Louis Guétant's violent criticism of Marchand). Yet the fact that they did not fit within this book's remit is no licence to omit their existence in this conclusion. We refer here to substantial works which are not only tales of greed, exploitation and horror but which also show the popular resonance that colonial scandals could achieve, whether about the massacres committed by the Voulet-Chanoine mission or the sadistic frame of mind highlighted by the Gaud-Toqué affair.[26] Echoes of some of these scandals could be found in some of the most influential anti-colonial works of the twentieth century, such as Joseph Conrad's *Heart of Darkness* or some passages of Octave Mirbeau's works.[27]

If African perceptions of imperial heroes were beyond the remit of this book, the chapters equally refrained from analysing what European minds made of the material about imperial heroes discussed here. This is dictated not only by the resolute focus, adopted here, on strategies intended to shape an 'imperial mindset' through the mass-media, which is in itself a vast subject, but it also reflects the nature of sources available. The absence of opinion polls is obviously a major factor for this choice, and newspapers alone provide little evidence as to how their articles were received and interpreted by their readers (letters to the editor being one of the rare exceptions). In spite of a few private sources that can offer original insights into individual perceptions, this type of evidence will always remain patchy and generally unsuitable to document perceptions beyond the elites, who are traditionally more

CONCLUSION

self-conscious and prepared to arrange their thoughts and private papers for posterity. So a full inquiry into the reception of imperial heroes is yet to come, dependent upon whether new sources become available.[28]

This book has endeavoured to show that imperial heroism was a phenomenon to be reckoned with when it comes to British and French popular cultures from the late nineteenth century onwards. More remains to be said about how these cultural artefacts changed European popular perceptions of the empire, of non-European worlds, of the encounter between the two and the influence it had on national identities. The postcolonial legacy of these imperial heroes is another major area of enquiry where many questions remain to be answered. The demise of empire did not mean that they always ended up in the cultural scrapyard of the ex-metropoles and the ex-colonies. For instance, General Gordon still commands an enduring fascination in the Western world. In 2009, and in spite of his ultimate military failure, he was the subject of a book in an American series looking at the 'significant and popular military figures drawn from world history'.[29] Marshal Lyautey inspired a biography by the politician and former Minister of Foreign Affairs Hervé de Charette.[30] Even if former colonizers generally refrain from orchestrating open commemorations that could be interpreted as apologetic of their colonial past, anniversaries are often used to revive public memories of these national heroes. The *Musée de la marine* mounted in 1980 an exhibition on Brazza to commemorate the centenary of his second mission, during which he signed the Makoko treaties.[31] Although it did not give rise to nationwide celebrations, the centenary of Brazza's death in 2005 generated two biographical studies retracing his career (and the reprint of a highly eulogistic biography by the Caribbean writer René Maran) and an online commemorative exhibition hosted by a website affiliated to the French Ministry of Culture.[32] He also inspired two novels, and was remembered in his native Italy, especially at the initiative of his descendants.[33] The beatification of Charles de Foucauld in 2005 was an excellent opportunity to refresh memories of his life and spiritual achievements, which had in any case remained vivid among the French Catholic community. And often, a stroll in an English city, or along the paths of a British university campus, will bring you face to face with a pastiche of Alfred Leete's Kitchener recruiting poster, whose pointing finger lends itself to a variety of injunctions: a century of celebrity has not diminished the appeal of this austere and authoritarian moustached hero endowed with inscrutable eyes.

Yet the resilience of heroic reputations of empire on the African continent itself is, quite legitimately, more surprising after the epic of decolonization that the continent witnessed from the 1950s onwards. Livingstone is still an important Zambian city endowed with a Livingstone memorial and its Livingstone museum (complete with a statue of the explorer at the front), whilst the largest city of Malawi has remained to this day named after the birthplace of the author of *Missionary Travels*. When President Kenneth Kaunda of Zambia attended a commemoration of David Livingstone at the Chitambo Memorial, he did not hesitate to re-write history and declare the missionary the 'first African freedom-fighter'.[34] If Northern and Southern Rhodesia have disappeared from world atlases to become Zambia and Zimbabwe, the Rhodes Memorial stands untouched on the slopes of Devil's Peak in Cape Town, a statue of Cecil Rhodes greets visitors at the University of Cape Town, the Muizenberg Historical Conservation Society (established in the cottage where he died) cherishes his memory, Grahamstown has been endowed to this day with a Rhodes University and his remains are still buried on the summit of a hill with a commanding view over the Matopos, in spite of the anti-white rhetoric of the current Zimbabwean president.[35] Even more surprisingly, the continent has witnessed in recent years a resurgence in the memorialization of imperial heroes. In 1999, the inhabitants of Ségou (Mali, the former French Sudan) staunchly opposed presidential plans to transfer the old statue of General Archinard from a town council backyard to Kayes. As a result of widespread popular mobilization (including from many young people), it now stands, fully restored, on the banks of the River Niger in Ségou. Historian Alpha Omar Konaré, who ran Mali between 2003 and 2008, decided to dedicate two squares of the presidential compound of Koulouba to the celebration of five French explorers of the area and of twenty-six colonial governors between 1880 and independence.[36] The most revisionist attitude came from the Congo-Brazzaville, where the Marxist-turned-liberal President Denis Sassou Nguesso orchestrated the rebranding of Brazza into a form of Congolese founding father. At least ten billion CFA francs (around £12.5 million) was invested by the Congolese government (with additional support from Congolese, French and Italian sponsorship) in a luxurious monument commemorating Brazza in the country's capital, still named after him – unlike, of course, its homonymic neighbour, which turned Leopoldville into Kinshasa after independence. A lavish purpose-built neo-classical building received in 2006 the ashes of the explorer and his family, transferred from the cemetery of Mustapha in Algiers.[37] It now hosts the headquarters of the *Fondation Pierre Savorgnan de Brazza*, and Congolese officials have unveiled ambitious development plans in an attempt to justify the expense – and the memorial itself. President Nguesso's initiative has attracted significant criticism, accused of

CONCLUSION

falling prey to the sirens of neo-colonialism and of mismanagement of resources in a country that still suffers from poor infrastructures.[38] Beyond the political controversy, the monument still stands in the centre of the city, with a majestic statue of the explorer, inspired by Nadar's famous 1882 photograph of the explorer, at the front of it. The whole story inspired French novelist Patrick Deville, who remarked wryly that Brazza decided to christen one of his children Antoine-Conrad following his reading of *Heart of Darkness*.[39]

The commemoration of great imperial figures in postcolonial countries does not seem exactly in line with the agenda set by the likes of Frantz Fanon or Ngugi Wa Thiong'o. Yet their versatility seems to have ensured their survival then and now, as their reputations were malleable enough to serve many purposes and interest groups. Their Promethean ability to retain a form of relevance in modern times offers yet another reason to analyse the origins and development of the legends surrounding these 'heroic imperialists'.

Notes

1 J. Darwin, 'Imperialism and the Victorians: the dynamics of territorial expansion', *English Historical Review*, June 1997, 642; G. Cubitt and A. Warren (eds), *Heroic Reputations and Exemplary Lives* (Manchester, 2000).
2 R. Williams, 'Fiction and the writing public', *Essays in Criticism*, 7 (1957), 422–8.
3 Personal conversation with Robert Darène, 10 June 2011.
4 J. Evans, 'Celebrity, media and history', in J. Evans and D. Hesmondhalgh, *Understanding Media: Inside Celebrity* (Maidenhead, 2005), pp. 17–19.
5 B. Sèbe, 'Aventurières et voyageuses en Afrique de l'Ouest', in R. Little (ed.), *Lucie Cousturier, les tirailleurs sénégalais et la question coloniale* (2008) pp. 163–86.
6 A. Blunt, *Travel, Gender and Imperialism* (1994), p. 149.
7 P. Bailey, *Leisure and Class in Victorian England: Rational Recreation and the Contest for Control, 1830–85* (1978), pp. 183–5, and J. M. MacKenzie (ed.), *Imperialism and Popular Culture* (Manchester, 1986), p. 9.
8 For a reflection on the influence of technical progress on text reception, see P. L. Shillingsburg, *From Gutenberg to Google: Electronic Representations of Literary Texts* (Cambridge, 2006).
9 A. S. Thompson, *Imperial Britain: The Empire in British Politics c. 1880–1932* (Harlow, 2000), pp. 52–60.
10 On the use of military villains against the army, see B. Taithe, *The Killer Trail* (Oxford, 2009).
11 G. Turner, *Understanding Celebrity* (2004), pp. 31–51.
12 P. Centlivres, D. Fabre and F. Zonabend (eds), *La Fabrique des héros* (1998), ch. 1.
13 A. Tessier, *Lyautey* (2004), p. 443.
14 C. Forsdick, *Travel in Twentieth-Century French and Francophone Cultures: The Persistence of Diversity* (Oxford, 2005).
15 R. Gildea, *Children of the Revolution. The French, 1799–1914* (2008).
16 T. Adorno and M. Horkheimer, *Dialectic of Enlightenment* (1944/1997), pp. 120–67.
17 J. A. Hobson, *Imperialism, A Study* (1902, repr. 2005), pp. 3–13; C. R. Ageron, *France coloniale ou parti colonial?* (1978); B. Porter, *The Absent-Minded Imperialists* (Oxford, 2004).
18 R. Dyer, *Stars* (1979), p. 3.

19 J. Darwin, *The Empire Project* (Cambridge, 2009), pp. 305–58.
20 R. Girardet, 'L'apothéose de la "plus grande France", l'idée coloniale devant l'opinion française (1930–1935)', *Revue française de science politique*, 18:6 (1968), 1085–114.
21 E. Balibar, *Race, Nation and Class: Ambiguous Identities* (1992), quoted in A. Burton (ed.), *After the Imperial Turn: Thinking with and through the Nation* (Durham, NC, 2003), p. 1.
22 On atrocities, see Taithe, *Killer Trail.*
23 F. Nicoll, *The Mahdi of Sudan and the Death of General Gordon* (Stroud, 2005). Two earlier attempts to describe the view of opponents to European conquerors were the novel by D. Brosset, *Un homme sans l'Occident* (1946) and the film by M. Hondo, *Sarraounia* (1986).
24 S. Hall (ed.), *Representation. Cultural Representations and Signifying Practices* (1997), pp. 16–19.
25 C. MacLeod, *Heroes of Invention. Technology, Liberalism and British Identity, 1750–1914* (Cambridge, 2007), p. 378. See also C. Andersen, 'Explorer-engineers take the field: imperial engineers, Africa and the late-Victorian public', in M. Harbsmeier et al. (eds), *Scientists and Scholars in the Field: Studies in the History of Fieldwork and Expeditions and Fieldwork* (Aarhus, 2012), pp. 169–91.
26 See for instance M. Mathieu, *La Mission Afrique centrale* (1996), or Taithe, *Killer trail.* On atrocities in the Belgian Congo, see A. Hochschild, *King Leopold's Ghost* (1999).
27 See for instance his article 'Colonisons' in *Le Journal*, 13 November 1892 (O. Mirbeau, *Contes cruels*, vol. 2 (1990), pp. 268–73); O. Mirbeau, *Les 21 jours d'un neurasthénique* (1901), ed. P. Michel, vol. 3 (2001), pp. 71–9; and 'Le caoutchouc rouge', in *La 628-E8* (1907), ed. P. Michel, vol. 3 (2001), pp. 377–80.
28 There is apparently an attempt to explore the actual reception of imperial heroes among the population in E. Berenson, *Heroes of Empire* (Berkeley and Los Angeles, CA, 2011), but primary written sources remain occasional (e.g. p. 193), whilst the bulk of the evidence is limited to printed sources, which offer insights into the senders' views, but not into the receivers' perceptions.
29 C. B. Faught, *Gordon, Victorian Hero* (Washington, DC, 2008).
30 H. de Charette, *Lyautey* (1997).
31 Various authors, *Savorgnan de Brazza (1852–1905). Catalogue de l'exposition présentée au musée de la Marine* (1980).
32 J. Martin, *Savorgnan de Brazza, 1852–1905* (2005); I. Dion, *Pierre Savorgnan de Brazza, au cœur du Congo* (Marseille, 2007); R. Maran, *Savorgnan de Brazza* (2009); www.brazza.culture.fr. [Accessed 15 April 2011].
33 P. Deville, *Equatoria* (2009); P. Besson, *Et le fleuve tuera l'homme blanc* (2009); various authors, *Una vita per l'Africa* (Florence, 2006); C. Pirzio-Biroli, *Pietro Savorgnan di Brazzà, esploratore leggendario 1852–1905* (Mariano del Friuli, 2006); F. Savorgnan de Brazza (ed.), *Pietro Savorgnan di Brazzà dal Friuli al Congo Brazaville* (Florence, 2006); M. Petringa, *Brazzà, a Life for Africa* (Bloomington, IN, 2006). On Deville, Besson and Maran, see N. Martin-Granel, '"Abracadabrazza" ou le roman du mémorial Pierre Savorgnan de Brazza', *Cahiers d'études africaines*, 50:197 (2010), 293–307.
34 Thanks to John M. MacKenzie for sharing this anecdote. It is also reported by M. Barrett in 'Presumed innocent: Michael Barrett on the contentious life and work of David Livingstone, "the First African freedom fighter"', *New Statesman*, 1 July 2002.
35 On the meaning of Rhodes's choice of his own resting place, see T. O. Ranger, *Voices From the Rocks: Nature, Culture & History in the Matopos Hills of Zimbabwe* (1999), pp. 30–3.
36 On Malian celebrations of the colonial past, see D. Konaté, 'Mémoire et histoire dans la construction des Etats-nations de l'Afrique subsaharienne: le cas du Mali', conference paper ('Expériences et mémoire: partager en français la diversité du monde', Bucharest, September 2006), www.celat.ulaval.ca/histoire.memoire/

CONCLUSION

    b2006/Konate.pdf [Accessed 14 July 2011]; R. de Jorio, 'Politics of remembering and forgetting: the struggle over colonial monuments in Mali', *Africa Today*, 52:4 (Summer 2006), 79–106.
37 Agence France Presse despatch, 24 May 2006; *Le Monde*, 3 October 2006.
38 See for example L. Atondi-Monmondjo, 'Pouvoir congolais et révisionnisme post-colonial: le cas Pierre Savorgnan de Brazza' (2006), www.congopage.com/IMG / Revisionnisme_P_nial_Atondi.pdf [Accessed 14 July 2011]; J. Tonda, 'Le mausolée Brazza, corps mystique de l'État congolais ou corps du "négatif"', *Cahiers d'études africaines*, 198-199-200 (2010), 799–821; F. Bernault, 'Colonial bones: the 2006 burial of Savorgnan de Brazza in the Congo', *African Affairs*, 109:436 (2010), 367–90, and 'Quelque chose de pourri dans le post-empire: le fétiche, le corps et la marchandise dans le mémorial de Brazza au Congo', *Cahiers d'études africaines*, 198-199-200 (2010), 171–98; S. Smith, *Voyage en postcolonie. Le nouveau monde franco-africain* (2010), pp. 262–80.
39 Deville, *Equatoria*, p. 184.

BIOGRAPHICAL SKETCHES

Archinard, Louis (1850–1932). A graduate of the *Ecole Polytechnique*, he started fighting in West Africa in 1880. As a military commander, and in his capacity as governor of the colony of the *Haut-Sénégal-Niger* (between 1888 and 1893), he was the founder of the French Sudan, which became part of French West Africa (AOF) when it was created in 1895.

Brazza, Pierre Paul François Camille Savorgnan de (1852–1905). Born in Rome into a wealthy family, Pietro Savorgnan di Brazzà joined the French navy to fulfil a wish to discover the world which the nascent Italian navy would have been unable to satisfy. A graduate of the Naval School of Brest, he was initially prevented from joining the navy on the grounds of his nationality. Having overcome this problem thanks to the help of a powerful patron, Admiral de Montaignac, he discovered Africa first in Algeria (as part of the expeditionary force which led the repression of the Mokrani revolt, 1871) and then in Equatorial Africa (1873). Inspired by Livingstone's and Stanley's writings, he was quick to fall in love with the continent. In three expeditions, he was to give France a considerable share of Equatorial Africa, in just a decade and against the chronic indecision of his government. Montaignac's nomination as Minister of Marine in 1874 facilitated the successful outcome of his first expedition project, which consisted in an exploration of the interior of the continent, along the Ogoué River (1875–78), which allowed him to establish a first contact with local populations and to make a name for himself in the metropole. The second expedition (1880–82) turned him into a hero as soon as he returned home: overtaking his rival Stanley on the right bank of the Congo, and going far beyond the orders he had received from the government, he claimed for France a vast territory through a treaty of protectorate signed with the king of the powerful Bateke, the Makoko. Widely acclaimed for his daring initiative, Brazza enjoyed wide popular support when he lobbied the Chambers to ratify a treaty they had never requested. Inflamed public opinion and national pride (badly wounded by the British intervention in Egypt) ensured that the *fait accompli* was finally given parliamentary backing. Brazza was sent for a third expedition (1883–85), the *Mission de l'ouest africain*, which laid the foundation of the future French colonies of Gabon and Congo. After the Berlin conference formally attributed the territory to France, he was sent back to the Congo with the title of *commissaire* *général du gouvernement*, to organize and administer the newly acquired territory. Perhaps better at exploring than administering, and certainly overwhelmed by the logistical challenge posed by the crossing of the Congolese colony by the Marchand mission, Brazza gradually crystallized growing criticism from his superiors, but also from the press. He was relieved of his functions in 1898 as his star seemed to fail, but a scandal involving the abuse of African prisoners on the occasion of Bastille Day led the government to recall him to investigate on the situation in the Congo. He was never able to hand in his damning report of the concessionary system (which he had contributed to establishing whilst being the *commissaire général*), for he died in Dakar, on the way back. His untimely death (which his wife always claimed resulted from poisoning) gave new impetus to his reputation, which retained definitely the features of the early 1880s: that of a peaceful conqueror, able to win hearts and minds through negotiation and respect for the indigenous populations. This attractive image was decisive in ensuring the resilience of the Brazza legend well into the postcolonial period.

Bugeaud, Thomas Robert, *marquis de la Piconnerie*, duke of Isly (1784–1849). An officer during the Napoleonic wars, Thomas Bugeaud, *marquis de la Piconnerie*, went down to posterity for his resolute military action in Algeria, where he was sent six years after the French landing in Sidi-Fredj. He signed the peace treaty of Tafna with Abd-el-Kader in 1837, before relaunching the French conquest of the Algerian interior during a seven-year war against the Emir (1840–47). His strategy of colonization was encapsulated in the Latin expression *Ense et Aratro* ('With sword and plough'), which advised that conquering soldiers had to be turned into settler peasants. He unsuccessfully advocated the combination of military colonization on the one hand and indirect rule on the other. For a long time, he epitomized the conquest of Algeria in French folklore.

Duveyrier, Henri (1840–1892). Coming from a background of disciples of Saint-Simon, educated partly in France and partly in Germany, Henri Duveyrier discovered the fringes of the Algerian Sahara aged seventeen. Backed by the great German explorer Heinrich Barth, he ventured into the depths of the Sahara for two and a half years (1859–61), developing close friendships with influential members of the Tuareg communities he met. Upon his return, the Legion of Honour was conferred upon him (1862), and two years later he published his masterpiece *Les Touareg du Nord* (with significant input from a mentor, as a result of ill-health following the hardships of his travels), in which he advocated close co-operation with the Tuaregs. He was awarded soon after the gold medal of the Paris Geographical Society, and reached the pinnacle of his career. He later produced an extremely critical analysis of the Sanusiyya brotherhood, which influenced generations of French colonial administrators. As the number of murdered explorers of the Sahara kept growing (especially with the massacre of the Flatters mission), he was increasingly criticized for his optimistic appraisal of Franco-Saharan relations. Depressed, he took his own life.

Faidherbe, Louis Léon César (1818–1889). A graduate of the *Ecole polytechnique*, and an officer of the Engineers, Louis Faidherbe started his career in Algeria, before being sent to Senegal (1852). In his capacity as governor-general of the colony between 1854 and 1861, and then again between 1863 and 1865, he considerably expanded French influence towards the interior, through a skilful use of locally recruited troops, alliances with local chiefs, and economic development based on trade (especially thanks to the building of a railway line). He was the founder of the *école des otages* in Saint-Louis, which was intended to train, and keep under French control, the next generation of African collaborators of the empire. He won a few decisive battles during the Franco-Prussian war at the head of the *armée du Nord*, and later became a Republican member of Parliament at the beginning of the Third Republic. A senator from 1879 onwards, he was also rewarded with the Legion of Honour. He was one of the great empire builders of the Second Empire, and was remembered under the Third Republic as the architect of the cheap but effective expansion of the colony of Senegal.

Foucauld, Charles Eugène de (1858–1916). A graduate of the military academy of Saint-Cyr and the cavalry school of Saumur, Charles de Foucauld started his career in North Africa, first with the Fourth Hussards and then with the Fourth *Chasseurs d'Afrique*. His eccentric way of life explained his change of posting (he had refused to part company with a mistress), and to many he appeared as an amateur officer only interested in spending a generous inheritance. Yet his time in Algeria near the Moroccan border instilled in him the wish to discover Morocco, then forbidden to Christians. Disguised as a Jew, he collected a valuable amount of information on the country in 1883–84. He was subsequently celebrated by the Paris Geographical Society, which bestowed on him its gold medal which propelled him among the famous explorers of the time. He also strengthened his status with his detailed account of his travels, *Reconnaissance au Maroc* (1885). Having witnessed Muslim fervour on many occasions during his travels, Foucauld underwent a spiritual conversion in the mid-1880s. After two months in the Holy Land, he joined the Cistercian Trappist order in 1890.

BIOGRAPHICAL SKETCHES

Constantly in search for an improvement of his faith through mortification, he made a point of living with less and less material well-being. After prolonged stays in monasteries in Alexandretta and Nazareth, Foucauld came back to Algeria in 1901, shortly after his ordination as a priest. He chose to settle in an area newly conquered by French troops, and built a small hermitage in Beni-Abbes. As a result of his friendship with General Laperrine, he travelled further south and developed links with the chief of the Kel-Ahaggar Tuaregs around 1905, built a new hermitage in Tamanrasset and, in 1910, another one in the middle of the Ahaggar volcanic mountains. He gained a deep understanding of the life, customs and language of the Tuaregs, producing a four-volume Tuareg–French dictionary. His assassination by a Senussist party on 1 December 1916 made him a martyr and paved the way for the heroization of his personal story from the interwar years onwards. Following a highly popular biographical account published in 1921 by René Bazin, this trend kept growing in the 1920 and 1930s, with a few major initiatives, such as Georges Gorée's *Sur les traces de Charles de Foucauld* and Léon Poirier's film *L'Appel du silence* (1936). Especially celebrated in colonial and Catholic circles, Foucauld became a major religious figure of the twentieth century, and contributed to the French fascination with the Sahara. Though he never converted anyone (in a striking parallel with David Livingstone, who had only one convert in his whole life), his spiritual legacy blossomed posthumously, with numerous religious congregations based on his writings, among them the Little Brothers and Sisters of Jesus. He was beatified in 2005.

Gallieni, Joseph Simon (1849–1916). Having completed his military training at the Saint-Cyr academy (and later at the *Ecole supérieure de guerre*), he quickly embarked on a string of military expeditions in the colonies, which led him to contribute decisively to the French wave of 'New Imperialism'. Though he operated in Indochina (where he chose Lyautey as his assistant), his main areas of activity were in Africa, first in the Western Sudan (1876–81 and 1885–88) and then in Madagascar, as governor general (1896–1905). He was with Lyautey a proponent of the 'oil spot' (*tâche d'huile*) pacification strategy, which purported that effective territorial expansion could take place only progressively from rigorously administered centres whose grip on the region would develop gradually. Limiting destructions in combat zones, co-operating with local leaders and promoting the supposed benefits of French colonization were key to this method. Recalled from retirement at the outbreak of the Great War, he successfully organized the defence of Paris (of which he had become the military governor) with a bold initiative: requisitioning taxis to help with the logistics of a daring counter-offensive on the von Cluck column (known as the *taxis de la Marne* episode). After six months as Minister of War under Aristide Briand, he resigned as a result of ill-health and died shortly afterwards.

Gordon, Charles George (1833–1885). Trained at the Royal Military Academy of Woolwich, Charles Gordon got his first opportunity to shine during the Crimean War. But it was further east that he gained the credentials that turned him into a national hero: sent to China with the Royal Engineers, he joined the Franco-British expeditionary force sent to Beijing during the Second Opium War and subsequently led a four-thousand-strong private force of Chinese fighters paid for by Shanghai's foreign merchants. The successes of the 'Ever Victorious Army' against the Taiping rebels made the fame of 'Chinese Gordon', as he came to be called in Britain in the early 1860s. After little more than half a decade back in Gravesend, he took up in 1873 the position of governor-general of the province of Equatoria, in the south of Sudan, then under Egyptian rule. Four years later, the khedive of Egypt appointed him governor-general of the whole of the Egyptian Sudan, a post he kept until 1880. After a short spell as private secretary to the new Indian Viceroy, he undertook archaeological research in the Holy Land, in search of the exact location of Biblical sites. As he was negotiating with King Leopold of Belgium his appointment in the Congo to develop the colony that would become the Congo Free State, the deteriorating military and political situation in the Sudan (nominally under Egyptian control, but British interests were involved too as a result of the British occupation of Egypt in 1882) threw Gordon into the limelight again, as a result of a press campaign led by W. T. Stead's *Pall Mall Gazette*, which made its headlines to the tune of 'Chinese Gordon to the Sudan' (9 January 1884). Gladstone reluctantly bowed to public opinion, and made him responsible for the Anglo-Egyptian withdrawal from the Sudan. Yet, rather than evacuating the garrison in Khartoum in order to operate an orderly retreat, Gordon organized the resistance of the city to the insurgents. After ten months of siege, the city fell on 26 January 1885 to the Mahdi's troops, who killed Gordon in the governor's palace: the reputation of 'Chinese Gordon' had been superseded for evermore by 'Gordon of Khartoum'. A relief expedition belatedly sent under the command of General Wolseley arrived two days later, only to confirm the fall of the city. Gordon's chivalric and often eccentric character, his boldness and his ability to lead troops (even foreign ones) and his final martyrdom made the legend of 'Gordon of Khartoum' one of the most enduring heroic reputations of Victorian times.

BIOGRAPHICAL SKETCHES

Gouraud, Henri Joseph Eugène (1867–1946). A graduate of the military academy of Saint-Cyr, Henri Gouraud led numerous military expeditions in Africa, and was famous for capturing the African leader Samory in 1898. He served in Dahomey (today's Benin), in Chad and Mauritania, and worked under Lyautey in Morocco (1911–14). After a distinguished contribution to the Great War (though he was not able to change the outcome of the Dardanelles operation when he took command of the French expeditionary corps), he enjoyed wide renown in the interwar years. He served as high commissioner in Syria and Lebanon between 1919 and 1923, before taking up the post of military governor of Paris (1923–37).

Kirk, John (1832–1922). A graduate of Edinburgh University, where he read Medicine, John Kirk assisted David Livingstone in his Zambezi expedition (1858–63). He went to Zanzibar in 1866 as the medical officer of the Zanzibar Agency, and quickly took up consular posts there for European nations (Britain, but also the Republic of Hamburg, as well as Portugal and Italy). Having won the trust of the sultan, he quickly acquired a position of power in Zanzibar. Alongside Livingstone and Gordon, he was deeply involved in the fight against the slave trade (he represented Britain at the African slave trade conference in Brussels in 1889–90).

Kitchener, Horatio Herbert (1850–1916). A former student of the School of Military Engineering of Chatham, Horatio Herbert Kitchener started his career performing surveying work, especially in Palestine where he learnt some Arabic. Both skills would prove valuable later in his career. Having been posted in Egypt in the wake of the British victory of Tel-el-Kebir, he served as intelligence officer in the expedition sent to rescue General Gordon in 1884. He persistently advised Wolseley that they should move south more speedily to increase chances of arriving before it was too late. Thanks to publicity by the press (and by his own father too), he was exonerated of the stigma left by the ultimate failure of the relief expedition, and enjoyed some fame in Britain: a promising prelude to his later status as a national hero, which also gave him the opportunity to develop useful social links with powerful potential supporters. After a spell in Zanzibar where he represented British views on the boundary-making commission for the sultanate, he became governor-general of Eastern Sudan and the littoral of the Red Sea (1886–88). Prime Minister Salisbury ensured that his next posting would be in Egypt again, and Kitchener spent three successful years in the Egyptian police and army. He was subsequently appointed commander-in-chief ('sirdar') of the Egyptian army (1892). He reformed it thoroughly, making it an increasingly effective force, which he saw as a prerequisite to any successful re-conquest of the Sudan. This was a legitimate goal for an officer like him, who had experienced first-hand the humiliation of General Gordon's death in 1885. The Italian defeat by Ethiopia gave a good excuse to advance south, and Kitchener was eager to make full use of the circumstances to get Salisbury's backing for his plans. In just two years, he strengthened the position of the Egyptian army in the Sudan, militarily through a string of victories along the Nile, and logistically with the building of a railway line crossing the heart of the desert. He defeated the Mahdi's troops at Omdurman on 2 September 1898, using the superior firepower of his machine guns to inflict extreme losses on the Mahdi's followers. The sheer extent of the massacre of under-armed fighters, and the subsequent destruction by Anglo-Egyptian troops of the Mahdi's shrine as part of a merciless repression, gave rise to widespread criticism in Britain (including from Queen Victoria herself). By contrast, Kitchener managed very tactfully his meeting with the leader of the French garrison installed in Fashoda (further south on the White Nile) since 10 July: his dealings with Major Marchand from 19 September onwards made it possible to avert open conflict between Britain and France. He was lionized upon his return to Britain, not least thanks to George Warrington Steevens's best-seller account *With Kitchener to Khartoum*, based on his dispatches for the *Daily Mail*. Popular acclaim was matched with official rewards (he was created Baron of Khartoum and Aspall and was awarded many honours). His role during the South African War (1900–02) was much more controversial, since his tactics included forcibly regrouping Boer families into camps which were later seen as prototypes of the concentration system. However, in the end, he was seen as the architect of the peace of Vereeniging, and widely celebrated in Britain. He was subsequently appointed commander-in-chief of the Indian army (1902–09), before coming back to Egypt as British consul-general (1911–14). In his capacity as secretary of state for war (1914–16), he played a pivotal role in readying British forces for the nature and scale of the conflict, especially thanks to his idea of volunteer force (the 'Kitchener armies'). He was lost at sea when his cruiser hit a German mine off Orkney. His tragic end immediately crystallized the legend that had developed around his figure as a disciplined, insightful and successful war leader, and even fuelled rumours that he might had escaped unscathed, only to help the warring nation further.

Laperrine, François Henry (1860–1920). A graduate of Saint-Cyr, his military career was entirely dedicated to North and West Africa: Algeria, Tunisia, Senegal and the Western Sudan. Commander of the

Saharan oases territories between 1901 and 1910, he played a pivotal role in expanding French paramountcy in the South of Algeria – especially through the *Compagnies sahariennes* which he created in 1902. He re-asserted French power in the Sahara during the Great War, and became in 1919 commander of the military division of Algiers. He was remembered particularly for his friendship with Charles de Foucauld, and for his accidental death when trying to undertake the first aerial crossing of the Sahara in 1920.

Lavigerie, Charles Martial Allemand (1825–1892). An ecclesiastical historian by training (he held doctorates in literature and theology from the religious Ecole des Carmes, and taught Church history at the Sorbonne between 1854 and 1856), Charles Lavigerie became Bishop of Nancy in 1863, before joining Algiers in 1867 as the archbishop of the capital of the French colony, upon the invitation of the Governor General Marshal MacMahon. Convinced that his mission was to advance the cause of Christianity in Africa, he repeatedly criticized Islam (sometimes making colonial authorities nervous about the reactions of Muslim colonial populations), tried to develop Christian humanitarian action, and vehemently fought the slave trade from the late 1880s onwards. He founded the order of the White Fathers in 1868, and the missionary Sisters of Our Lady of Africa in 1869, both of which have remained active to this day. He lobbied in favour of the French protectorate in Tunisia, and was subsequently made Archbishop of Carthage (1884–92), in addition to his Algiers see. Following a request by Pope Leo XIII in 1890, he was also an architect of the rapprochement between the Church and Third Republic France, especially through the 'toast of Algiers' of November 1890, which paved the way for the reconciliation of French Catholics with the Republic.

Lawrence, Thomas Edward (1888–1935). A graduate in modern history of Jesus College, Oxford, he later went on to write a doctorate whilst a Fellow of All Souls College, Oxford, from 1919 onwards. A promising scholar from an early age, T. E. Lawrence undertook excavations for the British Museum in Syria (1911–14) shortly after his graduation: this extended stay strengthened his fascination for the Arab world, which would never leave him and would lead him to favour an idealized Middle East for the rest of his military and political career. Joining in December 1914 the military department of the Egyptian expeditionary force to the Ottoman empire, he played an active role in fomenting the 'Arab revolt' which would spell the end of the 'old sick man of Europe' at the end of the Great War. From intelligence gathering to the leadership of military commandos through to negotiation with local chiefs, he was instrumental in co-ordinating the Arab uprising against the Turkish empire, making full use of his knowledge of Arabic and his deep awareness of local customs and ways of thinking. This made him all the more resentful when the terms of the Sykes–Picot agreement (1916) were implemented towards the end of the war, leading to French control over Syria, a country he had promised to his ally Emir Feisal, the son of the Emir of Mecca. He performed the role of private adviser to, and translator for, Feisal at the 1919 Versailles conference, where he tried to oppose French claims over Syria, which contradicted his own promises to Arab leaders during the war. At the same time, he was propelled to the status of global living legend by a series of illustrated lectures entitled 'With Allenby in Palestine and Lawrence in Arabia', given by the American journalist Lowell Thomas illustrated by short films and photographs by Harry Chase. It conquered the Anglophone world shortly after its premiere at the London Royal Opera House. In the early 1920s, as colonial secretary, Churchill called Lawrence to the Colonial Office to implement a durable political plan for the Middle East. Having resigned from the Colonial Office in 1922, he enlisted in the RAF under a false name in order to escape the scrutiny of the press. His willingness to escape publicity, whilst actually stimulating it through his enlistment under a variety of identities, has been variously interpreted. Upon enlisting into the RAF, Lawrence had finished rewriting his manuscript for his masterpiece *Seven Pillars of Wisdom* (of which he had lost the first manuscript in 1919), which was published privately by the author in 1926, and then as an abridged version under the title *Revolt in the Desert* (1927). Shortly after leaving the RAF, he died in a motorcycle accident which immediately led to speculation of a similar vein to that of Kitchener's legend. His elegant but often factually unrealistic prose and his eccentic personality, have attracted widespread interest and controversies, not least when it was radically re-appraised in 1955 with Richard Aldington's *Lawrence of Arabia: A Biographical Enquiry*, which sought to debunk the legend carefully preserved by Lawrence's own brother, Arnold Lawrence, as well as a handful of early biographers with personal sympathies for their subject, such as Robert Graves and Basil Liddell Hart.

Livingstone, David (1813–1873). The epitome of nineteenth-century exploration and missionary work, he came from a humble background and worked long hours in his early years to help his parents and siblings survive. His education had been rigorous thanks to the efforts of his family and he managed to get formal training as a licentiate of the Faculty of Physicians and Surgeons (1840), four years after he had started medical studies at Anderson's College in Glasgow. His early

BIOGRAPHICAL SKETCHES

contact with the London Missionary Society, through his congregational church, made it possible for him to undertake in parallel religious studies, which allowed him to be ordained almost at the same time as he completed his medical training. Shortly afterwards, he was dispatched to South Africa where he would stay for a little more than a decade, relentlessly exploring areas inland, establishing relations with powerful chiefs, learning Setswana and founding a family in the process with the daughter of fellow missionary Robert Moffat. Eager to explore the interior of the continent and to improve the fight against the slave trade, he organized several expeditions, often accompanied by his family who suffered from the dire living conditions imposed on them. In 1852, Mary Livingstone and her children sailed home, whilst Livingstone remained in Cape Town and organized another long and hazardous exploratory journey towards the Upper Zambezi which led him to Luanda (May 1854), before he immediately set out to reach the east coast of Africa, christening on the way the falls of Mosi oa Tunya as *Victoria Falls*. From Quelimane, he embarked for Mauritius, and arrived in December 1856 in England, where he was given a hero's welcome. Though Livingstone was often far afield, he had managed to send several reports to the Royal Geographical Society, which publicized them as widely as possible. Upon his return to England, the RGS president of the time, Sir Roderick Murchinson, ensured that Livingstone's exploits would enhance the public standing of the nascent geographical science. Shortly after receiving an exceptional RGS gold medal, and the honours of the London Missionary Society, Livingstone embarked upon writing his *Missionary Travels and Researches in South Africa*, in which the recounting of his years in Africa offered a convenient pretext to defend his views about the development of legitimate trade on the continent (which, in his eyes, would spread Christianity and would also reduce the prevalence of the slave trade), whilst at the same time presenting his own achievements in the best possible light. This book, a best-seller of the time, durably established Livingstone's reputation as an explorer, which he consolidated through numerous lectures. He used his heroic status to help organize (and, crucially, fund) his next expedition to the Zambezi (1858–64), which had the use of a dismantlable steam launch. Though Livingstone had left no stone unturned in exploring the possibility of developing an upriver trade route for British goods, it had been more costly and less successful than anticipated (and had cost the life of Livingstone's wife too). After two years in England (during which he faced mixed reactions to his relative failure with the Zambezi expedition), he embarked in 1866 on what would become known as his 'last journey', starting in Zanzibar and venturing into the Great Lakes area, in search for the sources of the Nile. Having to overcome logistical obstacles regularly, his expedition was slowed down and doubts about his whereabouts became more persistent, which led the *New York Herald* to commission the young journalist H. M. Stanley to 'find [him]'. Stanley's publicity stunt (driven by the journalist's own ambition) quickly gave Livingstone worldwide fame, which was further entrenched by his death from ill-health in Chitambo on 30 April 1873. His remains were given full honours and he was buried in Westminster Abbey, whilst the press, the public and missionary societies indulged in hero-worship. Though he made only one convert in his whole life, he was remembered as an exceptionally talented missionary and explorer who epitomized Victorian values.

Lugard, Frederick John Dealtry (1858–1945). A graduate of the Royal Military College of Sandhurst, Frederick Lugard started a promising career on the Indian subcontinent (1878–86). He resigned from the army to pursue a doomed love relationship, the failure of which led him to seek a dangerous and adventurous life. He was hired in 1888 by the Imperial British East Africa Company, which sent him first into Central Africa (Nyasaland) and then into Uganda, where he obtained for the company the right to intervene in local affairs. His action, which he defended in his book *The Rise of Our East African Empire* (1893), ultimately triggered the 1894 British protectorate over the country. He subsequently joined George Goldie's Royal Niger Company for a couple of years in West Africa, before going to southern Africa for the British West Charterland Company. In the summer of 1897, Joseph Chamberlain, then colonial secretary, offered him an imperial post in West Africa, where he would engineer the British colony of Nigeria, through two prolonged stays which totalled fifteen years of presence in what became a country (1897–1906 and 1912–18, only interrupted by a five-year term as govenor of Hong Kong). He married the colonial propagandist and *Times* journalist Flora Shaw (1852–1929) in 1902. Having retired in 1919, he published in 1922 *The Dual Mandate in British Tropical Africa*, in which he outlined his theory of indirect rule. Though he was the subject of a two-volume biography by the Oxford historian Margery Perham, following efforts by his wife to secure a biography of her husband, he never displayed the features of a popular hero in Britain, in spite of the fact that his action was decisive in adding two African possessions to the British empire.

Lyautey, Louis Hubert Gonzalgue (1854–1934). A graduate of Saint-Cyr, this cavalry officer with royalist sympathies dedicated most of his professional life to the expansion of the French empire, in Indochina, Madagascar, Algeria and, most famously, Morocco. Though he had served in Algeria between 1880 and 1882, his entry into the world of colonial affairs was marked by his article in the *Revue des deux-mondes*, entitled 'The social role of the officer in universal military service' (1891). He subsequently served under Gallieni in Tonkin (1894–97) and Madagascar (1897–1902). After a short spell back in France, he was sent to the South of Oran (Algerian territories near the Moroccan border), between 1903 and 1907. Having become gradually involved in the management of Algero-Moroccan affairs, he became Resident General in Rabat shortly after the signature of the Treaty of Fez establishing the French protectorate over most of Morocco. He performed this role during thirteen years, except for a short period during the Great War, when he was called to Paris as Minister of War (December 1916 to March 1917). An exceptional organizer, diplomat and strategist, he skilfully implemented the French protectorate over Morocco through a combination of military force, negotiation and respect for local customs. He was with Gallieni a fervent supporter of the 'oil spot' tactics. In disagreement with the French government about the conduct of the repression of the Rif War, he resigned in 1925. He organized the most successful colonial exhibition of the period, the Paris *Exposition coloniale internationale* held in the Bois de Vincennes (1931). Elected to the French Academy in 1912, he left a voluminous correspondence and several influential works on colonial government: *Du rôle colonial de l'armée* (1900), *Dans le sud de Madagascar, pénétration militaire, situation politique et économique* (1903), *Lettres du Tonkin et de Madagascar: 1894–1899* (1920) and a *Lettre circulaire sur la politique du protectorat* (1920) in which he foresaw the ultimate independence of Morocco. To a large extent, '*Lyautey l'Africain*' ('Lyautey the African') epitomized the figure of the Empire builder in early twentieth-century France, alongside Gallieni.

Mangin, Charles (1866–1925). A graduate of Saint-Cyr, he chose the French naval infantry, which opened many opportunities overseas. He served under Archinard in the Western Sudan in the late 1880s to early 1890s (he was made *chevalier* of the Legion of Honour as a result of his actions there) and joined the Marchand mission (1896–98) in its crossing of Central and East Africa. He then served in Indochina (1901–4), in Senegal (1906–8) and in Morocco under Lyautey (1912). He played a noted role during the Great War, especially as the architect of the recapture of the fort of Douaumont (battle of Verdun) and as commander of the First Army. After the war, he was Commander of the Rhine Army, and inspector general of colonial troops. In 1908, he published a noted book entitled *La Force noire* (1910), in which he advocated the use of colonial troops as a way of compensating the decline of French birth rates and population numbers inferior to Germany.

Marchand, Jean-Baptiste (1863–1934). A graduate of the military school of Saint-Maixent, this officer of modest family background joined the French naval infantry, which was at the time resolutely oriented towards overseas operations and, consequently, offered better career prospects than the territorial army. He embarked on a series of missions in West Africa from 1888 onwards, which took him into the areas of Senegal, Upper Niger and the interior of the Ivory Coast (1893–95). An audacious officer able to make the best use of the limited resources at his disposal, he was wounded twice in the Western Sudan: in 1889 when he led an assault on the citadel of Koundian and again in 1891 during the seizure of Diéna. Under Archinard's orders, he contributed to the capture of Ségou (on the Niger River). His *grand œuvre* is the *Mission Congo-Nil*, which he conceived, promoted and led in spite of the initial reluctance of the French government to risk provoking the British in the upper Nile region. However, the many connections in the Parisian establishment that he had developed whilst on leave from his African postings allowed him to lobby French government officials effectively, making the most of governmental instability to push forward a potentially explosive expedition project, making use of public funds to tease the British. Between June 1896 and May 1899, *la Mission Marchand* undertook a trans-African crossing from Loango to Djibouti, with the unofficial goal of pre-empting British paramountcy in the upper Nile, and therefore 'avenging' the 1882 unilateral intervention in Egypt. With extraordinary resilience in the face of often extraordinary logistical challenges, Marchand led his company of a dozen European officers and 150 African soldiers, carrying thousands of loads of supplies of food and ammunition as well as a steamer (the *Faidherbe*) requisitioned in the Congo and dismantled in order to transfer it from the basin of the Congo to that of the Nile. The eventful crossing of the Congo colony by the mission, which oftentimes applied a scorched earth policy to force local men to enrol as porters, ultimately cost Brazza his post as *commissaire général*. Marchand and his men reached Fashoda, on the upper Nile, on 10 July 1898, and immediately set out to renovate the old Turkish fort. The arrival of Kitchener and his five steamers on 19 September 1898 triggered one of the most acute Franco-British diplomatic crises since the Napoleonic wars. Against the backdrop of the Dreyfus affair and particularly unstable domestic politics, Foreign Affairs Minister Théophile Delcassé ordered the withdrawal from Fashoda, to the dismay of Marchand and his men as well as their nationalist supporters and significant sections of French public opinion. Dubbed 'the hero of Fashoda', which reflected widespread feelings of sympathy towards a valiant military leader supposedly betrayed by politicians and the Republic, and in spite of his widespread popularity, he refused to be the 'providential man' whose reputation would be used to inspire a *coup*. Besides, his limited political ability was reflected by the fact that his only electoral success was as a *conseiller général* in south-western France (1913–25). After the Fashoda incident, he contributed to the French expedition destined to repress the Boxer rebellion (1900), was promoted to colonel in 1902, and then left the army in 1904 after he had been denied the post of special adviser to a Russian general during the Russo-Japanese war. He volunteered to join the army again during the Great War, and the colonial troops under his command (the *Division Marchand*) distinguished themselves in the battles of Champagne, the Somme and Verdun. From 1898 onwards, press coverage of Marchand systematically included references to the Congo–Nile mission and Fashoda, which paradoxically appeared as the major *fait d'armes* of his career.

Rhodes, Cecil John (1852–1902). A graduate in Law from Oxford (though he received his degree quite late, aged twenty-nine), Cecil Rhodes gained first-hand knowledge of Africa from a very early age, thanks to one of his brothers, who lived in Natal. His discovery of southern Africa was a pivotal moment in his life, since his designs for his own enrichment and for the aggrandizement of the British empire would all revolve around this area. Thanks to his business acumen and his ability to conduct large African workforces, he quickly made the most of the diamond rush around Kimberley in the early 1870s. This offered him the means to get an Oxford education, which he had never ceased to seek. Through skilful amalgamation of claim holders over diamond mines, he engineered the irresistible rise of the De Beers mining company. He fervently used the considerable financial muscle of De Beers, and his own personal wealth, to further the cause of British imperial expansion in southern Africa and elsewhere, through military, political and educational action. His British South Africa Company, which had been granted in 1889 a royal charter which allowed it to administer and police territories north of the Limpopo River, whilst also concluding new treaties and concessions, spearheaded British expansion in southern Africa. His intense lobbying and dashing character allowed him to overcome the British government's reluctance to intervene in the region, and gave him the opportunity to carve up the territories that became North-Western and North-Eastern Rhodesia. A member of the Cape Parliament from 1880 onwards, he served as Prime Minister of the Cape Colony from 1890 until 1896. Lastly, the

'Rhodes scholarships' that he funded reflected his wish to train effective colonial rulers belonging to what he termed the 'Anglo-Saxon race'. His commitment to his imperialist goals, expressed repeatedly in 'Confessions of faith', had often embarrassing consequences, such as when his involvement in the calamitous Jameson Raid (1895) was demonstrated, causing considerable damage to his prestige and moral authority, and forcing him to resign from the Cape premiership. By contrast, his audacious handling of an African uprising in Southern Rhodesia (1896) included direct negotiations with Ndebele chiefs, much to the dismay of the settlers. During the South African War, his commitment to staying in a besieged Kimberley was noted, but the war itself reduced his ability to play a leading role in regional politics; he died before the Treaty of Vereeniging was signed. Though his dream to develop the 'Cape-to-Cairo' axis was not implemented until the end of the Great War and the disappearance of German colonies, he was remembered as a major architect of British imperial designs in Africa: an arch-imperialist whose towering reputation quickly became a matter of controversy.

Roberts, Frederick Sleigh (1832–1914). A graduate of the Royal Military College of Sandhurst (which he joined after two years at the service of the East India Company), Frederick Roberts started his military career during the Indian uprising of 1857, and his career developed mostly on the Indian subcontinent (Second Afghan War, commander-in-chief of Madras and of India). He became a popular military leader on the occasion of the South African War, when he replaced Sir Redvers Buller and worked very closely with Kitchener to redress a heavily compromised military situation. He subsequently became commander-in-chief of the British army. Rudyard Kipling's poems 'Bobs' (1898) and 'Lord Roberts' (shortly after his death from ill-health at the beginning of the Great War) did much to entrench in popular imagination his reputation as a valiant soldier.

Stanley, Henry Morton (1841–1904). Born John Rowlands, H. M. Stanley came from a humble background, which meant that he lacked formal education, and somewhat never overcame the social implications of these unpromising circumstances. Having tried a variety of low-skilled jobs in Britain, he found an opportunity to improve his life in the United States, where he was effectively adopted by a British trader established there. During the Secession war, he first enlisted for the Confederates (whom he served for ten months), before switching sides and joining the United States artillery. Shortly after the end of the war, he started a journalistic career, first for the *Missouri Democrat* and then, from late

BIOGRAPHICAL SKETCHES

1867 onwards, for the *New York Herald*. After a few assignments, the newspaper's owner, James Gordon Bennett, Jr, looking for a journalistic scoop that would sell well, famously asked him to 'find Livingstone'. Arriving in Zanzibar in 1871 after a long journey which offered him plenty of material to send to New York, he set out to join Livingstone in the African interior. He finally met him in Ujiji, on the Tanganyika lakeside, greeting him with the widely publicized (but certainly not spontaneous) opening 'Dr Livingstone, I presume?' Though his achievements, and especially his way of publicizing them loudly, were widely criticized upon his return to Britain, his book-length account *How I Found Livingstone* (1872) sold very well. He subsequently led the 'Trans-African expedition' (1874–77), which proved to be costly in lives and attracted widespread criticism in Britain for his heavy-handed treatment of all forms of African resistance (though it did contribute to the European geographical knowledge of the continent). He was hired in late 1878 by the Belgian King Leopold II to further his claims on the Congo, and spent five years trying to establish stations on the river, facing in the process the competition of Pierre Savorgnan de Brazza, busy creating a French Congo. He famously earned in the Congo the nickname of *Bula Matari* ('he who crushes rocks' in Kikongo). The dangerous situation in which Emin Pasha, the German-born governor of the Sudanese province of Equatoria, had been trapped as a result of the Mahdist triumph in Khartoum (following General Gordon's assassination) led to the dispatch of a relief expedition under Stanley's orders. The successful outcome of the mission (though they did not travel back together because of an accident which kept Emin in hospital for two months) was not enough to keep at bay echoes of atrocities and thirst for plunder. Once again, Stanley was confronted with a polarized reception of his public figure, with his book *In Darkest Africa* and his numerous lectures all highly successful, whilst growing criticism of the violence of his methods in Africa tarnished his reputation at the same time. Having married a well-connected artist in 1890, Stanley became involved in politics (he was an MP between 1895 and 1900), but, like Marchand at almost the same time, his influence in this domain was nowhere near that of his work relating to Africa.

Wolseley, Garnet Joseph (1833–1913). Coming from a family which suffered financial hardship as a result of his father's early death, Garnet Wolseley rose through the ranks thanks to his exceptional character and determination to succeed in life. He served in Burma, in the Crimean War, during the second Asante war (1873–74) and in many other colonial locations, including Egypt and the Sudan where he was in charge of the relief expedition which, having been sent too late and having progressed too slowly, failed to rescue General Gordon. He relentlessly tried to reform the army, especially in his capacity as commander-in-chief of the Forces (1895–1901). The expression 'All Sir Garnet' acknowledges popular recognition at the time of his ability as a skilful commander.

INDEX

Note: page numbers in **bold** refer to biographical sketches, page numbers in *italics* refer to images, 'n.' after a page reference indicates the number of a note on that page.

Adam, Juliette 235, 247
advertisements 71, 84, 97, 116–18, *118–19*, 131, 269, 271, 275
African reactions to imperial heroes 211–12
Allen, Walter J. 99
Archinard, Louis 226–7, 300, **304**, 315, 316
army
   popular image of (in Britain) 14, 28–30, 55, 98
   popular image of (in France) 31, 165, 226, 235, 239, 243, 293
Ashmead-Bartlett, Ellis 157, 231

Baker, Sir Samuel 61–2, 158, 231
Balfour, Arthur James 164
banal nationalism 194
Baratier, Albert 18, 81–2, 87, 201–2, 230–3, 235–6, 249, 255–7
Barrès, Maurice 82, 246–7
Behanzin (king of Dahomey) 187
Bennett, James Gordon Sr 61
Bennett, James Gordon Jr 62–3, 111, 318
Benoît, Pierre 85
Berkeley, Stanley 99–100, 113
Binger, Gustave 43, 58, 83, 227–8
Blackwood, William 16, 18, 70–2, 160–1, 264–86 *passim*
Blum, Léon 166
books *see* publishing
Boulanger, Georges 31, 65, 93n.102, 152, 237, 239–52 *passim*, 263n.114

Brazza, Pierre Savorgnan de 2, 35, 40, 103–5, *104*, 140, 148–152, 169, 175, 196, *212*, **304–5**, 316, 319
   advertisements using his name 118, *118*
   awarded gold medal of the Paris geographical society 43
   books on him 85–6
   cards featuring him *119*, 120
   city named after him 35
   cruiser named after him 206–7
   depicted liberating slaves 186, *197*, 197
   films on him 128–131, 208–9, 291
   and geographical societies 43–4
   in school textbooks 186–7
   official buildings named after him 40
   post-colonial reputation 299–301
   relationship with Marchand 232–3, 238
   relationship with the press 58
   song on him 124
   streets named after him 33–5, 50n.36
Briand, Aristide 166, 201, 307
Bruce, Alexander Hugh, sixth Lord Balfour of Burleigh 275–6
Bugeaud, Thomas Robert 11, **305**, 315
   as empire builder 186
   books on him 85–6
   streets named after him 35
Buller, Sir Redvers 69, 182, 317
Burleigh, Bennet 60, 265, 267, 272
Burton, Percy 63
Burton, Sir Richard 42
Butler, Elizabeth 97

[321]

INDEX

Caillié, René 11, 43
Carlyle, Thomas 8, 27–8, 59, 73, 174–5, 213
celebrity 14, 60, 62, 130, 179, 189, 211, 293
Chamberlain, Austen 167, 268
Chamberlain, Joseph 40, 109, 186, 314
charisma 84, 148, 176, 197, 247, 262n.94, 298
Chase, Harry 63–4, 114, 127, 312
Chautemps, Emile 227, 259n.10
chauvinisme 2, 84, 188, 198, 242
chivalric undertones of imperial heroes 2, 190, 194–5, 256, 308
chromos 118–20, *119*
Churchill, Winston 154, 172n.109, 284, 312
cinema *see* films
civilizing mission 15, 32, 40, 66, 174, 177, 183, 186–7, 194, 199, 208, 210–11, 254–5, 294
collectible cards 118–20, *119*, 258, *259*
commodification of imperial heroes 3, 185, 247, 290, 296
Copley, John Singleton 97
Coppée, François 238, 243, 246, 249, 251
Cromer, Earl of 141, 172n.109, 205, 274
Cust, Harry 268–9

Daily Graphic 55
Daily Mail 57–8, 70, 73, 264–85 *passim*, 310
Daily News 112, 267
Daily Telegraph 160, 261n.51, 265, 267, 272
Darène, Robert 291
Daudet, Léon 225, 245–6
David, Jacques-Louis 97
Delcassé, Théophile 141, 231, 235–8 *passim*, 244, 254, 316
Déroulède, Paul 65, 83, 163, 237–56 *passim*
Dickinson, Lowes Cato 98–100

Dinet, Etienne 102
Doumer, Paul 227, 253
Drapeau, Le 84, 243
Dreyfus affair 142, 225–6, 234–58 *passim*, 261n.53, 293, 316
Drumont, Edouard 163, 246, 251
Duveyrier, Henri 10, 92n.56, 185, 209–10, **305**
Duvivier, Julien 128

Elgar, Edward 124
Entente Cordiale 15, 199, 201
Etienne, Eugène 42, 166, 198
Ever Victorious Army 155–6, 161, 308

Faidherbe, Louis 35, 39, 86, **306**, 316
Fanon, Frantz 301
Fashoda 14, 16, 18, 65, *200*, 225, 231, 242–3, 248
  and Anglophobia 58, 89, 168, 235
  and Francophobia 198–200, 234
  and heroic reputations 89, 162–3
  influence of Fashoda on Jean-Baptiste Marchand's reputation 32, 66, 74, 79, 81, 105, 125, 133n.23, 163, 225–6, 246, 252, 254–8 *passim*, 316–17
  influence of Fashoda on Horatio Kitchener's popularity 279, 310
Ferry, Jules 41, 45, 146–51 *passim*, 168, 243, 254
Feyder, Jacques 128
Figaro, Le 66, 84, 130, 197, 237, 242, 252
films 19, 73, 126–31, 207–8, 213
First World War *see* Great War
Flatters, Paul 36, 186–7, 209, 230–1, 305
Forbes, Archibald 60, 113
Foreign Legion 32, 36, 124
Foucauld, Charles de 10, 203–4, 211, **306–7**, 310
  beatification 206, 299

[322]

INDEX

books on him 84–5, 219n.170, 257
films on him 114, *115*, 128–131, 208, 307
memorial *123*
official buildings named after him 40
relationship with local populations 203
relationship with the Sahara 67
sacrificial death 191
streets named after him 34–5, 50n.38
Foureau, Fernand 36, 43
Franchet d'Espérey, Louis 85, 129
Frankfurt School 54
Freemasons 65, 151, 235, 248, 251
Freycinet, Charles de 149, 151
Fripp, Charles Edwin 97

Gallieni, Joseph 10, 31–3, 39, 58, 165, 179, 196, 201, 226–7, 249, **307**, 314–15
books on him 82–6
métro station 1
theories of conquest and colonization 32
Gambetta, Léon 34, 57, 149, 151, 196, 258
Gaud-Toqué (affair) 105, 151, 298
Gaulois, Le 65–6, 84, 235, 243, 244
gender 9, 177, 194 , 291
Gentil, Emile 43
geographical societies 13, 28, 42–4, 84, 149, 183–5, 210, 228
Gladstone, William E. 61, 69, 99, 141, 155–62 *passim*, 178, 180–1, 267, 274, 293, 308
Goldie, Sir George 36, 187, 314
Goodall, Frederick 98–9
Gordon, Charles George 10, 30, 178, 211, 293, 299, **307–8**, 309, 319
advertisements using his name 116, *117*, *119*
books on him 47, 68–9, 85–6, 160–1, 190
and British interest in the Sudan 67

chivalric undertones of his legend 256
commemoration in Khartoum Cathedral 192–3
comments upon his legend 144, 177–8
compared to Henry Morton Stanley 156
critical appraisals of him 172n.109, 204–5
film on him 131
impact of his death on his reputation 62, 98, 134n.50, 187, 191–2
in school textbooks 187
in the illustrated press *111*, 112
Kitchener as Gordon's avenger 39, 162, 172n.111, 198, 234, 264, 266, 271
and 'newspaper government' 141
official institutions named after him 39
as a political argument *111*, 140, 154–62
promoted by the *Pall Mall Gazette* 61, 154–5, 308
religious undertones of his reputation 192–3, 206
represented in paintings 98–100
songs about him 124
statues of him 37–8, *38*, 192
streets named after him 1, 34–5
and *The Times* 56
use of his reputation by anti-slavery campaigners 143–4
and Victorian values 180–1
Gordon Memorial Service 100, 112, 273
Gouraud, Henri 31, 85, 201, 238, **308–9**
fort named after him 36
Graphic, The 107, *108*, *111*, 112, 267
Great War 12, 85, 101, *121*, 141, 178–9, 194, 199–206 *passim*, 220n.171, 255, 292, 297
Greenwood, Frederick 274–5

[323]

INDEX

Gros, Antoine-Jean 97
Groupe colonial 42, 142, 227, 231, 239, 241

Haig, Douglas 37, 202, 280
Hake, Alfred Egmont 160
Hanotaux, Gabriel 227, 230, 232, 247
Havelock, Henry 11, 37
Henty, G. A. 68–70, 162, 182–3, 202, 265, 281
hero-makers 10, 14, 17, 64, 82, 86–8, 96–7, 177–8, 213, 225, 244–51, 265, 285, 290–1, 294
Historia Magistra Vitae 175, 213
Hodgson, John Evan 98
Hugo, Victor 34, 48, 177, 183, 196
Huston, Walter 128

Illustrated London News 55–6, 111–17 *passim*, *117*, 134n.41, 198, 267
Industrial Revolution 2, 12, 14, 28, 35, 40, 49, 139–40, 174, 292
influence of America 61–4, 111

Jameson Raid 154, 188–9, 318
Jauréguiberry, Bernard 149
Jaurès, Jean 34, 151, 261n.71
jingoism 2, 46, 116, 198–9, 234, 277
Journal du Peuple, Le 250
Joy, George William 99–100, 191
Judet, Ernest 65–6, 243, 251, 254

Kelly, Robert Talbot 97
King, Henry 128
Kingsley, Mary 291
Kipling, Rudyard 16, 30, 32, 188, 198, 317
Kirk, John 62, 87, 143, 193, **309**
Kitchener, Horatio Herbert 10–11, 14, 16, 30, 178, 195, **309–10**, 312, 316, 317
  advertisements using his name 120
  as a hero of the Great War 179, 200 in France 199
  as a *proconsul turned hero* 140

as a role model 195
books on him 47, 68–73, 182, 264–86, 293
in the press 55–6
meeting with Marchand 201, 225, 233
official institutions named after him 39
political role 163–4, 195, 200
postcards featuring him 120, *121*, *200*
public disapproval of his 'concentration camps' in South Africa 195
role as Gordon's avenger 39, 162, 172n.111, 198, 234, 264, 266, 271
role of George Warrington Steevens in the making of his legend 264–86, 293
songs about him 124, 134n.51
statues of him 38
streets named after him 34, 51n.43
visual representations 101, 105, *107*, *108*, *110*, 111, 116
and war correspondents 60
Knight, Edward Frederick 267
knights *see* chivalry

Lamy, François-Joseph 36
lantern slides 49, 126, 129
Lanterne, La 252
Laperrine, François Henri 31, 196, 208, 219n.170, 306, **310**
  city named after him 35
  streets named after him 34–5, 50n.37
L'Appel du silence 114–16, *115*, 128–31 *passim*, 208, 307
Largeau, Victor 36, 227
L'Aurore 242, 250
Lavigerie, Charles Martial 10, **311**
  anti-slavery campaigns 147–8, 186
  as an *indirect promoter of imperial expansion* 140, 144–8
  books on him 86, 186, 257

[324]

INDEX

city named after him 35
proselytism 193
statues of him 39, *123*, 194
Lavisse, Ernest 46, 73, 166, 204
Lawrence, Sir Henry and John 11
Lawrence, Thomas Edward (a.k.a. Lawrence of Arabia) 10, 13, 63–4, **311–12**
  books on him 47, 87, 92n.50
  early promotion of his heroic legend 63–4
  film on him 64, 127, 131
  photographic representations of him 114
  relationship with local populations 203
Lean, David 64, 131
Leete, Alfred 116, 299
L'Eclair 229–30, 234–5, 254
Légion d'honneur 32, 227, 241
Le Hérissé, René 227, 239, 241, 246
Leroy-Beaulieu, Paul 41–2, 247
Libre Parole, La 76, 249–50
Ligue de la patrie française 243, 246, 252
Ligue des patriotes 238, 243, 248–9
Ligue des patriotes plébiscitaires 256
L'Illustration 207, 207, 229, 233, 255
L'Intransigeant 84, 163, 243, 249, 268
literacy rates 28, 45–6, 49
Livingstone, David 10, 38, 62–3, 142–3, 304, 307, 309, **312–14**, 318–19
  advertisements using his name 118
  American influence upon the making of his reputation 63
  and the anti-slavery cause 143, 144, 148
  as a moral example 180
  as an *indirect promoter of expansion* 140–4 *passim*
  awarded gold medal of the Paris geographical society 43
  belief in Britain's civilizing mission 186
  books on him 87–9, 91n.47, 176, 190
  comparison with Charles Lavigerie 147–8
  films on him 128–9, 208
  and geographical societies 42–3, 62
  heroic reputation of him 11, 23n.66
  in the illustrated press 111–12
  meeting with E. M. Stanley 111–12
  memorials 39, 300
  mission stations named after him 36
  Missionary Travels and Researches in South Africa 87, 143, 190, 300, 313
  museum 300
  official institutions named after him 39
  photographs (and magic lantern slides) 113, 126
  post-colonial reputation 300
  profits generated by books relating to/authored by him 87
  promoted by the *New York Herald* 62–3
  promoted by the Royal Geographical Society 42
  reception of his legend in France 43, 64, 92n.56
  religious meanings of his legend 186, 191, 205
  represented in paintings 100–1
  and Stanley 62–3, 181–2
  statues of him 1, 185
  streets named after him 34–5, 50n.4
Livingstone, Mary 313
Lugard, Flora (née Flora Shaw) 167, 211, 314
  as a colonial propagandist 56
  role in arranging the writing of her husband's biography 87–8
Lugard, Frederick 10, 30, 195, 211, **314**
  as a *proconsul turned hero* 140, 166–8

INDEX

Lugard, Frederick (*cont.*)
  books on him 87–8, 166–8, 178
  relationship with Hubert Lyautey 167–8
Lyautey, Louis Hubert 10, 307, 308, **314–15**, *314*
  as an example of Franco-British cooperation 167–8
  as empire builder 186
  as *proconsul turned hero* 140, 164–6
  books on him 85–6, 167
  city named after him 35
  in the illustrated press 196, *207*
  obsession with posterity 178, 293–4
  official institutions named after him 40
  political role 200–1
  postcards featuring him 122–3, *123*
  post-colonial reputation 299
  relationship with Frederick Lugard 167–8
  role in the colonial exhibition in Vincennes (1931) 122, *122*
  statues of him 36–7
  streets named after him 33–5, 50n.35
  support to Léon Poirier's *L'Appel du silence* 129, 208
  theories of conquest and colonization 32, 186
  transfer of his remains *207*, 207
  views on Louis Archinard 226

MacKinnon, Sir William 143, 156, 193
MacMahon, Patrice de 145, 196, 311
Mahdi, el (Muhammad Ahmad) 1, 105, 156, 191, 298, 308, 310, 319
  damage inflicted to his tomb by Kitchener 266
Makoko (Congolese king) 148–9, 186, 304
  French treaties with him 65, 149, 299

Mangin, Charles 31, 227, 237, **315**
  books on him 85, 201, 257
Marchand, Jean-Baptiste 10, 31, 66, 163, 187, 225–59, 305, 310, **315–17**, 319
  advertisements using his name 258–9, *259*
  and Albert Baratier 93n.103, 230
  as a hero of the Great War 179, 199–201, 255
  as a *hero used as political argument* 140, 163
  as a moral example 187, 198–9
  awarded gold medal of the Paris geographical society 43
  awarded the *Légion d'honneur* 32, 226
  books on him 74–84, 77, 87, 168, 189, 233–4, 243, 248, 255–7, 298
  celebrated in provincial towns 226, 237, 241
  compared to Napoleon 253
  development of his legend as a compensation to Fashoda 65, 89
  featured in an *image d'Epinal* 240
  and the Flatters massacre (1881) 230
  in the illustrated press 105, *106*, 111, *240*, 255–6
  in the press 65–6, 229–30, 234–44 *passim*
  links with Russia 252
  making of the Marchand legend 16, 225–59
  memorial 1, 257–8
  official celebrations of his return to France (May 1899) 237–41, *240*, 248
  official institutions named after him 33, 40, 247
  patronage to the Marchand mission 232
  political role 41, 163, 227–8, 248 54, 258

[326]

INDEX

represented in paintings 101, *102*
reputation after the Great War 254–5
role of geographical societies in promoting his legend 228
role of hero-makers in the promotion of his legend 244–51
self-promotion 142, 228, 230–1, 293
songs about him 125
statues of him *38, 39*, 226
streets named after him 33–5, 50n.34, 247–8
use of his reputation by the nationalists 64, 163, 235, 237, 239, 241, 243, 246–54 *passim*
use of his reputation during the Second World War 256–7
mass-media *see* press
Matin, Le 58, 130, 201, 235
Maunoir, Charles 185, 228, 291
McLuhan, Marshall 54
mediated personae 291
Melchior de Vogüé, Eugène 166
Michelet, Jules 73, 196
military activity 2, 8–15 *passim*, 28–32, 37, 55, 68, 71, 84, 89, 97–103 *passim*, 126, 144, 163, 176, 182–3, 187, 191–206 *passim*, 265, 270, 285, 292, 304–17 *passim*
Milner, Alfred 154, 159, 163, 270
mission civilisatrice see civilizing mission
Mistral, Frédéric 247
Moffat, John Smith 143
Moffat, Robert 100, 312
Monfreid, Henry de 178
Murchison, Sir Roderick 62, 143, 184, 291
music 15, 123–5, 130–1

Napoleon 29–30, 33, 68, 176, 183, 196, 253
Napoleon III 41, 101, 145

nationalism 1, 5, 19n.2, 57, 177, 193–4, 198
Nelson, Horatio 29, 34, 47, 51n.55, 68, 97, 176
Neuville, Alphonse de 97
New Imperialism 3–6, 11–16, 19, 27–8, 34, 97, 100–1, 123, 131, 139–40, 176–95 *passim*, 292–3, 297, 307
New Journalism 4, 60–2, 65, 155
New Penny Magazine 56
New York Herald, The 62–4, 111–12, 182, 313, 318
newyorkheraldisme 64
Nightingale, Florence 34, 291
Nouvelle Revue, la 235

Oliphant, Laurence and Margaret 71, 268–70
Orientalist school of painting 102
Outram, James 11

Pall Mall Gazette 61, 154–5, 167, 268–9, 274, 308
Pearse, Henry 267
Penny Illustrated Paper 105, 107, *107, 108,* 108, 112
Perham, Margery 87–8, 167, 178, 314
Petit Journal, Le 55–7, 65–6, 103–5, *104, 106,* 132, 196, 229, 235, 243, 247
Petit Parisien, Le 57–9, 76, 85, 103–5, *106, 110,* 111, 132, 196, 234–5, 238, 242–3
Peyré, Joseph 85, 94n.114
Phillips, Henry Wyndham 100–1
photography 113–16, 126
Pinker, James Brand 283
Poirier, Léon 85, 114–16, *115,* 128–32, 166, 208, 213, 291, 307
popular culture 4–7, 20n.18, 27, 45, 47–9, 90, 97, 127, 290–2, 298–9
popular imperialism 5–7, 205, 248, 255, 262n.97, 285, 291, 296–7

[327]

INDEX

postcards 74, 97, 118, 120–3, *121, 123*, 131, 134n.46, 199, *200*
Power, Frank 56, 60
Press 88–90, 141, 150,
   illustrated press 103–13
   political role of the press 28, 61, 141, 143, 145–9, 154–5, 167, 200
   popular press 4–5, 10–14, 184, 295–6
      in Britain 46, 54–7, 60–4, 198, 261n.51, 264–8, 273–5, 313
      in France 48, 57–9, 64–6, 84, 197–8, 229, 235–6, 242, 293, 317
Prinsep, Val 99
print-capitalism 3, 15, 54, 84, 293
print-runs 7, 14, 18, 57–8, 65, 69–76, 79–85, 87, 103, 105, 116, 161, 243, 266, 269–74 *passim*, 280, 295
Prior, Melton 113
Psichari, Ernest 84, 204, 257
publishing 5–17, 45–9, 54, 66–90, 130, 160–1, 205, 229–30, 244, 256–8, 264–86 *passim*, 295

Quinzaine coloniale, la 234

Rire, Le 107, *109*
Rhodes, Cecil 10, 87, 195, 292, **317–18**
   as a *direct promoter of expansion* 140, 152–4
   books on him 68, 72–3, 183, 187–9, 205, 210
   country named after him 36, 300
   film on him 128
   French criticism of him 107, *109*, 198
   official institutions named after him 39
   paintings of him 101
   political role 152–4
   portrait bust in Oxford 35
   Rhodes Memorial 39
   satirical interpretations of his legend 107, *109*
   statues of him 38–9
   streets named after him 34–5, 51n.42
Roberts, Frederick Sleigh 10–11, 47, 163, 178, **317**
   advertisements using his name 116
   books on him 68–70, 182
Rodin, Auguste 247
Royal Geographical Society 1, 36, 42–3, 62, 184–5, 210, 291, 313
Russell, William Howard 59–60

Sahara 32, 35, 36, 58, 67, 84–5, 94n.117, 128, 130, 145, 204, 206, 231, 246, 305, 307, 310
Saharomania 84–5, 255
Salisbury, Lord (Robert Gascoyne-Cecil) 141, 156–62 *passim*, 248, 267, 271, 309
Savorgnan de Brazza, Pierre *see* Brazza
school textbooks 17, 46–7, 175–7, 183, 186–8, 204, 293
Scudamore, Francis 60, 267
Second World War 9, 12, 37, 54, 119, 131, 168, 192, 210, 256, 291
Seldon, Charles 267
self-promotion 62–3, 226, 293–4
Siècle, Le 44, 146, 237–8, 242
Société des gens de lettres 82
Société de géographie 43–4, 73, 84, 92n.56, 130, 150, 183–5, 228, 238, 251, 256, 305, 306
   and its provincial equivalents 43, 228
Société patriotique et philanthropique des anciens militaries des corps de la Marine 248
Société de propagande coloniale 34
Speke, John Hanning 42, 71, 100, 270
Stanhope, Hester 13

[328]

INDEX

Stanley, Henry Morton 10, 62–3, 91n.45, 169, 195, 291, 304, 313, **318–19**
   as an example 181–2, 184–5, 195
   awarded gold medal of the Paris geographical society 43
   books on him 68, 181–2
   carte-de-visite photographs of him 114
   compared to Charles Gordon 156
   controversy about his actions 210
   films on him 128
   in the illustrated press 111
   promoted by the Royal Geographical Society 42
   publicity stunt 62–3, 132,
   reception of his legend in France 64, 149, 152
   satirical interpretations of his legend 70
   streets named after him 34
statistics *see* publishing; press
statues 1, 9, 14, 36–9, *38*, 96, 120, 122, *123*, 123, 139, 175, 185, 192, 194, 226, 300–1
Stead, William Thomas 46, 60–1, 153–5, 167, 268, 308
Steevens, Christina 264, 268–77 *passim*, 282–6 *passim*
Steevens, George Warrington 14, 16, 57, 70–3, 264–86 *passim*, 291, 293, 296, 310
Strachey, Giles Lytton 204
street names 1, 14, 19, 33–5, 40, 48, 50–1, 139, 247
Sunday schools 44, 47–8

Temps, Le 58, 84, 234–6, 241
Terrier, Auguste 84, 228
Thiébaud, Georges 243, 248–9, 253

Thiong'o, Ngugi Wa 301
Thomas, Lowell 63–4, 87, 114, 132, 312
   see also Chase, Harry
Times, The 55–61 *passim*, 112, 167, 198, 200, 256, 267, 275, 314
Tour du monde 103, 197, *197*, 212, *212*, 229–30
town names 14, 33, 35–6, 40
Tuareg 36, *115*, 130, 185, 203, 209, 211, 231, 305, 306, 307

Ujiji 38, 111, 318
urbanization (impact of) 14, 28, 32–5, 37, 44, 48–9

Vernet, Horace 101
Viertal, Berthold 128

Waddington, William Henry 149
Waller, Horace 42, 87, 143–4, 177, 185, 190, 193
War correspondents 10, 59–60, 86, 89, 103, 113, 132, 184, 264–85 *passim*, 295
Wellington, 1st duke of 29, 30, 34, 47, 68–9, 176
West, Benjamin 97
Wetherell, Marmaduke Arundel 128
Williams, Charlie 267
Williams, Raymond 291
Wingate, Sir Reginald 167, 270, 274, 277, 281
Wollen, William Barnes 97
Wolseley, Garnet Joseph 10, 69, 71, 124, 158, 178, 266, 308, 309, **319**
Woodville, Richard Caton 97, 100–1, 112–13
Wright, Henry Seppings 267